THE RISE OF ROME

THE RISE OF

ROME

❃ From the Iron Age to the Punic Wars ❃

KATHRYN LOMAS

THE BELKNAP PRESS OF
HARVARD UNIVERSITY PRESS
CAMBRIDGE, MASSACHUSETTS
2018

First published in the United Kingdom as The Rise of Rome:
From the Iron Age to the Punic Wars (1000 BC–264 BC) in 2017 by
PROFILE BOOKS LTD
3 Holford Yard
Bevin Way
London
WC1X 9HD
www.profilebooks.com

First Harvard University Press edition, 2018
First printing

Typeset in Garamond by MacGuru Ltd

Library of Congress Cataloging-in-Publication data is available from the Library of Congress
ISBN 978-0-674-65965-0 (cloth : alk. paper)

CONTENTS

Part IV: From city-state to Italian dominance

PREFACE AND ACKNOWLEDGEMENTS

The most common image of Rome is one of imperial power – a sprawling city of gleaming marble buildings ruling a world empire. This image is a long way from Rome's origins as a village on the banks of the Tiber, but by the end of the period covered by this book it was the most important state in Italy, dominating the entire peninsula and on the brink of becoming a world power. This rise from small village to world power is the theme of this book.

The question of why Rome became so dominant is an intriguing one. In its early stages of development it was a significant local settlement, but could not compare with its more powerful neighbours. It was only one of a number of emerging powers in central Italy during the ninth to the sixth century BC, and in many respects it was overshadowed by the Etruscan cities north of the Tiber, which achieved greater cultural and political development at an earlier date than Rome, and by the Campanian and Greek communities of southern Italy. A political pundit of the seventh century would probably not have picked out Rome as a candidate for domination of Italy, and still less could have imagined the empire it acquired during the second century. By examining its history in the context of these other Italian cultures, this book aims to explain Roman development in the light of similar trends elsewhere in Italy and will examine the exceptional aspects of Rome that allowed it to establish this dominance.

Perhaps the most obvious question that comes to mind about the very earliest history of Rome and its neighbours is, how do we know? Our information about this period is a dense thicket of archaeological information, augmented with an equally complex set of myths and narratives transmitted by ancient writers and additional information from inscriptions and coins. Sifting through this and creating a coherent picture of early Rome is a complex business, and there are no definite answers to many of the questions we might wish to ask – only a mass of intriguing possibilities. If some aspects of early Rome seem frustratingly vague, it is largely because of these difficulties posed by our evidence, which frequently throws up a mass of contradictions and requires us to read between the lines. Specific problems of interpretation are discussed in the text, but readers unfamiliar with this period of history may find it useful to consult A Note on Sources for a more general discussion of the issues posed by the evidence.

A new overview of the early history of Rome is timely for a number of reasons. There are a number of excellent scholarly studies in English, notably Tim Cornell's *The Beginnings of Rome* (London, 1995), Gary Forsythe's *A Critical History of Early Rome* (Berkeley, 2005) and Francesca Fulminante's archaeological study *The Urbanisation of Rome and Latium Vetus* (Cambridge, 2014), but there are few introductions available that are accessible to a more general readership. With the exception of Fulminante's book, much of the most recent archaeological research, and in particular the important and controversial work of Andrea Carandini, is published mainly in Italian. Many previous works also focus principally on Rome itself. The aim of this present volume, in contrast, is to examine the rise of Rome within its broader Italian context, and to explore the similarities and differences between Rome and the rest of Italy, in a way that is accessible to the non-specialist.

I would like to thank John Davey and the editorial team at Profile for inviting me to contribute to this series, and for their invaluable comments and support during the writing process. I would also like to thank my colleagues at Durham, Edinburgh, UCL and elsewhere for their comments and encouragement. In particular, I would like to thank Tim Cornell, Guy Bradley, Jeffrey Becker, Hilary Becker and Jamie Sewell, and my partner, Martin Hatfield, for their willingness to listen to discussion of early Rome well beyond the call of duty. Thanks are also due to Ruth Whitehouse and Martin Hatfield for permission to use their photographs, and to the staff of the Soprintendenza per i Beni Archeologici di Napoli, the Soprintendenza Speciale per il Colosseo, the Museo Nazionale Romano e l'Area Archeologica di Roma, the Soprintendenza Archeologia del Lazio e dell'Etruria meridionale, the Deutsches Archäologisches Institut, Rome, the Great North Museum, Newcastle upon Tyne, and the British Museum for assistance in obtaining images. I would particularly like to thank Andrew Parkin, Keeper of Antiquities at the Great North Museum, for permission to reprint images from the Shefton Collection of Greek and Etruscan Antiquities, a collection with which I have a long professional association.

Map 1. Ancient Italy: principal sites and settlements.

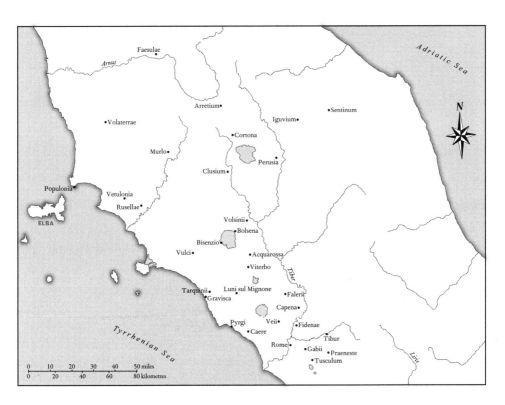

Map 2. Etruria: principal ancient sites.

Map 3. Latium: principal ancient sites.

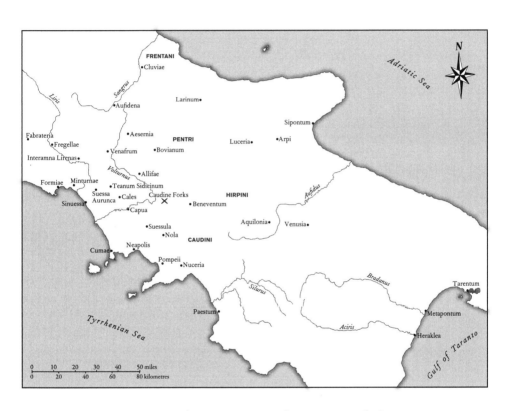

FRENTANI

•Cluviae

•Larinum

Liris

Sangrus

•Aufidena

Sipontum•

Fabrateria
•Fregellae

•Aesernia

PENTRI

Luceria• •Arpi

Adriatic Sea

Interamna Lirenas

•Venafrum •Bovianum

Formiae Minturnae

Volturnus

•Allifae

Suessa •Teanum Sidicinum

Sinuessa Aurunca •Cales Caudine Forks

•Capua X •Beneventum

HIRPINI

Aufidus

•Suessula

•Nola

CAUDINI

Aquilonia• Venusia•

Neapolis

Cumae•

Pompeii

•Nuceria

Bradanus

Tarentum

Tyrrhenian Sea

Paestum•

Silarus

Aciris

Metapontum

•Heraklea

Gulf of Taranto

| 0 | 10 | 20 | 30 | 40 | 50 miles |
| 0 | 20 | 40 | 60 | 80 kilometres |

Map 4. Campania and Samnium: principal ancient sites and ethnic groups.

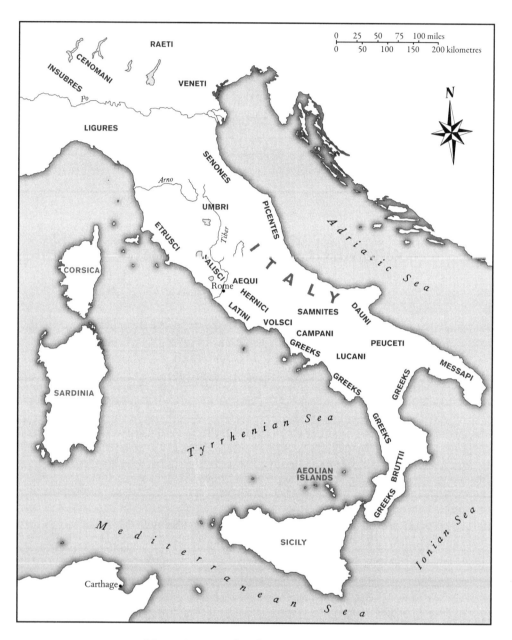

Map 5. Ancient Italy: ethnic groups, c. *400 BC.*

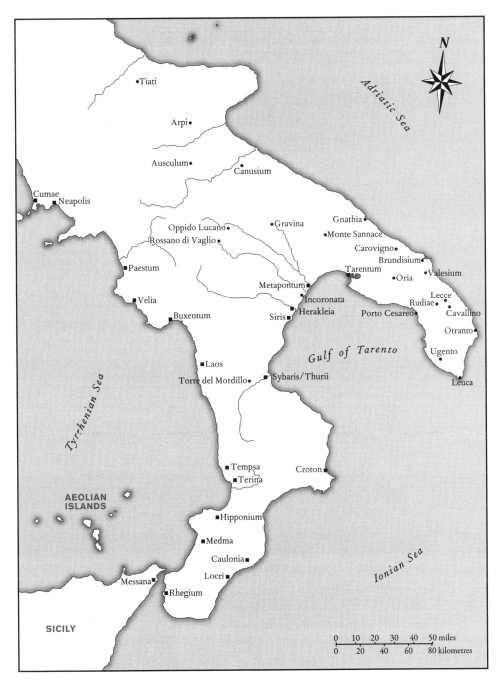

Map 6. Southern Italy: Principal ancient sites

LIST OF FIGURES
AND PLATES

❦

Figures

Plates

1 Biconical Villanovan funerary urn with incised geometric decoration. Eighth century BC (Shefton Collection, Great North Museum, reproduced by permission of Tyne and Wear Museums)

2 Italian bronze fibula, of *sanguisuga* ('leech') type, with geometric decoration. Eighth–seventh century BC. (Shefton Collection, Great North Museum, reproduced by permission of Tyne and Wear Museums)

3 Contents of a Latial IIA cremation burial from the Palatine, 900–830 BC. (Reproduced by permission Soprintendenza Speciale per i Beni Archeologici di Roma)

4 Pottery vessel with inscription, from Osteria dell'Osa, *c.* 775 BC. (Reproduced by permission Soprintendenza Speciale per i Beni Archeologici di Roma)

5 Greek cup with geometric decoration and inscription, known as 'Nestor's Cup'. (Museo archeologico di Pithecusae, reproduced by permission of the Ministero dei beni e delle attività culturali e del turismo, Soprintendenza per i Beni Archeologici di Napoli)

6 Rome: from the Capitoline, showing the Palatine hill on the right and the low-lying areas of the Forum below them. (Photograph: Martin Hatfield)

7 Foundations and post-holes of Iron Age huts on the Palatine hill, ninth–eighth century. (Photograph: Kathryn Lomas)

8 Cerveteri: tumulus grave, Banditaccia cemetery. (Photograph: Kathryn Lomas)

9 Cerveteri: interior of tumulus grave, showing funerary couch with chair, incised in low relief, at foot. Banditaccia cemetery. (Photograph: Ruth Whitehouse)

10 Etruscan bucchero *oinochoe* (wine jug), with incised decoration, early sixth century BC. (Shefton Collection, Great North Museum, reproduced by permission of Tyne and Wear Museums)

11 Etrusco-Corinthian amphora, with orientalising decoration. Sixth century BC. (Shefton Collection, Great North Museum, reproduced by permission of Tyne and Wear Museums)

12 Phoenican silver bowl (*lebes*) with incised decoration and serpent heads, from the Barberini Tomb, Praeneste. Seventh century BC. (Museo Nazionale di Villa Giulia, Rome. Reproduced by permission of the Soprintendenza Archeologia del Lazio e dell'Etruria meridionale)

Abbreviations

App., *Hann.*: Appian, *Hannibalic War*
App., *Samn.*: Appian, *Samnite Wars*
Arist., *Pol.*: Aristotle, *Politics*
Athen., *Deip.*: Athenaeus, *Deipnosophistae*
Aul. Gell., *NA*: Aulus Gellius, *Noctes Atticae*
Cic., *Am.*: Cicero, *De Amicitia*
Cic., *Att.*: Cicero, *Letters to Atticus*
Cic., *Balb.*: Cicero, *Pro Balbo*
Cic., *Div.*: Cicero, *De Divinatione*
Cic., *Dom.*: Cicero, *De Domo Suo*
Cic., *Leg.*: Cicero, *De Legibus*
Cic., *Leg. Agr.*: *De Lege Agraria*
Cic., *Nat. Deor.*: Cicero, *De Natura Deorum*
Cic., *Offic.*: Cicero, *De Officiis*
Cic., *Or.*: Cicero, *De Oratore*
Cic., *Phil.*: Cicero, *Philippics*
Cic., *Rep.*: Cicero, *De Republica*
Cic., *Sen.*: Cicero, *De Senectute*
Cic., Tusc.: Cicero, *Tusculan Disputations*
CIL: *Corpus inscriptionum Latinarum*
Dio: Cassius Dio, *Roman History*
Diod.: Diodorus Siculus, *Histories*
Dion. Hal.: Dionysious of Halicarnassus, *Roman Antiquities*
Festus: Festus, *De verborum significatu*
FRHist: T. J. Cornell (ed.), *The Fragments of the Roman Historians* (Oxford, 2013)
Front., *Aq.*: Frontinus, *De aquaeductu*

Hdt.: Herodotos, *Histories*
IG: *Inscriptiones Graecae*
Livy: Livy, *History*
Ovid, *Fast.*: Ovid, *Fasti*
Paus.: Pausanias, *Description of Greece*
Pliny, *NH*: Pliny, *Historia Naturalis* (= *Natural History*)
Plut., *Cam.*: Plutarch, *Life of Camillus*
Plut., *Cor.*: Plutarch, *Life of Coriolanus*
Plut., *Numa*: Plutarch, *Life of Numa*
Plut., *Pyrr.*: Plutarch, *Life of Pyrrhus*
Plut., *Rom.*: Plutarch, *Life of Romulus*
Pol.: Polybios, *Histories*
Propertius: Propertius, *Elegies*
SEG: *Supplementum Epigraphicum Graecum*
SIG: W. Dittenberger, *Sylloge inscriptionum graecarum* (Leipzig, 1883)
Strabo, *Geog.*: Strabo, *Geography*
Tac., *Ann.*: Tacitus, *Annals*
Tac., *Hist.*: Tacitus, *Histories*
Thuc.: Thucydides, *History*
Val. Max.: *Memorable Deeds and Sayings*
Varro, *LL*: Varro, *De Lingua Latina*
Varro, *RR*: Varro, *Res rusticae*
Vell. Pat.: Velleius Paterculus, *History*
Virg., *Aen.*: Virgil, *Aeneid*
Zon.: Zonaras, *Historical Epitome*

PART I

EARLY ITALY AND THE FOUNDATION OF ROME

I

INTRODUCING
EARLY ROME

In the ninth century Rome was merely one among a number of settle-ments developing in Latium.[1] It may have been larger than many of its neighbours, but it had no particular claim to prominence even within the region, let alone beyond it. The most powerful and dynamic communities in central Italy at this period were to be found in Etruria, to the north of the Tiber. By the third century, however, Rome had evolved into a powerful city-state, had established control over the rest of Italy and was poised to conquer a Mediterranean-wide empire. This book will explore the development of Rome from its origins to the mid-third century, the nature of its control over Italy and the reasons why it was able to achieve this level of domination. Although the earliest history of Italy and Rome is very distant in time, it addresses some surprisingly modern concerns. Problems confronting these societies include the stresses and tensions of multi-ethnic communities, how to deal with wide social, political and legal inequalities, and the interface between ordinary civil society and an international elite. By the third century Rome was also grappling with the moral and practical questions posed by rapid imperial expansion.

Rome did not develop in isolation, and it cannot be understood without this broader Italian context. One of the aims of this book is to introduce the wider history of Italy, its peoples and its cultures, as well as exploring their relationships with Rome. Our evidence for Rome is, of course, much more complex than for other Italian communities, as we have extensive ancient accounts of its early development as well as much archaeological evidence, although both pose interpretative problems. The principle on which this book is organised is to alternate chapters on Italy, which introduce the broad themes, with chapters examining Rome specifically, and eventually the relationship between Rome and its neighbours.

The sources for this early period are deeply problematic. There is a wealth of archaeological data from most areas of Italy, but the archaeological record from Rome itself is fragmentary and difficult to evaluate, thanks to the continuous occupation of the site since Antiquity. The textual sources pose equally difficult issues. There are some contemporary references to Italian and Roman history in fifth- and fourth-century Greek sources, but the earliest Roman historians, whose work survives only in fragmentary form, wrote in the late third and second centuries.[2] Some authors of the mid- to late Republic and empire whose work does survive, such as Polybios (second century), Cicero and Varro (both first century), included comments on early Rome in their work, but the earliest narratives of the period are those of Livy and Dionysios of Halicarnassus, writing in the late first century. This lack of contemporary textual evidence inevitably means that the writers of the surviving sources had, at best, limited knowledge of the period from the twelfth to the fourth century BC, and at worst, no authentic information. The Romans kept official state records and archives, but the date at which systematic record-keeping began is unclear, and private or public records and archives are likely to have been limited or non-existent before the beginning of the Republic, as well as vulnerable to damage. An introduction to the ancient accounts of early Rome, and a discussion of some of the problems posed by them, can be found in A Note on Sources.

Ancient Italy was a region of great diversity, with a broad range of climate, natural resources and topography, ranging from the alpine regions of the far north to the plains of Latium and Campania and the arid mountains of Calabria. Fertile plains along the coast and in some of the river valleys, notably that of the Po, are interspersed with more mountainous areas. The Apennines, which form the spine of Italy, are a ridge of high and inhospitable terrain stretching the length of the peninsula and dividing Italy into two distinct halves. The natural barriers to communication between the Adriatic and Ionian coasts ensured that these areas had different trajectories of cultural and economic development.

Italy occupied an advantageous position in other ways. It was at the crossroads of long-established trade routes: by sea, from Greece and the eastern Mediterranean to Spain, France and North Africa, and by land, across the Alps and into Europe. Its long coastline was well supplied with natural harbours, and it provided a short and convenient crossing point for people and goods travelling from western Greece and the Dalmatian coast, as well as for people travelling around the islands of the western Mediterranean. Italy and its inhabitants were connected to a wide-ranging network of contacts reaching from the Middle East and Egypt to central Europe, a fact reflected not just in Greek and eastern imports but also in the influence of Greek and eastern contacts on many Italian cultures. This is vividly illustrated by Rome's willingness to borrow and adapt cultural styles and customs from across Italy and the Mediterranean, while never losing sight of its own essential Roman identity.

how did Rome stay unique?

The coastal plains were densely populated, characterised by early development of the city-state as the main social and political organisation, and by a high density of urban settlement (map 1). During the period from the ninth to the seventh century, proto-urban settlements were established. Unlike Greece, however, where the natural territorial boundaries of each city were fairly clear-cut, the Apennines are the only major topographical barrier. Some lower-lying regions are divided by ranges of hilly terrain, but there are large areas where there are no clear natural boundaries, creating much potential for territorial conflict and inter-state wrangling. Most lowland areas were rich in fertile territory and mineral resources, so it is unsurprising that warfare in these regions was more or less endemic, as growing cities competed for an ever greater share of land and wealth.

Apennines are a mountain range

Urbanisation is a key concept for understanding the development of Italy, but it is a tricky one to define and there are a wide range of scholarly approaches to it. Even in the ancient world there was considerable variation: in Classical Greece the character of a city was defined by the character of its people as well as by the nature of its physical form, but later Greek writers defined cities in terms of possession of certain physical characteristics, while the Romans defined them in legal terms, as communities possessing a charter granted by Rome.[3] Modern approaches are no less varied, but the most recent and comprehensive attempt is that of the Copenhagen Polis project, which defines ancient cities as settlements with a population of no fewer than 1,000 people and a territory of not less than 30 km² (11.5 square miles), sharing a common name and common

"city" is a hard-to-define word

legal, social and political structures. All of these approaches agree that the ancient city was a city-state, comprising a central settlement and the surrounding territory controlled by it, which supported it economically. To be considered urban, a settlement must be large enough to have a degree of economic diversity and specialisation that lifted it beyond the level of a subsistence economy; political organisation and social hierarchies; and a concept of citizenship or state membership above and beyond membership of a family or kinship group. Features such as formalisation of urban layout, or monumental buildings, are not essential attributes of cities but frequently form part of urban development, and are useful diagnostic criteria as they demonstrate the existence of both an economic surplus and the political authority and collective will to harness it for large projects. Urbanisation was preceded, in many areas of Italy, by the development of settlements which were clearly larger and more substantial than villages but not fully nucleated, and which had not yet reached the level of complexity required by a city. These, which often consisted of interconnected clusters of habitations sharing communal space (often for religious use), are termed proto-urban settlements and regarded as the precursors of urban development.

Thanks to its rugged terrain, Apennine Italy developed on a very different pattern from lowland Italy. High-level valleys did not have the resources to support large concentrations of population. The peoples of the mountainous regions lived in smaller communities than those of the lowlands and relied on a mixture of small-scale agriculture and pastoralism. The isolation of the region contributed to the development of a distinctive social and cultural identity that was remarkably resilient in the face of pressure. Although it was well populated with small settlements, Apennine Italy remained largely non-urbanised until after the Roman conquest. Its indigenous political and social organisation was based on loosely knit federal organisations of small communities, which were well adapted to the nature of the region. The region developed at a different pace from that of lowland Italy, but these differences arose from adaptation to the local environment, not from backwardness or barbarism. Their effectiveness at resisting Roman expansion is in itself a testament to this. Apennine communities developed a form of statehood that was in many respects similar to that of the city-state but without the large population centres.

The ethnic and cultural diversity of ancient Italy was no less notable than its geographical variety. It was populated by many different groups, each with its own language, religious cults and material culture, mostly of indigenous origin, with the exception of the Greeks who settled in southern Italy and Campania (maps 5 and 6). The two most important groups in central Italy identified by ancient authors are those known to us as the Latins (*Latini*) and the Etruscans (*Etrusci* in Latin, *Tyrrhenoi* to the Greeks and possibly *Rasenna* in their own language). The cultures associated with these groups can be found (respectively) in central Latium and in the area between the Rivers Tiber and Arno from an early date. There are lingering questions about the origins of the Etruscans, thanks to their peculiar language, which bears little resemblance to any other Italian language and is probably not Indo-European, and to Herodotos' statement that they were colonists from Asia Minor, although this is contradicted by other ancient sources (Hdt. 1.93–96; Dion. Hal. 1.30; Strabo, *Geog.* 5.2.2–4).[4] They are now generally assumed to have been an indigenous people, although studies of ancient DNA samples reveal some intriguing findings. These show similarities between the populations of ancient Etruria and central Anatolia, as well as differences between Etruscan DNA and that of medieval and modern Tuscans. However, it is a step too far to take this as confirmation of Herodotos' belief that the Etruscans were colonists from Asia Minor, and DNA studies of Etruscans remain controversial, to say the least; other studies show that discontinuity between the DNA of people from different periods is common in Europe and should be attributed to population movements over long periods, not short-term colonisation of the sort envisaged by Herodotos.

In southern and upland Italy ethnic and cultural identities were more complicated. Sources for the location of Greek settlements in southern Italy, and about the culture and ethnicity of the inhabitants of the Salentine peninsula, are broadly consistent. Beyond this, however, it is impossible to draw an accurate ethnic map of Italy before the fourth century. Ancient sources, mostly written long after these cultures ceased to exist, disagree as to who lived where, and even on which parts of the peninsula could be defined as Italy.[5] A period of mass migration in the fifth century, during which some groups disappeared from the historical and archaeological record and new ones emerged, complicates the picture even further. Although it is clear from the archaeological record, and from inscriptions, that many different languages and cultures co-existed in Italy, it is much more difficult to pin down the concept of ethnicity. Ancient writers routinely describe Italy as a region of tribal societies to which they ascribe ethnic labels, but it is far from clear whether the Italians regarded themselves as belonging to well-defined ethnic groups, and archaeological evidence points to the city-state as the primary form of social and political organisation in the region. Many people may have identified themselves with their family, village or state, rather than with a broader ethnicity, and collective identities seem to have been fairly fluid. New groups emerged from the migrations of the fifth century, while others expand into new areas. The Volsci, Hernici and Aequi, all troublesome neighbours of Rome, appear at this date but disappear equally abruptly after the Roman conquests of the fourth century. Celts from beyond the Alps settled in northern Italy, Etruscans moved into the Po valley, and peoples from the central Apennines migrated en masse into Campania and southern Italy.[6] By the end of the fifth century the cultural map of Italy had changed considerably, and during the fourth century clearer ethnic identities began to emerge, but even at this point most people may have regarded themselves as primarily belonging to a particular state or community rather than an ethnic group – for instance, as a Tarquinian or Volaterran rather than as an Etruscan.

During the period of its rise to power Rome had only the administrative apparatus of a city-state at its disposal. Although this developed in complexity during the period from the fourth century to the second, administrative resources were limited. Roman power was maintained by a network of arm's-length relationships interspersed with areas of closer control, rather than by direct rule. Many Italian communities retained a measure of autonomy, although Rome was able to help itself to some of their resources, especially military manpower. Although Rome was indisputably the leader of the Italians by 270 BC, and dealt with any challenge to this position very firmly, Roman Italy was not a directly ruled empire. Regional and ethnic identities remained important, but were also fluid. Greek, Etruscan and Roman cultures all had an impact on the other peoples of Italy, just as Roman culture was itself influenced by those of the Etruscans and Greeks. The cultural Romanisation of the peninsula did not take place until the late second and first centuries; until then, the rest of Italy retained its own local languages and cultures, and the phenomenon of cultural convergence which is sometimes termed Romanisation was not yet prominent. Given the late date of most of our sources and our reliance on material written from the Roman point of view, it is easy to forget that Rome did not exercise Italian-wide dominance until the early third century, and that the establishment of this dominance was by no means a foregone conclusion. Even during the Punic wars there is a distinct sense that the will of Rome was only one factor among many in determining the actions of other Italians, and it is only with the reassertion of Roman authority after the defeat of Hannibal that Rome fully established domination of Italy. During the period covered by this book we can see the emergence of Rome from being merely one among many Italian states to a position of dominance, but the wider Italian context is essential for understanding this process.

2

SETTING THE SCENE:
IRON-AGE ITALY

❧❦❧

Prehistoric Italy was a very different place from the peninsula in later history. Around 1200 BC it was an area of small settlements with subsistence economies based on small-scale agriculture. Between the late Bronze Age and the Iron Age (c. 1000–800), larger and more complex settlements, often termed proto-urban settlements, developed, along with greater economic diversity, wider social divisions and distinctive regional cultures. This period also saw the establishment of the earliest known settlements on the site of Rome itself.

An important limiting factor is that we have no contemporary textual sources for this period and must rely entirely on archaeological evidence. There is no Italian equivalent of Homer or Hesiod, whose poetry offers vivid depictions of Iron-Age Greece, and the earliest inscriptions – which are few in number and in most cases very short – do not appear until the middle of the eighth century.[1] Nevertheless, archaeological evidence for the later Bronze Age and early Iron Age throws considerable light on Italian culture and society, although with some limitations. One of these is that much of our evidence comes from cemeteries. Because burials are ritual acts, funerary evidence tells us much about social relationships and organisation, economic development and the cultural priorities of a community, but relatively little about daily life. The publication of several cemetery excavations – notably those of Osteria dell'Osa, 18 km (11.4

miles) east of Rome, and Quattro Fontanili, one of the early cemeteries of Veii – has greatly illuminated Iron-Age society, and how it related to the later development of Latium and Etruria. Settlements are less well documented, but recent fieldwork has shed new light on where and how people lived, as well as how they were buried and commemorated.

However, there are limits to what we can do. We do not know, for instance, how Italians of the Bronze Age defined their own identities, or whether they perceived themselves as distinct ethnic groups. During the early Iron Age local differences developed in the form and style of manufactured goods, and in cultural customs such as burial practices, suggesting the emergence of regional cultures. Artefacts belonging to the Villanovan culture of Etruria are different in style from those of the Latial culture of the area around Rome, and this regional differentiation can be seen in other areas too, but we do not know what these groups called themselves or whether they shared a collective ethnic identity. Throughout this book terms such as 'Villanovan' and 'Latial' refer to the culture rather than the people. Unlike the later peoples of these regions, who identified themselves as Latins, Etruscans, Umbrians or Campanians, we do not know whether the possessors of Latial or Villanovan culture saw themselves as sharing any common identity or whether they just happened to adopt the same pottery shapes, metalware and other aspects of material culture for entirely different reasons. The ethnic development of Italy will be discussed elsewhere in this book, but at this early date ethnic identities had not yet emerged in archaeologically visible form.

Italy in the late Bronze Age

[During the Final Bronze Age (twelfth–tenth centuries) changes in economies and social organisation took place throughout Italy.] Settlements expanded, although with marked regional variations in type and size, and manufactured goods increased in quantity and variety[suggesting the work of specialised craftsmen] rather than items produced within the home. Many of the bronze objects, clearly produced by skilled artisans, are of notably high-quality workmanship. This increase in metal goods required access to mineral resources to provide raw materials, while the presence of imported pottery and metal items (mostly of Greek origin) demonstrates a network of contacts with the broader Mediterranean

lots of advancement

world. This was an era of social change, expanding trade and manufacturing, new craft skills and a more intensive approach to farming which permitted the growth of larger and more complex settlements. At the beginning of the Final Bronze Age most Italian settlements were villages, often of modest size, but by the Iron Age we can trace the earliest development of proto-urban settlements. These are characterised by larger size, more complex layout and a greater degree of both economic complexity and social hierarchy. They could vary in size, often between regions, and were not always a single nucleated settlement, but they all show signs of a greater degree of political and social complexity than the village sites of the Bronze Age.

[In Etruria we can trace settlement development in some detail.] Those of the earlier Bronze Age were aligned with tracks used as drove-roads and were short-lived, suggesting that the population was partly migratory, following livestock from winter to summer pastures. During the Final Bronze Age settled agrarian communities developed at locations selected for defensive potential and proximity to water sources – factors crucial for sustaining stable long-term settlements – rather than access to drove-roads. Two intensively excavated sites at San Giovenale and Luni sul Mignone, both near Viterbo (map 2), illustrate these changes. Each is located on an upland plateau, defended by steep slopes on several sides; Luni was further protected by artificial terracing and fortifications. Settlements of the Final Bronze Age were [generally limited in size and consisted of groups of small timber-framed huts] sometimes divided into several rooms, with a porch sheltering the entrance. At some sites, including Luni, larger and more substantial buildings have been found, measuring *c*. 15–17m by 8–9m (49–55 ft × 26–29 ft), with stone foundations. Their purpose is unknown, but their size and the use of stone – a more expensive and labour-intensive building material than wood or mud brick – for the base of the structures points to their importance, perhaps as houses for the community's leaders or as buildings used for religious rituals.

Elsewhere in Italy patterns of Bronze Age settlement varied. In Calabria open undefended villages situated on fertile plains, surrounded by intensively farmed territory, gave way to larger villages of *c*. 500–1,000 people, during the period between the twelfth and tenth centuries. These were situated on plateaux which offered better natural defences, and some, such as Torre del Mordillo, have yielded quantities of weapons and armour [In northern Italy some very large villages developed in the Final Bronze Age] such as Frattesina, in the Po plain, which covered an area of *c.* 200 ha (*c.* 495 acres). Overall, during the final phases of the Bronze Age, there is a trend throughout Italy towards the development of larger villages, and for the movement of settlements to more easily defensible locations, sometimes reinforced with man-made fortifications. The increase in weaponry and emphasis on defence in many regions imply a more aggressive society than in the previous period.

At the same time greater levels of social and economic inequality and the emergence of a social and political elite can be seen, reflected most clearly in changes in burial practices. The predominant funerary ritual was cremation, followed by the burial of the ashes along with grave goods that were relatively modest in both type and quantity. These typically consisted of pottery vessels and bronze fibulae, a type of brooch of a similar shape to a safety pin.[2] By the end of the Bronze Age, however, many cemeteries contain small numbers of burials with richer and more numerous grave goods, often including weapons or items of armour, weaving and spinning implements, and jewellery, implying a more socially, economically and politically stratified society and a greater visibility of women in the funerary record.

why?

Etruria and the Villanovan culture

The culture of Iron-Age Etruria is known as the Villanovan culture, named after the site at which it was identified, an Iron-Age cemetery at Villanova, near Bologna. It can be dated to the beginning of the ninth century, a period of important changes in patterns of habitation in Etruria. Settlements – already growing in the late Bronze Age – became much larger and began to cluster in groups, typically around the edges of plateaux or along ridges of high ground. The earliest phases of settlement on the sites of many Etruscan cities date to this early Villanovan period, although they are very different in form from the later cities.

In southern Etruria many smaller villages declined or were abandoned in the ninth and eighth centuries, and settlement became concentrated at a smaller number of large sites controlling greater areas of their surrounding territory. In the tenth century there were around fifty sites in the region, mostly between 1 and 15 ha (2.5–37 acres) in area, spread out at intervals of several kilometres. During the early ninth century these were reduced to ten larger areas of population interspersed with small settlements or individual farms, which may have been dependent on them. How and why this happened is unclear, not least because sites of this period are difficult to date (many can only be dated to a range between the late tenth and early eighth centuries). It is likely that communities merged, as neighbouring settlements competed for territory and resources and the stronger progressively swallowed the weaker, until only the larger centres remained. In some cases this may have been achieved by peaceful means, but in others it may have been a more violent process, involving the forcible takeover of some settlements by others. In the north of the region the change is less stark. During the ninth century, settlement concentrated around the sites of the later cities of Vetulonia and Populonia, and along the coast opposite the island of Elba, but a larger number of small settlements survived than was the case further south.

Settlements were larger than the preceding Bronze-Age villages, with estimated populations of up to 1,000 people. They clustered into groups,

Fig 1. Veii: areas of Villanovan settlement.

R. Valchetta

Quattro
Fontanili

R. Due Fossi

▲ Villanovan cemetery

● Villanovan settlement

0   500m

located only 1–2 km (0.5–1 mile) apart. At Caere, for instance, eight areas of settlement are known, and at Veii five substantial villages, each with its own burial area, were scattered around the perimeter of the area occupied by the later city (fig. 1). At Tarquinii and Volsinii there were at least two settlements in close proximity. The Calvario area of Tarquinii was occupied by at least twenty-five houses, built of wood or mud brick on stone foundations and roofed with thatch. The majority were small, although some larger structures may have been for communal use, possibly cult buildings, or have been private houses of wealthy individuals. Whatever their specific use, they point to the development of a more complex social hierarchy.

Villanovan cemeteries have been more extensively excavated than the settlements. At the cemetery of Quattro Fontanili, one of the cemeteries at Veii, around 650 burials have been excavated, dating to between the ninth century and the seventh. The earliest are on the summit of a hill, with the later ones spreading down onto the lower slopes, and are clustered into groups, believed to be family burial areas. The main funerary rite was cremation – in itself an indication that the deceased was a person of some status. The collection of fuel and construction of the pyre required an investment of labour and resources, and cremation ensured a funeral with some level of spectacle.

Ashes were placed in a pottery container (pl. 1), known as a biconical urn (its shape resembled two cones),[3] covered with a shallow bowl which was probably used for funerary libations and then inverted to form a lid. The urn was interred in a hole in the ground, sometimes lined with stone slabs, along with a modest set of grave goods, consisting of either fibulae (pl. 2), metal pins decorated with spirals, and spindle whorls; or of fibulae, knives and razors. This variation has been assumed to reflect gender, women being buried with spinning equipment and men with knives, but there is little surviving skeletal evidence to confirm this, and simplistic assumptions about gender based on grave goods are increasingly being challenged. The distribution of some of the finds within the grave may indicate that the urn was envisaged as a representation or symbol of the dead person, which was draped with jewellery and surrounded by personal possessions. It may even have been 'clothed' in fabric, fastened by fibulae, although since textiles do not survive this is conjecture, based on the distribution of the fibulae.

A small number of burials had significantly richer grave goods, including bronze weapons, armour and imported Greek pottery, and these became

Fig 2. Villanovan grave goods from a burial in the Quattro Fontanili cemetery.

more numerous from the middle of the eighth century. In one example, at Quattro Fontanili, the ashes were placed in a bronze vessel rather than the usual pottery urn, and accompanied by about fifty grave offerings, including pottery, jewellery, a bronze shield, an imposing helmet with a high pointed crest, weapons and a horse bridle (fig. 2). The weapons and horse harness alone indicate high rank, since horse ownership in early Italy was confined to the social elite. These burial patterns suggest that an elite may have been emerging, consisting of heads of families or even clans/extended families, and marked out by status symbols such as possession of weapons and control of greater degrees of wealth and resources. We are clearly still a long way from the urban society of the Etruscans, the later population of this area, but the scale of change indicates rapid political and social development.

Some eighth-century Villanovan communities were large enough to be within the range defined by Mogens Hansen as urban settlements, although they were very different in form from nucleated Greek or Roman cities. They consisted of clusters of settlements, which formed on the sites of Veii, Vulci, Tarquinii and other locations that later developed into cities, and are too close together to be fully separate communities.[6] Archaeological surveys by the British School at Rome in the 1960s and 1970s initially showed five separate areas of settlement on the site of Veii, which merged into a single nucleated settlement in the seventh century. However, more recent research has revealed Iron-Age occupation of the areas between the five main nuclei, as well as construction of a fortification in the mid-eighth century, suggesting that by the second half of the eighth century Veii had developed into a larger and more complex unified settlement. Similar signs that the clusters of villages were merging into larger, unified communities at this period can be found at Vulci, which acquired a fortification at around the same time as Veii, and at Tarquinii, where a cult place apparently shared by the various settlement clusters developed in the centre of the site.

A survey of Nepi (anc. Nepet), carried out by Ulla Rajala and Simon Stoddart, may shed further light on these developments. Here Villanovan communities formed on plateaux on which sub-groups within the community each controlled areas of territory containing a village, some dispersed houses and a cemetery.[7] One attractive hypothesis (although by no means the only one) is that each cluster of habitation belonged to a specific family or clan which divided up plateaux into separate territories, permitting each to maintain their own area within the wider community. Features such as shared cult places and large projects such as fortifications demonstrate that they were developing a shared identity and a sufficiently strong social and political organisation to undertake these works. Villanovan settlements do not show the levels of economic development, social complexity or political centralisation required by definitions of urbanisation. They can best be understood as proto-urban communities in which sub-groups such as clan or family units had their own areas, and which were much more complex than the villages of the Bronze Age but had not yet developed into city-states.

A small number of burials containing richer grave goods demonstrate that by the middle of the eighth century an elite was emerging. This showed its status by an increasing degree of conspicuous consumption, made possible by a flourishing economy. Etruria was a largely agrarian region, and the changes in settlement pattern entailed more intensive farming. Animal bones and botanical remains demonstrate cultivation of cereals and vines and the rearing of a range of livestock, including sheep, pigs and goats. There is also evidence for craft production and exploitation of raw materials. Mining was central to the economy of northern Etruria, around Vetulonia and Populonia, and Etruscan iron ore has been found on Elba and Sardinia. There was an increase in the quantity and variety of metal goods in circulation, including weapons, razors, jewellery and fibulae, continuing an established tradition of specialist craftsmen producing high-quality metal items. Etruscan metalwork is found as far afield as Sardinia and the area around Bologna, representing a considerable radius of circulation. Other forms of manufacture were less specialised. Most pottery was still impasto, a rough, handmade ware which was probably produced in the home rather than by specialist potters and for local use rather than trade. As in many ancient societies, textiles were produced in the household. Equipment such as loom weights and spindle whorls are widely found in both domestic contexts and female tombs, demonstrating not only that spinning and weaving were important to the domestic economy but also that they were important elements in a woman's status and role in the household. These items range from simple terracotta loom weights and spindle whorls to elaborately decorated distaffs made of expensive and exclusive materials such as ivory. Textile crafts were clearly practised by wealthy and privileged women as well as those of lower status.[8]

Villanovan Etruria was well connected and enjoyed regular contact with the wider Mediterranean world. From the eighth century onwards imported Greek goods are found in wealthy burials in southern Etruria, thanks both to direct links with the eastern Mediterranean and to trade with newly established Greek settlements in Italy. Many of these Greek imports were pottery vessels of types associated with the symposion, or drinking party, such as cups, serving jugs and large vessels for mixing wine and water. This does not necessarily mean the adoption of Greek social customs, such as the symposion, but it does suggest that the Etruscan elite was developing a taste for new types of consumer goods.[9] Local imitations were also manufactured. These wheel-thrown wares required more technical skill than the handmade impasto pottery and provide further evidence for specialised craftsmen, for the diffusion of new craft skills and technologies and for contacts between local and Greek artisans. The northern part of the region had less contact with the Greeks but maintained strong links with Elba and Sardinia and, through these connections, with the Phoenicians. Phoenician merchants had a well-established trade network with many areas of the western Mediterranean by the eighth century, shipping goods from Greece and the Middle East in return for metal ores, and there were well-established Phoenician communities on the islands of the western Mediterranean. Phoenician pottery and metal goods found in graves in northern Etruria demonstrate not only the circulation of new goods but also the importance of the export of mineral ores to the economy of northern Etruria, since the Phoenician communities on Sardinia played an important role in the trade in metals around the Mediterranean (see below, pp. 24–8).

In summary, Villanovan Etruria shows dynamic economic growth, a restructuring of communities and exploitation of resources. Large and complex proto-urban settlements had developed; families and kinship groups were central to social organisation, and more complex and steeply stratified social hierarchies were emerging. The Villanovan culture was also dynamic in other ways. Variants of it spread rapidly to other areas of Italy, especially the area around Bologna, and to parts of Campania, further demonstrating the wide network of contacts between Etruria and the rest of Italy. The population of Iron-Age Etruria had an active and flourishing network of contacts well beyond the region, and were exporting both their goods and their cultural influence in quantity.

Latium in the Iron Age

Latium, which developed on a similar trajectory to Etruria (although more slowly), played a vital role in the history of Rome. According to many versions of Rome's foundation myths, Romulus was the son of a princess of Alba Longa, a Latin settlement believed by the Romans to lie in the Alban Hills and to have founded several other states in central Latium. Although there is no archaeological evidence of a powerful state in the area of the Alban Hills at this time, these mythical and ethnic connections were important to Roman identity and were commemorated by

Roman participation in Latin religious festivals.[10] An understanding of the broader development of Latium is essential background to the early history of Rome.

Establishing dates is fundamental to our understanding of Italian prehistory, but the dating of the Latial culture, the culture of Iron-Age Latium, poses particular problems. Although most artefacts can be dated relative to each other, establishing absolute dates for this region has proved difficult, and the dates for the various phases of Latial culture – and therefore for the earliest settlement at Rome – are open to periodic revision. The extent of the variation can be seen in Table 1, which presents a comparison between the traditional chronology and a revised version based on dendrochronology presented by Marco Bettelli.[11]

Traditional Dates	Cultural Phases	Revised Dates
1100–1000	Final Bronze Age II	1150–1085
1000–900	Final Bronze Age III	1085–1020
900–830	Latial IIA	1020–950
830–770	Latial IIB	950–880
770–750	Latial IIIA	880–810
750–725	Latial IIIB	810–750

Table 1: **Chronology of Latial culture** (after Smith, 2005)

For present purposes, the traditional chronology will be used, but the dates for early Rome and Latium are fluid and may change in the light of new evidence.

The development of Latium follows a similar trajectory to that of Etruria, but the changes in settlement patterns in the early Iron Age are less radical. The Bronze Age was marked by a steady increase in the number of settlements, predominantly of c. 1–5 ha (1.5–12.5 acres) in area with populations of only a few hundred people. From around the tenth century the number and the size of settlements began to increase, suggesting an expanding population.

As in Etruria, the developments of the early Iron Age can be traced more easily in funerary than in settlement evidence. The earliest Latin cemeteries are those at Rome itself, which are discussed in the following chapter, and at various locations in the Alban Hills (map 3). Latial funerary practices were similar to those of Villanovan Etruria, although there are differences which allow us to distinguish Latial from Villanovan culture. Cremation graves contained an urn holding the ashes, which was placed in a large jar along with the grave offerings and then interred. Some of these cinerary urns were biconical vessels, as in Etruria, but others were shaped like huts, similar in form to the remains of structures found at Rome, Fidenae and Satricum. There were also differences in the grave goods that were buried with the urn, which in Latium typically included pottery and bronze objects and miniature replicas of items such as knives and razors (pl. 3). Other burials were inhumations, in which the body was buried intact in a trench grave, along with a similar range of grave goods.

Our strongest evidence comes from the cemetery at Osteria dell'Osa, on the shores of Lake Castiglione, 18 km (11 miles) east of Rome, and one of the most systematically excavated early sites in Italy. It was the burial place of a settlement that was the precursor of the archaic city of Gabii, and has yielded over 600 graves ranging from the tenth to the eighth centuries. Although little is known about the settlements to which it was attached,[12] it permits us to chart the social and cultural changes taking place in Iron-Age Latium. The graves are a mixture of cremations and inhumations, indicating a chronological change of burial ritual and the development of new social distinctions. In the later phases of Osteria dell'Osa, cremation graves were much smaller in number than inhumations and appear to have been reserved for the significant people. They were placed in the centre of clusters of inhumations, and often have remains of food associated with them. This distribution marks them out as special, quite apart from the fact that cremations in themselves involved a greater degree of outlay and funerary display. These grave clusters seem to be the burial places of different kinship groups in which the central cremation was the grave of the head of the family or founder of the clan. The traces of food suggest that it was the custom to make offerings of food or hold ritual feasts as part of funeral rites or the celebrations of a cult of the ancestors based around these tombs. As in Etruria, sub-sets of graves contain different goods – some people being buried with knives and razors, and others with spinning and weaving items such as spindle whorls, and personal ornaments – which were interpreted by the excavators as distinguishing male and female burials. All graves contained pottery vessels, especially drinking vessels, and fibulae. Some graves contained decorated pottery and some only undecorated vessels, which may be a further means

Fig. 3 Pottery vessel from Osteria dell'Osa, Latium, with inscription.

of distinguishing between social groups within the community, or even between people from different communities, if the cemetery was shared between several settlements.

A particularly important and intriguing find – the first known evidence of writing in Italy – came to light in a female cremation burial of the eighth century. This short inscription was scratched onto the side of a round, one-handled pottery vessel of local manufacture with a hole in the upper part (fig. 3 and pl. 4). It was written in a script that has been variously interpreted as a very early Greek alphabet or a form of modified Phoenician script and dated to *c.* 775.[13] The meaning of the one-word inscription, which reads *eulin* or *euoin*, has been the subject of much argument. It has variously been interpreted as a personal name (a shortened form of *eulinos*), the name of a god (*euios* is widely used in the Greek world as an alternative name for the god Dionysos), a ritual invocation to Dionysos (*euoi*) or an epithet applied to the owner of the object. Since most early Italian inscriptions are personal names – either of the owner or the giver of the object – this seems the most likely interpretation, although, given its unusual form, it is not impossible that it was a ritual object. Assuming that the inscription is written in the Greek language, an abbreviated form of *eulin*[*os*], it would form a Greek word meaning 'well-spinning', or 'a good spinner', which would be appropriate since spindle whorls are found in many female graves at Osteria dell'Osa. Whichever is the case, it poses some fascinating questions about how it got there. The vessel itself is of local manufacture and must have been inscribed by a Greek-speaker visiting the area, or by someone who had been taught to write by one. It is a striking demonstration of the connections between Latium and the Greek world, probably via a Greek settlement established on the island of Ischia, and has some fascinating implications for the development of literacy. It pre-dates the adoption of writing in Etruria, an area previously believed to be the first literate region of Italy, and is of similar date to the very earliest Greek inscriptions in Greece itself. Whichever linguistic interpretation is accepted, its presence demonstrates that Latium was in contact with the wider Mediterranean world from the early eighth century, and that new technologies such as literacy were being adopted at this date.

During the eighth century Latial burials containing richer grave goods increased in number. A female burial of *c.* 800–775 found at Castel di Decima (now on the southern outskirts of Rome) contained a collection of bronze fibulae and rings, amber and glass paste beads, and pottery cups, bowls and cooking pots, and more male graves contained weapons or armour. These burials suggest the emergence of a social and economic elite, and one in which warrior status was important. Society was becoming more unequal, with a small number of families controlling a greater proportion of wealth and power.

Latial settlements are much less documented than cemeteries, but their development into large and complex proto-urban settlements follows a similar trajectory to that of Villanovan Etruria. Traces of timber-framed huts dating to the ninth and eighth centuries have been found, at Rome, Fidenae and Satricum. These are similar to the Villanovan huts found at Tarquinii, which contained finds such as cooking and storage vessels, and weaving equipment, suggesting domestic occupation. At Satricum the forty-seven Iron-Age huts found on the acropolis offer a potential insight into how such dwelling places were used. They are arranged in two distinct clusters on either side of a water basin. The earliest huts (eighth century) are small (less than 10m²/107 square feet), but towards the end of the eighth century they were replaced by larger huts, *c.* 30 m² (322 square feet). In both phases they contained finds such as storage vessels and weaving equipment, suggesting that they were living-quarters, but are interspersed with smaller structures containing only fire-pits, which may have been used exclusively for cooking. A recent study by Colantoni, comparing Latin and Etruscan huts with ethnographic data,[14] casts doubt on whether the huts (particularly the earlier and smaller ones) could each have accommodated a nuclear family. Instead, Colantoni suggests that the two groups of huts may have housed two extended families, who used some huts for specialised purposes such as cooking, and others as storage and sleeping accommodation for individuals and couples, with much of the communal activities of daily life conducted in the open areas outside the huts.

The expanding number and size of settlements suggest more productive cultivation of land, and locally produced wheel-made pottery demonstrates more specialised craft production. However, the region lagged behind neighbouring Campania and Etruria in development. [Latium was neither as fertile as Campania nor as rich in mineral resources as Etruria, and was more peripheral to the principal trade routes of the eighth century.] We can see many similarities of social customs and organisation, but it developed at a slower pace.

Greeks and Phoenicians in Italy

The ninth and eighth centuries were an era of intense commercial activity and mobility throughout the Mediterranean, during which economic contacts and cultural influences between the eastern and western Mediterranean intensified. This was not a new phenomenon: Mycenaean Greek pottery, some of it dated as early as the sixteenth century BC, found at coastal sites in Puglia, Campania and some of the islands off the west coast of Italy, demonstrates that trade between Italy and the Aegean world had a long history.[15] In the eighth century, however, relations between Greeks and Phoenicians and the western Mediterranean moved to a different level. The effects of this greater Greek and Phoenician presence, and the commercial opportunities they brought with them, had a profound impact on Italy, which was felt throughout the peninsula.

The Phoenicians, a Semitic-speaking people originating from the area around Tyre and Sidon on the eastern shores of the Mediterranean, played an important role in the commerce of the Iron-Age Mediterranean. Trade was central to their economy from an early date. According to the Old Testament, ships from Tyre undertook long trading expeditions lasting up to three years, returning with rich cargoes of ivory, precious metals and exotic animals (2 Chronicles 9.21, and 1 Kings 10.22), as early as the tenth century, and this is corroborated by finds of tenth-century Phoenician goods in Spain and North Africa. From the ninth century Phoenician trade and settlement increased in volume and spread throughout the western Mediterranean, to southern Spain, Sardinia and Motya in western Sicily, as is confirmed by a fragmentary Phoenician inscription found at Nora in Sardinia. The Nora Stone commemorates a battle between Sardinians and Phoenicians, and the subsequent establishment of a peace between them, in the reign of the Phoenician king Pummay, who ruled Tyre between 831 and 785. The same wave of activity included the foundation of the Phoenician city of Carthage, one of the leading powers of the ancient Mediterranean and a bitter rival of Rome. Despite this interest in the west, no Phoenician settlements were founded on the Italian mainland. Thucydides says that 'they [the Phoenicians] occupied promontories and small islands off the coast [of Sicily] and used them as emporia for trading with the Sikels', implying that they deliberately avoided settlement on the mainland.[16]

The earliest permanent Greek settlement in Italy was Pithecusae (map 1), established at what is now Lacco Ameno on the island of Ischia in the mid-eighth century. Livy and Strabo (Strabo, *Geog.* 5.4.8; Livy 8.22) believed that it was founded by Greeks from the island of Euboea, refugees from the Lelantine war between Eretria and Chalcis, the principal settlements on Euboea, which took place at some point between 710 and 650. Although archaeological evidence suggests an earlier date for the first settlement on Ischia, probably *c.* 750, Euboean pottery decorated in Greek Geometric style confirms that at least some of the population was from Euboea. Strabo describes the settlers as being in search of a location to found a self-supporting colony, but this seems anachronistic and coloured by later Greek ideas about cities and city foundation. Ischia is an odd choice for settlers interested in founding a colony. It is rocky, dominated by the extinct volcano of Monte Epomeo, and arable land is limited, and more suited to cultivation of vines than other basic food crops. Palaeobotanical remains show that the diet of the population was based on the usual ancient Mediterranean crops of wheat, barley, vines and olives, suggesting that the community was agriculturally self-sufficient, but it was not a promising area for farming, particularly compared with the nearby Campanian mainland. Any Greeks who were primarily interested in agricultural land are unlikely to have settled on Ischia rather than heading straight for the mainland.

A more likely reason why the earliest Greek settlers opted for this island was Ischia's position on a trade route linking the eastern Mediterranean with Sardinia and Italy, an important and well-established route for exchange of metals and metal ores. Greece was not rich in mineral deposits, and there was a flourishing trade with areas of the western Mediterranean, which had deposits of metal ores, and of the Aegean world.

There were particularly close links between Sardinia, Cyprus and Elba, which can be traced through finds of distinctively shaped 'ox-hide' ingots. The ore for these came from the northern part of Etruria, the so-called *colline metallifere* or 'metal-bearing hills', and was shipped to Elba, where it was smelted down into ingots and then exported to Sardinia and finally to Cyprus. Ischia's role in this trade is confirmed by a complex of four buildings on the edge of the ancient settlement of Pithecusae. Three of these contained quantities of metal debris and fragments of iron, bronze and lead, as well as burned areas which may have been the site of smelting fires, suggesting that they were forges, while fragments of crucibles have been found elsewhere on the site. Pithecusae apparently had a flourishing metal industry, and was principally a trading community which owed its existence to its harbour and to its position on an important trade route.

The cemetery of Pithecusae offers insights into the way society was organised, as well as its economic activities. Grave goods were modest in quantity, but many were items of high quality, and their varied provenance suggests that it was an entrepôt for luxury goods from all over the Mediterranean. High-quality pottery from many parts of the Greek world, including Corinth, Rhodes and Euboea, is well represented, much of it decorated in the Geometric style. Finds include a pottery vessel decorated with a vivid scene of a shipwreck in which stylised humans are devoured by large fish (fig. 4). Drinking cups and jugs were popular offerings, an indication that the burial rites included pouring libations to the gods or to the dead. *Aryballoi* – small, finely decorated, flasks of perfume or

Fig. 4 Pithecusae: scene of a shipwreck from an eighth-century BC pottery vessel of local manufacture.

scented oils, which were a characteristic export of Corinth – are found in many graves. Other offerings included Egyptian scarabs, Phoenician seal stones and various forms of fibulae, jewellery and personal ornaments in bronze or silver. A particularly impressive drinking cup (pl. 5), known as 'Nestor's cup', carries one of the earliest known Greek inscriptions. It is of Rhodian manufacture, dating to the second half of the eighth century, and is decorated with patterns of diamonds and chevrons. It was inscribed by one of its owners with a short Greek poem or drinking song:

I am the cup of Nestor, good to drink from.
Whoever drinks this cup dry will immediately
Be seized by the desire of beautiful-crowned Aphrodite.

(*SEG* 14.604)[17]

The reference to Nestor demonstrates that awareness of Homeric legends and Greek mythology had already spread to Italy by the eighth century and – as Peter Wiseman has argued – may have had an impact well beyond the areas of Greek settlement. Mythical Homeric founders were attributed to many Italian settlements; Aeneas, whose role in the foundation legends of Latium is discussed in the following chapter, is the best-known, but Diomedes and Antenor were credited with founding settlements on the Adriatic coast, and Odysseus was linked to many areas of Italy.

Burials at Pithecusae were organised into groups which may have been family burial plots. There were different rituals for different age groups: children were buried, mostly accompanied by grave goods, while adults were mostly cremated with grave goods or, in some cases, buried without them. The cemetery also provides some intriguing insights into ethnic interaction on the island. A child burial of *c.* 750–725 was accompanied by fragments of an amphora with an inscription in Aramaic, the language of the ancient Middle East.[18] This, together with the profusion of Egyptian and Phoenician goods, reveals that Pithecusae was not just a Greek settlement but was inhabited by a mixture of Greeks and Phoenicians. Funerary evidence reveals that the local Italic population continued to live side by side with the newcomers. Most female burials included straight dress pins, which are a characteristic Greek form of dress fastening and are found in many female tombs in the Greek world, but others contained Italic fibula brooches instead, despite being part of groups of family burials that otherwise seem to be Greek. The interpretation of this data is complex,[19] but it suggests that Pithecusae was a flourishing trading community in which Greeks and Italians co-existed and intermarried, and which attracted residents from both the immediate locality and from the wider Mediterranean world. It was not unusual in this respect, as many eighth-century communities were of mixed population, particularly in ports. Al Mina in Syria, which was an important trading centre during the ninth and eighth centuries, had residents from many areas of the Mediterranean and Near East, including Greece, Phoenicia and Egypt. The mixture of locals and various types of incomer at Pithecusae is typical of the period.

Greek settlement in southern Italy

Towards the end of the eighth century the nature of Greek settlement in Italy changed, and the number of Greeks migrating there began to increase (map 6). Both historical and archaeological sources broadly agree that the first large-scale Greek settlement in the western Mediterranean dates to this period, although there are no contemporary accounts. Herodotos (Hdt. 1.163–65) offers snippets of information about colonisation, and Thucydides (Thuc. 6.1–6) lists the dates and the names of founders of colonies, but those authors were writing in the fifth century and other accounts such as those of Diodorus and Strabo (*Geog.* books 5 and 6) are even later. All agree that Greeks settled at Cumae, Rhegion, Sybaris, Croton, Taras and Metapontum as well as in southern and eastern Sicily between *c.* 725 and 700, and established further settlements in Calabria and Basilicata during the seventh century. The settlers are said to have come from many different areas of Greece, although the largest group are described with considerable vagueness as 'Achaeans'.[20] Most of these settlements are attributed to areas of Greece that were fairly peripheral to Greek history in the Classical period. Few of the cities that were prominent in Classical Greece were colonisers on a significant scale, with the exception of Corinth.

Ancient sources present the establishment of Greek settlements as a well-organised colonisation process, undertaken by fully developed city-states. Once a city had decided to found a colony, envoys were sent to Delphi to consult the oracle of Apollo as to the best place to settle. Colonists were then gathered, a leader (*oikistes*) was appointed, and the colonists set off to find the place indicated by the oracle. Once located, the oikists laid out the boundary of the new city, established the main cults

Colony	Founded by	Date
Pithecusae	Euboeans	*c.* 770
Cumae	Euboeans & Pithecusans	*c.* 725
Rhegion	Chalcis and Zankle	*c.* 720
Sybaris	Achaea	*c.* 720
Croton	Achaea	*c.* 710
Taras (Lat. Tarentum)	Sparta	*c.* 700
Metapontum	Achaea	*c.* 700
Neapolis	Cumae, Syracuse, Athens	*c.* 700–600
Caulonia	Croton	*c.* 700–675
Laos	Sybaris	*c.* 700–600
Temesa	Croton	*c.* 700–600
Terina	Croton	*c.* 700–600
Poseidonia (Lat. Paestum)	Sybaris	*c.* 700–675
Locri Epizephirii	Locri	*c.* 675
Siris	Colophon	*c.* 650
Hipponion	Locri Epizephirii	*c.* 625–600
Nicotera	Locri Epizephirii	*c.* 600
Medma	Locri Epizephirii	*c.* 600
Elea (Lat. Velia)	Phocaea	*c.* 535
Pyxus	Rhegion	*c.* 471
Thurii	Athens/ Panhellenic colony	444 or 443
Heraklea	Taras	433

Table 2: **Greek settlement in Italy, according to ancient sources**

and organised the division of land within the new city and its territory to ensure that the colonists all received a fair share.

This scenario has been subjected – rightly – to criticism, notably by the historian Robin Osborne, and many scholars now reject the idea that early Greek settlement outside Greece was a series of state-organised colonisations. The city-state had not yet developed fully in Greece in the eighth century, so the creation of Greek settlements designed to replicate a form of organisation that was still in the process of development at this date seems unlikely. Osborne and others propose that Greek cities in Italy developed gradually, over a period of time, just as Italian cities did, and that the descriptions of how to found a colony are later rationalisations reflecting the practices of the fifth and fourth centuries. This is not universally accepted, however, and the Israeli historian Irad Malkin has put forward a powerful counter-argument that the act of creating a new community, in itself, forces the development of new types of organisation. On current evidence, eighth-century colonisation should be viewed as a less structured process than that described by Thucydides, and one that involved the migration and settlement of individuals or small groups of people over a period of time rather than a state-run initiative, but it is possible – as Malkin has argued – that the act of founding new settlements forced migrants to think creatively about the way they structured their communities.

The motivations for this mass migration of Greeks to the western Mediterranean are equally vague. One view that has exercised a powerful influence is that population growth in eighth-century Greece had created a demographic and economic crisis, and that the early Greek settlers were motivated by a desire for arable land in quantities that were no longer available back home. Since both Greek and Italian societies were largely agrarian, and landholding conferred both wealth and social status, desire for more land is undoubtedly a plausible factor, but it does not entirely explain Greek migration.

One objection is that, although the increasing size of settlements and cemeteries suggests that the population of Greece was indeed growing, it was not doing so at a rate that could cause serious shortages of land. Another is that Greek settlements in Italy were not always chosen with land in mind. The earliest settlers, at Pithecusae, followed trade routes and selected a location for its proximity to these. Later settlers homed in on areas with a plentiful supply of farmland, but this was not inevitably the case. Settlements on the 'instep' of Italy, such as Metapontum, Sybaris and Croton, controlled very large amounts of land by the standards of Greece itself. Other colonies, however, had different priorities. Rhegion and Taras had relatively small territories, but each had a magnificent natural harbour and a strategic position on trade routes. Smaller colonies of the seventh century, such as Terina, Medma and Pyxous, developed on a rather unpromising stretch of the Calabrian coast, with only small coastal strips of arable land to sustain them. Land was clearly an important consideration, but sea-borne trade, exploitation of mineral resources and other strategic considerations were important factors too.

If we abandon the idea that Greek settlement in the eighth and seventh centuries was the result of state planning, we need to examine other motivations for individuals or groups of people to migrate in this fashion. The problem facing Greece may have been not an absolute shortage of land but inequalities of access to it. Someone who owned only a modest amount of land and had little prospect of obtaining more might find the idea of migrating in search of greater opportunities very attractive. Political strife often resulted in exile for defeated factions, and other socially marginalised groups might find a new start tempting. The Spartan Phalanthus and his followers, who founded Taras, were said to have been illegitimate children of Spartan mothers and non-Spartan fathers, and therefore ineligible for the full privileges of a Spartan citizen (Strabo, *Geog.* 6.3.1–3), and the seventh-century Greek poet Hesiod (*Works and Days*, 630–40) says that his own father was forced by poverty to leave his home in Kyme, in Asia Minor. The Greek settlement of Italy and Sicily cannot be attributed just to a shortage of land in Greece. It was driven by a range of factors, including social and political pressures, trading opportunities, economic ambition and the need to escape war or natural disasters such as a drought or a failed harvest.

We should not underestimate the sheer scale of mobility in the Mediterranean as a more general phenomenon. There is a tendency to regard early communities as static agrarian settlements, but both archaeological finds and the testimony of ancient writers suggest that, on the contrary, there was a high degree of movement around the archaic Mediterranean. There were flourishing international networks of trade, and skilled artisans seem to have travelled widely. Greek settlement in Italy was only one aspect of this wider phenomenon. What is undeniable, however, is that most of the Greek colonies in the west were highly successful ventures. Some smaller colonies struggled, but Taras and Sybaris in Italy and Gela and Syracuse in Sicily established themselves as some of the richest states in the Greek world.

The archaeological evidence for Greek settlement in Italy provides some insight into its date and its nature. Greek objects appear in significant quantities at Cumae, Rhegion, Taras, Croton, Sybaris and elsewhere in the last quarter of the eighth century, although there are small amounts of earlier Greek material at some of these sites. Some of the settlements later claimed by the Greeks as colonies appear to have been ethnically mixed at first. At Metapontum the cemetery of Pantanello offers fascinating insights into the early years of the colony. The earliest burials here, which are contemporary with the earliest phases of settlement, are a mixture of Greek and Italian. Most are Greek-style inhumations, in which the body is laid out supine, and accompanied by Greek grave goods, but others contain Italian grave goods. Italic-style objects do not, of course, necessarily mean the presence of Italian owners, and could have been acquired by Greeks by means of trade. Some of these burials, however, contain bodies placed on their side in a flexed position, which is an Italian rather than a Greek practice and suggests that the dead really were Italians. Neither can we assume that these burials are evidence of a local population enslaved or subordinated by the Greek settlers. The mere fact of receiving a burial, complete with grave goods, marks these out as people of some status, and the lack of spatial segregation between Greek and non-Greek burials suggests that the early population of Metapontum was socially and ethnically mixed. This is supported by evidence from the settlement that both Greek and indigenous pottery was produced there. Further out into the territory of Metapontum the same pattern is found at the important site of Incoronata. Here Greek and Italian house types co-existed, as well as Greek and Italian pottery and other objects, suggesting that this was a mixed community. Nor is Metapontum a unique case. Pithecusae was a mixed community, as was Siris/Heraklea.

During the seventh century this diversity disappeared, and by *c*. 600 Greek settlements had a more uniformly Greek identity. It is not clear whether this was because the local Italian populations were driven out or because they adopted Greek customs and became archaeologically indistinguishable from Greeks. In some areas Italian sites close to Greek settlements were abandoned in a manner that suggests that the Greeks had started to expand inland more aggressively and claim previously shared territory exclusively for themselves, but this is not the case everywhere. A more aggressive phase of expansion receives some support from Greek accounts which present colonisation as a violent process. Diodorus claims that the Greeks arrived with divine sanction to persecute the Italians, quoting what he claims to be a Delphic oracle relating to the foundation of Taras: 'I give to you Satyrion and Taras, a rich country to live in and to be a plague to the Iapygians' (Diod. 8.21.3). It is extremely doubtful whether this is the genuine text of an eighth-century oracular utterance. This – and similar narratives of conflict – are shaped by the attitudes of the fifth and fourth centuries, when warfare between the Greeks and their neighbours was endemic, and it is worth noting that some narratives of colonisation are much more peaceful. According to Thucydides, Megara Hyblaea, in Sicily, was founded because a local ruler, Hyblon, invited the Greeks to settle and generously offered them land. This variety of narratives matches the archaeological evidence, which reveals a diversity of experience suggesting that the impact of colonisation on the local population varied between different communities.

The arrival of the Greeks in eighth-century Italy seems to have resulted from piecemeal migration and settlement rather than organised colonisations, and the impact on the local populations varied considerably. In some areas Greeks and Italians co-existed peacefully, while in others the disappearance of indigenous Italian settlements shortly after the arrival of the Greeks reveals a more traumatic process. The impact of the Greeks on Italy was not confined to their immediate neighbours. Increasing quantities of imported Greek goods found throughout Italy demonstrates that they rapidly established commercial connections with other inhabitants of southern and central Italy. In addition to Greek pottery in Italian graves and settlements, finds of Attic amphorae are suggestive of a trade in wine or olive oil. The appetite of the emerging Italian elite for these luxury items is demonstrated by the alacrity with which Italian craftsmen adopted the new techniques and styles of decoration, producing local products in the Greek manner and adopting Greek styles to local tastes, as well as purchasing imported goods. This was not a case of Hellenisation, however, or the 'civilisation' of the primitive Italians by the more advanced Greeks. It is all too easy to think of the Greeks in terms of the Classical culture of the fifth and fourth centuries and imagine them as more advanced than their Italian neighbours, but in fact they were more or less at the same stage of development – a proto-urban society in the process of developing more sophisticated forms of social and political organisation.

To sum up, the foundations of later developments can be clearly seen in Iron-Age Italy. Burial evidence points to the importance of kinship and family groups in Iron-Age society, and the increase in numbers of burials with richer grave goods suggests the emergence of a social elite. Furthermore, we can see increasingly specialised craft production, exploitation of mineral resources and contact with traders from all over the Mediterranean. However, evidence from Veii, Tarquinii, Nepi and elsewhere demonstrates that complex proto-urban settlements were already developing by the time the first Greek settlements were established. It is no longer possible to view Italian forms of urbanism as something based on Greek forms of statehood, as many earlier archaeologists did. It is quite clear that cities of central Italy have their roots in the culture and society of the Italian Iron Age, not in Greek urbanism. The arrival of Greek settlers in Campania and southern Italy brought the Italian populations into contact with new cultural and economic influences which undoubtedly changed elite tastes but did not significantly affect the development of Italian societies. Eighth-century Italy was still a long way from the heights it later achieved, but it was already a region undergoing rapid development. It is against this background that we must consider the earliest development of Rome.

3

Trojans, Latins, Sabines and rogues: Romulus, Aeneas and the 'foundation' of Rome

⁂

⌊L⌋et us define a myth as a story that matters to a community, one that is told and retold because it has a significance for one generation after another. Such a story may be (in our terms) historical, pseudo-historical or totally fictitious, but if it matters enough to be retold, it can count as a myth.

T. P. Wiseman, *The Myths of Rome* (2004), pp. 10–11

According to the Romans, the city of Rome was founded on 21 April, some time around 750, by a Latin called Romulus, who became its first king.[1] He oversaw the establishment of a thriving city and then disappeared, having been transformed into a god, in 715, after a reign of thirty-eight years. A 'prequel' to this told the story of Romulus' descent from the Trojan hero Aeneas, founder of the royal dynasty of Alba Longa, which it identified as Rome's parent city. This version of the myth, which became widely accepted from the first century BC, was only one among many, and

Roman foundation legends are a chronologically complex collection of different traditions rather than a single myth, as will be discussed later in this chapter. Nevertheless, the foundation story involving Romulus and Remus, the descendants of Aeneas, form an important strand in Roman culture and identity.

One of the most contentious aspects of Roman history is whether – and if so, how – these stories about the earliest settlement of Rome can be interpreted and reconciled with the material evidence. Another is when and how the foundation mythologies developed. These traditions did not simply appear out of nowhere, but their antiquity and trajectory of development are matters of debate. The archaeologist Andrea Carandini argues that many have ancient origins, and rightly notes that they were a pervasive part of Roman culture. However, there were numerous different foundation myths for Rome, pointing to the development of a complex set of myths and legends over time, rather than an ancient tradition that reflects some sort of historical reality. Some historians, such as Cornell, believe that these traditions began to develop as early as the sixth century, while others, such as Wiseman, regard them as a complex mythology that developed from the fourth century onwards, and connect them with changes taking place in Roman culture at that time.

Carandini has, controversially, suggested that Roman cults and foundation legends preserve traditional memories of genuine historical events and people, and that Roman traditions of a single founder should be taken more seriously than has previously been the case.[2] His radical reconstruction of early Rome is based on his identification of early remains on the Palatine with locations and structures – such as the hut of Romulus – that form part of the Romulus myth. On the basis of this, he argues passionately that the new evidence supports the ancient tradition that the foundation of Rome was a single act by a specific individual, some time in the mid-eighth century BC. However, the identification of some of the new finds is contentious, and the theory as a whole remains highly controversial.

Most historians and archaeologists reject this approach in favour of an emphasis on just the archaeological evidence. Whether one accepts the fourth-century date or an earlier one for the development of Roman foundation myths, it seems impossible that they can be accepted as recording events or personalities of the eighth century. If we accept Wiseman's definition of a myth as a story important to a community, the importance of the Aeneas or Romulus foundation legends did not even lie in whether they were historically true. They were part of the Romans' sense of who they were and how they validated central aspects of their culture and political life. Locations in Rome with links to the foundation myths were venerated; ceremonies and festivals associated with the cult of the founders were important elements in the Roman ritual calendar, and the founders were invoked to legitimise successive regimes. To understand the earliest development of Rome we need to focus on the archaeological data, but the Roman mythological traditions cannot be dismissed. As myths they tell us a great deal about how Romans saw their history and identity, and how this changed over time, but they cannot be used to reconstruct a detailed history for the earliest centuries of Rome. For that, we must rely on archaeology.

The archaeology of early Rome

[handwritten margin note: Rome was not built in a day, nor was it built only by Romulus]

Although ancient tradition presents the foundation of Rome as a specific act attributed to a named founder, the archaeological record suggests a process of long-term development. The site of the later city was already occupied by the Middle Bronze Age, and this early settlement is not surprising, as the site offers many natural advantages. Its uneven topography made the later layout of Rome very idiosyncratic, but its seven hills (which are, in fact, composed of a larger number of ridges of high ground) provided defensible locations for settlements (fig. 5). The downside was that these were interspersed by areas of marshy ground which may have provided extra protection for the villages of the area but limited expansion and communication between them.[3] There was a ford across the Tiber just below the Aventine hill, so any settlement on the site could control major routes of communication between Etruria and Latium, while a position on a navigable river offered a means of water-borne transport both from the sea and from inland areas. The local tufa was good building stone, and other useful raw materials were available, such as deposits of clay close to the Palatine and Capitol and salt pans just downriver. All in all, the site of Rome offered many advantages.

[handwritten margin note: Rome is unique and (mostly) advantageously geographical]

On current evidence, there were at least three Bronze-Age settlements on the site of Rome. Pottery dated to the Middle Bronze Age

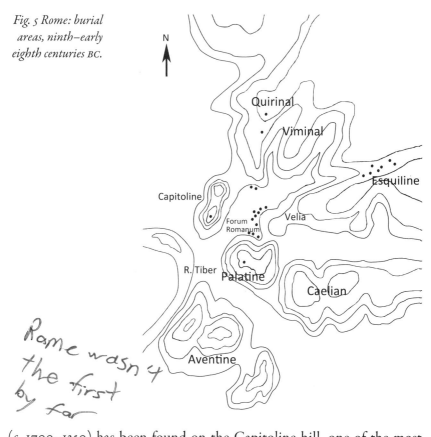

Fig. 5 Rome: burial areas, ninth–early eighth centuries BC.

N

Quirinal

Viminal

Esquiline

Capitoline

Forum Romanum

Velia

R. Tiber

Palatine

Caelian

Aventine

Rome wasn't the first by far

(*c.* 1700–1350) has been found on the Capitoline hill, one of the most important areas of the later city, and near the church of S. Omobono close to the later Forum Boarium. Potsherds of the Recent Bronze Age (*c.* 1350–120) have come to light in the valley between the Capitoline and Palatine, the site of the later Forum (pl. 6), and on the north-eastern slope of the Palatine hill. However, these Bronze-Age finds are small in quantity and most lack an archaeological context, so it is unclear whether they were grave offerings from burials or domestic debris from settlements.

Evidence for the Final Bronze Age (*c.* 1200–975) is more substantial. Pottery deposits from the Forum, Palatine and Capitoline demonstrate that these areas were occupied and recent excavations near the Capitoline Museum have unearthed artificial terracing and a possible fortification. Andrea Carandini has speculated that there may have been settlement on other hills, including the Janiculum, Quirinal and Aventine, based on pottery found near the foot of the Aventine, near the ford over the Tiber, and on ancient accounts of rituals and festivals associated with the foundation of Rome. Because of the very limited nature of the evidence, the precise number of settlements, their organisation and the relationship between them remains unclear, but there is growing evidence that Rome was occupied in some shape or form from the Middle Bronze Age onwards.

From the early Iron Age (Latial Culture IIA, *c.* 900) we find ourselves on firmer ground. Several sites within the area of the later city were settled by this date. An area of the Forum, close to the later Temple of Antoninus and Faustina, was used as a cemetery in the tenth century, possibly as a burial area for settlements on the Palatine and/or the Capitoline hills, and further burials have been found in the area of the imperial fora. Most of these were cremations, of a type familiar from other sites in Latium. The urn containing the ashes of the deceased was placed inside a large earthenware jar, along with grave goods, and then buried in a cavity cut into the ground and covered with a capstone. The most frequent items buried with the dead were pottery vessels, both miniature and full-size, but some burials contained metal objects such as knives and fibula brooches. One even contained a piece of gold, while in another the ashes of the occupant were placed in an elaborately modelled hut urn. There were also a small number of inhumation burials, in which the body was buried rather than cremated.

Other cemeteries, on the Esquiline, Quirinal and Viminal hills, were established in the ninth century, but our knowledge of these is limited by the circumstances of discovery. They came to light during the nineteenth-century (AD) redevelopment of Rome, and many problems in understanding them arise from a lack of scientific excavation. Finds were not accurately recorded, and we may only have a fraction of the actual grave goods. On the basis of what was recovered, the graves were inhumations containing pottery, including some imported Greek vessels, fibulae and other bronze objects. Inaccurate records mean that most finds cannot be linked to any particular burial, but they suggest a funerary culture very similar to that of Osteria dell'Osa, Castel di Decima and other major settlements in Latium. The recent excavations in the Giardino Romano, close to the Capitoline Museum, have revealed burials on the Capitoline which have been more systematically investigated. In most of these cemeteries there are no pronounced variations in the wealth of grave goods, but some of the burials in the Forum have more elaborate goods, suggesting a higher or special status. On current evidence it is likely that burials in the Forum ceased some time in the late ninth century, and that the Esquiline cemetery replaced it. The use of a different burial rite, inhumation, suggests that the Esquiline graves belong to a later period than the cremation burials in the forum. There may have been a period of overlap, during which the forum and Esquiline were burial areas for different communities, but the change from cremation to inhumation found at Rome is similar to that elsewhere in Latium.

The remains of a group of ninth- and eighth-century houses found on the Cermalus, one of the two ridges of the Palatine, reveals that buildings of the period were oval wooden huts with thatched roofs. The best preserved of these is a roughly square structure of 4.9 × 5.6 m (16 × 18 feet), with a wooden frame, a thatched roof and a shallow porch (pl. 7; for a reconstruction, see fig. 6).[4] A larger oval hut of *c.* 8 × 12 m (26 × 39 feet) of similar type has been found in the same area. It is possible that this was earlier than the smaller huts, and that it was replaced by them some time around 775–750, but there are many uncertainties about the dating of this group of buildings.[5] Francesca Fulminante estimates, on the basis of the most recent excavations on the Palatine and Capitoline, that by the late ninth century the Capitoline/Quirinal settlement occupied a site of *c.* 54 ha (133 acres) and that on the Palatine occupied *c.* 37 ha (91 acres).

By the early eighth century the development of Rome gathered pace, and the Palatine, the Capitoline and much of the area between was occupied, although with varying density of settlement. At least four nuclei

Fig. 6 Reconstruction of Iron Age hut, ninth–eighth century BC.

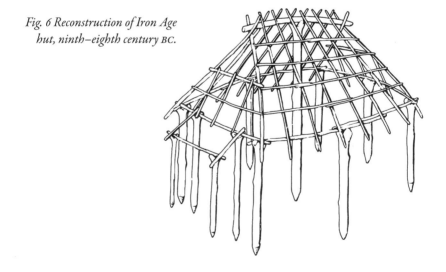

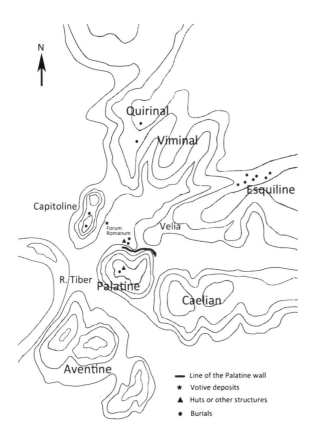

Fig. 7 Rome: key areas of development by the late eighth century BC.

of settlement have been identified, on the Palatine, Capitoline, Quirinal/ Viminal and the Caelian/Oppian/Velia area, with evidence of sparser settlement between them. Estimates of the size of eighth-century Rome range from 100 to 203 ha (247–500 acres), but a figure towards the upper end of this range would be consistent with developments at nearby Villanovan sites such as Veii.

The Forum was no longer used as a cemetery for adults, although an area near the later Temple of Antoninus and Faustina was reserved for infant and juvenile burials (fig. 7). Instead, the first finds on the sites of key public buildings point to a transformation of the Forum from cemetery to public space. Part of the Forum was paved over – evidence that it had a special status as a public area. The earliest finds in the area of the Comitium (the area in which the Roman assembly met) and the Volcanal (shrine of Vulcan) located next to it, are eighth-century votive offerings, which indicate that a religious cult was celebrated there. Objects and the remains of huts on the site of the House of the Vestals and those of a substantial house of *c.* 4–5 m × 8 m (15 × 26 feet) on the adjacent site of the Domus Publica (the official residence of the chief priest, the *pontifex maximus*), previously believed to be seventh century, are now dated to *c.* 750–700. By *c.* 700, finds in several areas of the Forum that were later connected with public life provide the first signs that the Forum was a special area devoted to the civic life of Rome.

The Capitoline, one of the key religious areas of Rome, also underwent important changes. In later periods it was the site of temples of the Capitoline cult (Jupiter, Juno and Minerva, a cult closely identified with the Roman state), Juno and Jupiter Feretrius, said to be the oldest temple in Rome. Even the Romans did not understand the name of the cult – Feretrius may refer to Jupiter as bearer of arms or as wielder of thunderbolts – but it was of high importance as the temple was where spoils of war were dedicated, treaties concluded and solemn oaths sworn. Votive offerings dating to *c.* 750–725 demonstrate that religious activity was established on the Capitoline by the middle of the eighth century. The location of these is particularly evocative because of the antiquity and importance of Jupiter Feretrius and the Capitoline cult. Livy's belief that the temple of Jupiter Feretrius was founded by Romulus himself cannot be substantiated, but the presence of early votive deposits demonstrates that the Capitoline was a site of religious significance from a very early date. Eighth-century religious activity was not confined to the Capitoline, however. Votive deposits at S. Omobono, in the Forum Boarium, contained offerings of imported Greek pottery, including Euboean, Corinthian and Pithecusan items, which demonstrate that Rome's range of contacts outside Latium was increasing, and specifically that it had connections with the Greek settlement of Pithecusae, an important entrepôt for Greek goods.

In the mid- to late eighth century new developments took place on the Palatine. A stretch of eighth-century wall has been excavated at the foot of the hill, on the north side, as it runs down towards the Forum. It consisted of a stone and earth foundation topped with a narrow wall approximately one metre (just over three feet) wide, made of wood and compressed clay, and flanked by a ditch. A gateway in the wall, which Carandini identifies with the Porta Mugonia mentioned by Livy as one of the ancient gates of Rome, and the route of an early street were also found. Finds from the foundations of the gateway date the initial construction of the wall to *c.* 730–720, although it was extended and rebuilt twice during the seventh and sixth centuries. Further to the north-east, excavations have revealed an early street and crossroads, marked by two votive deposits containing objects of the eighth and seventh centuries, and an open precinct marked with tufa blocks. The excavators suggest that this may have been the Curiae Veteres, the location at which the earliest assembly of the Roman people met.

The odd location of the Palatine wall, its narrow dimensions and the presence of boundary stones and a possible votive deposit all raise questions about its purpose. At one level this seems obvious – to defend the settlement on the Palatine. If this was its main function, however, both the structure and position of the wall are a little odd. A more robust structure built on the top of the Palatine, rather than at its foot, would have been a much more effective fortification. It seems more likely that it had a dual purpose, as a rudimentary defence work and as a way of marking the formal boundary of the settlement. The marking out of such ritual boundaries was an important part of founding a city in later times, and the myths associated with the foundation of Rome describe Romulus demarcating the boundary of his city. Some of the finds associated with the wall have been deeply controversial. Carandini argued that human remains found near the gateway were those of a sacrificial victim buried beneath the gate as a ritual act, and are evidence that the wall and gateway were indeed the ritual boundary of Rome. The custom of burying a human sacrifice beneath the walls or gate of a new settlement is known in early Italy, and could explain the human remains at the foot of the Palatine, but remains of several other burials were found in this area. The human remains on the Palatine may be a ritual sacrifice marking the gateway, but they may also be an ordinary burial which had been disturbed by the new structure. Nevertheless, the position of the wall suggests that it was not just a fortification but also marked the boundary of the Palatine settlement. The Romans themselves associated the Palatine with the ancient boundary of Rome (Roma Quadrata – literally 'Square Rome'), which they believed was established by Romulus.

As discussed in the previous chapter, the dating of the Latial culture is more fluid than the chronologies for most other areas of Iron-Age Italy. This inevitably means that there are areas of uncertainty and the chronology may be open to revision in the light of future discoveries. Despite this, the evolution of eighth-century Rome is becoming clearer. Although the Iron-Age settlements at Rome occupied a group of hills rather than a single plateau, the pattern of development is very similar to that of contemporary Etruria and Latium, with the growth of a number of settlements in close proximity which gradually merged into a single community. There were several substantial settlements, on the Palatine and Capitoline and probably on other hills; remains of huts on the Quirinal support the thesis that these were not the only hills that were settled. The construction of the Palatine wall, the placement of boundary stones and the evidence of a crossroads all suggest that it had acquired a defined boundary and some form of street layout, evidence of a more sophisticated level of social and political organisation. The abandonment of the Forum cemetery during the eighth century in favour of new burial areas and the use of the Forum as public space point to the development of these areas as shared civic and ritual spaces for the inhabitants of all communities, demonstrating an increasing level of centralisation. Like Veii and other Villanovan centres, Rome was a proto-urban settlement, probably organised around families or clans that each maintained their own area, but which converged into a single settlement during the course of the later eighth century.

A visitor to Rome at the end of the eighth century would have found a group of substantial settlements of wood and clay huts, occupying several hills. These had defined boundaries and defences, cemeteries and an area reserved for public and ceremonial activities. It may have been composed of several interdependent villages, possibly dominated by specific clans or families, but maintenance of separate burial areas suggests that the various settlements retained their own separate identities within the wider community. The increasing evidence for the development of the Forum in the late eighth century suggests that these settlements were well on their way to developing into a single community. Eighth-century Rome was, like Veii and Nepi (anc. Nepet), 'proto-urban', a community that was more complex than a village but which had not yet become fully urban.

Romulus, Remus, Evander and Aeneas

If the archaeology of early Rome is complex, the myths and traditions that preserve the Romans' own understanding of their origins, and those of others, are no less so. There are two distinct strands, each with a long and complicated history: the foundation of Rome by Romulus and Remus, and the 'prequel', which focuses on their ancestor the Trojan hero Aeneas.

Perhaps the best-known foundation myths concern Romulus, the grandson of Numitor, the king of the Latin city of Alba Longa. There are several variations of this, but in the best-known, Numitor was deposed by his brother Amulius, and his daughter, Rhea Silvia, was forced to become a Vestal Virgin to prevent her marrying and producing a rival heir to the throne. Despite this, she became pregnant – by the god Mars, in some versions – and gave birth to twin sons, Romulus and Remus. Amulius gave orders to expose them and leave them to die on the slopes of the Palatine, but they were suckled by a she-wolf and rescued by a herdsman, Faustulus. They were brought up by Faustulus and his wife, Acca Larentia, and lived as herdsmen until they reached adulthood, when their true origins were revealed. They ejected the usurper Amulius from Alba and reinstated Numitor as king, but then left to found a city of their own on the site of Rome.[6] Remus disappears from the story, killed by his brother during a quarrel in some versions, although there are several variants. Romulus then went on to lay out the boundaries of the new city, and in order to increase the population he declared it to be an asylum – an area in which displaced or exiled people, criminals fleeing justice or runaway slaves could seek sanctuary and settle. Although this increased the size of the settlement, it resulted in a predominantly male population, so, to rebalance this, Romulus invited the people of neighbouring settlements to allow their women to intermarry with the Romans. When these overtures were declined, he used the religious festival of the Consualia, which was attended by people from the area outside Rome, as a pretext to abduct the women of the neighbouring Sabines. Needless to say, this did not endear him to the Sabine men, who sent an army to fetch their womenfolk back. According to Livy, this counter-raid was foiled by the women themselves, who were distressed at the war between their birth families and their new ones, and insisted that the two sides make peace. From this point onwards, Romulus reigned as co-ruler along with the Sabine king Titus Tatius.

Romulus is credited with an implausibly long reign of thirty-eight years, and many key features of the Roman state are attributed to him. His foundation of the city involved laying out a square boundary, the *pomerium*, which he marked by a furrow, and which retained huge symbolic significance to Romans.[7] According to Ovid (*Fast.* 1.25–30), he was responsible for creating the Roman calendar and founding some of the most significant festivals. He is also credited with the division of the Roman people into three tribes and thirty subdivisions of these, known as *curiae*, creating laws and governing with an advisory council which was the forerunner of the later senate. Finally he disappeared and was assumed to have been carried off to become a god. After his apotheosis, various cults and festivals in his honour were established.

Aspects of the Romulus myth, such as the rape of a mortal woman by a god, the abandoned babies raised by animals and [the foundling princes raised by a poor family] are similar to myths found in many other societies throughout the Mediterranean and Near East, but it is difficult to pinpoint the date at which the specific legend of Romulus and Remus first appeared in Italy. Wolf legends seem to have existed in a number of early Italian societies, and representations of she-wolves are found in Etruscan art, although the famous bronze statue of the Capitoline wolf, often used as evidence for the presence of wolf legends as early as the sixth century, is now the subject of some controversy. It is conventionally believed to be of Etruscan manufacture, but in a fundamental reappraisal the art historian Anna Maria Carruba has argued that it is in fact of medieval date, undermining its relevance to this issue. Even if the original Etruscan attribution is accepted, the figures of the twins are later additions and it does not offer conclusive evidence for the early development of the Romulus legend. An Etruscan bronze mirror from Bolsena, engraved with a scene featuring a she-wolf, along with a shepherd and several deities, has been interpreted as a depiction of a scene from the Romulus myth, featuring Faustulus, the wolf and the twins. However, there are key differences between the scene as depicted here and the legend, and the mirror is of fourth-century date, leaving us with no secure evidence linking the legend to the sixth century. By the third century, however, the wolf and the twins were established as a symbol of Rome. The Ogulnius brothers set up a statue of them near the *ficus ruminalis*, the fig tree associated with the legend, in 296 (Livy 10.32.12), and they were sufficiently widely recognised for an image to appear on one of the earliest issues of Roman coinage, issued in 269 (see pl. 21), but the earlier development of the legend is now less clearly attested.

Ancient tradition also included a 'prequel' to the Romulus myth which conferred added prestige on him by tracing his descent from the Trojan prince Aeneas. Stories about the foundation of Rome, connecting it with the heroes of the Trojan War, were known in the wider Mediterranean world from at least the fifth century, and the Nestor cup demonstrates that the Homeric myths were known in Italy from at least the eighth century. The Greek historian Hellanicus, whose works survive only as fragments, knew of a story of a foundation by Aeneas, Odysseus and a Trojan woman called Rhome, suggesting that legends concerning Rome were established in Greek literature by this date. Greek writers knew of at least sixty different versions of Rome's foundation, attributing it to various groups of wandering Greeks, but the preferred version in Rome took the story back to Aeneas.

Aeneas' role in Rome's foundation can be traced in Roman tradition at least from the time of Ennius and Naevius, writing in the third century BC. Livy (1.1) briefly recounts how Aeneas, the semi-divine son of the Trojan Anchises and the goddess Venus, escaped from Troy after its sack by the Greeks and sailed to the western Mediterranean accompanied by his son, Ascanius (sometimes also called Iulus), and a group of companions. On arriving in Italy, he made an alliance with the local ruler, Latinus, and married Latinus' daughter Lavinia. He became leader of both the native Italians and the Trojans, now collectively renamed Latini (Latins), and founded a new city, Lavinium. A series of wars with other central Italian princes followed, notably against Turnus, king of the Rutuli, and Mezentius, ruler of Caere, during which the Latini gained control of the Alban Hills and the surrounding area. After the death of Aeneas, during or shortly after this war, Ascanius became king of the Latins and founded Alba Longa in the Alban Hills as their main city. After several generations, during which Alba became established as a major power in Latium, civil war broke out between Numitor and Amulius, brothers and rivals for control of Alba Longa. Numitor was exiled, but his grandsons Romulus and Remus went on to found Rome.

Like the foundation myths about Romulus, the Aeneas myth has a long history in both Greek and Roman culture. There are references to Aeneas' journey to Italy in Greek literature and depictions of it in Etruscan art. Perhaps the most concrete evidence is a hero-shrine to Aeneas that was established at Lavinium by the sixth century. Greek historians were keen to prove that the Italians in general, and the Romans in particular, were Greek in origin and thus fit them into the Greek world. Dionysios of Halicarnassus ascribes fictional Greek origins to many Italic peoples and places, including attributing the first settlements at Rome both to the Greek demigod Herakles and to Evander, a Greek from Arcadia, and his followers. Probably the best-known version, however, is that of Virgil, whose epic poem the *Aeneid* narrates Aeneas' journey to Italy after the fall of Troy, his marriage to the Latin princess Lavinia and his alliance with Evander. The poem foretells the foundation of Alba Longa and Lavinium, portrays Aeneas as the ultimate founder of Roman greatness, even though he did not found the city itself, and describes him as having a divinely ordained destiny to found Rome:

> It was not for this that she [Venus] twice rescued him from the swords of the Greeks. She told us that he was the man to rule Italy, pregnant with empire, and crying out for war, passing the high blood of Teucer to his descendants and subduing the whole world to his laws. If the glory of such a destiny does not fire his heart, if he does not strive to win fame for himself, ask him if he grudges the citadel of Rome to his son Ascanius?
>
> (Virgil, *Aeneid* 4.229–35 [trans. D. West])[8]

[handwritten marginal note: plebian = common folk / patrician = high class]

All these traditions about Roman origins are clearly in the realms of myth rather than history, but they are important – not as historical evidence for the foundation of Rome but for what they tell us about the Romans' own beliefs about their past. Some aspects of the Romulus myth are distinctly odd. Although most states in the ancient Mediterranean had similar myths of a heroic founder, almost all of these attributed their foundation to someone of high distinction: Homeric heroes such as Aeneas or Odysseus, or demigods such as Herakles, for instance. Roman foundation myths, in contrast, are morally ambivalent tales. Romulus was a man of doubtful parentage who grew up in obscurity, and the establishment of his new city involved fratricide, recruitment of outsiders and criminals, and mass abduction and rape. This idea of the founding hero as an outsider is not uncommon in ancient mythology, and other cultures have similar myths of heroes who are illegitimate or carry some sort of stigma, but the Romulus myth carries these features to extremes – in particular, in the ethnically mixed nature of the settlement he founded.

The fate of Remus particularly bothered the Romans and illustrates the complex and multilayered nature of the various traditions. There are a number of different versions of his involvement in the foundation of the city, and of his death, but the idea that he was the victim of fratricide had particular significance in the violent years of the late Republic. Romulus' motives, and whether his action was justified, were debated by figures as various as Cicero and St Augustine. Cicero concluded that Romulus acted entirely from political expediency, while Augustine (*City of God* 3.6) admits that this aspect of the story was difficult for the Romans, saying that 'many brazenly deny it; many question it in shame; many find it too painful to admit'. However, there were other versions, in which Remus was not the victim of his brother but died in a riot when his supporters and those of his brother clashed. In this retelling, his death symbolised self-sacrifice and the need to protect Rome rather than fraternal violence. Evidence for Remus is thin on the ground before the early third century, but in later versions of the foundation myth he is said to have founded a settlement on the Aventine hill, a centre of popular protest during a power struggle in the fifth to third centuries, and Wiseman has argued that his increased prominence was because he became a symbol of plebeian resistance to patrician power at this period.[9]

It is possible that Remus is a dramatisation and rationalisation of important features of early Rome. Many aspects of the myths play on ideas of duality. Rome has two founders (Romulus and Remus) and two kings (Romulus and the Sabine Titus Tatius); it includes two main ethnic groups; it is founded on more than one site, with settlements on several hills. The foundation by twins and the presence of Remus as part of the myth are an important part of this, providing a rationalisation for dualities and divisions of power within the city. Nevertheless, Remus remains a more marginal figure than Romulus, and his presence raises some troubling questions.

Although some aspects of the Romulus myth may seem strangely negative for a city that took such pride in its imperial power, they include aspects that the Romans regarded as fundamental to their collective identity. A willingness to incorporate outsiders by making them Roman citizens is an important feature of Roman culture, and was central to establishment of Roman power. Levels of mobility, both of individuals and groups, were high in archaic Italy, and it seems to have been fairly easy to cross state and ethnic boundaries and to live in communities to which one did not belong by birth. Rome, however, took this to a higher level by extending Roman citizenship fairly generously to non-Romans (see Chapter 13). As Emma Dench has demonstrated, Romulus' asylum and inclusion of Sabines in the new city was a powerful validation of openness to new cultures and ethnic groups as a core aspect of Roman identity. The Sabines were equal partners in the new Roman state, represented by the dual kingship of Romulus and Titus Tatius, and their incorporation was cited by later Romans to justify the granting of Roman citizenship to outsiders. Such openness about citizenship was one of Rome's major strengths when it came to incorporating conquered peoples, but it was not universally approved of by later writers. Cicero, in one of his letters to Atticus (Cic., *Att.* 2.1.8.3) refers sourly to the Roman people as the 'faex Romuli' ('the dregs of Romulus'). Nevertheless, by ascribing a high degree of ethnic and cultural flexibility to Romulus, the myth emphasises the importance of these aspects of Roman culture and validates them by this association. Romulus' story also contains many elements of violence and confrontation. In some versions the father of Romulus and Remus is human, but in others Rhea Silvia is raped by Mars, the god of war, and Romulus' later career involved abducting the Sabine women and making war against Latins and Sabines. The symbolism of Mars as father of Rome's founder has obvious resonance in the light of Rome's later imperial conquests. Aggression and territorial expansion are implicitly justified by association with a revered founder, and the placing of Mars at the centre of the foundation myth gives an added sense of Rome's destiny to rule.

These were not matters of merely antiquarian interest to later Romans. The foundation myths continued to have resonance for them, but they were not static; they changed in response to changes in Roman culture or political circumstances. Even the foundation date of 753 BC did not become widely accepted until the later first century BC; earlier historians such as Fabius Pictor and Cincius Alimentus dated its foundation to other years in the eighth century (748/7 or 729/8 BC). Others, such as Ennius and Naevius, favoured a much earlier date, and the Alban kings who filled the gap between Aeneas and Romulus were suggested as a way of reconciling the date of foundation with the chronology of the Trojan War.

Emphasis on the role of Aeneas was particularly strong during the first century. By then Rome was a dominant Mediterranean power and in contact with Greek cities and kingdoms in the eastern Mediterranean, and a heroic Trojan founder was a mythical past that Greeks would recognise and understand. Aeneas acquired other political overtones in the era of Augustus, the first Roman emperor. He presented himself as a re-founder of Rome, restoring the state after a prolonged period of civil war; he even considered taking the name of Romulus. He had a personal connection with the legend, as his family, the Julii (he was the maternal grand-nephew and adopted son of Julius Caesar), claimed descent from Aeneas. Aeneas, therefore, became a powerful symbol of the new regime, and references to the Aeneas legend are frequent in Augustan art and literature. Virgil's Aeneas and his destiny to establish Roman greatness clearly prefigure

Augustus and his mission to restore Rome after a long period of civil war. The foundation legends of Rome were constantly evolving, remaining important to the Romans' own changing self-identities, and could be reinterpreted to suit new circumstances or appealed to as validation for many aspects of Roman life. They can tell us much about who the Romans believed they were, and about their views on their own culture and history. What they cannot do, however, is offer genuine historical evidence for the earliest history of the city.

History and archaeology

These ancient traditions about the foundation of Rome present their own problems, not least because they changed and evolved, are frequently self-contradictory and were sometimes questioned even by some Romans.[10] As indicated above, I believe that for this earliest period of Roman history these should be examined for what they say about the Romans' own views of their past, their identity and their place in the world, rather than as a repository of information about the earliest settlement. The importance of foundation myths to the later culture of Rome, and to the Romans' sense of themselves, is demonstrated by the number of locations in Rome that remained closely associated with aspects of these stories. Many of these were the focus of important rituals and cults which were celebrated until well into the period of Christianisation in the fourth century AD. Romulus and the foundation myths were woven into the topography of the city in a very real and immediate sense, and the Romans continued to revere the locations associated with them. Although many of these rituals appear to be very ancient, the forms they took, the significance attached to them and the places with which they were associated were not set in stone but changed over time, demonstrating both the power of these myths and the ways in which they were manipulated to meet changing needs.

A number of rituals and festivals illustrate this point. The Parilia, celebrated on 21 April, was a festival honouring the ancient god Pales, but within Rome it also commemorated Romulus' foundation of the city. There were a number of other festivals, particularly the Septimontium, which was a series of sacrifices dedicated to seven hills and their inhabitants, and which may well date back to a pre-urban period when Rome was composed of several settlements. The festivals of the Argei, at which figures made of straw were collected from key points in the city by a procession of priests and magistrates and ritually thrown into the Tiber, falls into the same category.[11] However, both events seem to be linked with purification of ancient sacred boundaries. Many of these festivals continued to be celebrated throughout Antiquity; the Parilia was still going strong in AD 121, when Hadrian renamed it the Romaia. The festivals and rituals connected with Romulus and the foundation of Rome continued to play an important role in the ritual life of the city until Late Antiquity.

Romulus was a powerful presence in the urban landscape of later Rome, and sites associated with him were closely linked to the well-being of the city, as is demonstrated by the long-lived House of Romulus on the Palatine,[12] which was a hero-shrine to the mythical founder. This is described by Dionysios of Halicarnassus and Plutarch as a wattle-and-daub hut with a thatched roof, which was preserved on the Palatine and believed to have been the house of Romulus. These descriptions are very similar to the appearance of the hut urns found in Latial burials and to the ninth- and eighth-century huts found at Fidenae and Rome. If it fell into disrepair, it was replaced in the original style and materials, and any damage to it was perceived as a bad omen. It was listed in a fourth-century AD catalogue of Roman buildings, which suggests that it continued to be maintained until Late Antiquity.

On current evidence, the site of Rome was occupied by *c.* 1200, and other small settlements developed in nearby areas during the early Iron Age. By the middle of the eighth century there were well-established settlements at Rome and other key Latin sites, although the smaller communities in the Alban Hills failed to grow and were abandoned or eclipsed. The Palatine wall implies a reorganisation of the settlement with greater emphasis on boundaries and territorial demarcation. This in itself suggests concentration of social and political authority at Rome into the hands of a person (or more likely a group of people or families) powerful enough to instigate such a reorganisation.

Proto-urban settlements throughout central and northern Italy were organised into clusters of houses, each with its own burial area, a pattern of development similar to that of Rome and at sites elsewhere in the region, such as Osteria dell'Osa. Terrenato's suggestion that the settlements on the Palatine and Capitoline were the territories of different clans is an attractive one. The organisation of Rome into *curiae*, based on family/clan ties and attributed in ancient tradition to Romulus, is regarded by many as a very ancient feature of Roman society. If Terrenato is correct, it is possible – although not provable on current evidence – that the *curiae* preserved memories of Rome's early origins as a group of settlements by different clans which co-operated and eventually merged into a single community. However, it is impossible to leap from evidence for a substantial eighth-century proto-urban settlement to acceptance of the tradition that Rome was founded in 753 or thereabouts by Romulus, or the deeds ascribed to him. The Roman mythological tradition offers fascinating insights into Roman beliefs about their own past and their rationalisation of this, but it cannot be interpreted as a history of the foundation of the city.

4

THE RISE OF THE INTERNATIONAL ARISTOCRACY: ITALY AND THE ORIENTALISING REVOLUTION

In 1836 a priest and a local landowner, Alessandro Regolini and Vincenzo Galassi, made a spectacular discovery near Cerveteri in northern Lazio, close to the site of the Etruscan city of Caere. Underneath an earth mound they found a seventh-century Etruscan tomb – now known as the Regolini–Galassi tomb, after its discoverers – containing a huge collection of over 300 rich grave goods. The tomb consisted of four chambers cut into the rock and linked by a corridor. It contained two burials, the principal one being an Etruscan woman of very high status,[1] and the accompanying grave offerings included inlaid furniture, a ceremonial carriage, many finely worked vessels of metal and pottery, and a large collection of gold jewellery, all of it intricately decorated.

The burial illustrates some of the key features of what is termed the orientalising period (*c.* 700 to 575). This was an era of rapid social and economic change during which contact intensified between Italy, Egypt, the Near East and the wider Mediterranean. It was marked by the development of steep hierarchies of wealth, social status and political power. If the main trend in the eighth century had been the development of proto-urban settlements structured around families and elites with a warrior identity, the seventh century was dominated by the emergence of a hugely wealthy and powerful international aristocracy. As well as exercising growing domination over their own communities, the families belonging to this group established social networks with their peers across state and ethnic boundaries to form an international super-elite. The material culture of Italy was transformed by their wealth and appetite for luxury goods, some of which were manufactured locally and others imported. Changes to settlements, connected with this boom in wealth and the restructuring of social and political power, provided further impetus towards urbanisation.

These changes were most marked in Etruria, but all communities – including Rome – show a similar pattern of growing prosperity accompanied by a concentration of resources, social status and political power into the hands of a small and dominant elite. Princely burials such as the Regolini–Galassi tomb are found throughout central Italy and show remarkable similarities in their construction and contents. A pan-Italian aristocratic culture was developing, marked by access to, and conspicuous consumption of, luxury goods. By far the richest and most comprehensive evidence we have comes from Etruria, but the trends we find there are true of most areas of Italy, and in particular of Latium and Campania.

Princely burials and conspicuous consumption

The most conspicuous demonstration of this concentration of social and political power is found in changes in burial practice. In the eighth century the spatial layout of cemeteries emphasised family groups. Richer burials for some individuals in the late eighth century suggests that a social and political elite was starting to develop, and that warrior status was central to the self-image of this elite. In the seventh century, however, elite burials were no longer about maintaining social identities within a community. Instead, they were displays of conspicuous consumption, and about competing for status with their peer group on an international level. Warrior status, although still significant, became secondary to the importance of displaying family power and identity.

From *c.* 700 the elites of Etruria and adjacent areas began to build chamber tombs intended for multiple burials. Typically, these consisted of underground tomb chambers (or, where the rock was unsuitable for excavating underground chambers, burial chambers constructed from stone blocks) covered by an earth mound, or tumulus (pls 8 and 9). Some were relatively simply structures, with only an antechamber or entrance passage and a single tomb chamber, but it was not uncommon for tombs to have suites of two or more burial chambers (fig. 8). Many of the interiors mimicked houses, with ceilings carved to resemble house beams, carved stone furniture and even stone representations of pillows and coverlets on the couches and household goods on the walls (see pl. 9). In regions where the predominant burial rite was inhumation, burial chambers were lined with stone funerary couches on which the bodies of the deceased were placed. Where cremation remained the norm, as in northern Etruria, Picenum and the Veneto, the ashes were placed in bronze or pottery containers, sometimes moulded to resemble the head and upper torso of the deceased, which were then placed on a ceremonial chair or couch (pl. 25).

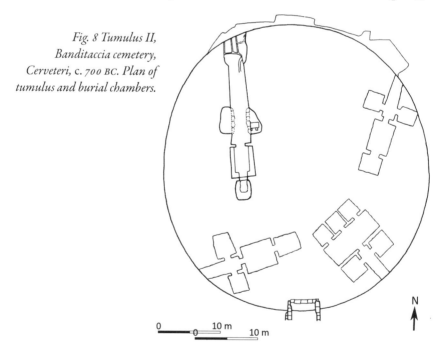

Fig. 8 Tumulus II, Banditaccia cemetery, Cerveteri, c. 700 BC. Plan of tumulus and burial chambers.

0   10 m
0   10 m

N

These tombs and their contents represented a major outlay by important families, and their monumental size ensured maximum visibility.

This type of tomb remained in use throughout the seventh and sixth centuries, and cemeteries outside major Etruscan cities contained many tumulus burials, but they were not confined to Etruria. Similar burials are found in Latium (for instance, at Praeneste and Castel di Decima), in Campania (Cumae, Pontecagnano), parts of Samnium and in the Veneto (Este). A study by Sarah Willemsen of forty tombs from Crustumerium demonstrates similar changes in burial customs in Latium Vetus between *c.* 650 and 550. Grave goods become less copious and conspicuously wealthy during the course of this period, but tomb architecture becomes much more monumental and elaborate, and multi-burial tombs become the norm. Willemsen speculates that these changes may have been driven by, among other things, increasing social competition between elite families, which channelled expenditure into construction of monumental tombs. In southern Italy, in contrast, simple inhumations in trenches, sometimes lined and capped with stone slabs, remained the main burial rite, and grave goods were less ostentatious. Other evidence suggests that the societies of southern Italy were just as dominated by wealthy aristocrats, but conspicuous funerary display was a less important status symbol in this region.

The difference in scale and ambition between tumulus tombs and the burials of the preceding era is enormous. Although some small chamber tombs may have been intended for a single occupant or a couple, most were intended for multiple use by an extended family over several generations. The development of clan burial is illustrated by two tumulus burials at Satricum. Burial mound C (*c.* 775/750–600) covered a large group of burials arranged in a circle, segregated by status with the richest depositions in the centre and the poorest on the periphery. Mound F, also dating to the seventh century, was closer in type to the Etruscan tumuli. The depositions were fewer in number, although it included one princely burial, and the dead were placed in stone burial chambers. Both of these seem to have been the burial places of powerful clans. The priority was no longer to commemorate notable individuals but to create monuments to an entire noble family. The warrior ideology of the eighth century did not disappear and continued to be reflected in some grave goods, but the emphasis was now on monuments showcasing family status.

Aristocratic tombs of this type became the focus of cults designed to celebrate the history, identity and importance of the family, and to

*Fig. 9 Gravestone of
Avele Feluske, Vetulonia,
late seventh century.*

honour its founder. In northern Italy carved gravestones were displayed outside tombs. The late seventh-century Tomb of the Warrior at Vetulonia was marked by a stone stele showing a warrior armed with a double axe, probably celebrating the founder of the dynasty (fig. 9). It was inscribed with his name, Avele Feluske, along with those of his parents, and that of the dedicator of the monument, Hirumina of Perusia (mod. Perugia). Elsewhere, we find altars set up outside tombs, such as the Tomb of the Cima (Caere), but the most striking evidence for a tomb cult comes from the nearby Tomb of the Five Chairs. Five throne-like stone chairs are lined up in a side-chamber of the tomb, flanked by tables, an altar, baskets and lower seats, all carved out of stone and mimicking a room set up for religious ceremonies. Fragmentary painted terracotta statues found in the tomb were probably originally placed on the chairs to represent the dead family. All the figures wear ankle-length tunics, decorated with a chequer-board pattern, and a cloak pinned on one shoulder and draped across the body, while the women wear large hooped ear-rings and their hair is drawn back into a long braid. The figures are posed with one hand outstretched, as if holding an offering or poised to pour a libation.

Many tombs were excavated in the nineteenth and early twentieth centuries by enthusiastic amateurs who did not record finds and associations with the precision of modern best practice. Others attracted (and continue to attract) the attentions of *tombaroli*, professional tomb robbers who sold their contents on the international art market.

Nonetheless the grave goods we have from such tombs are impressive. Many male burials contained horse bridles along with ornate weapons and armour more likely to have been used for ceremony than in battle. Most tombs were provided with banqueting services of pottery or bronze vessels. These generally included vessels in bucchero, a characteristic Etruscan pottery with a high-gloss black glaze, often with incised motifs (pl. 10), together with a mix of Greek pottery and local wares decorated in Greek style (pl. 11). Other exotic finds included carved ostrich eggs, ivory ornaments, faience beads and amulets. Jewellery such as fibulae, ear-rings and necklaces was sometimes made of gold and encrusted with granulated decoration. Tombs were houses of the dead, and were equipped with richly decorated furniture as well as personal ornaments. Usually, only the decorated inlays of ivory or bronze survive, but some high-backed ceremonial chairs were so completely encased in sheet bronze that they are preserved more or less intact. The most impressive tombs contained carriages or chariots which, like the furniture, were richly decorated (pl. 26).

The Bernardini and Barberini tombs at Praeneste in Latium give a flavour of the extravagance of princely tombs. Grave gifts included bronze tripods and cauldrons, silver jugs and bowls decorated in Greek and Syrian style (pl. 12), gold fibulae and clasps of large size and elaborate decoration, weapons decorated with silver and amber, and a large amount of carved ivory, probably decorative inlays for wooden furniture which has not survived, as well as a high-backed chair encased in sheet bronze. They also contained numerous items of tableware, and long decorated poles, probably the remains of at least one chariot.

These tombs and their contents reveal a trend towards conspicuous consumption as a demonstration of family status. As well as impressing the mourners and providing the dead with a comfortable afterlife, they demonstrated the wealth of the families, although they prioritise the symbolic value of luxury items as status symbols over their intrinsic economic value. Many items were imported from Greece, the Near East and Egypt, or show the influence of eastern styles and craft techniques, and an elite that owned such things was not just rich. It controlled access to international trade networks and could employ skilled craftsmen from all over the Mediterranean and beyond. Grave goods also reveal changes in social values. Iron-Age burials were those of a warrior elite, but orientalising weapons and armour were for show rather than use, and the chariots and carriages were not military equipment but processional vehicles, designed for ceremonial display. Corinna Riva's study of these burials has described the orientalising princes as cultivating an image of the 'civilised warrior'; their image as warriors – represented by decorative ceremonial armour – co-existed with that of munificent princes, entertaining their peers and followers.

Settlements, sanctuaries and palaces

For many years one of the puzzling aspects of orientalising Italy was the disparity between the funerary evidence, with its wealthy burials, and the much less impressive evidence from settlements. This posed intriguing questions about where, and how, this wealthy elite lived. These questions were partly answered in 1970, with the discovery of a complex of monumental buildings at Poggio Civitate, near Murlo, 20 km (12.5 miles) south of Siena. There are traces of Iron-Age settlement in the area, but in the early seventh century a group of much larger buildings was constructed, from c. 675–650 (fig. 10). The main building was of mud brick on a stone foundation, with a floor of beaten earth. It contained numerous fragments of painted terracotta sculptures and mouldings, decorations from the eaves and ridge of the roof, which would have given the building an imposing appearance. The lifestyle of the inhabitants was lavish. Finds included fragments of dinner services of imported Greek pottery

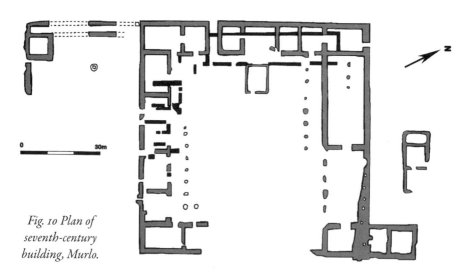

Fig. 10 Plan of
seventh-century
building, Murlo.

and locally produced ceramics, personal ornaments and bone and ivory objects, probably inlays from items of furniture.

There were two other structures on the site. To the south, another large building was divided into three parts, with a spacious central hall flanked by two smaller chambers. The finds included fine pottery, some of it inscribed with personal names and the formula *mini muluvanice* ('I am the gift of ...'). To the south-east, an even larger structure contained industrial debris, food remains and tools, and was probably a workshop producing a wide range of food items and manufactured goods for local consumption.[2] All three buildings were destroyed by fire at the end of the seventh century. A tray of tiles in the workshop was covered with footprints, as if workers fleeing the fire had run across it as they left. Other nearby settlements were undamaged, suggesting that the destruction of Murlo was an accident, not the result of enemy action, although both scenarios are possible. Recent excavation has revealed a fourth building, possibly the earliest of all, on the site. This was a long, rectangular building, with two rooms, and open at one end. Its stone walls and tiled roof, and finds – which included fine pottery and spindle whorls – suggest that it may have been an imposing elite residence.

Despite the scale of the damage, this was not the end of Murlo. In the sixth century the three earlier buildings were replaced by a single massive structure *c.* 60 m (197 ft) square, consisting of four wings enclosing a central courtyard, and an additional courtyard to the south protected by a fortification. Like its predecessor, it was decorated with terracotta statues and reliefs. It was in use for a relatively short time, however, and seems to have been abandoned and demolished some time around 550.

Murlo is often described as a palace, but its function is ambiguous, and it has been variously identified as a religious sanctuary, a public building used for political meetings or an aristocratic house. The tripartite building is similar in form to Etruscan temples, which have a central chamber divided into three parts, and the gift-giving formula inscribed on some of the pottery suggests that they were votive offerings. However, finds from the main building include many high-quality personal and domestic items, suggesting that it was the residence of someone of high rank. This is corroborated by the terracottas. The statues from the roof depict men wearing high-crowned and wide-brimmed hats, a form of headgear that occurs in art throughout central and northern Italy as a mark of status. The terracotta plaques recovered from the later phase of the building are decorated

Fig. 11 Scenes from a terracotta frieze, depicting banqueting
and a ceremonial occasion, Murlo. Seventh century BC.

in low relief with scenes of aristocratic pastimes such as banqueting, horse-racing and processions (fig. 11). The answer may be that religious, political and domestic uses were not mutually exclusive at this date. In a world of dominant aristocrats, buildings such as the Murlo complex had to accommodate political activities, official visitors and religious ceremonies as well as providing living-quarters. Murlo is the best-excavated of such residences, but it is not the only example. Similar large courtyard houses have come to light at Acquarossa, near Viterbo, in Etruria, and at Ficana, Gabii and Rome in Latium. The elites of the seventh century invested in large and impressive buildings which combined private accommodation with public and ritual space and were located in the countryside, not in the emerging cities.

From around 650 there were changes in more modest housing throughout Italy. Most were rectangular structures with thatched or tiled roofs, built of dressed stone or mud brick on stone foundations. Houses excavated at Ficana in Latium and San Giovenale in Etruria had an inner room, a courtyard and a porch supported on columns. At San Giovenale, a small settlement near Caere, it is possible to trace the development of some houses from simple thatched wooden huts in the early seventh century to more substantial stone houses with tile roofs and courtyards by *c*. 600. In Latium, Satricum offers an insight into how new forms of domestic architecture might have been used as social spaces. The two groups of huts on the acropolis were each replaced by a single house with stone foundations and a tiled roof, consisting of rows of small rooms opening off a central courtyard. Colantoni's study of these suggests that they were used in a similar fashion to the huts that they replaced, with couples, individuals or small families occupying the rooms and the courtyard used for communal activities such as cooking by the entire extended family or clan. Some archaeologists, notably Carmine Ampolo and Gabriele Cifani, see the development of courtyard houses (and particularly the larger examples, such as those at Murlo and Acquarossa) as a new development influenced by Greek and Syrian architecture and introduced by craftsmen from the eastern Mediterranean. As Colantoni has pointed out, however, the development of Satricum suggests a higher degree of continuity than this implies. The extended families living there had created more monumental forms of housing but retained traditional uses of space, suggesting that continuity was just as important as innovation, and that the roots of the courtyard house lie just as much in Italy as in the eastern Mediterranean. Additionally, the similarities between houses throughout Etruria and Latium demonstrates that, particularly among the aristocracies of central Italy, there were many shared aspects of elite culture and are an indication that Rome was not exceptional, but part of a central Italian cultural milieu.

Settlements in general grew in size and complexity in the seventh century and acquired many urban features. The proto-urban centres of the eighth century grew into larger nucleated settlements with several thousand inhabitants, many with urban features such as fortifications and more structured use of space, such as street plans and public buildings. At Satricum, for example, a small cult building on the acropolis was replaced at the end of the seventh century by a larger and more monumental temple, and a street layout is discernible. The best-excavated of the larger Etruscan centres, Tarquinii, shows a similar pattern. Houses were larger, streets more systematically organised and a building with a courtyard in which votive offerings were found may have been a temple. Similar processes were at work in parts of southern Italy. By the end of the seventh century Greek settlements had adopted an organised urban layout, with regular street plans and areas set aside for religious or civic use. This is particularly clear at Metapontum, which has been extensively surveyed. Although these sites had not yet expanded to anything like their later importance, they were growing rapidly in size and complexity. As discussed in Chapter 1, this pattern of nucleation, growth in size and greater signs of complexity in both settlement and territorial organisation are all indicators of urbanisation, and demonstrate the emergence of greater social and economic complexity and stronger political authority.

Key religious centres become visible in Italy for the first time in the seventh century. We know considerably more about cults and rituals from some regions than others, but some general trends can be identified. The earliest traces of religious activity are deposits of votive objects, including small figurines (often with hand outstretched in a gesture of offering), drinking vessels and clay models of votive cakes. These are found from the late eighth century onwards, sometimes accompanied by remains of animal bones. The concept of the *votum* (vow or promise), in which the worshipper makes, or promises, an offering to the gods in return for divine favour, is central to Roman and Italian religion, and, as these objects demonstrate, animal sacrifice, offerings of food and drink and the donation of small objects to secure divine help or favour were practices of great antiquity. Since most sacred places remained in use over long periods, it is possible to trace the development of religion and changes to religious customs. At Satricum votive deposits show that a spring became the focus of cult activity from *c.* 800. During the period between 800 and 400 an increasingly extensive complex of buildings was constructed on the site, including a stone temple dedicated to Mater Matuta. The votive objects included pottery vessels, weaving tools, weapons and figurines, many of which (particularly from the late sixth century onwards) depicted nursing mothers. Its position, the size and long chronology of the votive deposits, which included thousands of votives, and the size and location of the temple suggest that the worship of Mater Matuta was the main cult of Satricum. The nature of the cult is obscure, but the votives imply that Mater Matuta was a goddess of healing and fertility, although the presence of weapons suggests that she protected warriors as well as women in childbirth.[3]

Each region or ethnic group in Italy had its distinctive deities, often very localised. Many are connected with important elements in the life of the community, such as fertility, warfare, healing, protection of crops and animals, and protection of boundaries. The Romans had a complex calendar of festivals dedicated to deities such as Pales (protection of flocks), Robigus (protection from crop blight) and Terminus (protection of boundaries), which they believed to be very ancient, although the origins and meanings of these festivals were disputed even by Roman writers such as Varro and Ovid. Other Italian cultures had deities that played similar roles: Mater Matuta (at Satricum) seems to have protected both warriors and women; Mefitis (worshipped in Campania and Lucania) was a chthonic deity associated with fertility; while Reitia (worshipped at Baratella, near Este in the Veneto) was responsible both for healing and literacy. Although votive deposits can reveal the whereabouts of sacred places and sometimes the identity of the gods worshipped, we know little about the organisation of religion or what sort of rituals took place.

There is little sign of the monumental architecture that was later associated with both Greek and Roman religion. Most religious sites were open-air enclosures, often focused on natural features in the landscape, such as mountain tops, lakes and springs, or wooded areas. Some, such as Nemi and Lucus Feroniae in Latium, were sacred groves, while others, such as Aqua Ferentina (Latium) and the shrine of Mefitis at Rossano di Vaglio (Lucania), were the sites of sacred springs. The important sanctuaries of Mons Albanus (the Alban Mount) and Mount Soracte were hilltop sanctuaries, and many ritual sites in Puglia were located in caves. Worship did not require buildings, and the important features of a sanctuary were a defined boundary, to separate sacred from secular space, and an altar at which the priest could conduct sacrifices, pour libations and make other offerings to the gods. Augury was an important aspect of religious practice in some areas of Italy, so an enclosure with a good view of the horizon was important to some cults, as the augur needed to be able to observe the flight of birds as a means of gauging the will of the gods. Religious rituals may also have taken place elsewhere, such as the 'palace' at Murlo, which combined religious and domestic use, rather than in purpose-built temples. Huts seem to have been constructed at some sanctuaries from the ninth century and to have developed, in several phases, into specialised temples constructed on the same site, a pattern found at several Latin sites (for instance, Lanuvium and Gabii). However, these monumental temples are a sixth-century phenomenon, and any buildings at earlier sanctuaries were extremely modest.

Italian cult places were not purely religious but had a range of uses. Many of the earliest and most important sanctuaries were located not in cities but at significant locations in their territories. This was sometimes dictated by the association between cults and natural phenomena, but many were placed on political or natural boundaries in areas that marked the transition from one state to another, or from city to countryside. River mouths and promontories were also frequent sites of temples and cult places: for instance, the sanctuary of Hera Lacinia on Cape Lacinium in the territory of Croton, or the Heraion at Foce del Sele, near Paestum. Despite the rural setting, these were important centres of religious and political activity. They acted as a forum for economic activities, for legal hearings and for political meetings and negotiations as well as for religious rituals and festivals. Aqua Ferentina, for instance, was the regular meeting place of a league of Latin states until its dissolution by Rome in 338. The rural nature of many of these sanctuaries enhanced their role as meeting points for people from a wide area. Other sanctuaries and religious rituals may have been for marking boundaries and excluding other peoples. From our perspective they show the growing level of social organisation and state development. They were public locations which were accessible by people from different states and acted as important points of contact and dissemination of goods, ideas and information. Conversely, they can demonstrate a greater hardening of boundaries as communities developed a stronger sense of collective identity.

By c. 600 settlements were larger and more complex than their eighth-century counterparts and developing many more urban features. They were dominated by an aristocracy that lived in some style, owning lavish houses and burying their dead in prominent family tombs. The greater visibility and prominence of shrines and sanctuaries is a further indication of the formalisation of territorial boundaries between settlements.

The rise of the elites

So who were these aristocrats who lived in such splendour? And what was their relationship to the rest of society in this period? The level of domination exercised over the rest of society by a small number of aristocratic families seems to have been extensive. The lavish burials and large houses display family wealth and status, and tombs were the focus of cult practices and rituals devoted to celebrating family identity and probably the founder (real or fictive) or ancestors of the group. These developments go hand in hand with the increasing importance of the clan, or extended family, as a key element in Italian society. In this context a clan[4] can perhaps best be defined as a group of families claiming descent (real or not) from a common ancestor, sharing a common name, and worshipping a shared family cult, often honouring a mythical or semi-mythical founder of the family, as a means of reinforcing their identity. The enhanced importance of the clan as a source of status and power is demonstrated in changes in personal names. In Etruria, the region where we can trace this most securely,[5] there was a change during the seventh century from use of a single personal name – such as Larth, Avele or Velthur – to use of a two-part name. This consisted of a personal (given) name and an inherited clan name: for instance, Laris Velthie and Laucies Mezenties, known from inscriptions from Caere; or Velthur Talumnes and Pasna Nuzinaie, from Veii. Compound personal names of this type became the norm throughout Italy during the seventh and sixth centuries. The significance of this change is that it demonstrates that membership of a specific family was now an important part of social identity, and that the family and clan one belonged to were highly significant.

Despite the importance of the clan in orientalising Italy, we know frustratingly little about how they organised themselves. A clan consisted of several collateral families, the heads of which wielded considerable power, determining social alliances and political behaviour and ensuring that the status of the clan was maintained. It is often assumed that one such head of family was accepted as the head of the entire clan, but we have little evidence for whether this was the case (and if so, how he was chosen, or what powers he exercised). Iconography and archaeology confirm the social dominance of small groups of leading men, but not the relationship between them, or their subordinates. It is possible that the situation was fluid, with overall clan leaders emerging at certain points, or in some clans, while in other contexts the heads of the constituent families acted collectively. Membership of the group was not restricted to immediate family, but included junior branches of the family and poorer relatives and their families. It also included people who were clients of the clan or its members, but we know little about whether they were clients of the clan as a collective body, acknowledgeing the clan head as their *patronus*, or were clients of its constituent families within the clan, owing their allegiance to the heads of such families.

The relationship between patron and client was pervasive and powerful. There are many uncertainties about it, particularly for the earliest periods of Italian history, because it was essentially based on bonds of social rather than legal obligation, but the patron seems to have held quasi-paternal authority over his clients, which gave him extensive power over many aspects of their lives. He was expected to provide protection and assistance, in return for which they owed him obedience and support in a range of ways. These might include political support, acting on his behalf in economic transactions, or even fighting for him. Large houses and villas such as the 'palace' at Murlo, or an archaic villa (the 'auditorium' villa) found near Rome, can best be understood as the houses of men who headed such groups. Land may have been owned collectively by the clan, which ensured that most clan members depended on the head of the clan for receiving their fair allocation, although evidence for this from an Italian context is very slight, to say the least.

This domination by small, tightly knit aristocratic groups which gained their social and political legitimacy from tracing their descent from mythical founders was not confined to Rome or Italy. Many Greek cities of this period were dominated by hereditary aristocracies which controlled political power, social influence and access to economic resources. Corinth was ruled by the Bacchiad clan, an extended noble family who were ejected by a popular revolt in the mid-seventh century, and this social system was replicated in the Greek colonies of the western Mediterranean. At Locri, the so-called Hundred Families, a group of nobles claiming descent from the first group of settlers, controlled land ownership and political power, and Syracuse was ruled by a similar faction called the Land-Sharers (*Gamoroi*). A key characteristic shared by the Greek and Italian nobility of the seventh century is that they were largely hereditary. Membership was very restricted, probably to those who were born into particular families, and it was very difficult for outsiders to become members of such an elite. As a result, they exercised a very high degree of dominance over their communities.

This exclusivity created an almost impenetrable boundary between those who belonged to the aristocratic class and those who did not, but there was a dense network of interconnections between those families which did belong to it, both within communities and across political and ethnic boundaries. This was partly based on intermarriage. The essence of a closed elite is that its members only marry among their own class, and since the number of elite families in each individual area was, by definition, small, marriages and connections of kinship between noble families from different areas were frequent. The consequence was a network of family ties between families of high status, which not only linked families but also linked communities and regions.

Ties of friendship between aristocrats were another important feature of elite social life. These were not primarily based on personal attachment but were formalised relationships which carried specific obligations of support and hospitality and were underpinned by social and religious sanctions. Harming someone with whom one had ties of friendship and hospitality, or failing to fulfil one's obligations to them, incurred disgrace and, potentially, divine displeasure. Friendships of this type (often termed guest-friendships) could be hereditary, linking families over several generations and connecting families from different areas. In this way they sustained a network of links between regions and communities. Among the debris from the main building at Murlo excavators found a number of ivory tablets, carved in low relief into the shape of a lion on one side and inscribed with a personal name on the other. These were *tesserae hospitales* – tokens denoting a formal guest-friendship between two people or families which could be produced if need be, as proof of the relationship and to act as a visiting card or form of introduction. Their presence demonstrates that whoever lived there had cultivated a network of relationships with their peers elsewhere. These relationships enhanced social status – the more guest-friends a person had, the more important he was seen to be – but also had a practical application. An extensive collection of guest-friends facilitated travel (as the name implies, they were obliged to provide hospitality) and acted as a network of diplomatic or political contacts.

The result of this networking was an international elite class of wealthy families which shared a luxurious material culture and lifestyle, but which was largely closed to anyone outside their peer group. This interconnectedness goes some way to explain why the contents of princely burials were so similar in all areas of Italy. Usually, regional variations would be expected in the types of object buried and the styles in which they were made. The level of homogeneity found in the orientalising princely tombs suggests a common source of luxury goods and close interaction between the people who possessed them and circulated them within the group. Some rich grave goods were objects circulated as gifts, since competitive generosity and exchange of lavish gifts were an essential element in any formal contact between people of this status. Valuable items changed hands on many social occasions, symbolising friendship and goodwill and demonstrating the wealth and generosity of the giver. Others may have been transferred from family to family as part of a dowry.

Another effect of interconnection between elite families throughout Italy is the development of a shared aristocratic culture. Symbols of high status are common to many areas of Italy that are otherwise ethnically and culturally distinct. Similar marks of rank (large hats, sceptres, ceremonial chairs) are found throughout central and northern Italy, and the prevalence of drinking vessels in tombs and depictions of banquets in art suggest that ritualised feasting was important to aristocrats in most Italian cultures. The possession of horses, chariots and carriages is a common feature of the way aristocrats are depicted in the art of many regions, and the horse or chariot as a powerful status symbol is backed up by finds of chariots, horse trappings and even the remains of horses in princely tombs.

We can get a flavour of the culture and lifestyle of the archaic aristocracy from the art of the period as well as the funerary remains. Etruscan reliefs are revealing, as are a series of bronze vessels produced in northern

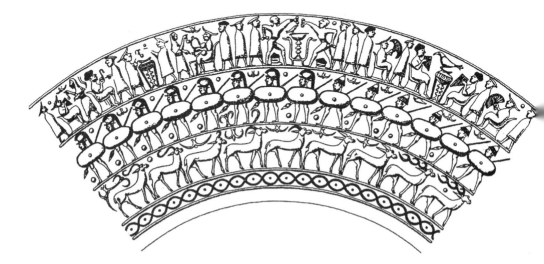

Fig. 12 The Benvenuti situla. Este, c. 600 BC.

Italy which were decorated with elaborate scenes of aristocratic life.[6] Orientalising art is very formulaic, consisting of friezes of stylised figures, and we cannot regard it as a naturalistic depiction of reality. Nevertheless, these items give us some idea of how the wealthy elites of this period lived and what sort of activities were important to them. The Benvenuti situla (fig. 12), one of the most complex examples, was found in a tomb at Este, in the Veneto. It dates to *c*. 600 and depicts a victorious army leading some prisoners on one register and an aristocratic banquet, probably a victory celebration, on another. Men of different rank are differentiated by dress: attendants at the banquet are bare-headed while diners wear beret-style headgear, and the most prominent figures are seated on high-backed ceremonial chairs and wear extravagantly wide-brimmed hats as insignia of power and status. This type of chair and the large hat are symbols of status, marking out figures of power, in art and sculpture throughout northern and central Italy. The Murlo friezes show scenes of aristocratic life drawn in similar style, including feasts, horse-races, a procession in which a couple ride in a chariot and a scene in which a nobleman appears to hold audience. They show a range of activities of importance to the aristocracy of seventh-century Italy: prowess in war and a culture of social ceremonies such as processions, athletic competitions, horse-races and banqueting, which allowed them to show off their wealth and power.

Women are often assumed to have little power in traditional societies such as those of archaic Italy, but in a situation in which power and status depended on belonging to the right family, women of those families in fact had considerable status and importance. Marriages were a way of maintaining connections and alliances between families, so women had an important role to play in dynastic politics. These highly unequal societies, paradoxically, conferred more influence and higher status on women of elite families than was the case in more democratic societies such as those of Classical Greece. Membership of an important family placed women in a potentially influential position, although only as members of a family rather than because they wielded power in their own right. This is perhaps most strikingly illustrated by the Roman practice of not giving women personal names but only giving them the female version of the clan or family name, emphasising that their status derived entirely from their membership of the group.[7]

That said, women in many areas of Italy enjoyed a degree of visibility and social status much greater than that of women in some other areas of

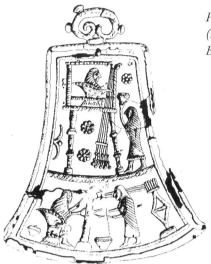

Fig. 13 Bronze tintinabulum *(rattle) showing women weaving. Bologna, late seventh century* BC.

the Mediterranean. A significant number of 'princely' burials commemorated women, either on their own or as part of a couple, and these include some of the wealthiest burials of all. Giving a lavish funeral and large tomb to a female relative was, of course, a way of demonstrating family status, but nevertheless it is significant that women of the highest social class were commemorated nearly as frequently and lavishly as their menfolk. Italic art gives some insight into the life of a seventh-century noblewoman. A bronze rattle from Bologna embossed with scenes in the style of situla art shows a group of women weaving (fig. 13). They all wear the characteristic dress of northern Italian women at this date – an ankle-length tunic with a voluminous shawl draped over the head and upper body – but two are of higher status, seated on high-backed ceremonial chairs, and are apparently supervising their servants. This appears to be a domestic scene, but other items suggest that women lived a much less secluded life than was the norm in the Greek world. The Murlo friezes and many tomb paintings show women – clearly of high rank – participating in public occasions, reclining at banquets or riding in chariots alongside men. Later Greek writers took a dim view of Etruscan women and their freedom to appear in public, regarding this as a sign of licentiousness and decadence, but orientalising art and funerary practice suggest that, far from being loose women, the aristocratic ladies of the period played an important role in society.

The nature of political power and forms of government in seventh-century Italy are less clear. The aristocrats are often assumed to have had royal powers and to have ruled as kings, but we do not know whether individuals governed as monarchs, ruling for life, or whether power was shared collectively between families. The notion that they were royal dynasties arises from the gulf in wealth and status between the elite and the rest of the population. Objects sometimes seen as symbols of kingship were found in princely tombs and in depictions of high-status individuals in Italic art. These include carriages and chariots, the high-backed chair and large hat described above and a staff or sceptre with a characteristic curved top. All of these are indubitably symbols of high rank, but none of them proves that the owners were kings. The sceptre, or *lituus*, is a ceremonial staff used by priests, so it may be a symbol of religious authority rather than political office. On current evidence we do not know whether seventh-century communities were ruled by a sole ruler or a group of men who shared power between them. What we can conclude with certainty is that the Italian aristocracies were a closely knit and all-powerful group who dominated Italian society.

How these families related to people outside their own peer group – the vast majority of the population – is uncertain. Greek writers compare the status of ordinary Etruscans to that of the *penestai* of Greek Thessaly, a serf class who did not have full citizen rights and worked their land as tied labourers who were dependent on their landlords.[8] Some Greek cities, both in Greece itself and in the western Mediterranean, were run by similar restricted elites which maintained the rest of the population in a state of dependence and serfdom during the Orientalising period. The seventh-century poet Hesiod makes scathing reference to all-powerful aristocrats who ruled like kings, giving a vivid description of corruption in a property dispute, in which he alleges that the ruling 'kings', who clearly had the final word on the matter, were bribed: 'we split our property in half, but you grabbed the larger part and praised to heaven the kings, eaters of bribes, who love to try such a case as that' (Hesiod, *Works and Days* 38–9, 220–21).

The problem, as ever, is lack of sources for seventh-century Italy, and it can be dangerous to extrapolate from conditions in Greece. Since most resources, including land, were owned and controlled by a narrow elite, it is very likely that the rest of the population – or such of it as made their living by farming – were effectively tied tenants of this elite. However, the flourishing trade and craft production of the period demonstrates that there were also a substantial number of people who made their living as merchants and artisans and were not tied either to the land or its owners. These groups were highly mobile, and their movements can be traced via movements of goods, artistic styles and production techniques, as well as the occasional inscription. Men such as this were unlikely to have been bound by ties of serfdom or clientship but were nevertheless reliant on finding wealthy patrons to purchase their goods and services. The society of seventh-century Italy can perhaps be best envisaged as a steep pyramid, in which the bottom 90 per cent of the population were tied to the wealthy 10 per cent by a network of obligations ranging from outright serfdom to less formal bonds of clientship and patronage, while the 10 per cent formed an international elite with shared tastes and lifestyles.

This steep social and political hierarchy was reflected in the military organisation of the period. Equipment found in burials suggests that most warriors fought wearing a bronze helmet and armed with a round or oval shield, swords and spears or javelins. Horses and their accoutrements are limited to high-status graves, and fighting on horseback was the preserve of the rich. This is consistent with what ancient writers tell us and with how soldiers and armies are depicted in the art of the period. Ancient descriptions of warfare are of infantry battles fought by heavily armed foot soldiers, although none of these is contemporary. The nearest evidence we have for warfare at this period comes from the Greek world. The seventh-century Greek poet Archilochos (Archilochos frag. 5 [West]), who fought as an infantryman, describes abandoning his cumbersome shield to escape a defeat, and what he says is consistent with the evidence from Italy. Visual representations of armies are illuminating. A pottery jug in Etrusco-Corinthian style from Tragliatella near Caere is incised with one of the earliest representations of a group of soldiers (fig.

Fig. 14 Incised decoration from an Etrusco-Corinthian oinochoe, showing marching warriors (after Spivey and Stoddart 1990). Caere (Tragliatella), late seventh century BC. The inscription reads 'Mi Mamarce' ('I belong to Mamarce') or possibly 'Mi Amnuarce'.

14).[9] They march along in formation, all identically armed with a bunch of spears and a round shield painted with an emblem of a wild boar. The leading figure is empty-handed, and the last man in line carries a curved staff, which is a sign of religious or political office. Some of the bronze situlas from northern Italy also show military scenes. One register of the Benvenuti situla shows groups of soldiers armed with helmets, shields and spears.

These scraps of evidence give us some idea of how soldiers might have fought but tell us little about how armies were organised. By the fifth century Italian armies were militias in which all male citizens who could afford armour and weapons were obliged to serve, but in the seventh century it is more likely that they were effectively private armies, consisting of the armed retainers of powerful men, or of tenants and other dependants who fought when instructed to do so by their patron. The device on the shields of the warriors on the Tragliatella jug suggests they belonged to a single band of soldiers, and the Benvenuti situla uses differences in armour and weapons to distinguish between different groups of warriors, possibly to denote followers of different men.

Literacy: a new technology

The seventh century was the period at which literacy spread into Italy, revolutionising the possibilities for record-keeping and bureaucracy as well as literature. The earliest writing consists of a handful of eighth-century inscriptions, including the inscription from Osteria dell'Osa, but these are few and far between. In the seventh century inscriptions become more numerous and literacy spreads more widely, although the Etruscans and Greeks were still the most copious writers. The number of Etruscan inscriptions rises from about twenty eighth-century examples to over three hundred dating to the seventh century, and we see a similar increase in areas of Greek settlement. The Etruscan alphabet (fig. 15), which was based on Greek and Phoenician scripts and developed in the early eighth century, became more established, and the high concentration of inscriptions in the area of Caere and Veii has led the philologist Aldo Prosdocimi to speculate that reading and writing may have been taught there, probably by priests at one or more of the sanctuaries.

Many inscriptions are limited to the name of the owner and sometimes also of the object inscribed: for instance, a plate from Caere inscribed 'mi spanti nuzinaia' ('I am Nuzina's plate'). Others are gift inscriptions, such as the seventh-century jug, also from Caere, dedicated to 'beautiful Titela' or the wine jar dedicated by Aranth to Ramutha Vestiricinala.[10] Most inscribed objects are found in graves and were probably either offerings to the dead or are prized possessions buried along with the deceased. Others are found at shrines and were votive offerings, inscribed with the name of the god to whom the item was offered. The brevity and formulaic nature of many of these inscriptions do not imply that writing was of low value. Many are painstakingly written, and some of the longer examples are cleverly worked into the decoration of the objects on which they are inscribed, forming elaborate patterns. Most are written on objects of some

	Etruscan	Phoenician
a	Ꭿ Ꭺ	⅄ Ⲕ
b		ꟼ
c	⟩ ⟩	ꓹ ꓥ
d	ꓝ ◁ △	△ △
e	ⅎ ⅃ ⅎ	⅄ ⅁
v	ⅎ ⅎ	Ⲩ
z	ꓩ Ꮖ ⵜ ✝	Ꮖ ⵣ
h	⧗ ⧗	⊟ ⊟
th	⊗ ⊕ ⊙	⊕ ☺
i	⎮	ⵣ ⵣ
k	⅄	⅄ ⅄
l	⌋	⌐
m	⋔	⋔ ⋔ ⋔
n	⋔	⅄ ⅄
š	⊞ ⋈	╪
o		Ο
p	ꓶ ꓶ ꓵ	⌣ ꓹ
ś	Ꮇ Ꮇ	Ⲙ
q	Ⓠ	⦾
r	◁ ◁ ◁	ꓻ
s	ⵣ ⵎ ⵞ	Ⲱ Ⅴ
t	Ⲧ Ⲧ Ⲧ	✛ ✗
u	Ⲩ Ⅴ ⅄ Ⲩ	
ks	✛	
Ph	Ⓠ Ⓞ	
kh	Ⲯ Ⲯ	
f	𐌚	

Fig. 15 The early Etruscan alphabet, c. 750–500 BC, and its Phoenician model.

value, such as bucchero, painted pottery, or metal items. This in itself suggests that writing was prestigious, associated with high-class items and produced by skilled craftsmen.

The content of the inscriptions also places writing in the context of elite lifestyle. The exchange of gifts was an important aspect of orientalising society, taking place as part of ceremonies such as marriages and funerals, or to commemorate formation of guest-friendships and other forms of social and political alliance. Personalising the gift by adding the name of the giver, or of the recipient, to the object conferred even more kudos on both parties, and acted as a record of the transaction. The inscription on the Nestor cup found at Pithecusae offers another angle on this. Banquets and drinking parties were a common part of aristocratic life. There is a wealth of evidence for these, both from ancient descriptions and from depictions in art, and the Nestor cup, with its little verse referencing the *Iliad* and showing off its owner's learning and sophistication, was probably manufactured for such an occasion.

Inscriptions are the only direct evidence of early literacy. Perishable media such as wooden writing tablets or papyri do not survive, but there is other evidence that literacy was important in aristocratic society. Writing implements were buried as grave goods and dedicated in sanctuaries as votive objects, suggesting that they were valued possessions. The earliest example is an ivory writing tablet, decorated with traces of gold leaf and inscribed along one edge with an alphabet, and with an indentation to hold the wax writing surface. This dates to *c.* 675–650 and was found in a rich burial, probably of a woman, at Marsiliana d'Albegna.[11] Alphabets are also found incised on small pottery vessels, sometimes of high quality, which may have been used as inkwells (pl. 24). Clearly, writing tools could be an indication of prestige.

The reason why literacy is so important is that it has many implications for the organisation of ancient states and societies. At this early date the number of people who were literate was very small. Seventh-century aristocrats may not have been literate themselves and may have delegated reading and writing to specialist scribes or priests, but the presence of inscriptions on their possessions demonstrates their wish to associate themselves with a prestigious new technology. Although most seventh-century inscriptions were marks of ownership or record rituals such as votive offerings, the Marsiliana tablet shows that writing may have been used for a broader range of purposes. The adoption of literacy enabled record-keeping and accounts, facilitating the development of religious and state bureaucracy.

The orientalising economy

The affluence of the emerging aristocracies depended on factors that varied from region to region, although some common themes can be identified. Throughout Italy, exploitation of agricultural land intensified. In Etruria land was more systematically cultivated. There are signs that the population was growing, and many small rural settlements developed, but we know little about who farmed the land or owned these farms and villages, or their relationship to larger settlements. The greater diversity of crops and the new patterns of rural settlement suggest new divisions of land, which in turn points to the emergence of new forms of political and social authority with the power to determine these. Given the steep social hierarchy of the seventh century, it seems plausible that the aristocracy controlled most of the land, cultivating it as large estates, either through tenant farmers, a tied serf population or use of slaves. Cultivation of more land and more intensive farming resulted in greater production, and although most people still farmed at subsistence level, large landowners were able to produce a significant surplus. In central Italy cereals, legumes, vines and olives were all grown, and olives and grapes were cultivated particularly intensively from the middle of the seventh century. Banqueting was central to the aristocratic culture of conspicuous consumption, requiring a steady supply of high-quality food and wine, and any surplus formed a valuable export. Most seventh- and sixth-century shipwrecks found in the western Mediterranean contained Etruscan amphorae transporting wine, oil and olives, some helpfully inscribed with their contents (mainly 'vinum', wine, and 'eleiva', oil), to Sicily, Spain, southern France and beyond. The popularity of Etruscan wine throughout the western Mediterranean ensured a lucrative trade for those who controlled production and shipping.

In the areas of Greek settlement in southern Italy the seventh century was a period of consolidation. The Greeks exercised increasingly systematic control of the territory in the hinterland of their settlements, and there were changes to the settlements themselves. At Metapontum a regular grid of land divisions and boundaries appears in the territory by *c.* 600, a sign that the land was being systematically surveyed and allocated to settlers. Italian villages disappeared from the area as the Greeks extended their control over the surrounding territory, apportioning it among themselves and exploiting its resources. At the same time the layout of the city became more formalised. Both changes point to the growth of a stronger urban organisation.

Alongside this there was an intensification in the exploitation of mineral resources, especially in Etruria. The metal-rich hills near Pisa continued to be mined, and ox-hide ingots of Etruscan metal found in Sardinia show that the trade route linking Italy to Sardinia and the eastern Mediterranean continued to flourish. Trade in foodstuffs and manufactured goods was healthy. Large quantities of Greek and eastern imports are found in Italy, particularly central Italy, but Etruscan goods and produce were also exported throughout the Mediterranean and central Europe. Trade in wine and olive oil can be traced via finds of Greek and Phoenician amphorae in Italy. At the luxury end of the market many small round flasks (*aryballoi*) for perfume or scented oil are found. They were produced in large quantities in Greece, particularly in Corinth (pl. 13), which also just happened to produce perfumes. These are signs not just of a trade in pottery but of a far more lucrative trade in expensive scent. Trade routes across the Alps and into central Europe provided Italy with a source of raw materials, including some luxury items such as amber, and a European market for Italian goods. Etruscan bronze vessels were widely traded and are found throughout the Greek world, but they also made their way into central Europe. Shipwrecks, explored thanks to advances in underwater archaeology, provide a fascinating snapshot of international commerce. A Phoenician trading ship sunk *c.* 600 off the coast of Etruria, near the island of Giglio, carried rich and diverse exports. Its primary cargo was a shipment of metal ingots, but it also carried Etruscan and Phoenician amphorae (probably containing olives and/or wine), perfume flasks and Greek and Etruscan pottery. This mix of metal ingots, agricultural produce such as wine and olives, and high-end manufactured goods is typical of the contents of other shipwrecks and gives an insight into the volume and diversity of Mediterranean trade at the end of the seventh century.

The advances in craft production and techniques, and the international reach of artisans, can be seen in changing artistic styles. The orientalising period takes its name from a particular style of art adopted in the Greek world in the seventh century but derived from Egypt and the culture of the Near East (see pls 10–12). It is characterised by friezes of animals, often mythological beasts such as griffins and sphinxes, or exotica such as lions and panthers. Backgrounds are densely filled in with rosettes and floral motifs. Human figures are represented with stiff poses and gestures and stylised wig-like hair in a style similar to that of Egyptian art. These styles and conventions originated in the east but were rapidly taken up by Italian craftsmen and incorporated into local production. The ubiquity of the style is a striking demonstration of the interconnectedness of the Mediterranean world in the orientalising period, and of the mobility and skill of the craftsmen of this era.

Migration and colonisation

The seventh century was characterised by a lack of social mobility between the elite and the rest of society but by a high degree of geographical mobility, driven by the new opportunities for trade and craft production. Artisans, especially, were very mobile, as demonstrated by the ease with which new artistic styles, craft skills and technologies such as literacy were transmitted.

This connectivity is vividly illustrated by the career of Demaratos of Corinth. According to tradition, he was a Corinthian nobleman who was forced to go into exile when the ruling Bacchiad clan, to which he belonged, was ousted from power by the tyrant Kypselos in 657 (Pol. 6.11a.7; Dion. Hal. 3.46.3–5; Pliny, *NH* 35.43.152). Rather than moving to another Greek city, he emigrated to Italy, accompanied by a group of retainers and craftsmen, and settled at Tarquinii, where he married into a noble Etruscan family and continued a successful career as a merchant. He is said to have derived his personal wealth, as well as the social contacts that enabled him to settle at Tarquinii, from trade with the Etruscans, and his companions were credited with introducing the Etruscans to Greek styles of pottery and painting, as well as the art of writing. His son Lucumo later migrated to Rome, where (renamed as Lucius Tarquinius Priscus) he became the fifth king of Rome. Demaratos may or may not have been a historical figure,[12] but the story personalises several trends that are present in the archaeological record: the close connections between Greek and Italian craftsmen, the adoption of writing and the importation of large quantities of Greek goods. It offers an insight into how the intensely hierarchical society of the period enhanced opportunities for mobility in some social contexts. A man of rank such as Demaratos could migrate across regional and ethnic boundaries by exploiting networks of social contacts and guest-friendships, and ultimately forged ties with families of equivalent status which enabled him to settle in a different community. If a man of rank decided to move, he did not do so unaccompanied, but took companions and dependants with him. Personal names suggesting mixed ethnic origin may also give a clue to patterns of migration. A grave offering from Tarquinia was inscribed to (or by) a man named Rutilius Hipukrates, who has a Latin first name and an Etruscanised Greek second name and apparently lived in, or had travelled to, Etruria at the time of his death.

On a broader level the impact of this fluidity can be seen in larger-scale movements of peoples and cultures. Connections between Etruria and Campania had been established in the ninth and eighth centuries, but during the seventh and sixth centuries Etruscan culture became more prominent in central and coastal Campania. Studies of votive objects and grave goods have shown that the region was in close contact with many neighbouring areas, with artefacts showing influences of Latin and Apennine culture, but Etruscan imports and influence on local culture were increasingly prominent at Capua (the principal settlement of the region) and at other important centres such as Nola, Nuceria, Fratte di Salerno and Pontecagnano (map 4). Whether this meant that they were Etruscan colonies, as some Romans (notably the historian Cato) believed, is another matter. Current evidence – especially that of inscriptions which demonstrate the use of the Etruscan language and presence of people with Etruscan names[13] – points to an Etruscan presence, either as settlers or regular visitors such as traders, but this does not support the idea that Etruscans colonised the region or dominated it politically. There was widespread adoption of Etruscan culture by the local Campanian population, and in the seventh century it was probably transmitted via contact between Etruscan and Campanian aristocrats. At Rome there is a similar pattern: the cultural influence of Etruria was important between *c.* 650 and 500, and there were close connections between Etruscan and Roman aristocrats, but it was not an Etruscan colony. The picture is more complex in northern Italy, especially in the area around Bologna. Funerary monuments and burials from Bologna demonstrate the widespread adoption of Etruscan culture and the presence of Etruscan settlers, but even here 'Etruscan colonies' seem to have been inhabited by a mixture of local people and Etruscan migrants.

In the south there were further waves of Greek settlement. A second wave of colonisation took place from *c.* 650 to 600, and new settlements were established along the coast of Calabria and Lucania. Other changes suggest a greater exclusiveness and a more hostile attitude towards the local population. At Metapontum the cemeteries, which had previously included both Greek and Italic burials, become purely Greek. At the same time there are important changes in the territory. These can be illustrated by the fate of Incoronata. Although buildings and finds from the site suggest a flourishing mixed community of Greeks and Italians for much of the seventh century, by the end of the century it had been abandoned, only to be reoccupied as a Greek village and religious sanctuary shortly afterwards. The Italian presence disappeared. Similar patterns can be found in the hinterland of Locri and Sybaris, where Italic settlements abruptly disappear from the territory around the Greek settlements. In some cases the Italians were driven out of Greek territory, and in others they may have been absorbed so thoroughly that they are no longer archaeologically distinguishable from the Greek population, but there is a general pattern of greater cultural and ethnic exclusivity.

To conclude, the seventh century was a period of rapid social and economic change throughout Italy. It was marked by increasing urbanisation in many regions, and by the rise of an increasingly wealthy elite which displayed its power and status through conspicuous consumption. During the early part of the century this can be traced by the increasingly rich burials, but by the end of the seventh century priorities had started to change, and self-advertisement and competition for status were beginning to be expressed in different ways. The construction of large houses, impressive new religious buildings and early types of public building demonstrate that the elites of Italy were beginning to invest in their communities as a form of self-promotion.

5

ORIENTALISING ROME AND THE EARLY KINGS

According to Roman tradition, the city had seven kings – Romulus, Numa Pompilius, Tullus Hostilius, Ancus Marcius, Tarquinius Priscus, Servius Tullius and Tarquinius Superbus – whose reigns spanned the period from the foundation to the late sixth century, when Tarquinius Superbus was ousted by a group of nobles who abolished the kingship and established Republican government. Kings were appointed rather than being hereditary, and each reign was separated by at least a one-year interregnum during which the new king was chosen. Needless to say, there are many problems with this, not least, as noted in chapter 3, the fact that these traditions had many variants and a complex chronological development. The historical existence of the early kings is highly questionable, and there is little or no reliable historical evidence for them.

These traditions credit Romulus with many of the fundamental elements of the Roman state.[1] He is said to have instituted a council of leading men to advise the king and an assembly of the Roman people, divided into three tribes and thirty units (*curiae*) to vote on key matters. The creation of a citizen army with an organisation based on the tribes and *curiae* was also attributed to him. His supposed successors Numa Pompilius, Tullus Hostilius and Ancus Marcius continued to refine and elaborate on these institutions as well as expanding Roman power against its nearest neighbours. Numa Pompilius is said to have been a Sabine who placed the Roman state on a stronger legal and religious footing. He was credited with establishing the basis of the Roman calendar, the creation of most of the key priesthoods and the foundation of the temple of Janus, the doors of which were closed when Rome was at peace and left open during wartime. He established some of Rome's most ancient religious festivals and ensured that his innovations were imbued with divine authority by attributing them to a goddess, Egeria, who he claimed had advised him on everything.

Tullus Hostilius, in contrast, was supposedly a Latin, and is portrayed as a formidable warrior whose aim was to establish Roman domination over the surrounding region. He is said to have fought wars against Alba Longa and the Sabines and to have established Rome's pre-eminence in central Latium. These events formed the background to the legendary exploits of the Horatii and Curiatii, two sets of triplets who challenged each other to single combat during the first war against Alba Longa, resulting in a victory for the Roman Horatii over the Alban Curiatii. After the fall of Alba Longa some of the leading Alban families were absorbed into the Roman aristocracy, and the ancient Latin religious festival, the Feriae Latinae (sometimes also called the Latiar), was taken over by Rome. The festival honoured Jupiter Latiaris, sometimes identified with Latinus, the eponymous founder of the Latins, and was held on Mons Albanus (Monte Cavo), the highest of the Alban Hills. It was a ceremony shared by both Rome and the Latins, acting as a symbol of kinship between them. Shorn of the narrative details furnished by later writers, the development of shared rituals celebrating a greater sense of shared community, enacted at a site out in the open countryside, is perfectly consistent with the archaeo-logical evidence for sanctuaries elsewhere in central Italy. Ironically, Tullus Hostilius is said to have neglected religious duties, particularly in contrast to the piety of his predecessor, and to have died in a house fire caused by a lightning strike – a clear sign of Jupiter's displeasure in Roman eyes. His successor was Ancus Marcius, the grandson of Numa, who reputedly combined the strengths of his predecessors. He is said to have initiated successful campaigns against the Latins, expanded the territory controlled by Rome and established a legal and religious framework for warfare and diplomacy, as well as reinforcing law and order within Rome itself. He and Tullus both extended the boundaries of Rome to include the Caelian and Aventine hills, reinforced Rome's defences and established a colony at Ostia, near the mouth of the Tiber.

These early kings cannot be viewed as historical figures. Many aspects of the Roman tradition of seven kings, reigning from the mid-eighth century until *c.* 508, are inherently implausible, not least the fact that the average length of reign would have been an unrealistic thirty-four or thirty-five years.[2] Despite Carandini's view that the foundation stories of Rome contain elements of historical truth, Numa Pompilius, Tullus Hostilius and Ancus Marcius can best be understood as legendary archetypes rather than real people. The priest, the lawgiver and the warrior king are figures that frequently turn up in foundation stories in the ancient world, and Numa, Tullus and Ancus fit this pattern suspiciously neatly.

The surviving narratives are best understood as later rationalisations of the early development of Rome. Livy presents Rome as having multiple founders, responsible for establishing key aspects of the state: boundaries and territory, priesthoods and religious festivals, law and military credibility. This narrative arc of increasing legal and political sophistication, and the evolution of a more complex community, is broadly plausible, but the details and the personalities must be treated as mythical. These, and other Roman traditions, tell us much about what later writers thought was important about early Rome, but their vision is filtered through later assumptions about cities and statehood which cannot be applied to the seventh century. The last three kings may be a different matter (see chapter 7). At some point during the seventh or early sixth century Rome had developed into an organised political community, attested not just by Roman traditions, but by Etruscan art and by archaeological evidence which sheds light on the period associated with the Tarquins and Servius Tullius. The first archaeological evidence of kingship, in the form of a sixth-century potsherd found in the Forum, inscribed with the word 'rex' ('king'), belongs to this period. The earlier kings, however, are much more nebulous figures whose historical existence must be doubtful, and we cannot even be sure if Rome was a monarchy before the late seventh century.

Power and status in orientalising Rome

The archaeological evidence for Rome in the seventh and early sixth centuries is less plentiful than that from Etruria and from some other areas of Latium but suggests a similar trajectory of development, marked by increasing wealth, a steep social and political hierarchy and domination by powerful clans (*gentes*, to use the Roman term). Princely burials have been found in the surrounding area, notably at Castel di Decima, but the extremes of wealth found in elite burials elsewhere are not matched by funerary evidence from Rome. The cemetery on the Esquiline continued to expand as the main burial site, but seventh-century graves contained relatively modest grave goods compared with those found in some neighbouring areas, and were mostly simple inhumations. The tumulus-covered chamber tombs of the type used by the Etruscans and others were either not adopted by the Romans or (perhaps unsurprisingly, given the poor preservation of Roman evidence) have not survived. However, there are signs of aristocratic conspicuous consumption in other ways. The expanding size and complexity of the city is in itself a demonstration that the community was growing in wealth and power, and that it had a sufficiently well-developed political organisation to mobilise the community's resources and undertake significant changes and reorganisation of the central area of settlement.

Although social organisation is less well documented in orientalising Rome than elsewhere, it is probable that a small and dominant elite of the sort found in Etruria and in Greece had developed, and what evidence we have suggests that the clan was an important element in society (on clans see above, pp. 66–8). Large palace-like buildings such as those at Murlo, which may have been the residences of heads of clans and the meeting places of their followers, are not found in seventh-century Rome, but a similar building of slightly later date (sixth century), which was found on the northern outskirts of Rome, may have served a similar purpose.[3] Instead, the growing importance of family identity, at least for the elite, can be demonstrated by changes in personal names. By the end of the seventh century aristocratic male Romans had two names: a personal name (*praenomen*, e.g., Gaius, Lucius) and a clan name (*nomen gentilicium*, e.g., Claudius, Junius, Tarquinius).[4] As in other areas of central Italy, family identity had become closely entwined with social rank and power.

Although ancient tradition describes seventh-century Rome as a monarchy, the nature of power, and of social and political organisation, is far from clear. Our sources describe a system, established by Romulus, in which the king, supported by a senate or council of the heads of leading clans, ruled over a population divided into three tribes, the Ramnes, Tities and Luceres,[5] each of which was subdivided into ten units called *curiae*, giving thirty *curiae* in total. The tribes and *curiae* formed the basis of military and political organisation. Each tribe contributed a force of 100 cavalrymen and 1,000 infantry to a common Roman army. The *comitia curiata* was an assembly of the Roman people organised by *curiae*, which came together to ratify laws.

Much of this account is anachronistic, framed in terms of the later Republican government by senate and assembly, but the *curiae* themselves seem to be of ancient origin. They were associated with specific geographical neighbourhoods,[6] although membership may have been based on kinship and membership of particular families as well as geographic location. Monarchical rule in the seventh century, in contrast, must be open to question. Our sources (Livy 1.17–18, 31) acknowledge that monarchy was punctuated by periods during which the heads of leading *gentes* ruled collectively, appointing one of their number as an *interrex* to select the next king, and the earliest corroborating epigraphic evidence for kings at Rome dates to the sixth century. As noted in the previous chapter, the distinction between priest, head of clan and king is fluid in the orientalising period.

The role of the *curiae* as essential elements of the state and the possibility that political power was exercised by a small elite rather than by a single monarch are compatible with the archaeological evidence for Roman development, and with social developments in other areas of Italy. As Nicola Terrenato has pointed out, the development of Rome in the ninth to early seventh centuries is similar to that of Villanovan settlements in Etruria, which were composed of clans who occupied specific areas within the settlement, and whose heads formed a ruling elite. If Rome followed a pattern of development similar to that of Veii or Tarquinii, it may have been ruled at this period by an elite composed of heads of clans who shared power, rather than exclusively by kings, and the *curiae* may have been a relic of the earlier proto-urban phase, in which each clan was associated with its own area of the city.

Early Roman religion

As in all ancient societies, religion was an important aspect of early Rome. The Romans worshipped a large number of minor deities, responsible for specific actions (gods of ploughing and sowing, for instance) or specific locations (such as the lares, the gods who protected each household), and had a ritual calendar of festivals connected with important aspects of the life of the community, such as protection of the army, the boundaries, fertility and agrarian production. Festivals, such as the Robigalia (25 April: protection against crop disease) and the Parilia (21 April: purification of livestock, and later believed to be the anniversary of the foundation of Rome), were associated with agrarian life, although they continued to be celebrated in later periods of Roman history. Others were linked to the need to mark out boundaries or celebrate community cohesion in ways that gave divine sanction. The Terminalia (23 February) was dedicated to protecting the boundaries of Rome, and the festival of the Argei (15 May) involved sacrifices at various locations, and was clearly associated with ancient divisions within the city and the need to establish their identity.[7] The Romans themselves believed that they were of archaic origin and credited Numa with creating a calendar that divided up the year and established this cycle of religious rituals and observances.

All the evidence for these festivals is from a much later period, so it is impossible to discover when they were established and why. An early origin seems plausible, although the attribution of some developments to Romulus or Numa lies in the realm of legend rather than history. Agrarian festivals, rituals for the protection of boundaries and festivals such as the Argei and Septimontium, which were connected with areas of early settlement, may well have had an ancient origin, and the early development of an established calendar of festivals can be reasonably assumed. A number of inscribed versions of the Republican calendar have survived, listing the key festivals and sacrifices and the dates on which they were to be performed. All of these are much later than the seventh century, and connections with the early history of Rome cannot be proved, but there are good grounds for thinking that many religious ceremonies and rituals were of considerable antiquity.[8] However, the Roman tendency to trace many cults and rituals back to the very earliest history of the city makes it difficult to reconstruct the earliest development of Roman religious practice with any certainty.

The Romans also worshipped a pantheon of gods, including Jupiter, Juno, Minerva, Mars, Vesta, Diana, Ceres, Vulcan and Janus, who exercised powers over many aspects of daily life, and cults of these deities are already attested in the seventh century. The Volcanal (shrine of Vulcan) and the sanctuary of Vesta were first established in the Forum during the orientalising period, and there was a structure on the Capitoline that may have been dedicated to Jupiter. Although these gods bear a strong resemblance to Greek Olympian deities, the development of a Roman mythology about them seems to have been a later phenomenon, probably as a result of greater contact with the Greek world from the fourth century onwards.

Religion was not confined to specific occasions. It was all-pervasive and central to the Roman way of thinking about the world and was perceived as influencing all aspects of life. Maintaining the *pax deorum* (favour of the gods) and therefore the health and well-being of the state and its people were of paramount importance. Religion was highly ritualised, and divine favour was secured by performance of the correct rituals accurately and at the proper times. The will of the gods was established by various means of divination, and every important action or occasion (public or private) was accompanied by the appropriate sacrifices.

By the beginning of the Republic, colleges of priests had been established to oversee public sacrifices and rituals. The most important of these, the college of pontifices, was headed by the *pontifex maximus* (chief priest). However, there is very little evidence for priesthoods, or about how religious rituals were conducted and supervised, in seventh-century Rome. One possibility is that the kings or heads of clans acted as religious as well as political leaders. Later Romans believed that the practice of augury, conducted by specialist augurs, was already established under the early kings:

> according to tradition, Romulus, the father of this City, not only founded it in obedience to the auspices, but was himself a most skilful augur. Next, the other Roman kings employed augurs; and, again, after the expulsion of the kings, no public business was ever transacted at home or abroad without first taking the auspices.
>
> (Cic., *Div.* 1.3)

However, there is no contemporary evidence to support this. By the end of the sixth century religious authority seemed to reside with the king, and a priesthood with the title of *rex sacrorum* had to be created after the end of the monarchy to take over the religious duties of the king, but the organisation of religious life of orientalising Rome is very unclear.

The urban development of Rome

The seventh century at Rome saw development at many of the key political and religious locations. This was a period of urbanisation, during which the settlements on the various hills merged more clearly into a single community, with many of the attributes of a city-state (fig. 16). Fulminante estimates that the city may have reached *c.* 320 ha (790 acres) in area during the course of the seventh century.[9] Cemeteries on the Quirinal moved further away from the centre of Rome, suggesting that the areas of settlement were expanding and pushing the burial areas outwards, and burials near the Caelian hill show that it was occupied. The expansion of the population was accompanied by major changes in the area of the later Forum, a rebuilding of the Palatine wall, the first phases of some large private houses and an upsurge of activity at two important religious sites, the temple of Capitoline Jupiter and the archaic sanctuary near the church of S. Omobono.

The changes to the area of the later Forum Romanum are particularly significant, as it was the political and juridical centre of the later city, and the site of key temples and public buildings. It occupied the low-lying area at the foot of the Capitoline and Palatine, located between the settlement areas of the ninth and eighth centuries. By the late seventh century it had

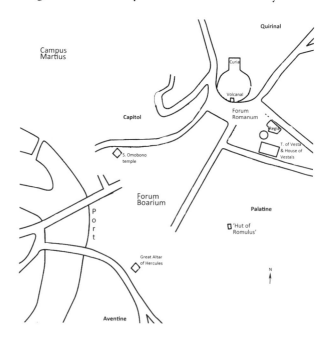

Fig. 16 Plan of central Rome showing areas of seventh-century development.

developed into a central area of the community, marked out as an open space for public usage. The ground level of the Forum was raised significantly in some places in order to overcome the problems of poor drainage, and in the mid-seventh century the huts on the route of the Sacra Via – in later times the main processional route through the Forum – were demolished. By the end of the century the area of the Forum had been covered by a pavement of beaten earth, and there were new developments at several key locations.

Investigation of the western side of the area, below the Capitoline and Palatine, has revealed seventh-century structures on the sites of many later buildings. Some time around 650–630 the site of the Comitium was excavated into a deep triangular depression, which was paved with a beaten earth pavement, replaced a few years later with a more substantial gravel one. It may even have contained a precursor of the Rostra, the platform from which Roman officials addressed the people. Near by was a small rectangular pit and elliptical basin cut into an outcrop of tufa, which has been identified as an early phase of the Volcanal, an archaic sanctuary dedicated to Vulcan.[10] These are highly significant: the Volcanal was closely connected in the Roman mind with the early days of the city, and the Comitium – where the Roman people met to vote, and to be addressed by their leaders – was central to political life (see fig. 16). A formal public space is not in itself proof of urbanisation, but clearing and formalisation of this area demonstrate that Rome was developing a collective identity that required space for public life. The importance of this area to Roman self-identity can be seen from the ancient sources. These attributed the foundation of the Comitium and Volcanal to Romulus himself and the first *curia* (senate house), which was located near by, to Tullus Hostilius. The senate house continued to be known as the Curia Hostilia until the first century. There was an undeniably close link in the Roman mind between this area and the public life of the community, and archaeological evidence supports the possibility that it was an important area of public space from early in Rome's history.

At the western end of the Forum, excavations near the House of the Vestals and the sanctuary of Vesta have revealed an important group of seventh-century buildings. The excavators of these structures have identified them as the early phases of the Regia ('House of the kings'), House of the Vestals and Domus Publica (official residence of the *pontifex maximus*), but these attributions remain merely speculative. Their size

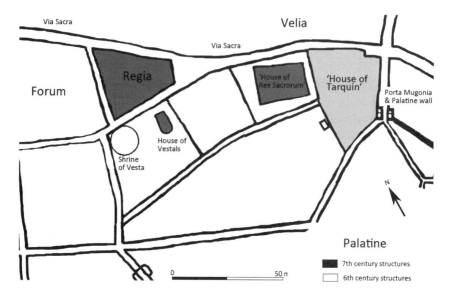

Fig. 17 Rome: plan of the Regia and associated buildings c. 600–500 BC.

and complexity, however, demonstrate their significance. The importance
of the Regia (fig. 17) is demonstrated by both written and archaeological
evidence. The building initially identified as the Regia is a wedge-shaped
structure. It has a complicated architectural history and was remodelled
and extended at least three times during the seventh and sixth centuries,
and then more radically rebuilt around 500. The seventh-century phases,
dating from *c.* 625, consist of an enclosed courtyard with two rooms at the
back and a colonnaded porch in front of the entrance, constructed in brick
and stone with a tiled roof. It was clearly a building of some importance,
and the late seventh-century Regia was decorated with painted terracotta
mouldings, in the Etruscan manner. However, it now seems unlikely that it
was ever a house, and it may have been the place where the king performed
certain rituals.

Investigation of the site of the later House of the Vestals and Domus
Publica, located near the Regia, has uncovered several substantial seventh-
century buildings.[11] An eighth-century structure on the site of the Domus
Publica was rebuilt *c.* 650–640, using stone foundations and a tiled roof,
and more drastically remodelled around 600, when the open area in front
of it became an enclosed courtyard (later converted into a roofed atrium)
surrounded by rooms. Developments on the site of the adjacent House of

the Vestals follow a similar pattern, in which huts with earth walls were replaced in the mid- to late seventh century by a larger structure and a more complex building with stone foundations and a tiled roof.

There is much confusion over the purpose of these buildings. According to Roman tradition, Numa Pompilius established the Regia as the official residence of the king.[12] Later, it housed the offices and archives of the *pontifex maximus* and the college of pontifices, as well as two important cults dedicated to the gods Mars and Ops Consiva. Until relatively recently, the Regia was identified as the wedge-shaped building to the east of the temple of Vesta, but this has been challenged by Carandini, who believes that the building/banqueting complex located in the sanctuary of Vesta was the first royal residence, arguing that it was later handed over to the *rex sacrorum* and replaced as the official house of the king by a new building next to, but outside, the sanctuary of Vesta.[13] Given that the early kings cannot be regarded as historical figures, and the many uncertainties about the political organisation of Rome before *c.* 600, this identification cannot be accepted, but the Regia and House of the Vestals/Domus Publica complex clearly had a ceremonial and ritual function. The eighth-century building of the Domus Publica contained wall-benches, cooking pots and tableware, suggesting that it was originally a banqueting suite, and an infant burial found within it suggests a foundation ritual, which indicates that the building had special status. A combination of ritual use and aristocratic residence would be consistent with evidence from Murlo, Acquarossa and Ficana, where large seventh-century buildings acted as aristocratic residences, places where a clan's cults were celebrated, and meeting places for the members of the clan.

The seventh century saw some other important developments in Rome. The burial areas were now confined to the outlying hills, the Esquiline and Quirinal, and the more central areas around the Palatine and Capitoline were now reserved for public buildings or private houses. On the Palatine, the eighth-century wall was demolished *c.* 625 and replaced by a new and more elaborate wall with a different type of construction. This new structure consisted of two parallel stone facings filled with a mixture of mud and rubble to give a more robust fortification. Some of the key religious sites of Rome also continued to develop. Many seventh-century finds have been made on the site of the later temple of Jupiter on the Capitoline, suggesting that the cult of Jupiter Capitolinus was already established, and seventh-century pottery and votives, and traces of an early structure, have been unearthed at the sanctuary of S. Omobono, close to the Forum Boarium.

The boundaries of the territory of Rome at this date are a matter of conjecture. Ancient writers associate a number of archaic cults with locations at a radius of approximately 5 Roman miles (*c.* 7 km or *c.* 4 imperial miles) from the city. A number of religious festivals, in particular the Robigalia, Terminalia and Ambarvalia (Strabo, *Geog.* 5.3.2) were concerned with reaffirming the boundaries of Rome. They involved a procession of priests that walked a route round the boundaries of the ancient territory of Rome, which, on this estimate, amounted to *c.* 150–200 km² (*c.* 58–77 square miles).[14]

Demographic estimates are notoriously difficult to arrive at, and those for early Rome vary wildly according to the criteria used and how they are interpreted. Some suggest that the population at the end of the seventh century was as low as *c.* 4,500 people, but others place it very much higher. The figures are suggested by demographic modelling, based on density of occupation and number of people per household, estimated size of territory and estimated productivity of territory, to arrive at a figure for the number of people who could have fitted into the settlement area and been supported from the produce of the land. The problem is that settlement size, territory size and population size all have to be extrapolated from incomplete data and weighted for factors such as variations in population density, variations in cultivation and productivity of territory, and many other factors.[15] Extrapolation from estimates of the population and territory of Rome in the late sixth century suggests that a territory of *c.* 150–200 km² may have been able to support a population of up to *c.* 8,000 people, but this cannot be more than a rough estimate. Ultimately we cannot be sure how large Rome was in the seventh century. It is clear, though, that it was now much larger and more complex than a mere village, and that it controlled a territory of significant size. Rome at the end of the seventh century was a substantial settlement which had acquired a grip on a good amount of the surrounding area, and was larger than most of its Latin neighbours.

Although the evidence for seventh-century Rome is perhaps not as spectacular as that for the sixth century, there are signs that Rome was steadily developing into a nucleated urban settlement with a strong collective identity. There seems to have been something of a surge in development in the last quarter of the seventh century, as many of the changes outlined above date from *c.* 625 to 600.[16] There also seems to have been a change in the priorities of the Roman aristocracy, with less emphasis on lavish burial and personal commemoration towards the end of the century. Instead, they seem to have been putting their energies into developing the public areas of Rome, and in investing in private houses. In general, seventh-century Rome follows roughly the same trajectory as the emerging cities of Latium and Etruria, although it seems to have lagged behind the larger Etruscan centres in development. Finds of pottery and metal objects demonstrate that Rome was in touch with the orientalising culture of the rest of Italy, and developments in the structure of the settlement are very much in line with those which took place elsewhere in the region. A seventh-century Greek vase found in the Esquiline cemetery has an inscription in the Greek language and script, which suggests that there were Greeks living in Rome and further underlines Rome's contacts with other areas of Italy and the Mediterranean. Taken together with ancient accounts of Rome's territorial ambitions from an early date, it seems that seventh-century Rome was a vigorous society and that the infrastructure of the settlement was beginning to develop to reflect the increasing degree of social and political complexity. By the end of the seventh century it had evolved from a collection of interlinked settlements into an urban centre of some importance.

PART II

WAR, POLITICS AND SOCIETY: ROME AND ITALY, 600–400

6

THE URBAN REVOLUTION: CITY AND STATE IN SIXTH-CENTURY ITALY

clan
↓
elite
↓
community

※⬤⬤⬤⬤⬤⬤⬤⬤※

If the seventh century was an era of domination by powerful aristocrats, the sixth century was a period in which the city-state became the most important form of social and political organisation throughout much of Italy. Although this period was still dominated by dynamic and competitive elites, their focus shifted from their clan or family to the wider community, and this change shaped social interactions, cultural changes and the political and military organisation of cities. The development of Rome will be discussed in the next chapter, but it shares many of the characteristics of urban development happening elsewhere in Italy.

This rise of the independent city-state raises important questions about inter-state relations and contacts. State identity appears to have been stronger than broader ethnic identities during the sixth century, and people thought of themselves primarily as Romans, Tarquinians, Caeretans, Cumaeans and so on, rather than as members of wider communities of Etruscans, Latins or Campanians. There is some evidence that groups of neighbouring states formed loosely knit leagues or federations which celebrated shared religious festivals and offered scope for intermittent military co-operation, as well as fostering a sense of kinship and common ethnicity. However, regional identities based on language, culture and a sense of shared kinship were relatively weak, and there is little sign of city-states banding together into larger political units.

Settlements in most areas of Italy had already begun to grow in size and complexity in the seventh century, but from around 575 onwards there was a marked change of pace. Key settlements grew more rapidly in size, emerging as central places controlling substantial areas of territory. Comparison of the size of urban centres demonstrates further that cities throughout Italy were growing, and also that Rome was now comparable to some of the larger cities of Etruria and Latium (Table 3). In the process, many cities acquired features such as an organised layout, monumental architecture and specialised areas for religious ceremonies and political life. Monumental buildings and spatial organisation are not essential defining characteristics of urbanisation, but they are useful signs of political, and administrative complexity, and of more diverse economies which could generate a surplus to fund large projects. Communities that could generate this type of infrastructure were more complex than a collection of tribes or families.

The size of the population of Italy, or even of individual cities, in the archaic period is very difficult to estimate, but ancient cities were small by modern standards. Few had a population of more than $c.$ 30,000, and many were much smaller than this, although Rome was at the upper end of the scale.[1] The estimates of Ampolo and Cornell suggest that Greek and Etruscan cities occupied large amounts of territory (possibly as much as 500 km^2 [193 square miles] in some cases), but most Latin communities were of more modest size (typically in the 25–100 km^2 range as seen in Table 4), although some, such as Tibur, Praeneste and Rome itself, were much larger. Ampolo has estimated that by the end of the sixth century Rome controlled an area of $c.$ 822 km^2 (317 square miles), which could have supported a population of $c.$ 35,000 people.

Ability to exploit this territory effectively was essential to the growth of larger communities, but relationships between city and territory were complex and varied from region to region. The territory of Metapontum in southern Italy, for example, was divided into regular plots of land, arranged on a regular grid, a sign that it had been systematically divided up among the citizens. Many of these lived in the city itself, but numerous farmhouses and several large villages found in the territory suggest that

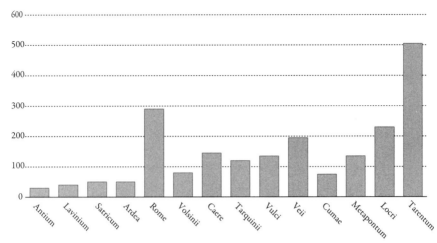

Table 3: **Estimated size (in ha) of the urban areas of leading cities of Latium, Etruria and Magna Graecia, c. 500** (after Cornell 1995)

small cities but lots of land

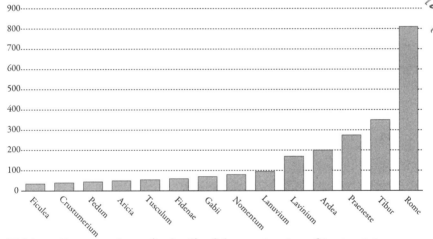

Table 4: **Estimated size (in km²) of the territories of Latin cities,** *c.* 550–500 (after Cornell 1995)

a significant proportion of the population lived out in the countryside. Other cities organised their land differently, and in some areas there are few traces of rural houses or villages, despite signs that the land was intensively cultivated. Here the owners of the land lived mainly in the city and 'commuted' out to their farms.

One notable change at this period was that cities developed a more monumental physical appearance. Their increasing size generated surplus wealth and manpower, making large construction programmes possible, and the social and cultural changes taking place were reflected in changes to the urban landscape. Whereas the aristocrats of the seventh century had invested in imposing tombs that showcased their family status and power, [the elites of the sixth century invested their wealth in their communities.] The cities of this period were still a long way from the grandeur of imperial Rome or even Classical Athens, but they were much more impressive and complex settlements than their seventh-century precursors. Stone city walls make their first appearance, replacing fortifications of earth or mud brick, throughout Etruria, Latium, Campania and Greek areas of Italy. These had the obvious benefit of providing better defences and marking the boundary between town and countryside, but they were also a statement of collective identity and self-confidence. Within the walls, houses became larger and more substantial, built of brick and wood on stone foundations. Public buildings began to appear, and cult centres were monumentalised. Throughout Etruria and Latium temples of stone and/or brick, decorated with elaborate and brightly painted terracotta mouldings and statues (see pls 15 and 16) were built, while the Greek cities of the south boasted some of the largest and earliest stone temples anywhere in the Mediterranean. Anyone approaching such a city would be well aware that this was a place of some significance.

This new level of central organisation of communities is reflected in their layout. Greek cities in Italy were reorganised along regular lines, with a grid of streets which divided the cities into rectangular blocks, a central area (*agora*) for public business, and religious sanctuaries with stone altars and temples, a so-called Hippodamian plan, attributed to Hippodamos of Miletos. By the end of the century, and throughout the fifth century, the Greeks invested in buildings that symbolised collective identity, such as the Ekklesiasterion, a circular structure with stepped seating built to house meetings of the citizens, at Metapontum. New Etruscan cities founded in the Po valley in the sixth century – notably Marzabotto – followed suit and adopted regular town plans, although these were not simply an adoption of Greek practices (fig. 18).[2] In central Italy, in contrast, many cities developed on sites that had been occupied since the Iron Age, and had a much less regular layout than that of their Greek counterparts. Rome is typical in this respect. The irregular topography, sprawling over a group of hills, and the organic growth of the community over many centuries made it impossible to impose a formal structure, and many Etruscan cities,

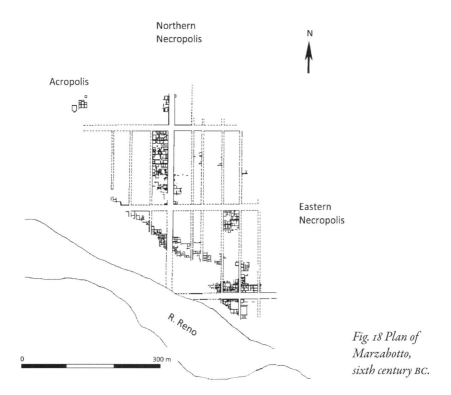

Fig. 18 Plan of
Marzabotto,
sixth century BC.

including Veii and Tarquinii, had the same problem. This is somewhat ironic, since the Etruscans – and later the Romans – were renowned for their expertise in surveying and planning communities. There was an extensive body of Etruscan lore on how to survey and set out a community in accordance with appropriate ritual observances, which formed the basis of Roman practices when founding colonies during their conquest of Italy.

Urbanisation went hand in hand with investment in other aspects of infrastructure. The Etruscans, in particular, were eager builders of roads and bridges. The latter were especially necessary in this region, which is one of rugged plateaux separated by steep gorges and river courses. At Veii a network of *cuniculi* – small tunnels – was constructed covering much of the territory. Most were drainage channels, enabling previously poorly drained areas to be cultivated, but some functioned as aqueducts, carrying drinking water into the city. Although there were no roads as impressive as the later Roman road network, there are signs in many areas of Italy that communities were investing in transport, drainage, water supply and other major projects.

Non-urban Italy

Although the city was the predominant form of organisation in many areas of Italy, this was not the case everywhere. Upland areas such as Calabria, the Apennines, parts of Umbria and the areas north of the River Po remained largely non-urban until a much later date. The central southern Apennines, a region later associated with the Samnites, who were notable enemies of Rome, was underdeveloped, and relatively little is known about settlements here before the fifth century. The region is one of mountains and high but fertile valleys. Field surveys have revealed an increasing number of small and medium-size villages during the seventh and sixth centuries, each consisting of twenty to forty houses, mostly of wattle-and-daub construction. These were frequently located on ridges and hilltops, making the most of the defensive advantages of the region's geography, and depended on a mixture of agriculture and stock-rearing. This area of Italy is associated by both ancient and modern historians with pastoralism, involving long-distance transhumance of flocks from winter pastures on the Adriatic coast to the summer pastures of the high Apennines, but there was also a well-established agrarian economy. At Arcora, the only settlement to be extensively excavated to date, the inhabitants grew cereal crops, legumes, vines and olives, as well as keeping sheep and cattle.

The monumental religious sanctuaries that were a feature of the central southern Apennines in later periods were not yet established, but the location of sacred places can be established from votive deposits, often in mountainous areas. The votive objects are mostly small figurines, often of the god Hercules, who was widely worshipped in this region, but are not associated with any buildings or structures. The monumental buildings associated with cults and cult places elsewhere in the sixth century are not found here until much later.

Most of our knowledge about the early history of the Apennines comes from cemeteries, some of which were extremely large. The cemetery at Alfedena, one of the most extensive, contained around 12,000 burials, of which only around 2,000 have been excavated. Burials were simple inhumations in which the body was wrapped in a shroud fastened with fibula brooches and sometimes placed in a wooden coffin. They were accompanied by an assortment of personal objects and sometimes bowls containing the remains of food – part of a ritual meal or food for the journey to the afterlife. Large vases found near graves may have been buried over the grave, as a marker or as a vessel for libations to the dead. From the middle of the sixth century, graves or clusters of graves in some parts of Apennine Italy were covered with large earth tumuli, a more dramatic and visible form of commemoration.

Both the layout of cemeteries and the grave offerings paint a familiar picture of a society organised into family groups but with a growing degree of social stratification in the later sixth century. Burials are organised into groups, probably family burial plots. Grave goods included local and imported pottery, bronze bowls and razors, jewellery in female burials, and bronze weapons and armour in male burials. The practice of burying valuable bronze items was a way of marking social and economic status. As in many other areas of Italy, the sixth century saw the rise of a social and political elite, but in the Apennines they remained a warrior aristocracy for whom weapons were an important status symbol. However, we know little about the political organisation of the region at this date or whether the people of the area had developed a clear ethnic identity.

Sanctuaries, priests and ritual

During the seventh century religious sanctuaries had few buildings. The important elements were the boundary that separated sacred and secular space, and the altar at which the main rituals of libation, sacrifice and burned offering were carried out. During the sixth century, communities poured money into converting these sacred precincts into monumental complexes, complete with impressive temples.

In Magna Graecia large stone temples in Doric style proliferated in the sixth and fifth centuries. These were built on a low platform with a colonnade running around the entire building, and many were decorated with sculpted stone panels (metopes) inset into the structure above the columns. The best-preserved examples are the three temples at Paestum, one dedicated to Athena at the northern edge of the city and the other two dedicated to Hera at the southern edge (pl. 14). Since temples were not essential to Greek worship,[4] temple-building was not driven by ritual requirements but by local pride, representing an investment in money, labour and expertise to demonstrate civic ambition and sense of importance.

Elsewhere, we can trace similar trends, although Italic and Greek temples differed in form. Temples in central Italy were built on raised podiums, with steps along the front for access, and had a deep porch with one or more rows of columns but no surrounding colonnade. Smaller examples had a single inner chamber, but many larger temples had an internal division into three parallel chambers, permitting the worship of groups of three gods, a common custom in Etruria and some other areas of Italy. The roof was typically wide and low-pitched with deep eaves, and ornamented with terracotta drainage spouts, antefixes along the eaves and sculptures along the roof ridge.

At Rome a massive new temple to Jupiter, located on the Capitoline, was begun in the sixth century, and the sanctuary of Apollo at Veii was equipped with a temple decorated with painted terracottas. Terracotta statues depicting the god (*akroteria*) were placed along the roof ridge, and the eaves were decorated with painted terracotta plaques covering the beam ends (pl. 15). Two major sanctuaries at Lavinium developed along similar lines. At the Sanctuary of the Thirteen Altars, located to the south of the town, the first altar was built *c.* 550. Two more were added in the later sixth century, and by the middle of the fifth the total had increased to nine, with four more being added in the fourth century. The complex did not have a temple, but an L-shaped building with a portico, which together with the array of large stone altars, must have made an impressive appearance. An archaic votive inscription honouring Castor and Pollux gives us the identity of at least one of the cults worshipped there. There was also a small tumulus grave close to the complex which was associated with a cult of Aeneas, although this connection may not have been made until later, probably around 300. Another sanctuary, on the eastern edge of Lavinium, was dedicated to Minerva. No temple has been found, but copious terracotta sculptures of types similar to those found in Etruria and some Greek cities suggest that it had a monumental building (pl. 16).

Not all temples were located in cities. Two of the best-documented sanctuaries are those at Pyrgi and Gravisca, which were located respectively in the territories of Caere and Tarquinii, close to the ports of these cities. Pyrgi (mod. Santa Severa) was the most important of Caere's three ports. Its sanctuary (fig. 19) had three temples: Temple A, built in Etruscan style, had a porch and tripartite chamber, but the largest, Temple B, constructed *c.* 510 as part of a major rebuilding, had a single chamber and a Greek-style colonnade. It was decorated with painted terracotta sculptures, and was dedicated to the Etruscan goddess Uni and her Phoenician

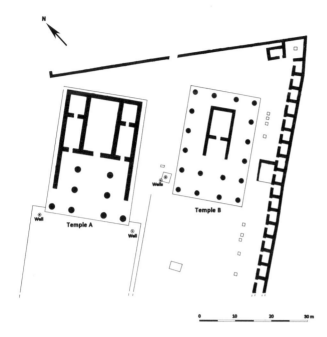

Fig. 19 Plan of the sanctuary at Pyrgi, sixth century BC.

counterpart, Astarte. A set of inscribed gold tablets, written in both Phoenician and Etruscan and found buried just outside the temple, commemorated its dedication to Uni and Astarte by Thefarie Velianas, ruler of Caere. Sacred prostitution was practised at temples of Astarte elsewhere in the Mediterranean, and a set of small cubicles along the boundary wall of the sanctuary may have been used for this purpose. A range of Greek, Etruscan and Phoenician deities were worshipped at Pyrgi. As well as Etruscan Uni and Astarte, there were the Greek deities Herakles, Eileithya and Leukothea, and the Etruscan deities Ino, Thesan, Cavtha, Tinia and Suri. Some common themes can be identified: Tinia and Suri were gods of the underworld, while Thesan and Cavtha were bringers of light, and Uni, Ino, Astarte, Eileithya and Leukothea were mother goddesses who protected women and children but also had responsibility for protecting sailors. According to a tradition reported by Herodotos, Herakles, whose deeds were represented in the sculptures of Temples A and B, was the ancestor of Tyrrhenos, the founder of the Etruscan people.

Excavations at Gravisca, the port of Tarquinii, have not revealed any buildings as significant as Temple B at Pyrgi, but they have uncovered deposits of votive offerings, dedicated to the Etruscan goddess Turan and to a number of Greek deities. Most were made by people with Greek names and consisted of pottery or other small objects of Greek manufacture.

One of the most intriguing is part of a stone anchor, dedicated to Apollo by one Sostratos. The votive inscription is written in the alphabet and dialect of the island of Aegina, and it is possible (although not provable) that the dedicator may be the merchant Sostratos of Aegina mentioned by Herodotos (4.152).

Trade was an important part of the local economy, and the presence of Greek and Phoenician merchants and craftsmen living in, or visiting, Etruria is shown by the high proportion of Greek dedications at Gravisca and Pyrgi. The bilingual inscription of the Pyrgi tablets is a vivid demonstration of the close links between the Etruscans and the Phoenician world, and the multicultural nature of sixth-century Etruria. However, the concentration of foreigners at these port sanctuaries, rather than temples in the city, suggests that the relationship between citizens and visitors was changing. In the seventh century Greeks and other non-Etruscans are found throughout Etruria, but by the middle of the sixth century Greek and Phoenician inscriptions and objects are mainly found in the ports. There is still evidence of interaction and even intermarriage between different ethnic communities, but the refocusing of activity by the non-Etruscan populations suggests that their own cult places and communities had an increasing importance to them.

Cult places were important points of contact where people from different cities and ethnic groups could meet. A religious festival was not just a celebration of a particular set of rituals but an opportunity for markets and fairs to be held, for legal disputes to be settled and for political and diplomatic negotiations to take place, under the protection of a god or a sacred truce. Sanctuaries – particularly those in rural areas – acted as meeting places which enabled economic and political contact between people in the region and beyond. The Latin festival held at Mons Albanus was, for instance, a celebration of common Latin identity, while the sanctuary of Lucus Feroniae was frequented by Latins, Sabines and Etruscans.

Other religious practices were associated with the political identity of city-states. The ritual formula used at Rome to begin some ceremonies was 'the foreigner, the chained prisoner, the woman, the girl, out!', excluding anyone who was not a free adult male Roman. The Iguvine tables, a long Umbrian inscription recording rituals from Iguvium (mod. Gubbio), had similar esxclusions, banning the neighbouring Sabines and Etruscans from attending some ceremonies.[5] Temples and sanctuaries, and the rituals associated with them, could be important in bridging boundaries between communities, but they could also be used as a means of exclusion, to emphasise the distinction between citizens and outsiders.

Other aspects of Italian religion that are obscure before the sixth century now come into focus. With better evidence from votive and ritual inscriptions and iconography, it is possible to identify some of the deities worshipped. These could be purely local, but there are signs that some cults spread more widely, and in regions of cultural contact there were levels of syncretism between cults of different ethnic groups. The Etruscan deities Tin, Turan and Uni are sometimes identified with Jupiter, Venus and Juno, and in Puglia there were cults of Damatira, Zis and Aprodita, which were local versions of the Greek cults of Demeter, Zeus and Aphrodite. Despite the similarities, however, rituals, votives and forms of worship were often specific to particular local areas. A cult site located in a cave, the Grotta della Poesia, near Rocavecchia in Puglia, offers an illustration of syncretism between different strands of religion, as well as the international nature of the devotees at some sanctuaries. The use of caves as sacred places has a long history in the region, dating back to the Neolithic period, but inscriptions found in the cave, mostly dating to the sixth and fifth centuries, showed that it was used by both the local Messapian population and by Greeks. The deity honoured is identified as a local god, Batas, in the Messapic votives, but conflated with Zeus and honoured as Zeus Batios by Greek worshippers.

Deposits of votive offerings from sanctuaries demonstrate the importance of the gods. These often ran to hundreds of items, of varying value, offered in the hope of divine favour or assistance. Some show signs of wear and tear from daily use and were probably personal possessions of the worshippers, while others were specific to particular cults and were manufactured specifically as offerings at a particular temple or sanctuary. Items offered include small figurines, pottery or bronze objects, sometimes with inscriptions giving the name of the giver or of the deity to which the offering was made. Votives may represent the gods and goddesses themselves, the worshippers or items relevant to a particular cult. Sanctuaries of deities who were reputed to have healing powers, for instance, frequently yield models of the afflicted body parts, no doubt offered in the hope that the god would heal the damaged limb or organ.

One aspect of Italian religion we know little about is how it was organised. We can deduce a certain amount about Etruscan practices, but the only state for which we have much evidence for priests and their activities is Rome itself, and even here it is difficult to be certain how far later practices can be traced back to the sixth century. In Republican Rome there was a close connection between political and religious life, and most priests were not religious specialists but were members of the aristocracy who held priesthoods alongside secular offices as part of a political career, but whether the same was true in the Regal period, or in other Italian societies, is unknown. According to Livy, the Etruscan cities banded together and elected a priest to undertake rituals on behalf of all members, something that suggests a connection between religious and political power, but other aspects of Etruscan religion required specialist knowledge. Forms of divination such as haruspicy (interpreting the entrails of sacrificial animals) or augury (observing and interpreting natural phenomena) were central to it, and these involved considerable study. Religious knowledge – particularly that connected with divination, which the Romans termed the *disciplina Etrusca,* or Etruscan scholarship – was recorded in sacred books written on linen. One of these, known as the Zagreb mummy roll (the linen was reused as wrappings for a mummified body), has survived, although in a very damaged form,[6] as have study aids such as the Piacenza liver, a model bronze liver marked up with the meanings of different areas of the organ. However, individuals known to have held office as a haruspex or an augur were mostly members of the aristocracy who had chosen to make a study of this knowledge. With a small number of exceptions, priests in ancient Italy were not set apart from society as special religious orders but undertook their religious duties – conducting sacrifices and rituals, and interpreting the results – alongside other public and private occupations.

Politics and society

From *c.* 600 the dominance of the closely knit aristocracies of the orientalising period was challenged by a wider group of wealthy and influential men who aspired to share power and influence. This was still an era of powerful and competitive aristocracies, but there were changes in the ways they behaved and how they interacted with the wider community. Changes in funerary customs offer some insight into this. In Etruria tumuli with their multiple burial chambers fell out of favour, although existing tombs of this type remained in use. Sixth-century tombs were more modest in size and appearance, and were constructed in regular terraces, forming 'streets of the dead' outside the cities they served (pl. 17). The tombs themselves present a more uniform and modest external appearance and consisted of two or three burial chambers leading off a small antechamber, each with two stone platforms to accommodate bodies or sarcophagi. At Orvieto (ancient Volsinii) numerous examples of these terraces of medium-size tombs can be seen in the Crocefisso del Tufo cemetery, each inscribed along the lintel with the name of the family that owned it, and at Caere 'tomb terraces' were built among the tumuli in the Banditaccia cemetery. At Tarquinii painted chamber tombs continued to be built, but they were more modest in size than the seventh-century examples.

These changes were related to the changes taking place within the aristocracy,[7] but we should not interpret these developments as a growth in social equality. Italian societies were still very hierarchical. The extravagant princely burials may have disappeared, but the elite were still buried in substantial tombs, with substantial amounts of grave goods and commemorative inscriptions to record their names and families. The manufacture of luxury goods in copious quantities and the lavish private houses of the sixth century, such as those found at Acquarossa or the archaic houses on the Palatine at Rome, show that the Italian elites were every bit as competitive as they had been in the orientalising period. Status was no longer primarily displayed by competitive funerary rituals and tombs but by investment in the new urban infrastructure of walls, temples and public buildings, as well as large and opulent private houses.

Within these elites women in archaic Italy had a more prominent social role than they did in some other Mediterranean societies. This was deeply shocking to Greek historians, some of whom comment disapprovingly. The Greek historian Theopompus took a particularly dim view of the apparent freedom enjoyed by Etruscan women, who are portrayed as decadent and party-loving:

Theopompus in the forty-third book of his *Histories* says that it is customary with the Etruscans to share their women in common: the women bestow great care on their bodies and often exercise even with men, sometimes also with one another; for it is no disgrace for women to show themselves naked. Further, they dine, not with their own husbands, but with any men who happen to be present, and they pledge with wine any whom they wish. They also drink a lot, and are very good-looking. The Etruscans rear all the babies that are born, not knowing who is the father in any single case. These in turn pursue the same mode of life as those who have given them nurture, having drinking parties often and consorting with the women.

(Athen., *Deip.* XII, 517 d–f)[8]

The tone of prurient outrage, and characterisation of Etruscan women as promiscuous and immoral, tells us far more about the social anxieties of the fourth-century Greek male than about women in sixth-century Etruria. Depictions of high-ranking women in Etruscan art confirm that they had a more visible role in society than Greek women. They were not segregated from men, as Greek women were, but are shown participating in social gatherings such as banquets, richly dressed and reclining on banqueting couches alongside their menfolk. Tomb paintings from Greek cities in Italy, in contrast, depict all-male drinking parties (pl. 28). Etruscan epitaphs often include the names of both the dead person's parents, which is unusual in Italy. It suggests that Etruscan society was not exclusively patrilineal, and that mothers, as well as fathers, were an important source of status and family identity. This prominent social role for elite women can be traced, although not in as much detail, elsewhere in northern Italy. In the Veneto and the Po valley, some of the richest burials are those of women, and many votive figurines and bronze plaques found in sanctuaries depict female worshippers and priestesses. There is a lot of variation in the visibility of women between different areas of Italy – women are commemorated far less frequently in the funerary and votive inscriptions of some parts of southern Italy than they are in the north – but the overriding impression is that many Italian women of this date played a more active and visible role in society than those of the Greek world.

Whether this translated into power and influence is, of course, another matter. The only role open to women in the wider life of the city was that of priestess. This was not negligible: priestesses such as the Vestal Virgins at Rome, or the priestesses of Reitia, the chief deity of some Venetic communities,[9] held prestigious and influential positions, but they were limited to one particular sphere. Women could not hold other public offices, and there is little evidence that they were able to own and manage their own property. Even what little evidence we have is much later than the third century.[10] At Rome, women required a male guardian to act for them in legal and financial matters. In societies such as those of archaic Italy aristocratic women may well – despite their lack of formal power – have exercised considerable informal influence. In a world dominated by a small number of powerful families, women who belonged to such families had considerable powers of patronage and behind-the-scenes influence simply by virtue of belonging to the ruling elite.

Another sign that the tightly knit aristocracy of the orientalising period was changing is the emergence of a greater variety of forms of government, some involving greater participation by the citizens. These are best documented in the Greek communities of Italy, which were ruled by elected magistrates from the late seventh century. These were the main executive officers of state, supported by a council selected from the older and wealthier citizens, and subject to varying degrees of control by assemblies of the people. The division of power and responsibility between these three elements changed over time and varied from city to city. Some were effectively oligarchies, in which the wealthier citizens dominated, while others gave a greater degree of legislative power and influence to assemblies of the citizens.

The situation elsewhere is less clear. The first evidence of Etruscan political organisation is a highly decorated stone pillar from Rubiera, near Bologna, which dates to the beginning of the sixth century. This was decorated with relief sculptures in an orientalising style and carried an inscription stating that it was set up by a *zilath* – the Etruscan title for a magistrate. Depictions of rulers – whether kings or elected magistrates – in contemporary Etruscan art show a number of symbols of office, including a curved staff (*lituus*) which was carried by a ruler or priest, a special chair or throne and a robe similar to a Roman toga. Roman sources are unhelpful, as Livy mostly refers to the leading Etruscans just as 'leaders' (*principes*), but a Greek account of Etruscan symbols of power is strikingly similar to those found in Etruscan art:

> [the envoys] returned after a few days, not only with words, but also bringing the insignia of sovereignty with which they decorated their own kings. These were a golden crown, an ivory throne, a sceptre with an eagle perched on it, a purple tunic embroidered with gold, and an embroidered purple robe like those the kings of Persia and Lydia wore except that it was not rectangular like theirs, but semicircular.

This kind of robe is called a toga by the Romans and a *tebenna* by the Greeks.

(Dion. Hal., 3.61)

The picture is no clearer for Latium. Some Latin cities elected their rulers, and we have references to various magistrates, of which the best-known is the dictator. At Rome, however, there is epigraphic evidence for rule by a king during the sixth century. The most likely explanation is that there were local variations, and that some cities had a monarch who ruled for life while others elected their leaders for fixed periods of office, or even that communities alternated between elective and monarchical rule. For both Rome and the rest of Italy the period between *c.* 550 and 470 was an era of transition, as communities began to experiment with different forms of government which gave a greater say to a larger cross-section of the community.

These changes had a profound impact on military organisation and styles of warfare. Previously armies were organised around aristocrats supported by groups of armed retainers. In the sixth century, in contrast, units of heavy infantry equipped with – typically – helmet, circular shield, lance and short sword became more usual. These well-armed infantry-men fought in co-ordinated units, as part of larger and better-equipped armies with a greater degree of organisation. This style of warfare (so-called 'hoplite warfare') was widely adopted throughout Italy and the Greek world. Armies were citizen militias drawn from the peasantry and property-owning classes who could afford substantial bronze armour and weapons, and men fought in close formation. At Rome the reforms of Servius Tullius, discussed in the following chapter, created just such a system, organising the male citizens into classes based on wealth, each of which had defined military duties and obligations. We know less about armies and military organisation in Etruria and in other areas of central Italy, but representations of warfare on vases such as the Tragliatella vase from Caere (see fig. 14) show units of heavy infantry armed with shields, helmets and spears, and similar items are found in burials. The heroic warrior figure was still a popular subject in art, particularly funerary art, and being seen as a warrior remained an important part of noble status, but actual warfare was now a matter for state-organised armies, in which most male citizens had to fight. These changes reflect a greater need for larger armies as developing states sought to protect their territories and assets, but they also reflect changes in social organisation.

The aristocratic clan was still central to the way in which archaic society operated. Heads of clans were still a dominant force in society, and relationships within, and between, clans were influential in the ways in which states developed. However, the ways in which these clans expressed their power had changed. They no longer invested their wealth in prestigious princely burials but in houses and in the infrastructure of their communities.

The urban economy

The sixth century was a period of economic growth, and the agrarian economy of Italy flourished, partly as a result of higher levels of urbanisation. City-states needed agricultural produce to feed their growing populations and provided ready markets for the farmers of the surrounding areas. They controlled wider territories, and were better able to exploit them more effectively, than the smaller settlements that they replaced. Archaeological surveys of the Albegna valley, Tuscania and Veii in Etruria, the territory of the Greek city of Metapontum and the territories of the Messapic settlements of Valesium and Vaste in Puglia all show similar developments. The number of rural settlements around these cities increased, more land was brought under cultivation, and farming was more intensive, though with many local variations. The connection between this intensification of production and the central authority of the city-state can best be seen at Veii. A comprehensive drainage system, which would have required state organisation, was constructed. A network of small drainage channels or tunnels, covering a wide area of the territory, was dug, enabling the cultivation of formerly waterlogged land and, in some cases, acting as aqueducts to carry water into the city.

Excavations of farmsteads provide valuable insights into rural life. Podere Tartuchino, in the Albegna valley in central Etruria, was a medium-size farmhouse built in the middle of the sixth century and greatly enlarged around forty to sixty years later. The owners grew cereal crops, grapes for wine-making and olives, and kept sheep and pigs. Estimates of the output of the farm at Podere Tartuchino concluded that it had the capacity to produce more than a subsistence level of crops, generating a surplus that could be sold.[11] Although the owners of such farms were far from wealthy, they were generating a reasonable income. Studies of plant and animal remains, and human skeletons from other areas (including Rome) suggest that Podere Tartuchino was typical and that the diet of sixth-century Italians was based on legumes, cereals, fruit, olives and wine, supplemented by fish and shellfish where people had access to them.[12] Most people ate little meat, other than on special occasions.

Trade and manufacture flourished, but with significant changes. Etruscan craftsmen had a reputation for fine workmanship, and there was a lively demand for their products from both outside and inside Etruria. Vulci was noted for its output of intricate bronze ornaments, tableware and household objects, which were in demand by the Etruscan elite and manufactured for export. Decorated pottery – both bucchero and painted pottery using Greek black-figure and red-figure techniques – was manufactured in large quantities. These luxury goods give a strong sense of the opulence of the aristocratic lifestyle of the period, and personal ornaments suggest that wealth was to be displayed. Etruscan jewellery of the period is often made of gold, decorated with semiprecious stones and intricate granulation, and many pieces are of substantial size. New prestige items appear, such as carved gemstones intended to be worn as seal-rings, and bronze mirrors and other toilet items decorated with incised mythological scenes. The sixth-century tomb paintings of Tarquinii (pl. 18) depict richly dressed couples, often shown reclining on dining couches, surrounded by wreaths and other trappings of a lavish banquet, and entertained by dancers and musicians. Styles had changed, and the banqueters now wear elaborately draped and embroidered cloaks and tunics, similar in style to those of the contemporary Greeks, pointed shoes or boots and fine jewellery, rather than the big hats and straight tunics of the orientalising period. Grave goods were not as opulent as those of the seventh century, but this reflects social change and a more mature economy, in which the intrinsic value of prestige objects was more important than their symbolic worth. The aristocracies of sixth-century central Italy clearly lived in some style, and the decline in the value of grave goods reflects a change in priorities, not a lack of wealth.

Elsewhere, some of the Greek cities of the south prospered so mightily that they became a byword for wealth. The term 'sybarite' is derived from Sybaris, which was notorious for the luxurious lifestyle of its citizens. Surveys and excavations reveal that Greek cities exploited their territories ever more intensively, with an increasing density of settlement in the hinterland of many colonies during this period. Similar developments are found in Puglia, on the fringes of Greek Italy. The early coinage of Meta-pontum was even stamped with a symbol of ears of barley to advertise the city's agrarian wealth.

Commerce also flourished. Imports from Greece and the Aegean continued to arrive in quantity in all areas of Italy, and from the end of the seventh century new markets began to open up for Italian traders. Both Etruscans and Greeks had a lively export trade with southern France and beyond. Etruscan and Greek goods are found in quantity, and trade in wine and oil can be traced via finds of Etruscan amphorae. Several Greek colonies were founded in southern France from *c.* 540, the most important of which was Massalia (Marseille), and the region was a fertile point of contact for exchange of goods between Greeks and Etruscans as well as with the indigenous peoples of the region.

Two factors allow us to trace these interactions: the survival of lead tablets inscribed with commercial agreements, and the excavation of a number of shipwrecks off the southern French coast. A lead tablet from Pech-Maho, inscribed with a Greek contract on one side and an Etruscan inscription on the other, clearly shows that there were important commercial dealings taking place between Greeks and Etruscans. Although this inscription is somewhat later than the time-frame of this chapter (probably dating to the early fifth century) and its meaning is much debated, it illustrates the strength and importance of commercial interactions, while finds from ancient shipwrecks demonstrate trade in a wide range of Greek and Etruscan goods which made their way into France and Spain, and also up the Rhone valley into central France and Germany.

Another sixth-century innovation was coinage. The first coins were minted in Asia Minor, but by 530–510 Greek cities of the south – Rhegium, Croton, Sybaris and Tarentum – had adopted the habit. Their coins were silver and most were of high value, although smaller denominations were also issued.[13] Typically they were stamped with symbols of the issuing city, often the head of a patron deity or founder on the obverse and a symbolic image such as the Metapontine barley on the reverse. Struck coins with a recognisable image remained restricted to the Greeks and their immediate neighbours until the late fourth century,[14] but rudimentary bronze coins and stamped bronze ingots in standard weights appear in some Etruscan areas around the same time as the first coinage, and Romans such as Pliny the Elder believed that ingots of this type were first issued at Rome by Servius Tullius in the late sixth century. The fact that early coins and ingots were high-value items, even in their smaller denominations, gives us a clue to how they were used. These were not for making small payments but to facilitate large-scale transactions. One possible explanation for the development of coinage is that it was a medium for paying troops or making similar large payments which offered quality control, as coins were of a standard weight, and authentication by a named state, the emblem of which was stamped on the coin. Another use was to facilitate large commercial transactions. A high concentration of standardised ingots has been found in peripheral communities such as Mantua and Marzabotto, both of which depended on international trade. The Italians did not have a monetary economy as we would understand it, but the appearance of the first coins demonstrates a growing economic sophistication. Minted coins and bullion bars were used as a means of payment and exchange alongside other modes of transaction such as barter, like-for-like exchange of goods and services, and credit agreements.

Inter-state connections

By the sixth century the individual city-state was the principal political and social unit in Italy, but this raises questions of how these states interacted, whether they co-operated in times of war and whether collective identities over and above those of the individual city developed.

Religious connections were an important factor. Shared sacrifices and festivals, celebrated by groups of communities at communal shrines, were vital to creating and sustaining a sense of shared culture and identity. The sites chosen were often rural sanctuaries which, being out in the countryside, were readily accessible to people from a wide area. The Latin festival, the Feriae Latinae, which was held each year on Mons Albanus is one of the better-known examples:

> he [Tarquinius Superbus] nominated as the place of assembly a high mountain located almost in the centre of these peoples, and commanding the city of the Albani; he enacted a law that an annual festival should be celebrated upon this mountain, during which they should all refrain from acts of war against all the others, and should make joint sacrifices to Jupiter Latiaris, as he is named, and should feast together, and he laid down the share which each city was to contribute to these

sacrifices, and the share that each was to receive. The cities which shared in this festival and these sacrifices numbered forty-seven. The Romans celebrate these festivals and sacrifices to this day, and call them Latin festivals; some of the cities which take part bring lambs, some cheeses, and others a certain quantity of milk, and others offerings of similar kind. One bull is sacrificed jointly by all of them, with each city receiving its designated share of meat. The sacrifices which they offer are on behalf of all cities, and the Romans oversee them.

(Dion. Hal., 4.49)

Other sources describe it as a much older festival, which pre-dated Rome's conquest of the Alban region, suggesting that it was indeed of great antiquity. Its association with Jupiter Latiaris, the principal god of the Latins, and with the eponymous founding hero Latinus, confirms that it fostered a shared identity and sense of community between the Latins. Other Latin sanctuaries used in a similar manner are known at Lucus Feroniae, Lavinium, Tusculum, Lucus Ferentinae and Aricia, and most were established by the sixth century. Although we know more about those of the Latins than of other Italian peoples, the general pattern seems to have been common to most of Italy. The Etruscans had an important shared sanctuary of Voltumna, near Volsinii (mod. Orvieto), for instance, which was of great cultural and political importance.[15]

Religious confederations based on shared rituals and festivals were important aspects of cultural and ethnic identity, but some had practical significance as well. The Etruscans were said to have organised themselves into a league of twelve cities, representatives of which met at the shrine of Voltumna. This league had a military purpose as well as a religious one. Livy describes how, in 434, during the war between Veii and Rome, Veii and Falerii were so alarmed that they called a meeting of the twelve members of the league to solicit military support from the rest of Etruria against the Roman advance. Similar leagues of twelve states existed in Campania, one of which was headed by Capua, and the Hernici, a people occupying the southern part of Latium may have had a league headed by Anagnia. The best-documented, however, were the Latin league, an association of Latin states, and the Italiote league, a confederation of some (or possibly all) of the Greek cities of Italy.

Working out what leagues of states actually did and how they functioned is problematic. Ancient accounts are sparse, and there is little epigraphic or archaeological evidence to supplement them. We have a fairly clear account of the Italiote league, which first appeared in the late sixth century, was dissolved in the late fifth century, and was re-established in the mid-fourth century. It maintained a meeting house and treasury for league finances at the temple of Hera Lacinia in the territory of Croton, the leader of the league at that time, and was primarily an alliance of the Greeks of Calabria and Basilicata. However, it is unclear whether this was the case for the whole of its history or only applies to its fourth-century version. Federations of states were an established part of Greek political and diplomatic life from the mid-fifth century onwards, and most Greek leagues involved regular meetings of a league council, election of league officials and generals, a treasury funded by financial contributions from members and regular military co-operation. Whether the same is true of the sixth century is less clear.

The so-called Latin league (although this is a modern usage) played an important role in Roman history in the sixth and fifth centuries. The name used by Roman sources – the *nomen latinum*, or Latin name – shows a strong perception of shared culture and ethnicity, as do the shared cults and festivals described above, but these tell us little about the ways in which specific joint activities were organised.

As well as sharing a language, religion and culture, the Latins shared some specific legal rights and privileges. These included the right to own property in another Latin state, make commercial contracts with Latins from other states and legally to marry someone from another Latin community. These rights linked Latins – including Romans – into a web of property ownership and intermarriage that cut across the boundaries of individual communities.

The political and military activities of the league, and particularly Rome's role in it, are more problematic. The Romans were full participants in the league's religious festivals and believed them to be ancient. Most accounts suggest that the league met at Lucus Ferentinae, a sanctuary of the goddess Ferentina that was probably a mile or so (2 km) from Albano Laziale. The league does not seem to have acquired a political and military role until the sixth century, and even then meetings for the election of a common war leader were a response to emergencies rather than a regular occurrence. Although Rome eventually emerged as the leader of the league, there were occasions when the other Latins sought to exclude it, and Dionysios of Halicarnassus implies that they used the league to counteract the growth of Rome's power. The elder Cato (*FRHist* 5 F36) recounts an incident in which Latin cities (he lists Tusculum, Aricia, Lavinium, Lanuvium, Cora, Tibur, Pometia and Ardea) banded together under Egerius Baebius of Tusculum as leader (*Dictator Latinus*) and dedicated a new shrine of Diana in a wood near Aricia as a common Latin sanctuary. The shrine in question is probably the sanctuary of Diana at Nemi, an ancient and famous cult place presided over by a priest who was by tradition a runaway slave.[16] This rededication of the shrine at Nemi as a federal sanctuary suggests that the Latin league was reorganised as a focus for resistance to Roman expansion, possibly under the leadership of Tusculum, and that when the situation required, they elected a common leader and fought as a common army. In the later sixth century, Rome began to expand its power into Latium, and this seems a likely context for the organisation of Latin resistance.

The evidence suggests that from the sixth century onwards, as state organisation grew stronger, the Italian communities began to make common cause with their neighbours, although it is hard to be sure whether this took the form of short-term alliances or more complex federal structures. In either case their military and political functions seem likely to have grown informally out of shared religious occasions. Nevertheless, they seem to show an increasing degree of contact and co-operation on a regional level.

The Etruscans abroad

The sixth century saw a change in the balance of power in Italy. The Etruscans expanded their political reach and their cultural influence beyond the confines of Etruria itself; the Greeks extended their territory at the expense of their neighbours; and other Mediterranean powers, especially Carthage, began to take an interest in Italy.

There had been contact between Campania and Etruria from the eighth century, but from *c.* 625 this became much more intensive. Throughout the seventh century Etruscan luxury goods were found in many princely tombs in the region. The areas around Capua and Pontecagnano had particularly close cultural and economic connections with Etruria, which co-existed with a flourishing local culture. Towards the end of the seventh century Etruscan pottery – especially a type of fine bucchero produced at Caere – appears in greater quantity in Campanian burials and Etrus-can-style goods began to be produced in Campania. Flourishing local bucchero and terracotta industries developed during the sixth century. Painted terracotta mouldings suggest that Etruscan styles of architecture had also spread to the region. These developments were in part due to the influence of Etruscan craftsmen and to the adoption of Etruscan styles by the peoples of Campania, but there are signs of more direct Etruscan influence. Capua and Pontecagnano were reorganised in the sixth century, and new settlements were established at Fratte di Salerno and Marcina. Capua rapidly established regional dominance, controlling trade and com-munications between Campania and the Greek areas of Italy. It grew to a substantial size, and the richness of its material culture and the copious output of its craft workshops, producing bronze and pottery vessels and terracotta items that were traded throughout Italy, demonstrate its wealth and power.

The presence of Etruscan people as well as Etruscan goods is estab-lished by sixth-century inscriptions written in the Etruscan language and alphabet which have been found in Campania. There are around a hundred of these, compared with about eighteen inscriptions in other local languages.[17] Most are short texts inscribed on pottery vessels, giving the name of the owner or giver of the object, which provide evidence of people with distinctive Etruscan names. One of the longest-surviving Etruscan inscriptions – a text many lines long incised on a clay tile – comes from Capua. This intriguing document appears to be a ritual calendar listing festivals and sacrifices. If this is correct, it suggests that Etruscan gods and religious practices were known in central Campania. The Greek geographer Strabo (*Geog.* 5.4.3) even speaks of a league of twelve Etruscan cities in Campania, headed by Capua.

While it would be rash to take this at face value and interpret the Etruscan presence in Campania as conquest or colonisation, there was clearly a significant level of Etruscan settlement there in the sixth and fifth centuries, as well as close economic and cultural connections between these areas. Capua and several other cities were socially and politically dominated by aristocrats who had adopted many elements of Etruscan culture, some of whom may have been of Etruscan origin, but there is no sign that there was a direct Etruscan takeover or mass colonisation. Instead, sixth-century Campania seems to have been a melting-pot, where Greek, Etruscan, Latin and Apennine cultures mingled with that of the local Campanians. Studies of the Fornaci cemetery at Capua show that there was considerable continuity of cultural and funerary practices in the sixth and fifth centuries, undermining the notion of an Etruscan takeover. The multicultural nature of the region is perhaps best illustrated by the development of flourishing pottery and terracotta industries, which produced bucchero and red-figure pottery, and terracotta figurines and architectural decorations, using Etruscan techniques but in distinctive local styles. Etruscans settled in, or had regular contact with, Campania, no doubt attracted by commercial opportunities and a plentiful supply of fertile land. The depth of Etruscan influence on the region, however, was due to cultural and economic influence. The importance of Etruscan commercial power and political influence cannot be underestimated, but it was not achieved by anything as direct as a process of colonisation. At Rome too we can trace Etruscan influences on Roman culture and society, which will be explored in detail in the following chapter, yet levels of direct migration and settlement were much lower than in Campania.

Etruscan influence was not limited to central Italy but began to expand northwards into Lombardy and the Veneto and towards the Alps, and eastwards to the Adriatic coast. Connections between the Etruscans and the Po valley had been established since the eighth century, and there were Etruscan settlements at Bologna and Verucchio. Felsina (mod. Bologna) was a large and impressive settlement with a flourishing metalwork industry and control of an extensive territory. Excavations in the S. Francesco area of the city revealed an industrial quarter with workshops producing high-quality bronze vessels. Cemeteries with over two thousand tombs dating from the eighth to the fourth centuries provide a profile of a society dominated by a small but powerful aristocracy. In the middle of the sixth century, however, the pattern of settlement in this region changed drastically. New settlements were founded at Spina, Marzabotto and Mantua, and many Etruscans settled at Adria, as demonstrated by both Etruscan goods and Etruscan inscriptions.

Adria, a mixed community of Greeks, Etruscans and Veneti; and Spina, a predominantly Etruscan city, were ports on the Po delta. They quickly established themselves as important entrepôts, exporting goods from Etruria and other areas of northern Italy to Greece and the wider Mediterranean world, and importing Greek goods into Italy. The cemeteries of both are rich in burials containing goods from a wide area, and in particular many items of fine imported Greek pottery. Marzabotto, founded just outside Bologna, provides a fascinating insight into Etruscan city life, as it is one of the few cities where both the burial areas and the urban area have been systematically excavated. Unlike most Etruscan cities, it was a planned community with a regular street grid dividing houses and other buildings into long narrow blocks, closely modelled on contemporary Greek town planning. The streets had central drains and pavements along the sides. The blocks were constructed of brick and wood on stone foundations and were subdivided into private houses, reached via a narrow entrance and fronted by shops or workshops. The houses themselves had a central courtyard with a series of rooms opening off it, and were not unlike the atrium houses found at Rome and elsewhere in Etruria. The economic importance of the city can be judged from the large areas of workshops producing pottery and metal vessels on an industrial scale.

The urban area of Spina is less well explored, but there are signs that it was a planned city. Large stones inscribed with the word *tular* were probably markers used in the surveying and planning of the city. In Etruscan, *tular* indicates a benchmark or boundary stone marking points fixed as part of the planning process. There are signs of a systematic network of streets and canals, suggesting that the population of Spina was taking care to improve land and water-borne transport, as well as drainage. Around the same time Felsina underwent a major reorganisation, acquiring a more regular street layout, new public buildings and a fortified citadel with temples, which was the ceremonial and defensive core of the city, and which was located on a spur of the Apennines, above the centre of the city.

This intensification of interest in the Po plain and the Adriatic coast was prompted by changing conditions in coastal Etruria and central Italy. The Etruscans had a reputation in the Greek world as a seafaring people, noted for naval power which sometimes led to piracy.[18] Strabo says that: 'before that time [the eighth-seventh centuries] men were so afraid of the bands of Etruscan pirates and the savagery of the barbarians in this region that they would not even sail there to trade' (Strabo, *Geog.* 6.2.3). Much of their early success had been based on sea-borne trade in the Mediterranean, but by the middle of the sixth century their grip on this area was becoming shaky. The Greeks of Sicily and coastal Campania had begun to challenge Etruscan control, and the Carthaginians posed an additional threat. Some time around 500, Thefarie Velianas, the ruler of Caere, signed a treaty with Carthage, and Rome may have done likewise at some point in the fifth century.[19] An alliance of Etruscans and Carthaginians certainly existed *c.* 540 BC, when their fleets combined to fight a naval battle off Alalia (mod. Ajaccio) on Corsica against Greeks who had settled there. Although the Greek settlers were forced to abandon Alalia, the Etruscan fleet suffered heavy losses, and by the late sixth century the Etruscans could no longer dominate trade in the western Mediterranean. Adria and Spina provided a handy alternative access to the Mediterranean by shipping goods down the Adriatic coast. Trade routes through the Po valley, Lombardy and Liguria gave access to overland routes into Europe, and to shipping routes via Massalia and the River Rhone. These became yet more important during the course of the fifth century, as Etruscan power in Campania was eroded. Reorganisation of the territories of the cities in the Po plain, the establishment of a network of roads and canals in the Po delta, and the large 'industrial quarter' at Marzabotto all point to a fundamental reorientation of Etruscan priorities in this area, from exploitation of agricultural resources to trade and manufacture. Agricultural produce and natural resources remained important, and at least some of the export trade flowing out of Spina and other Adriatic ports was of grain, metal ores and amber, as well as manufactured goods, but it was no longer the only consideration.

There is some debate about whether Spina and Marzabotto are evidence for a policy of Etruscan expansion and colonisation in the Po plain in the late sixth and early fifth centuries. The regular layout of the cities of the Po plain and delta, which differ strikingly from the organic and haphazard growth of earlier Etruscan cities, has prompted speculation that they may have been founded as colonies by one or more of the city-states of Etruria. However, settlement in the Po valley seems more likely to have been the result of a steady stream of Etruscan migrants intermingling with local populations, as it was in Campania, rather than a process of formal state-organised colonisation. Many Etruscan names found in local inscriptions have a distinctive suffix, -alu (e.g., Rakalu, Kraikalu), which is only found in this area, suggesting that most of the population of Marzabotto were locals who had moved there from other parts of the Po plain, not colonists from Etruria. The more regular layout of the communities reflects changing ideas about urban organisation in the sixth century, influenced by Greek Hippodamean planning and a growing body of Etruscan ritual and practice connected with foundation of settlements. The planned layout of Marzabotto, Spina and some other cities reflects greater use of these ritual practices rather than colonial origins.

The changes in Etruscan settlement in the Po plain and Etruscan links with northern Italy were connected with changes in the balance of power in Etruria itself, although not as direct cause and effect. During the seventh and sixth centuries the cities of southern and coastal Etruria – Caere, Vulci, Veii and Tarquinii – were the dominant powers in the region. Towards the end of the sixth century, as trade routes shifted away from these cities and towards northern and Adriatic Italy, the inland cities of northern Etruria, such as Perusia, Arretium, Volsinii and Clusium, became more dominant. The balance of power within the region shifted towards the cities that controlled trade and communication with continental Europe and with northern and eastern Italy. By the beginning of the fifth century the likes of Veii and Caere were beginning to decline. Their economic power was undermined by changing patterns of trade and by the rise of two new powers in the western Mediterranean: Carthage and Rome.

The dominant themes of the sixth century in all parts of Italy are the increasing importance and complexity of city-states and the changes in the behaviour of elites, from investing in symbols of personal and dynastic power to investing in urban infrastructure. These two developments go hand in hand, as cities of increasing size and importance offered new opportunities for both displays of elite magnificence and for the exercise of elite power and influence. It was also an era of cultural and economic changes, in which Etruscan influence expanded into areas stretching from the Po delta to Campania, a development that had a huge impact on sixth-century Rome.

7

TYRANTS AND WICKED WOMEN: ROME, THE TARQUIN DYNASTY AND THE FALL OF THE MONARCHY

According to ancient tradition, Rome was ruled in the late seventh and sixth centuries by the Tarquinius family, who were of Etruscan origin (fig. 20). The first of them, Tarquinius Priscus, was said to be the son of Demaratos of Corinth, who moved to Rome and exchanged his Etruscan name, Lucumo, for the more Roman Lucius Tarquinius Priscus.[1] We are told that he became the right-hand man of the king, Ancus Marcius, held several important military commands and succeeded Marcius in *c.* 616. After a lengthy and successful reign he was succeeded by his son-in-law Servius Tullius. In Roman sources Servius Tullius was the son of a slave, a noblewoman captured in Tarquinius' wars in Latium. Portents in Servius' childhood marked him out and helped him gain the favour of Tarquinius and his wife, Tanaquil, becoming a trusted lieutenant of the king. His accession is described as having been stage-managed by Tanaquil, bypassing

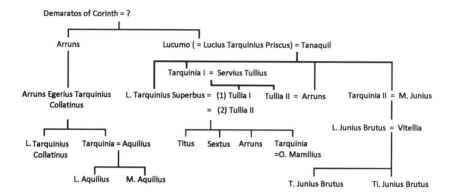

Fig. 20 The Tarquin family tree.

the normal formalities, but he became Rome's most notable king, whose reign was marked by a number of far-reaching reforms. The seventh, and last, king of Rome was Tarquinius Superbus, the son of Tarquinius Priscus and also the son-in-law of Servius Tullius. His wife, Tullia, encouraged her husband to murder her father and usurp power by force. Although Tarquinius Superbus was an effective ruler, he was also cruel and oppressive, and was overthrown in 509, after which Rome became a Republic.

These last three kings, Tarquinius Priscus, Servius Tullius and Tarquinius Superbus,[2] seem at first glance to have more historical substance than their predecessors, but the specific actions and personalities attributed to these later kings must be regarded as largely fictitious. They contain many elements of mythologising, folk-tale and anachronism, such as Servius' origin as the son of a slave/deposed princess and the divine portents that singled him out, or Tarquinius' original name, Lucumo, closely related to the Etruscan word for 'king' (*lauchume*). The traditions also contain many internal inconsistencies, such as the discrepancies between the dates of Demaratos and Tarquinius Priscus and those of Tarquinius Superbus, who would have to be a more distant descendant of Tarquinius Priscus to fit the traditional chronology. Livy's descriptions of their accessions and actions contains many implausible and possibly anachronistic elements, and the depiction of the characters of these kings and their families owes much to stereotypes of the good king (Servius Tullius), virtuous and wicked women (Tanaquil and Tullia) and the tyrant (Tarquinius Superbus).

Nevertheless, there are reasons to accept at least the historical existence of the Tarquin dynasty, even though much of the narrative of their reigns cannot be substantiated. The history of the Tarquins, particularly after their exile in 509, is entwined with that of Aristodemos, the tyrant of Cumae, who was a character of some interest to Greek historians. Later historians may have had access to accounts of his reign based on Cumaean sources, now lost, and if some of the material about the later history of Tarquinius Superbus comes from this source, it provides non-Roman corroboration of at least part of the story. The general picture of a vigorously expanding Rome, ruled by an elite influenced by Etruscan and Greek culture, fits with contemporary archaeological evidence, and the establishment of kingship as an institution at Rome by the sixth century is confirmed by contemporary inscriptions. The Forum inscription, a stone block inscribed with a sixth-century ritual or sacred law, found near the Comitium (see pl. 20), mentions a king (*rex*), and this is corroborated by a sixth-century pot inscribed with the word 'rex'.

A more substantial alternative tradition for the Tarquins and Servius Tullius can be pieced together from Etruscan sources. In a speech made in AD 48 by the emperor Claudius, and recorded in an inscription from Lyon (*CIL* 13.1668), the emperor urged the senate to admit members from Gaul, citing historical examples of Roman willingness to extend citizenship and even high office to non-Romans.[3] One of these examples is Servius Tullius, who was, according to Claudius, one and the same person as an Etruscan warlord called Mastarna.

Further evidence for Mastarna comes from the late fourth-century François Tomb at Vulci. One wall of the main burial chamber is painted with scenes from the *Iliad*, while on the other there is a scene of combat between pairs of warriors, labelled with their names and (in the case of some) their place of origin (fig. 21). The scene depicts the rescue of a group of captured Etruscans, including the well-known heroes Aulus and Caelius Vibenna, by Mastarna and a group of companions. Most of the protagonists are Etruscans, but the scene includes Gneve Tarchunies Rumach (Gnaeus Tarquinius of Rome) being struck down by Marce Camitlnas (Marcus Camitilius, or possibly Marcus Camillus).[4] These scenes show an Etruscan tradition involving a skirmish between the Vibennas of Vulci and their supporters and a group of warriors from Suana, Volsinii and Rome, but, although elements of this same tradition were evidently known to Claudius, we do not know what legend or historical episode it depicts.

Given that the tomb dates to *c.* 300, the frescoes give us an insight into fourth-century traditions about earlier heroes and warriors rather

Fig. 21 Tomb paintings depicting Mastarna and companions freeing prisoners,
François Tomb, Vulci. Fourth century BC. The figures are labelled as Mcstrna
(Mastarna), Caile Vipinas (Caelius Vibenna), Larth Ulthes, Laris Papthnas Velznach
(from Volsinii), Rasce, Persna Aremsnas Sveamach (from Suana), Avle Vipinas (Aulus
Vibenna), Venthi Cal[...]plsachs, Marce Camitlnas (possibly Marcus Camillus),
and Gneve Tarchunies Rumach (Gnaeus Tarquinius the Roman).

than contemporary sixth-century evidence. However, there are many
other sources, both Roman and Etruscan, for the exploits of the Vibenna
brothers, some of which pre-date the François Tomb. Some writers derived
the name of the Caelian hill from that of Caelius Vibenna, who is said to
have migrated to Rome along with his followers.[5] Another tradition, a
version of which was known to the third-century historian Fabius Pictor,
claimed that the name of the Capitoline was derived from *caput oli* ('head
of Olus'), after Olus (an alternative spelling of Aulus), an Etruscan from
Vulci, who could be identified with Aulus Vibenna. Etruscan evidence for
the Vibenna brothers includes depictions of their exploits on funerary
urns from Clusium and mirrors from Volsinii. A fifth-century pottery cup
inscribed 'Avile Vipiienas', found in the Portonaccio sanctuary at Veii, may
be a sign of a hero cult dedicated to him and demonstrates that the traditions surrounding the Vibennas were not an invention of the late fourth
century.

One solution proposed to the problematic identification of Servius
Tullius and Mastarna is that Mcstrna is an Etruscanisation of the Latin
title *magister*, indicating the leader of the war band (i.e., Servius Tullius),
which was later mistaken for an alternative, Etruscan, personal name.
Cornell notes that it would be difficult to reconcile an Etruscan tradition
that Mastarna/Tullius had a previous career as an Etruscan warlord before
he became king with the Roman tradition that he was a follower and eventually right-hand man of Tarquinius Priscus. However, the discrepancies

between the two traditions are not irreconcilable. Roman and Etruscan sources both suggest that the Vibenna brothers had connections with Rome, and in the context of the picture they present of bands of warriors, drawn from different states and moving from place to place, a Roman who became the right-hand man of an Etruscan warlord, and then of a king of Rome, before becoming king himself is not impossible. Ethnic and state boundaries in archaic Italy were permeable, and there is much evidence of mobility between cities, including those of different ethnicity or culture. A mixed Latin and Etruscan background for Rome's rulers is consistent with what we know about the nature of Italian society.

Servius Tullius and his reforms

Although Servius Tullius' background, personality and deeds may be at least partly later traditions, the reforms ascribed to him are central to understanding how the Roman state worked. As presented by our sources, the political organisation of sixth-century Rome consisted of three elements: an executive power (the king and, later, annually elected magistrates), an assembly of the Roman people (the *comitia curiata*) and a deliberative council (the senate), although the development – or even the existence – of all of these elements before the foundation of the Republic is very unclear.

The powers of kings are obscure, as is the way they were selected. Livy describes a complex procedure for appointing a new monarch. Following the death of the ruler, an interregnum of one year was declared, during which Rome was ruled by the heads of the patrician families, who took turns to hold power for a period of five days each. At the end of this period an election was held, in which the new king was chosen, and formal executive power (*imperium*) was conferred on him by a *lex curiata*, a law of the *comitia curiata*, the assembly of the Roman people. It is not clear whether Livy envisaged the people choosing between several candidates, or accepting or rejecting a single candidate selected in advance.

The ancient sources present two kings as exceptions to this. Servius Tullius is said to have taken power without a vote by the people, thanks to his family connections as Tarquinius' son-in-law and his role as a prominent political and military leader. After the assassination of Tarquinius, the succession is presented by Livy as stage-managed by his widow, Tanaquil, who addressed the people from the window of her house, proclaiming Servius as king without an interregnum or a vote by the people. The accession of Tarquinius Superbus was an even more violent event, a murky tale of treachery and murder. Servius Tullius had married his daughters (both called Tullia) to Arruns and Tarquinius, sons of Tarquinius Priscus. The younger Tullia, wife of Arruns, plotted with her ambitious brother-in-law Tarquinius Superbus to murder both her husband and her sister and marry him. She then egged on her husband to seize the throne by force. After Servius Tullius' assassination, Tullia even drove her chariot over her father's corpse. Although Tullia is the villain of this episode, Tarquinius is presented as ruthless and devious, and Livy's account prepares the reader for his later bad reputation for oppressive and ruthless behaviour.

These traditions involve a high degree of melodrama and implausibility and cannot be accepted as historical. Roman accounts seek to establish the moral characters of the main protagonists rather than to record fact, and the procedure for choosing a king looks suspiciously as though it may have been inferred by Livy's sources from later procedures for coping with gaps in the consulship, which involved an *interrex*. Cornell has argued that ancient accounts of the accessions of Servius Tullius and Tarquinius Superbus, which lacked the usual ratifications, indicate that they were usurpers, analogous to the Greek tyrants of the seventh and sixth centuries, who held power by virtue of popular support rather than legal right. However, it is more likely that Livy's account of the procedure for choosing a monarch is both formalised and anachronistic, and that the normal process was no less ad hoc for the other kings than it is said to have been for Servius Tullius and Tarquinius Superbus.

The forms of government at this date are impossible to establish with certainty. The existence of kings is corroborated by the '*rex*' inscription described above, but we know little about their powers, although it is probably reasonable to assume that they were the chief executive power. Our sources refer to an influential senate, almost certainly an anachronism, and an assembly of the Roman people. This assembly, the *comitia curiata*, was believed by the Romans to have been of very ancient origin. It was organised by (and voted in) *curiae*, the bodies to which all male citizens belonged. Under the Republic, the assemblies elected magistrates and approved or rejected laws, but we know little about the functions of the *comitia curiata* in the sixth century.

The organisation of Rome comes into sharper focus with the military and political reforms that later traditions attributed to Servius Tullius (Livy 1.41–6; Dion. Hal. 4. 14–23). These changes implied a radical transformation of the Roman state. Servius is said to have held a census, at which all citizens of Rome were divided into new units and allocated to *tribus* or tribes. These were based on place of residence and census registration, and transformed the Roman definition of citizenship, which now became a matter of legal status rather than birth or ethnicity: this made it much more easily extendable and transferable with the institution of subsequent censuses, which came to be held periodically (later, roughly every five years).

In the later Republic (after 241 BC) there were thirty-five tribes, four in the city and thirty-one in the country districts. Fourteen of the latter were created in a series of stages between 387 and 241 BC, but the history of the earlier ones is less certain. Livy tells us that the first twenty-one tribes were in existence already in 495 BC (2.21.7), but we cannot be sure how many of these (if any) date back to the regal period.[6] Some sources say that Servius divided the city (and perhaps also the surrounding territory) into four tribes, but others suggest that he also created some of the so-called rustic tribes as well; but the relevant texts are confused and contradictory (especially Dion. Hal. 4.14–15), and no firm conclusion is possible on this matter.

Additionally, Servius is said to have fundamentally reorganised both military and political life by distributing adult male citizens into five classes based on wealth and property. These in turn were subdivided into *centuriae* (centuries) of *iuniores*, the younger men who formed the main fighting force, and *seniores*, those over the age of forty-five, whose role was to defend the city. Each man had to equip himself at his own expense: from a full set of bronze armour, sword, spear and shield for the highest class; to slings and javelins for the lowest.

This scheme looks both artificial and anachronistic. The discrepancies between sources suggest that the Romans themselves were unsure about the details, and in general their accounts seem to conflate two different reforms – one military and the other political. For instance, both describe an army consisting of centuries of a hundred men each, but this is incompatible with the notion of classes containing all citizens who met the wealth qualification. It is more likely that all men who qualified for a particular property class were divided into units of equal size, but whatever

---

Class	Property	Armour	Weapons	Number of centuries		
				Iuniores	Seniores	Total
I	100,000 asses	Helmet, shield, greaves, Breastplate	Spear, sword	40	40	80
II	75,000 asses	Helmet, shield, greaves	Spear, sword	10	10	20
III	50,000 asses	Helmet, shield	Spear, sword	10	10	20
IV	25,000 asses	[shield]	Spear, javelin, [sword]	10	10	20
V	11,000 asses	None	Sling stones, [javelin]	15	15	30
Total infantry centuries						170
Supernumerary centuries: Cavalry (equites): 18; Engineers: 2; Musicians: 2; Proletarians: 1						23
Total number of centuries						193

Table 5: **The organisation of centuries** (according to Livy 1.43 and Dion. Hal. 4.16–18)

the size of the population they are unlikely to have amounted to a hundred men per century in any of the classes.

Although the wealthiest class must have been far less numerous than the poorer ones, it had four times as many centuries as the three classes below it and nearly three times as many as the lowest class. This unequal distribution is impossible for a military force. However, it is compatible with a political organisation in which centuries acted as voting units, and which was weighted to ensure that the rich could outvote the poor and the old could outvote the young. It is likely that the sources were describing Roman political organisation as it was before a reform in the third century,[7] and attributing it to Servius Tullius.

On the other hand, the organisation into five classes makes little military sense, although a basic division – between the better-off who served as heavy infantry, with a full set of armour, sword and shield; and those who could not afford armour and served as lightly armed support troops, armed with javelins or slings – is plausible. The idea that such a division of the people was also given a political function, in which the

centuries formed voting units in a citizen assembly, is a reasonable speculation, and the possibility that it originated in the regal period cannot be
ruled out. The calculation of the citizens' property holdings in *asses* may
be an anachronism, but although Rome did not start minting coins until
c. 300, the use of the *as* (a unit of bronze weighing a pound) as a measure
of value is likely enough before the introduction of coinage, and may go
back as far as the sixth century.

The most important point about a reform of this kind is that it could
have introduced an organised army and a new style of fighting. As noted
in Chapters 4 and 6, the boundaries of the state in archaic Italy were relatively weak. Powerful nobles supported by bands of armed clients and
retainers could (and frequently did) pursue their own private conflicts,
either entirely on their own behalf or on behalf of the state. The frescoes
of the François Tomb (see fig. 21) may depict just such a conflict between
bands of these powerful warlords and their followers. The Servian reforms,
whether by accident or by design, would have had the effect of strengthen-
ing the military organisation of the state and making it less dependent on
powerful individuals. Whether they would have wiped out private military
enterprise is, however, another question; as it happens, we have examples
of private military activity from the fifth and fourth centuries, but the
reform would have created a stronger state army. The reorganisation into
artificial units based on property classes had the effect of cutting across
other loyalties – for instance, to a powerful patron or family – and would
have further strengthened state control over the fighting force.

The reforms would also have introduced a new and highly effective
form of warfare based on the use of heavy infantry fighting in close
formation. This technique of hoplite warfare (see pages 114–15) developed
in Greece during the seventh century, alongside social and political reorganisations similar to the Servian reforms at Rome. From the end of
the seventh century scenes of men armed with hoplite-type armour and
weapons, fighting in organised ranks, are found in Etruscan art (see fig.
14), and bronze armour and weapons of the types depicted are found in
Etruscan graves, suggesting that this form of combat had been adopted by
the Etruscans. There is less archaeological evidence from Rome, mainly
because there are fewer wealthy burials of this date, but the argument that
the hoplite style of fighting had spread throughout central Italy by the
sixth century is persuasive.

We are told that Servius' military reforms went hand in hand with political reforms that replaced the *curiae* with *centuriae* and tribes as the main voting units of the Roman assembly. In the Republic, Romans had three assemblies: the old *comitia curiata* still existed, but it was eclipsed by the *comitia centuriata*, in which the citizens met and voted in their centuries, and the *comitia tributa*, in which they met and voted in their tribes. The dates of these changes are unknown, however, and it is worth repeating that the link with Servius and his military reforms is unclear. The sixth-century date of these reorganisations is consistent with changes taking place elsewhere, such as the development of hoplite warfare and the consequent political influence of the hoplite class, but it is unclear whether it was a single programme of reform or a series of longer term changes rationalised by later historians and attributed to a charismatic figure. Ancient accounts of systematic reform do not fit well with the fragmented and turbulent social and political realities of archaic Italy, and some of the details may be anachronistic. The version given by ancient historians is likely to be, at best, a conflation and rationalisation of longer-term changes.

Conflict and conquest in Latium

Roman tradition links the kings, and especially the last three, with wars against the neighbouring Latins and Sabines and expansion of Roman territory. Tarquinius Priscus is said to have campaigned successfully against Sabines and Latins, capturing the settlement of Collatia and extending Roman control into Latin territory. He is also credited with raids on the territory of Veii, Rome's most powerful neighbour to the north. This conflict between Rome and Veii continued during the reign of Servius Tullius, alongside other military successes against the Latins, but it is Tarquinius Superbus who enjoyed a high reputation as a military leader. He is credited with the capture of Gabii, although it put up a considerable fight and Livy attributes its capture to a trick rather than defeat in battle. Perhaps more significantly for the long-term expansion of Roman power, he is said to have begun the war against the Volscians, which continued throughout the fifth century and paved the way for Rome's conquest of southern Latium. His capture of Pometia was particularly significant as the spoils provided funds for his ambitious rebuilding of Rome.

This narrative of expansion poses problems, and many of the conquests listed in our sources may be apocryphal, but it is generally accepted that Roman territorial expansion had already begun well before the end of the sixth century. Veii, for instance, occupied a large territory on the north bank of the Tiber, and the establishment of Rome as a regional power was a threat to its position. A long but intermittent war between Veii and Rome broke out in the 480s, and it is possible that this was preceded by a period of tension and cross-border raiding dating back to the sixth century. There is good reason to suppose that by the time Tarquinius Superbus was over-thrown Rome had established a foothold on the other side of the Tiber, and controlled territory stretching as far as the sea and the Alban Hills.

According to Livy and Dionysios (Livy 1.50–75; Dion. Hal. 4. 45–60), Rome negotiated treaties with some defeated enemies, although Pometia was sacked and plundered. The leading men of Gabii who had opposed Rome were executed or exiled, leaving it under the control of Tarquinius Superbius' supporters, and groups of Roman colonists were sent to Ostia, Cora, Signia, Circeii, Pometia and Fidenae. Corroborating evidence is slight, and much of this description seems to be based on later Roman practices for dealing with defeated enemies. However, the earliest Roman treaty, the Foedus Cassianum, a text of which was extant in the first century BC, is traditionally dated to 493 BC, so it is not impossible that Rome was already building alliances in Latium during the late sixth century.

Archaeological evidence for colonisation is more problematic At Ostia there are traces of an early road system that may date to the sixth century, but the earliest structures are later, probably early fourth-century. Cora, Signia, Circeii and Pometia were all hilltop sites ringed with stone defensive walls, and a temple in the case of Pometia (if it is correctly identi-fied with Satricum/Borgo Le Ferriere), but there is no persuasive evidence for whether these were linked with Roman settlement.[8] Termeer's study of the sites in this area named in the sources as early colonies reveals a typical pattern of development. This is characterised by a sixth- to fifth-century phase of territorial reorganisation, in which clusters of small sites developed, and by changes to religious architecture, usually involving the building or redecorating of a temple which may have acted as a focus and meeting place for new settlers. Although sources describe Roman campaigns and subse-quent colonies as organised, state-led events, the reality may have been messier. As Bradley and Rawlings have pointed out, warfare in archaic Italy was just as likely to have been raiding conducted by condottieri with armed bands of followers, acting on their own initiative, and many early 'colonial' settlements may have been the result of such condottieri seizing land and parcelling it out among their followers. There is little doubt that Roman power was expanding, but it may have done so as the result of action by individual war bands, rather than through organised state campaigns.

Although our sources present relations between Rome and its neighbours as a narrative of conquest, peaceful contacts – either on a personal level or between states – were just as important. In societies such as those of early Italy, dominated by powerful clans, connections between leading men and their families were a powerful diplomatic tool. This pattern was already established in the orientalising period, and throughout the sixth century leading men cultivated a network of connections with their counterparts elsewhere by forming family alliances and friendships. Livy, for instance, tells us that Tarquinius Superbus sought to extend his influence in other Latin cities by cultivating good relations with their ruling aristocracies, notably by marrying one of his daughters to Octavius Mamilius of Tusculum, and this pattern of behaviour is corroborated by material evidence. Inscriptions found at Rome include a sixth-century ivory tablet in the shape of a lion, which was probably part of a *tessera hospitalis* – a record of a formal agreement of friendship and reciprocal hospitality between two people. The name inscribed on the tablet is Etruscan, suggesting that this may have been a declaration of friendship between an Etruscan and a Roman. Agreements of this type went far beyond the modern concept of friendship as a purely private and informal relationship based on personal liking. Being declared a *hospes* ('guest-friend') of someone involved formal responsibilities of mutual hospitality and support for each other in both public and private matters. When such relationships of intermarriage and hospitality existed between nobles from different states, they were a way of building up networks of influence and support in other cities.

Rome's growing status in the region and in the western Mediterranean as a whole is corroborated by a treaty between Rome and Carthage. Carthage had a keen interest in central Italy, as demonstrated by the Pyrgi tablets, dating to *c*. 500. These thin gold tablets found in the sanctuary of Uni at Pyrgi, the port of Caere, record, in Etruscan and Punic, an agreement between Thefarie Velianas, the ruler of Caere, and the Carthaginians concerning the sanctuary. The fact that the ruler of Caere was willing to establish this shared sacred space, and that the Carthaginians felt the need to do so, indicates the importance and long-term nature of Carthage's connections with Etruria. Rome's relationship with Carthage

Plate 2. Italian bronze fibula, of sanguisuga ('leech') type, with geometric decoration. Eighth–seventh century BC.

Plate 1. Biconical Villanovan funerary urn with incised geometric decoration. Eighth century BC.

Plate 3. Contents of a Latial IIA cremation burial from the Palatine, 900–830 BC.

Plate 4. Pottery vessel with inscription, from Osteria dell'Osa, c. 775 BC.

Plate 5. Greek cup with geometric decoration and inscription, known as 'Nestor's Cup'.

*Plate 6. Rome: from the Capitoline, showing the Palatine hill on
the right and the low-lying areas of the Forum below them.*

Plate 7. Foundations and post-holes of Iron Age huts on the Palatine hill, ninth–eighth century.

Plate 8. Cerveteri: tumulus grave, Banditaccia cemetery.

*Plate 9. Cerveteri: interior of tumulus grave, showing funerary couch
with chair, incised in low relief, at foot. Banditaccia cemetery.*

Plate 10. Etruscan bucchero oinochoe (wine jug), with incised decoration, early sixth century BC.

Plate 11. Etrusco-Corinthian amphora, with orientalising decoration. Sixth century BC.

Plate 12. Phoenican silver bowl (lebes) with incised decoration and serpent heads, from the Barberini Tomb, Praeneste. Seventh century BC.

Plate 13. Orientalising oil/perfume flasks (aryballoi). Greek, seventh century BC.

Plate 14. Paestum: sanctuary of Hera. Temple II (c. 460–50 BC) is in the foreground with the earlier Temple I (c. 550 BC) in the background.

was even more momentous, leading eventually to three bitter wars and opening the way to Roman domination of the western Mediterranean. The first connections were a series of treaties between Rome and Carthage, the first of which is dated by Polybios to 508/7, the first year of Republican government at Rome. The treaty sets out the conditions on which Romans were permitted to trade with Carthaginian settlements in Sicily, and also establishes that Romans were not permitted to sail into areas along the coast of Carthage. More interestingly, it states that:

> The Carthaginians shall do no wrong to the peoples of Ardea, Antium, Laurentium, Circeii, Terracina or any other city of the Latins who are subject to Rome. With regard to those Latins who are not subjects, they shall keep their hands off their cities, and if they take any city, they will hand it over to Rome undamaged.
>
> Pol., 3.22.11–12

The matter is confused by conflicting evidence on how many treaties there were between Rome and Carthage, and their dates,[9] but Polybios not only claims to have read the treaty but also comments on its difficult and archaic language, suggesting that he had consulted a genuinely early document. The significant point is that, if an early date can be accepted for this treaty, other major powers in the region, such as Carthage, recognised Rome's domination over much of Latium and acknowledged Roman leadership of the Latins by the late sixth century.

The economy and society of archaic Rome

Latin cities grew quickly at this date, and Rome became by some way the largest city in the region, although its size and population are difficult to establish. The so-called 'city of the four regions' (i.e., the four tribes attributed to the Servian reforms) measured *c.* 285 ha, or *c.* 700 acres, if reconstructed on the basis of Varro's description (*LL* 5.45–54). The question is complicated by the ongoing debate (the evidence for which is discussed further below, p. 145) about whether Rome was fully fortified at this date and, if so, how large an area was enclosed by the so-called 'Servian Walls' of the sixth century. Estimates by Cifani suggest that these fortifications were *c.* 11 km (*c.* 7 miles) in circumference, and enclosed an area of *c.* 427 ha (1,055 acres). Other scholars, notably Cornell, reject this as too large for the regal period. Cornell and Ampolo have argued for a population of *c.* 30,000–35,000 by the sixth century, partly on the basis of comparison with Etruscan cities for which the evidence is more secure. Even if these figures are an overestimate, there is little doubt that sixth-century Rome was significantly larger, in population and area, than other nearby settlements such as Lavinium, Satricum and Gabii, and was comparable to Etruscan cities such as Caere and Tarquinii, although smaller than the Greek cities of southern Italy (see Tables 3 and 4, page 101).

Like most city-states in ancient Italy, Rome depended on the produce of its surrounding territory, and the importance of land is demonstrated by the Servian reforms, which linked social status and military obligations to a valuation of property holdings. However, it was not exclusively dependent on farming, but had an extensive range of economic contacts with other areas of Italy, and with the wider Mediterranean. Imported Greek pottery, mainly from Athens, demonstrates trading links and cultural connections with the Greek world.

Socially, Rome was a highly stratified society, like most contemporary societies in Italy, and powerful clans played a central role. Activities that we naturally assume to be prerogatives of the state, such as war or diplomacy, were frequently carried out by private individuals, using their own resources and social contacts with their peers in other cities. Individual aristocrats could call on armed bands of retainers – in effect, private armies consisting of clients and dependants. In some circumstances these clearly fought as parts of larger forces, as part of the army of a city-state. In others they may have acted at the behest of an individual rather than the state. When this happened, we find evidence of individual aristocrats pursuing private conflicts, or sometimes combining in ad hoc alliances with other similar individuals, sometimes not from the same city, to achieve their objectives – whatever these happened to be at any given time. The scenes on the François Tomb depict a situation of this type, in which warriors from a number of states – including Mastarna/Servius Tullius and the Vibenna brothers – together with their followers, fight each other. Another example is provided by the so-called Lapis Satricanus, an early inscription from the Latin town of Satricum. The stone on which it was written was reused as building stone for the rebuilding of the temple of Mater Matuta at Satricum, which dates it to *c.* 500 at the latest. It is a dedication to Mars, the god of war, by the companions (*sodales*) of Poplios Valesios – an archaic spelling of the Roman name Publius Valerius – and is probably a dedication by a private army of this type led by Valesios. Other examples of actions by private armies include a war against Veii in 479 by the Fabii, the arrival in Rome of the Sabine aristocrat Appius Claudius in 504, accompanied by 5,000 armed men, and the famous defection of Gnaeus Marcius Corio-lanus to the Volscians, along with a large band of armed clients, in the fifth century (Livy 2.15–17, 2.35–41, 2.45–7). This was not an unusual or small-scale phenomenon but an important aspect of archaic society. The fact that the dedicators of the Satricum inscription identify themselves as the com-panions of a particular person is significant, as it implies that their loyalty was to the leader of the group rather than to a particular state. Groups of this type, and their leaders, seem to have found it relatively easy to move across political and ethnic boundaries, and to attach themselves to a par-ticular state as and when it suited their personal interests.

Archaic Italy was a region of considerable personal mobility, both social and geographical, especially for people of high rank such as Demaratos, Tarquinius and the more historical Appius Claudius and Poplios Valesios. Networks of personal contacts between high-ranking individuals could enable such people to move effortlessly between different cities and regions. Friendship inscriptions (*tesserae hospitales*) provide evidence of formal connections of friendship and hospitality between families from different cities, and the use of Etruscan language on tesserae found at Rome, for instance, implies strong bonds between Roman and Etruscan families. It seems to have been relatively common for the aristocratic families of neighbouring cities to intermarry, reinforcing the impression of a highly mobile society.

The structure of the clan, and how such an organisation might have operated, are not entirely clear. Christopher Smith has argued that the Roman *gens* was a more loosely knit structure than previously suggested, and that bonds between individual nuclear family groups within the clan would inevitably loosen over time, meaning that the coherence of such a group would be difficult to maintain for more than a small number of generations. It is certainly difficult to see how some of the aspects of the *gens* as traditionally conceived could have worked in practice – possibly because they were describing an idealised and anachronistic version of it. Total dominance by a single head of the clan over all subordinate branches would have been difficult to sustain, and we should be wary of seeing political behaviour as something entirely determined by family relationships. The complicated family tree of the Tarquins indicates how complex family structures could be, and the downfall of the Tarquin dynasty, described in the final section of this chapter, illustrates the instability of dynastic politics. The way that *gentes* were organised and operated clearly changed over time. *Gentes* remained central to the ways in which archaic Roman (and other Italian societies) operated, but by the mid-fifth century important aspects such as communal ownership of land had disappeared.[10] Nevertheless, the clan was an essential element of society in archaic Rome and Italy, and many aspects of military, diplomatic and political business were conducted as interpersonal or inter-family transactions.

Women of noble families appear to have been influential in archaic Rome. One of the striking features of traditions about the Tarquins is the prominent role of royal women. Tanaquil is depicted as exercising considerable influence over her husband, and played a vital role in securing Servius Tullius' accession to the throne. Tullia, despite being an archetypal 'wicked woman', was an active participant in securing the throne for Tarquinius Superbus. Lucretia, the wife of Tarquinius Collatinus, was a virtuous and loyal wife. These are clearly literary stereotypes, contrasting the virtuous Lucretia with the wicked Tullia, and Livy seems to give prominence to women when he wants to imply a breakdown of order – female influence being inherently a bad and unnatural thing. However, Roman women – unlike ancient Greek women, who were expected to live in seclusion – played an active part in the life of aristocratic families. The Roman matron was expected to lead a virtuous life, largely confined to the domestic sphere, but in the world of archaic Rome, where many activities of state were closely bound up with the actions and family connections of powerful individuals, women could exercise considerable influence, albeit indirectly and via their menfolk.

Archaeological evidence corroborates the notion that aristocratic women, at least, enjoyed high social status. Some of the most lavish burials from Rome and from the surrounding Latin communities are those of women. In a society where women were commemorated by a formal, marked, burial much less frequently than men, the prominence of the graves of some of these aristocratic women is striking. The archaeological evidence for prominent women is less striking at Rome than in Etruria, but this is principally because we have less funerary evidence at Rome from the relevant period of history. The high status of aristocratic women in archaic Rome is clearly not a figment of Livy's imagination, and it is not at all implausible that they exercised influence – however indirect – via their male relatives.

The 'Mighty Rome of the Tarquins'

The changes in the institutions of Rome in the sixth century, and the wider cultural and economic changes taking place, were accompanied by changes in the physical development of the city. An exhibition of archaeological finds from the archaic period held in Rome in 1990 was given the title *Il Grande Roma dei Tarquini* ('The Mighty Rome of the Tarquins'), and this reflects the rapid expansion of the city, its acquisition of monumental buildings and the wealth of its culture.

A visitor to Rome at the beginning of the seventh century would have found a community consisting of huts of wood and thatch, interspersed with areas of burials and sacred areas, and the beginnings of civic buildings in the Forum. Visitors to Rome in the late sixth century, however, would have encountered a very different city (fig. 22). They would have entered a city that may have been enclosed by a defensive wall, although this is still a matter of some debate (discussed later in this section). Walking along the Sacra Via, the processional way through the centre of the city, they would have passed along streets below the Palatine hill lined with large houses decorated with painted terracotta mouldings. Passing into the newly drained Forum, they would have found more monumental buildings and, on the Capitol, a massive new stone temple. Beyond this, the Forum Boarium boasted a new temple in the Etruscan style. Rome was well on its way to becoming a monumental city.

Some of the key religious sites within the city were already in use during the seventh century, but the sixth century was a period of major development for areas of Rome associated with important aspects of public life. Earlier collections of votive offerings have been found at the sites of many later temples and sanctuaries, but the sixth century was a period of rebuilding and elaboration. Monumental temples were constructed at some of the important religious sites, the most important of which was a large stone, wood and terracotta temple dedicated to Jupiter Optimus Maximus, constructed on the Capitol in the late sixth century. The stone foundations of this measure a massive 61 × 55 m (*c.* 200 × 180 feet), and it

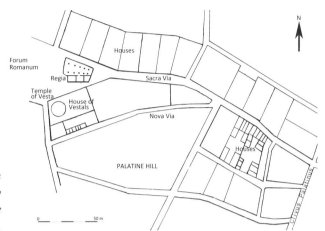

Fig. 22 Rome: plan of sixth-century building around the Palatine and Forum.

was the largest temple construction of its date in the ancient world, comparable with any of the temples of the archaic Greek world. The sanctuary of S. Omobono, in the Forum Boarium, was also monumentalised by the addition of a new temple, probably dedicated to Fortuna or Mater Matuta. Little of the structure of this survives, and the chronology of the development of the S. Omobono temples is extraordinarily complex, but the later sixth-century building was decorated in the Etrusco-Italic manner, with painted terracotta statues and friezes, which have survived in fragmentary form. A group of statues depicting Athena and Heracles decorated the roof of the temple. Deposits of votive offerings from elsewhere in Rome demonstrate that other cults were flourishing, but three temples are of particular importance. The cult of Jupiter Optimus Maximus (sometimes also referred to as Jupiter Capitolinus) was an iconic symbol of Roman identity and the centre of many important rites connected with the life of the state, while that of Diana (see below, p. 189) was politically significant. The S. Omobono sanctuary, on the other hand, was particularly important for contacts between Rome and the outside world. The large number of fragments of Greek and Etruscan pottery found there suggest that the area was frequented by both foreign visitors and some of the city's non-Roman residents.

Other public areas of Rome underwent major developments at this time, and can be linked to what the sources tell us about the last three kings. Construction of a drain, the *cloaca maxima*, to drain the Forum area, and the creation of a more formal layout of the Forum, setting aside areas for porticoes and shops, are variously attributed to both Tarquinius

Priscus and Tarquinius Superbus. Servius Tullius is said to have enlarged the ritual boundary of the city – the *pomerium* – to enclose several of the hills of Rome, and to have built a defensive wall around the city. However, the evidence for this is contentious. A study of the fourth-century walls of Rome (confusingly known as the 'Servian Wall', although it is of much later date) by Gabriele Cifani has revealed sixth-century fortifications beneath some sections of it. Cifani believes that there is enough evidence to reconstruct the line of a perimeter fortification, 11 km (*c.* 7 miles) in length and enclosing an area of *c.* 427 ha (1,055 acres), consisting of a mixture of stone walls, earth-works and ditches. The extent and completeness of these fortifications are, however, open to question. Seth Bernard's review of the evidence concludes that the walls were not a single fortification enclosing the whole of Rome but a series of fortifications enclosing individual hills, and that Rome was not a fully walled city until the fourth century. Cornell has also expressed scepticism that the urban centre of Rome was as large as 427 ha in the sixth century, and hypothesises that the figure of 285 ha (704 acres), derived from Varro, is more plausible. Both the size of the urban area of Rome and the extent of its fortifications at this date are still very much open to question.

Archaeologically, there is substantial evidence for the development of the Forum. Several sections of sixth-century paving have been found and a large number of fragments of terracotta decorations from this area suggests that buildings around the Forum were becoming more elaborate and highly decorated. A stone with a sixth-century inscription – from beneath the so-called *Lapis Niger* – was found close to the site of the Regia and Comitium, and seems to record a religious law or set of rituals connected with a sanctuary (possibly to be identified with the Volcanal) and led by the king, supported by a herald (pl. 19). The Comitium was the later heart of the Roman state, and was the area where the senate house stood and where the Roman people met to elect magistrates and to pass laws, and it is probably no accident that this area was monumentalised and redeveloped at the time when the political organisation of Rome was becoming more complex. Even leaving aside the problems of the city wall, these public works represented a considerable outlay of money and manpower, demonstrating Rome's wealth and civic ambition, and also a degree of centralised political authority which could plan and carry out such an undertaking.

Expenditure on fine buildings was not restricted to public buildings such as temples. Excavation on the Palatine has revealed large stone buildings, private houses as well as public buildings. The houses had a narrow entrance, and rooms opening off a central atrium or courtyard, although the fragmentary state of survival means that many details of the internal layout are uncertain. Carandini's reconstruction, which suggests that they are prototypes of the Roman atrium house, is controversial. Nevertheless, they were large and complex structures, and must have been residences of aristocratic families. Their location on the Sacra Via, the street that led to the Capitol and was a processional route for religious ceremonies and for military triumphs, was one of the most prestigious areas of Rome. One of a group of buildings uncovered during excavations on the Palatine and the Velia has been identified by the excavator, Andrea Carandini, as the house of Tarquinius Priscus himself. However, this is extremely problematic. The building is probably a private house of the sixth century, but its location does not match the sources' description of the whereabouts of Tarquinius' palace.

There were also developments outside the city boundary. The sanctuary of Diana on the Aventine hill, which was just outside the *pomerium*, is said to have been founded by Servius Tullius, and an inscription recording this was apparently still in existence during the reign of the emperor Augustus. An interesting feature is that the sanctuary is explicitly said to have been founded not just for use by Romans but as a common religious centre for all the Latin peoples. Its location outside the *pomerium*, and therefore technically outside the city, would have facilitated access by non-Romans. What form it took is not clear; during the sixth century it may have been an open-air precinct with an altar, with a temple added later, but it was an important shrine and one that became politically significant during the fifth century.

The port of Rome, the Portus Tiberinus, which was just below the Aventine, was first developed around the same time. The construction of the *cloaca maxima* drained the area, enabling construction of the three temples of Fortuna, Mater Matuta and Portunus close to the port.[11] A temple of Fortuna or Mater Matuta is said to have been established by Servius Tullius (Dion. Hal. 4.27.7; Livy 5.1.9.6), and the sixth-century finds under the church of S. Omobono confirm the existence of temple construction at that period. Little remains of the structure, which appears to be only a single temple at this date, but the associated architectural terracottas suggest that it was an impressive building.[12]

Further afield, remains of a large sixth-century villa have been discovered outside the later Porta Flaminia, on the north side of Rome and well outside the sixth-century boundaries. This was a structure of impressive dimensions, covering 20 m² (215 square feet), with a layout similar to that of the Palatine houses. The purpose of the Villa Auditorio is not known, but there is a strong possibility that – like the building at Murlo in Etruria – it acted as an aristocratic house, a cult site and a centre of economic production. The aristocracy of archaic Italy did not just invest their money in a display of wealth in towns but also created opulent villa-style residences away from major settlements.

The changing architectural styles of the sixth century reflect Rome's expanding cultural horizons. New buildings, both public and private, were closely based on Etruscan models, in both form and decoration. The temples of the Capitoline and S. Omobono were of Etruscan type, with a deep porch, and a main chamber divided into three parts. They – and many other public and private buildings – were decorated with painted terracotta mouldings in the Etruscan manner, some of which may have been made by Etruscan craftsmen. Famously, Tarquinius is said to have commissioned an Etruscan sculptor, Vulca of Veii, to make the cult statue of his new temple of Jupiter on the Capitol.[13] Pliny's description of this gives a vivid impression of the grandeur of the new temples:

> Having summoned Vulca of Veii, Tarquinius Priscus ordered him to place a statue of Jupiter in the Capitolium; it should be made of terracotta and painted with vermilion; at the gable ends of his temple were four-wheeled chariots of terracotta, about which we are often told.
>
> (Pliny, *NH* 35.157)

The scale of the rebuilding taking place in the Forum and at some of the major religious sanctuaries demonstrates the increasing wealth, ambition and political clout of archaic Rome. Projects of this size require significant investment of both money and manpower, as well as a high level of administrative and political organisation. The spoils from successful campaigns against the Latins and the Sabines, attributed to Tarquinius Priscus and his successors, may have paid for much of the new building. However, the debate between Wiseman and Carandini over the so-called 'House of Tarquin' illustrates the impossibility of linking the monumentalisation of Rome with specific individuals, particularly when these may not even be historical. Livy's description of Tarquinius Superbus as an enthusiastic rebuilder of Rome is consistent with the archaeological evidence for a period of redevelopment in the sixth century, but this cannot 'prove' the existence of Tarquinius as a historical figure.

Etruscan or Roman?

The substantial evidence for Etruscan culture at Rome, the presence of kings of Etruscan origin and the expansion of Etruscan power beyond Etruria itself have given rise to a lively debate about the relationship between Rome and the Etruscans. Was Rome actually conquered by one or more of the Etruscan states during the sixth century? Or was the 'Etruscanising' phase a result of cultural influence rather than political domination? The argument runs broadly as follows: the Etruscan expansion into Campania could not have taken place without domination of Latium and Rome as well; the Etruscan origins of some of the kings demonstrates that Rome was governed by puppet rulers installed by whichever Etruscan city had conquered it; and the Etruscan elements in Roman culture were the result of this process.

The problem with this, however, is that it requires a major reinterpretation of ancient sources, none of which mentions an Etruscan conquest. During the twentieth century various historians argued vigorously that they represent a cover-up, rebranding the Tarquins as immigrants to Rome to disguise the unpalatable fact that the flourishing Rome of the sixth century was under Etruscan domination. None of this, however, amounts to proof that Rome fell under the control of any of the Etruscan cities.

In order to make sense of the situation we need to unpick the various political and cultural aspects of the problem. Our sources agree that there were influential Etruscan families in Rome – notably the Tarquins – but they lived in Rome for several generations and ruled Rome in their own right, asserting Roman power at the expense of their Etruscan neighbours. The presence of Etruscans can be explained by the high degree of personal mobility in this period, which meant that it was perfectly possible for individuals, sometimes accompanied by substantial groups of followers, to migrate from one city to another and even to hold high office there. The presence of Etruscans at Rome is a demonstration of mobility, not of conquest by a foreign power.

That said, the connections between Rome and Etruria were undoubtedly close during this period. Roman culture, particularly the culture of the elite, was heavily influenced by that of the Etruscans, but this pervasiveness was not the result of conquest. Etruscan culture was the dominant aristocratic culture of central Italy during this period, and its influence can be seen on the indigenous cultures of regions as far afield as the Po valley, Liguria and Campania. The term 'Etrusco-Italic' is used by some scholars to describe the art and material culture of this period, reflecting the extent to which Etruscan and other Italian elements had merged into a hybrid culture shared by elites from many areas of northern and central Italy. It would have been more surprising if Etruscan culture had been absent from Rome and Latium. Technical innovations, artistic styles and new types of artefact were spread by contact between the aristocracies of central Italy and by the movement of craftsmen between different cities. Many of the most eye-catching objects, such as the orientalising silver or bronze vessels and Greek and Etruscan pottery found in wealthy burials throughout central Italy, were circulated between elite families – exchanged as part of marriage dowries or as gifts, spreading a taste for new artistic styles and luxury goods along with them. Adoption of Etruscan styles of architecture and of architectural decoration may also have been a form of 'keeping up with the neighbours', by emulating the styles current in the powerful and well-established Etruscan cities such as Caere and Tarquinii. Buildings in this style demonstrated that the person commissioning them had international tastes and also the wealth and influence to import leading craftsmen from Etruria. What they do not do is prove that Rome was an Etruscan dependency at this stage in its history.

By the late sixth century, Rome had developed into an expanding city with monumental architecture. The extensive programme of building demonstrates both the economic prosperity of the community and the ambition to establish itself as an important regional power. The impressive private houses indicate the dynamism and social ambition of the ruling elite, and there is evidence of close networks of contacts between Roman aristocrats and those of neighbouring cities. At the same time, the city was undergoing the first stages of organisational changes which transformed the relationship between citizen and state. The expansion of both territory and population is a striking testament to the economic prosperity of the city, and the presence of both imported luxury goods and foreign craftsmen indicates that it was part of an international network of trade that stretched across central Italy and the Mediterranean. All of this underpinned a period of growing regional prominence that saw Rome become established as the most powerful of the Latin cities, and a possible rival to Etruscan Veii. All of this, however, was a prelude to a period of turbulence and change at the end of the sixth century, which saw the ejection of the kings and the establishment of the Roman Republic.

The Fall of the Tarquins

According to Roman traditions, the end of the Tarquin dynasty came at the end of the sixth century (traditionally 510/09, or 508/7 according to Polybius), when the last Tarquin king, Tarquinius Superbus, was deposed and replaced by two elected consuls. The portrayal of Tarquinius Superbus is uniformly hostile, and the later Roman distaste for kings and kingship stemmed from his behaviour and reputation.[14] Our sources describe him as a usurper who conspired with his wife to murder his father-in-law, Servius Tullius, and seize power. He is depicted as an effective ruler, responsible for extending Roman influence throughout significant areas of Latium and for much of the new building and monumentalisation of Rome itself, but also as cruel and high-handed, autocratic, reliant on an armed bodyguard to protect him and intimidate enemies, and lacking respect for laws and traditions. His character and actions are closely modelled on those of ancient Greek tyrants, and, as has frequently been noted, many of the traditions about his reign are very similar to those of other tyrants such as the sixth-century Athenian ruler Peisistratos.

Superbus' ultimate downfall and deposition are said to have been triggered by the actions of Sextus Tarquinius, one of Superbus' sons, who raped Lucretia, the wife of his cousin, Tarquinius Collatinus. Lucretia subsequently committed suicide, and this outrage prompted Collatinus and a group of his relatives and friends, including Lucius Junius Brutus, Publius Valerius Poplicola and Spurius Lucretius, to stir up the Roman people against Superbus, denouncing him as a tyrant, and depose him. The king, who was conducting a military campaign against Ardea at the time, arrived back at Rome only to find the city gates closed to him and the rebellious group of aristocrats in charge. Envoys from Brutus, Collatinus and their collaborators persuaded the army to back the rebels, and Superbus and his sons were forced into exile. The king was replaced by two magistrates, elected for a period of one year.

This was followed by a volatile period of warfare with Tarquinii and Veii, and various attempts at the restoration of Tarquinius. The situation worsened in 508. Lars Porsenna, ruler of Clusium, declared war in support of Tarquinius and marched on Rome. He got as far as the Janiculum, on the far side of the Tiber, and laid siege to the city. This episode supplied many famous tales of Roman heroism in defence of the Republic, including an epic defence of the Sublician Bridge over the Tiber by Horatius Cocles, who held out until the Romans managed to demolish it. Other notable exploits included the defiance of Gaius Mucius Scaevola, who allowed Porsenna to burn off his right hand rather than reveal information to the enemy, and the escape of a group of captured Roman women. Cloelia, the leader of the escape, encouraged the women to swim across the Tiber to safety and became an iconic example of female virtue and heroism. A statue of a woman on horseback, located at the top of the Sacra Via, was widely believed to commemorate her – a rare honour, as there were very few other equestrian statues of women. Despite having Rome at a disadvantage, Porsenna abandoned the siege and marched further into Latium. He was decisively defeated at the battle of Aricia in 505 or 504, by a combined army of Latins and Cumaeans. After the failure of this attack on Rome, Tarquinius and his son-in-law, Octavius Mamilius of Tusculum, persuaded the Latin cities to make war against Rome in a last-ditch attempt to regain his throne, but they were defeated at the battle of Lake Regillus (variously dated 499 or 496), a battle at which Rome reputedly received divine assistance from Castor and Pollux. Tarquin finally gave up and spent the rest of his life in exile at Cumae, while Spurius Cassius, the consul for 493, negotiated a peace treaty with the Latins.

There are many inconsistencies and puzzles in this narrative. The first magistrates are variously named as Brutus and Collatinus (Livy), Brutus and Horatius (Polybios) and Brutus and Valerius Poplicola (Cicero and Pliny). The powers of the new elected rulers, and even their title, are unclear, and will be discussed further in Chapter 9. The wars with the Etruscans and Latins – in particular, Porsenna's abandonment of the siege of Rome at a point where he clearly had the upper hand – do not make sense, particularly if his main aim was to restore Tarquinius to power, and the details were disputed even in Antiquity. Livy and Dionysios of Halicarnassus insist that Rome did not fall to Porsenna, but Pliny and Tacitus mention an alternative tradition that he captured Rome and imposed humiliating peace terms.[15] The political relationships within

Rome pose interesting questions, most notably: what were the real reasons for Tarquin's expulsion? Two of the leaders of the coup are identified by our sources as members or associates of the Tarquin family (Brutus was the king's nephew and Tarquinius Collatinus was a cousin: see the family tree in fig. 20), which raises the question of why were some Tarquins more unacceptable than others. Why did Brutus and (briefly) Collatinus manage to hold office within the new Republic at a time when the family was apparently so deeply unpopular, and how did Brutus manage to escape the decree exiling all Tarquins?

Roman historians presented the fall of the Tarquins and the establishment of the Republic as an act of liberation, replacing a tyrannical monarch with elective government, but this seems an unlikely scenario. The most prominent leaders of the coup against Superbus were his relatives, and, despite the rhetoric of liberation, the expulsion of the Tarquins looks more like an outbreak of strife within the ruling family itself.

One approach is to reject ancient accounts of the period as later inventions, imposed in order to give greater narrative power and coherence to the political changes taking place. Another is to view the transition to Republican government as a process rather than a single event, in which the powers of the kings were gradually eroded and shared between the aristocracy on a wider basis, a process onto which later historians imposed a shorter time-frame and a dramatic personal narrative (see further below, pp. 172–5). On the other hand, the idea of a dramatic coup and even the possibility of an internal family dispute are not to be dismissed out of hand. As Tim Cornell has pointed out, in a society such as that of Rome, where social and political influence was essentially dynastic, conflicts and feuds of the sort described in the sources between (and even within) powerful families were not uncommon, and personal insults and vendettas could have far-reaching consequences.

The disappearance of the Tarquins as the result of dynastic politics is consistent with our understanding of Roman – and broader Italian – society. In a world where extended families were central to the social and political fabric, coups as the result of power struggles within a ruling family are not unknown. This does not rule out the possibility that Roman government was in a state of evolution. The powers and role of the king may have changed during the sixth century, and the early Republic was perhaps a period of experimentation in which we can see aspects of both continuity and innovation. However, the evolutionary approach does not explain why the idea of kingship became associated with tyranny in the Roman mind, and so revolting that the title of king (*rex*) was permanently tainted. This deep-rooted aversion to kingship suggests that the transition from monarchy to Republic was triggered by a crisis associated with the last king. There is no way of securely disentangling the facts of Porsenna's campaign against Rome, but an attack by the Etruscans on Latium and Campania fits the general pattern of turbulence and changing balance of power outlined in the previous chapter and is consistent with what we know about the breakdown of Etruscan power in Campania. The balance of evidence points to a traumatic upheaval in the late sixth century which left lasting bitterness at Rome and brought about conflict in the wider region.

8

The 'Fifth-Century Crisis' and the Changing Face of Italy

The troubles at Rome in the late sixth and fifth centuries were not unique. There are signs of disruption throughout Italy, along with ethnic and cultural change (map 5). The Etruscans were in retreat in Campania, although less so in the north. Many of the ethnic groups known to later history appear for the first time, or display a new level of self-conscious ethnic identity, and there are signs of both economic stress and social tension. The fifth century has often been described as a period of crisis, and this chapter will examine the changes taking place in Italy, their impact on Italian society and whether they really did constitute a crisis.

Widespread conflict was a feature of the late sixth and fifth centuries. Rome was engaged in a struggle against powerful Etruscan enemies to the north and the peoples of Latium to the south. Etruria was in a turbulent state as cities fought for dominance, and the sixth-century powerhouses of Caere, Veii and Tarquinii were eclipsed by the northern centres of Perusia, Volsinii, Arretium and Clusium. Clusium, under the leadership of Lars Porsenna, was in particularly expansionist mood: a Clusine army raided Latium and Campania in 508–505, and may even have captured Rome.

Warfare was also endemic in southern Italy. There were several bitter wars between Greek communities, and between the Greeks and some of their Italian neighbours. Siris was destroyed by an alliance of Rhegium, Metapontum and Sybaris, probably *c.* 550–530, and Sybaris itself fell to Croton in 510. In Apulia, Tarentum was engaged in intermittent warfare with the Iapygians throughout the early fifth century. The Iapygian community of Karbina (probably mod. Carovigno) was savagely sacked during the 470s, although the Greeks suffered a major reverse in 473, when a joint force of Rhegines and Tarentines was crushingly defeated by the Iapygians. Nevertheless, the Tarentines managed to extend their grasp on southern and central Apulia, commemorating their victories by two large monuments set up in the sanctuary at Delphi.[1]

In Campania, Cumae, ruled by the tyrant Aristodemos, was at the height of its influence. Aristodemos rose to power after leading a successful campaign against the Etruscans in 524 and set about building an anti-Etruscan alliance of Greeks and Latins to push back against their dominance in central Campania.[2] The Cumaeans and Latins won a battle near Aricia in 505 or 504, curbing Etruscan power in Campania, and in 474 a combined fleet of Cumaean and Syracusan ships defeated an Etruscan fleet, curtailing Etruscan naval power. These two set-backs cut off the Etruscans of inland Campania from the coast and began to erode their control of the region, effectively ending Etruscan domination. The archaeological record shows a decline in Etruscan goods and objects in burials, and in Etruscan inscriptions.[3] This had a profound impact. The decline of Etruscan power was an important factor in the transformation of Campania into an area dominated by Oscan-speaking peoples from the Apennines, a dramatic cultural and ethnic change. For the Etruscans it marked the end of their long period of cultural and political influence south of the Tiber, and an intensification of their engagement with northeast Italy and the Po valley. This was established in the sixth century, with the foundation of an Etruscan settlement at Marzabotto and the growth of Adria and Spina, which had mixed Greek and Etruscan populations. During the fifth century these developed rapidly as new centres of trade and manufacture, and as entrepôts for Greeks and others trading with the Po valley and northern Italy. This change in the trade routes between Greece and Italy was a factor in the greater cultural and economic isolation of Latium and southern Etruria in the fifth century.

Many areas of Italy were under threat from further afield. Magna

Graecia suffered from encroachments from other parts of the Greek world, as Syracuse expanded its influence throughout the fifth century, culminating in the capture of Locri, Rhegium, Caulonia and Croton by Dionysios I in the 390s, and Athenian interest in the west grew stronger. The new colony of Thurii, founded on the site of Sybaris in 444/3, was nominally a pan-Hellenic venture but had a strong Athenian presence. The foundation of Heraklea in 433 by Tarentum was an assertion of Tarentine power in response both to this and to Italic aggression. An Athenian admiral, Diotimos, visited Naples with a squadron of Athenian ships, probably around 450, and is said to have settled new colonists there.[4] In 415, Athens almost dragged the Greeks of Italy into its disastrous military expedition against Syracuse. The Athenians landed in Italy on their way to Sicily and appealed to ancestral ethnic connections to try to drum up support. Tarentum, which claimed to be a Spartan colony, refused to allow the fleet to land, but other cities were less intransigent and Rhegium provided some assistance.

Social unrest and political strife

Throughout Italy inter-state conflict was accompanied by civil unrest within communities. Aristodemos, the tyrant of Cumae, was deposed some time around 490, despite his success in fending off the Etruscans and building up Cumaean influence. In Magna Graecia a new cultural and philosophical movement based on the philosophical teachings of Pythagoras had sprung up.[5] Pythagorean clubs, dedicated to an austere and restrained lifestyle, were founded, but, although these seem to have formed as a reaction to conspicuous consumption and aristocratic excesses, their members were themselves part of the elite. Two strands of aristo-cratic culture – conspicuous wealth versus Pythagorean austerity – came to symbolise factionalism and social tensions within the elite. By c. 500 these Pythagorean groups had become politically dominant in some cities, notably Croton, Sybaris and Metapontum, but were also deeply disliked. According to Polybios (Pol. 2.39), there were outbreaks of popular unrest during which Pythagoreans were exiled and the meeting houses in which they gathered were burned down. After a period of civil strife many cities in Magna Graecia adopted some form of elective government based on annual magistracies, although the extent to which the mass of the people could exercise power varied greatly. At Tarentum most male citizens were permitted to vote and to stand for office, while other cities, notably Locri, restricted this to members of the higher social and economic classes.

In Etruria we have less information about political unrest, but there are signs of social change. The growing number of modest-sized family tombs, such as those found in the Crocefisso del Tufo cemetery at Volsinii or the cemeteries around Caere (see pl. 17), imply the growth of a new elite of families with more modest personal habits than the aristocracies of the seventh and sixth centuries. The nature and effects of these changes are difficult to determine, but the common thread is that cities and states in several regions suffered from power struggles between various elements within the elite.

'Crisis? What crisis?'

These political and social tensions were exacerbated by economic change. There are reports of frequent food shortages, droughts, crop failures and epidemics. Changes to patterns of trade and the draining effects of wide-spread conflict placed further strain on some areas of Italy. Economic hardship was enhanced by other factors such as growing debt or inequalities of land distribution.

Throughout Italy there were changes in settlement patterns and burial practices which may point to economic stress. The relationship between settlements and their surrounding territories changed. Land became less intensively cultivated and less productive, and the number of farms and small rural settlements fell. Imports from overseas declined after *c.* 450, particularly imports of luxury goods, and urban development was scaled back. At Rome very little public building took place between *c.* 480 and 400, and the development of the city slowed down sharply. Even the mighty cities of Etruria suffered an economic downturn, particularly in the south of the region. The destruction of Sybaris, a major trading partner, and the decline of Etruscan influence in Campania disrupted trade between southern Etruria and the Greek world. Imported Greek pottery became rarer, especially items connected with an aristocratic lifestyle, such as high-quality drinking sets and tableware, and the output and quality of Etruria's own pottery and painting workshops declined.

The north of the region, around Populonia, Rusellae and the cities of the Po valley, continued to prosper. Here Greek goods continued to be imported in large quantities, and bronze vessels and other luxury goods are found in both domestic and funerary contexts. Many of these were made in Vulci, suggesting that northern Italy was now a major market for luxury goods. Populonia even started to mint its own coins. Silver and even gold coins stamped with a lion's head or the head of a gorgon and dating to *c.* 450–425 have been found in various parts of Etruria and as far afield as Tarragona in Spain, demonstrating a considerable commercial reach. This new economic order is consistent with a broader shift in the balance of power in the region, with the emergence of the northern cities as the economic and political powerhouses of Etruria, and a decline in the strength and influence of Caere, Tarquinii and Vulci.

The development of fifth-century Campania is particularly complex. During the early fifth century Capua, Cales, Nola and Nuceria prospered. The output of the pottery and bronze workshops of Capua and other cities was notably high. Fine pottery was produced in quantity, much of it in the Etruscan bucchero style, and a cauldron-shaped bronze vessel known as a *lebes* was particularly in vogue. The quantities of decorated architectural terracottas found at many sites suggests that sculptors in terracotta were enjoying a boom, and that buildings grand enough to warrant this type of decoration were being constructed. Capua and Cumae both undertook wide-ranging programmes of public works in the late sixth and early fifth centuries, with improved water supplies and fortifications, a reorganisation of urban space, and new temples in both cities. Culturally, Etruscan influence remained dominant in the early fifth century. Even the more isolated and less developed inland areas on the border of Samnium, historically associated with the Oscan Caudini, had a period of expansion, marked by manufacture of Etruscan-style bronzes and pottery, and an increase in the quantity of Greek imports into the area. In the mid-fifth century, however, craft production declined sharply, burials contained fewer and less valuable grave goods, and the number and quality of votive offerings at sanctuaries diminished. Building activity slowed down, and the number of farms and settlements in rural areas decreased. Etruscan language and cultural influences disappeared, and new elite burial practices became prevalent.

There is persuasive evidence for an economic downturn in much of Italy during the fifth century, but whether this constituted an Italy-wide crisis is much less clear. Some of the changes observable in the archaeological record may reflect new social and cultural behaviour rather than economic hardship. In many regions notable burials declined in number, and both the quantity and quality of grave goods diminished, but these can be interpreted as the effects of cultural change, with fewer people accorded a commemorated burial and less conspicuous consumption focused on burials and grave goods. In the sixth century aristocrats were already moving away from the lavish funerary displays of the orientalising period and towards a culture of greater restraint. Perhaps the most striking examples of this are the Pythagorean communities of the late sixth century, which championed a more austere lifestyle, and the fifth-century Roman law code of the Twelve Tables, which specifically limited the lavishness of funerals and burials. There was a new social climate of austerity, in which conspicuous displays of wealth and status were frowned upon. Changes in burial practice may be the result of these cultural changes rather than economic decline, and may even indicate the development of a more advanced economy. In the orientalising period, luxury objects were valued more for their social display than for their intrinsic value, but by the end of the sixth century the economic value of high-status objects outweighed their symbolic value as grave goods.

There is good reason to believe that the fifth century was a time of recession, but economic stresses may have been more localised than the model of an Italy-wide 'fifth-century crisis' suggests, and regional variations are perceptible. In Etruria, for instance, changes in patterns of trade and contact with the rest of the Mediterranean had cultural and economic implications for the cities of southern Etruria, which showed signs of stress, but the north of the region continued to flourish. There seems little doubt that the fifth century was a period of change and disruption to some communities but was by no means a period of universal economic 'crisis'.

Migration or cultural transformation?

The fifth century was a period of ethnic and cultural change throughout Italy. In the north the Celtic populations from beyond the Alps had an increasing impact on local cultures and settlements. The dynamic and warlike Samnites, who played a pivotal role in Italian history and posed a serious challenge to Rome for control of Italy, can be identified for the first time. Ancient sources describe mass migrations, often with violent

THE RISE OF ROME

consequences, from the central Apennines into Campania and southern Italy, and from the Alpine areas into northern Italy, but the archaeological evidence is more complex and nuanced. New ethnic groups – the Samnites, Campani, Lucani and Bruttii – emerged in central and southern Italy, as well as the Volsci, Hernici and Aequi in areas closer to Rome. Rome's wars against these groups dominated the fifth century, as wars against the Samnites dominated the fourth. A greater level of ethnic self-definition is apparent, and the ethnic composition of Italy becomes clearer, but the underlying processes are less dramatic than our sources suggest.

The Hernici of the Trerus valley occupied the area around Anagnia, *c.* 60 km (37 miles) south-east of Rome. Archaeological evidence is limited to the remains of fortifications, mostly on hilltop sites, although the dating of these is highly insecure and it is not clear whether these mark small towns or simply hill forts used for defensive purposes. Surviving examples, such as those at Alatri, consist of walls of massive polygonal stone blocks, which suggest that the towns or hill forts were heavily fortified. Ancient writers describe the Hernici as being organised in a league led by Anagnia, the main settlement of the region. The Aequi are even less well known, but remains of hilltop fortifications in the mountains above eastern Latium suggest that, like the Hernici, they built heavily defended hill forts. The origin of both of these groups is obscure: ancient tradition says that they were migrants from Apennine Italy, but archaeology shows no clear evidence of mass migration or invasion.

Livy's version of the Volscian expansion is that they migrated down the Liris valley from the Apennines, taking control of Cora, Pometia, Antium and Velitrae during the 490s, and eventually dominating the coastal strip between Antium and Terracina, the Pomptine plain, and upland areas around the Liris and Sacco valleys. Archaeological evidence, in contrast, suggests considerable continuity of population in this region, although a third-century inscription from Velitrae, the sole evidence for the Volscian language, is written in a language related to Umbrian. As with the Hernici and Aequi, Volscian identity probably developed from a pre-existing local population combined with some migrants from the Apennines. Further afield, the cultural and linguistic make-up of Campania, Lucania and Bruttium was transformed, and the peoples of these regions developed into distinctive ethnic sub-groups – Campani, Lucani and Bruttii – recognisably similar in language and culture but with their own ethnic identity. In order to understand this transformation, and to understand the Roman conquest of Italy, we must examine both the Samnites and the broader cultural changes taking place in southern Italy.

The Samnites

The key development in the central Apennines between *c.* 500 and 350 was the emergence of the Samnites as a clearly identifiable ethnic group. Burials show that the aristocracies of Apennine Italy still presented themselves as warrior elites. Many male graves contained weapons, as they did in the preceding period, but the deposition of armour became increasingly common in the fifth century. Aristocratic tombs contained helmets and cuirasses as well as wide belts made of bronze plates stitched onto a leather backing, all serving as a display of wealth and as a statement of warrior status. Towards the end of the fifth century these rich burials declined in number and became less ostentatious in what they contained.

During the same period the fairly homogenous culture of the sixth century diversified into distinctive regional sub-cultures. There are localised changes in burial customs, with changes in the types and structures of tombs, and regional variations in types of armour found in graves. The typical Samnite breastplate, consisting of three bronze discs joined to a back-plate of the same design by shoulder straps, is fairly ubiquitous in the Abruzzi and northern Molise. In southern Molise, in contrast, burials contain a breastplate formed from a single panel of metal, similar to Greek breastplates. Also, cremation – a Greek custom – was adopted as the main funerary ritual. This diversification in the archaeological record is linked to far-reaching changes in the ethnicity and culture of the central Apennines. Before the fifth century it is impossible to identify ethnic groups in this area, but from this point Samnite identity becomes more archaeologically recognisable. Strictly speaking, we do not know what these people called themselves. Romans referred to them as *Samnitae* and Greeks as *Saunitai*, but a small number of Oscan inscriptions include the word *safinim* or variants of it, and this may be the Samnites' own word for themselves. They spoke a language that is referred to by modern scholars as Oscan, or Sabellian, and is linguistically related to Latin, although it looks very different to modern eyes.[6] By the fifth century they had adopted writing and produced inscriptions in a local alphabet adapted from that of the Etruscans.[7] Several hundred of these survive, mainly votive dedications,

lots of Greek influence

laws and decrees of various officials. Most date from the fourth to the second century, and although they are limited and formulaic in form and content, they are an important resource for understanding Samnite society and how it worked.

Roman sources subdivide the Samnites into several groups: the Pentri, who were the largest grouping, Hirpini, Frentani, Carraceni and Caudini (map 4). This is broadly consistent with what the Oscan inscriptions tell us – that between *c.* 450 and *c.* 350 the Samnites subdivided into a number of well-defined states. Unlike most of the population of Tyrrhenian Italy, the Samnites did not adopt an urban way of life, and Samnite states were not city-states. Some of the larger settlements were developing urban char-acteristics by the late fourth century, but, by and large, urbanisation of the region largely took place after – and partly as a result of – Roman conquest. Until then, most of the population still lived in villages, but we can trace the development of a wider state infrastructure through the construction of numerous hill forts and religious sanctuaries.

Nearly a hundred hill forts are currently known, varying in type and function. Many are small, with defensive walls only 200–300 m (656–984 feet) in circumference and serving as defensive refuges for the surrounding people in times of trouble. Others are larger, with walls of up to 3 km (1.5 miles) in circumference. Two of the largest – Monte Vairano and Monte Pallano – enclose an area that is clearly well beyond that required for a defensive enclosure and contains evidence of houses and other buildings, suggesting that they had a permanent population as well as acting as a defensive refuge. This network of hill forts grew massively in number, size and complexity during the fourth and third centuries, but some may have been established in the fifth century, although dating is imprecise.

This network of defended strongpoints was complemented by new cult centres. Many religious sanctuaries were located in open countryside, close to a hill fort and to routes of communication, and at this date were little more than open-air enclosures with few buildings. The main gods honoured were Hercules, Jupiter and Mars, as well as Ceres (Oscanised as Kerres) and various local gods, especially Mefitis. The significance of these sanctuaries, even in their rudimentary fifth-century state, goes far beyond the purely religious. They served as a focus for the sort of state activity that would – in a city – have been conducted in the forum, and provided a venue for elections of magistrates, political meetings and law hearings, as well as religious rituals. Surveys of the landscape around some sanctuaries, notably San Giovanni in Galdo, demonstrate that rural settlements tended to cluster in the areas around sanctuaries, reflecting their role as foci of local activities, and suggesting that they primarily served the local community. Their importance is underlined by their later development. During the period from the fourth to the second century stone temples, porticoes and even theatres were added to sanctuaries. Dedicatory inscriptions show that, although some of these were paid for by wealthy private individuals, many were paid for by magistrates, underlining the political as well as the religious significance of these sites. The fact that monumental structures were built in an apparently planned and coherent manner suggests the emergence of a strong state organisation from the fifth century onwards.

Most of these features were at an early stage of development in the fifth century and did not reach their full development until somewhat later, but we can perhaps see the emergence of both a stronger Samnite ethnic identity and the emergence of Samnite states. The establishment of political/religious centres, and the mere fact that the Samnites could field large and well-organised armies on a regular basis, implies that by the fourth century, they had effective forms of political and administrative organisation. Samnite inscriptions mention an organisation called a *touto*, a word that seems to denote 'the people' or 'the state' (roughly equivalent to Latin *populus* or Greek *demos*).[8] It appears to refer to a state, analogous to city-states elsewhere in Italy, rather than a tribal society and demonstrates the development of state organisation and rule by magistrates in Oscan and Umbrian-speaking areas of Italy. The *touto* was governed by an elected magistrate known as the *meddiss tuvtiks* (chief magistrate of the *touto*, latinised by ancient sources as the *meddix tuticus*).

Some scholars, notably E. T. Salmon, have hypothesised a hierarchical structure in which each *touto* was subdivided into smaller units called *pagi* or *vici*, which consisted of a village or group of villages governed by minor magistrates, also with the title Mediss. The problem with this scenario is that it is difficult to substantiate, particularly for the period before the Roman conquest. The evidence for *pagi* and *vici* comes primarily from inscriptions post-dating the Roman conquest, in which these terms seem to refer to regions or subdivisions of cities, not to rural areas, and it is difficult to demonstrate a connection to the pre-Roman *touto*. As Tesse Stek has convincingly argued, organisation based on *pagi* or *vici* was a later development, which took place after the Roman conquest and was related to urbanisation, not to the pre-Roman political structures of the region.

Nevertheless, many factors support the view that the Samnites developed a coherent state organisation during the fifth and fourth centuries even though the *pagus*/vicus model seems to post-date the Roman conquest.

The Romans tended to view the Samnites through the prism of an ethnic stereotype which presented them as rugged mountain men, whose non-urban lifestyle was a sign both of lack of sophistication and of a warlike and austere nature. Livy refers to:

> The Samnites, who at that time lived in villages in the mountains, ravaged the places on the plain and along the coast, whose cultivators they despised as softer and, as often happens, similar to their place of origin, just as they themselves were rough mountain men.
>
> (Livy 9.13.7)

However, it would be a mistake to accept this view of a backward rural society. Samnite states were well suited to the geography of the region, in a way in which urban life was not. Many of the high valleys of the Apennines could support village-sized populations comfortably, but not larger, city-sized populations. The Samnites developed effective legal, administrative and political organisation, but separating this from large concentrations of population was an effective strategy for this particular region.

Marauding hordes or peaceful settlers?

The influence of the Samnites was not confined to the Apennines. According to ancient tradition, they migrated en masse into surrounding areas during the fifth century, rose up against the local populations and took over. Our sources describe a ritual, shared by many Italic peoples but particularly associated with Oscan areas, known to Roman historians as the *ver sacrum*, or Sacred Spring. It entailed dedicating all the offspring – human and animal – born in a particular year to a god (usually Mars), and when this group born in a sacred year reached adulthood, they were obliged to leave home and migrate elsewhere. This sounds suspiciously like a later rationalisation, but whatever the truth of the Sacred Spring, we do not need to resort to divinely inspired mass migration to explain the demographic changes of the fifth century. There was a long history of contact, migration and mingling of cultures between peoples of neighbouring areas, and the chances are that long-term but small-scale population movements had taken place throughout the sixth and fifth centuries in areas such as southern Latium and Campania. There are obvious reasons why people from mountainous areas with limited arable land, such as the Celts in northern Italy and the Samnites in the south, would have been attracted to areas with better resources. This was also an era of personal mobility, and it was not uncommon for people to move around from one region to another, either as individuals or as groups. The Sabine Appius Claudius, for instance, migrated to Rome with a large band of followers and settled there at the end of the sixth century. There could be many different reasons to migrate, ranging from military or economic opportunism to social and political tensions that made it expedient to move.

The effects of the migrations from the central Apennine were felt most acutely by the people of Campania. People from the Apennines had settled peacefully in the Capua area over a period of many years, but in 423 these incomers staged an uprising and seized control of Capua, the principal city of the region. From there they spread out across Campania, taking control of the main cities and exiling or murdering their inhabitants. Cumae was overrun in 421, after which much of its Greek population decamped to Naples, and a similar fate befell Poseidonia (thereafter known as Paestum) in 410 (Livy 4.36; Diod. 12.76).

Ancient accounts leave us in no doubt that the Samnite takeover of Campania was a violent and deeply traumatic event. The problem, however, lies in the lack of archaeological support for this. Coinage, inscriptions, art and architecture all point to important cultural changes in Campania in the fifth century. The difficulty is that these occurred gradually and there is no trace of the destruction and sudden change that would accompany a violent uprising and takeover of the region.

One possible explanation is that the conflict was social rather than ethnic – not Oscans versus Etruscans and Greeks but tension between an unpopular ruling class and an excluded and resentful population. The elites of sixth-century Campania were an ethnic mixture of local and Etruscan families that had adopted Etruscans styles of architecture, visual arts and crafts, Etruscan religious cults and forms of urbanism and Etruscan lifestyles. The rural population, in contrast, was a mixture of local Campanians and Oscan-speaking peoples from the Apennines. The roots of the transformation of Campania may lie in tensions between an excluded and increasingly Oscanised people and an over-dominant Etruscanised elite.

It is clear, however, that these developments transformed the culture of the region. At Capua, Oscan language and culture became predominant, and Etruscan inscriptions, goods and burial customs were replaced by Oscan ones. By the middle of the fifth century a distinctive form of Campanian tomb began to appear. These stone-lined chamber tombs were decorated inside with frescoes depicting the afterlife or the journey of the dead to the underworld. Many show their owners as armed warriors wearing distinctive Samnite style of armour and dress, and contained rich collections of grave goods (pl. 27). Campanian cities were reorganised on lines familiar from other Oscan communities – rule by elected magistrates known as the *meddices*. Personal names in inscriptions are mostly Oscan, suggesting that the people who were wealthy and important enough to commission an inscription – in other words, the socially and politically dominant group – were ethnically Samnite or had adopted their language and customs.

Similar developments took place at most of the inland Campanian cities and at Cumae. Naples, however, took a different path. The Neapolitans voluntarily absorbed the new population, and Strabo (*Geog.* 5.4.7) records that from the end of the fifth century the lists of *demarchoi*, the chief magistrates of Naples, included both Greek and Oscan names, demonstrating that the Oscan migrants were given full citizen rights and that the social and political elite had become mixed. Funerary inscriptions from chamber tombs corroborate Strabo's statement that the elite included people of Oscan descent, but Greek culture remained dominant in many areas of civic life. Temples and public buildings continued to be built in the Greek style, and Greek remained the predominant language.

Perhaps the strongest evidence for the complexity of the aftermath of the Oscan invasions comes from Paestum (Greek Poseidonia, renamed after the Oscan takeover), one of the best-preserved ancient cities in Italy. A fragmentary account by the third-century historian Aristoxenos, quoted by the later essayist Athenaeus, gives a vivid picture of the oppression and cultural dispossession supposedly suffered by the Greeks, although the archaeological evidence is more mixed:

These people [of Poseidonia], who were Greek in origin, became barbarised, becoming Etruscans or Romans, and changed their language and their other customs; and today they meet to celebrate only a single

Greek festival, at which they recall their former names and ancient customs, lamenting over these; and then, having shed many tears, they leave.

(Athenaeus, *Deipnosophistai* 14.632a)

As at Cumae and Capua, the city's magistrates adopted the Oscan title *meddix*, and Oscan inscriptions show that Oscan language and cults were prominent. However, Greek was still spoken, many people with Greek names appear in inscriptions, Greek cults were still worshipped at the two great sanctuaries of Hera and Athena, and production of high-quality Greek red-figure pottery continued. There is little sign of violent destruction, as would be expected if the city had been taken by force, and there are contemporary Greek and Oscan burials. Ancient accounts painting a picture of mass migration with violent consequences grossly oversimplify a more nuanced and complex situation. Nevertheless, there is no doubt about the impact of these cultural changes and stronger ethnic identities. The Volsci and the Campani presented Rome with a considerable challenge, and the emergence of the Samnites as a major power in southern Italy was even more significant. Their wars with Rome were pivotal moments in the Roman conquest of Italy, and they pushed Rome to the limit.

Similar cultural changes can be seen in northern Italy. The Celts (or the Gauls, as Roman sources called them) began to migrate across the Alps from what is now France, Germany and Switzerland. Their origins and culture have been a matter of controversy in recent years, as scholars – notably Simon James – have tried to strip away layers of mythologising and misconceptions imposed by nineteenth-century scholars, intent on co-opting the Celts into their own nationalistic histories of western Europe. They are generally agreed to correspond to regions where the Iron Age Hallstatt and La Tène cultures predominated from the seventh to the first century – i.e., France, Britain, Switzerland, western Germany and Austria.[9] Many other suggestions – in particular, the notion that they were Aryan invaders from further east – are now widely rejected. On the yardstick of civilisation versus barbarism applied by Greeks and Romans, the Celts were barbarian. They lived in villages rather than cities, and although brave, hardy, and endowed with a strong warrior ethos, they were rough and lacking in many aspects of civilised life. The account by Cato the Elder (*FRHist* 5 F33) adds that they were highly industrious and

[handwritten margin note: downplaying threats]

prized eloquence as well as military prowess. Despite this damning with faint praise, it is clear that the Celts were neither ineffective nor unsophisticated, and they were formidable warriors who posed a serious threat to the Romans on several occasions.

As with the Samnites, ancient writers believed that the Celts overran northern Italy, suppressing the indigenous population and driving out the Etruscans who had settled in the Po valley. Livy (5.33; see also Pol. 2.17 and Dion. Hal. 13.10–11) pins the blame on a disgruntled Etruscan called Arruns, from Clusium. The story goes that Arruns' wife had been seduced by an aristocrat called Lucumo, who was too powerful to be challenged or punished by law. Arruns hit on the idea of shipping a cart full of fruit and wine across the Alps. Celts were notorious in Roman eyes for their love of strong wine (drunk unwatered, which further demonstrated their barbarian character), so he easily persuaded them that territories that produced such products would be well worth having, and personally guided the first invaders across the Alps and into Italy. The reality was rather less colourful. Livy himself admits that the truth was both more complex and more prosaic and acknowledges that there had been Celts in Italy for a good 200 years before they attacked Clusium, settled in areas ranging from the Ticino to the Romagna.

Archaeological evidence points to a pattern of gradual long-term Celtic settlement, starting in the sixth century, and reaching a critical mass that changed the culture of parts of northern Italy, by the fourth century. The indigenous culture of Lombardy and Piedmont, termed the Golasecca culture, was lively and flourishing. Large settlements at Como, Castelletto Ticino and Sesto Calende had regular street plans and substantial houses and tumulus burials with copious grave goods. They had flourishing economies, close contacts with other areas of Italy and wide-ranging commercial and cultural contacts. Celts and locals lived side by side – for example, at the important settlement of Monte Bibele – and the language of the region is believed by linguists to be related to Celtic. The Celts did not suddenly appear from nowhere; the population of north-west Italy was already mixed. During the fifth century more artefacts belonging to the La Tène culture are found in north-west Italy, accompanied by changes in burial customs, from cremation to inhumation, and in grave goods, which suggest migration into the region. Around the same time established settlements collapsed and much of the population moved to smaller sites, often on defensible hilltops. Trade routes were disrupted;

Etruscan imports declined drastically, although imports from some parts of France, continued. Wine amphorae from the Greek colony of Massalia (now Marseille) demonstrate that there was still a trade in some goods for elite consumption. However, it is undeniable that the material culture of the region became poorer.

However, none of this adds up to a convincing case for a mass Celtic migration. The fortified hilltop villages that replaced the proto-urban towns were already occupied, not newly founded responses to a military threat, and the distribution of Celtic goods and their owners from the fifth century onwards is very localised. In some areas Celtic goods, settlement patterns and burial customs became predominant, but in others, particularly in western Lombardy and south of the river Po, the indigenous culture continued to predominate. As the archaeologist Ralph Häussler has argued, there are many reasons that could account for the changes to Golaseccan society. Given the difficulties faced by some regions of Italy during the period *c.* 450–400, north-west Italy may have been faced with similar social unrest, the disruptive effect of wars and changes in international trade. The more visible Celtic presence in some areas was the result of a long-term process rather than invasion and conquest.

The Celts had a fearsome reputation because of their wars against the Etruscans and Rome, but they were not necessarily a destructive presence. Periodically, Celtic armies pushed south and enjoyed some successes, such as their annihilation of the Roman army at the battle of the Allia and subsequent sack of Rome in 390, an event that left long-term scars on the Roman psyche and made Rome permanently nervous of the Celtic threat, but the practical effects were short-lived. Celtic settlements, concentrated around Milan, Como and the lakes, flourished, and networks of trade with other areas of Italy, north-west Europe and the Mediterranean revived. Judging from the contents of their graves and debris found in settlements, the elite of the area had access to a plentiful supply of wine, mostly imported via Massalia, which they drank from fine imported pottery. Dinner services of the same pottery suggest that feasting was still an important social ritual, and food remains suggest that their diet was varied and plentiful. Far from being barbarised by the arrival of the Celts, north-west Italy was a vigorous and dynamic region.

To sum up, the fifth century was a period of change and even recession in many areas of Italy, but it was not an era of crisis. Some states and social groups did quite well out of it, while others struggled. The power of the

sixth-century aristocracies was challenged by new elite groups, trigger-
ing political strife, social unrest and major changes in elite culture. The
ethnic map of Italy changed as stronger collective identities developed,
but these were not the result of invasions and violence. Instead, new ethnic
identities began to emerge out of a fusion of indigenous populations with
well-established groups of incomers. Some of these newly visible ethnic
groups were major players in the history of Rome: wars against the Celts
and the struggle with the Samnites for dominance in central and southern
Italy were important episodes in the history of Rome in the fourth century
and paved the way for Roman control of Italy.

9

A DIFFICULT TRANSITION: THE EARLY ROMAN REPUBLIC

Like the rest of Italy, Rome underwent a period of economic hardship and social and political strife during the fifth century. The early part of the century was dominated by the aftermath of the ejection of the Tarquins, while the so-called Struggle of the Orders, a social, political and economic conflict between the patrician elite and the rest of Roman society, lasted throughout the fifth century and well into the fourth.

Ancient sources for this period remain problematic. We have narratives by Livy and Dionysios of Halicarnassus, and comments by other historians of the late Republic and empire, but many aspects of their accounts are suspect and cannot be relied on. Roman traditions concerning the fifth century may contain a kernel of factual information, but much of the material still contains a large amount of anachronism, later rationalisation and mythologising. One key problem, which is central to understanding the development of government in the early Republic, is the reliability and authenticity of the *fasti*, the lists of magistrates and of military triumphs awarded. These are preserved in a number of sources, including inscribed lists commissioned by the emperor Augustus. These different versions of the list name the magistrates from the foundation of the Republic, but it is disputed whether the names of the earliest magistrates are genuine or whether they are based on invented or miscopied material. The arguments for and against these positions are discussed in A Note on Sources, but in this chapter I broadly follow Christopher Smith's view that the *fasti* – however imperfect and subject to later reorganisation – cannot be dismissed as later invention.[1]

In Roman tradition the break between monarchy and Republic was regarded as a fundamental change, in line with ancient political theory, which conceptualised political development as a natural progression from monarchy, via tyranny, to aristocratic government. Despite the sources' stirring rhetoric and presentation of Brutus as a liberator, however, there was considerable continuity between the monarchy and the early Republic. The power (*imperium*) of the king remained, but instead of being held by a single man for life it was held by elected magistrates who served for a limited term of one year.

Livy's account of the transition (Livy 2. 1–2) is based on the assumption that Rome was governed, from the earliest years of the Republic, by two consuls, elected by the assembly and supported by the senate – the system of government that was characteristic of the middle and later Republic. However, there is significant doubt over how many annual magistrates there were in the fifth century, what they were called, how they related to each other and what their powers were. The Livian tradition of replacement of the king by two consuls is probably oversimplified. It is more likely that the early Republican government was a work in progress and that the fifth century was a period of experimentation.

It seems fairly clear that one or more elected annual magistrates replaced the king as chief executives of the Roman state, holding *imperium* (right of command), commanding armies, presiding over meetings of the senate and assemblies, and exercising civil and criminal jurisdiction. *Imperium* was essential to the senior magistracies, since it was the basis of both civil and military power and right of command. Many of the royal symbols, which denoted the sacred nature of these powers, were transferred to these magistrates. They had the right to wear a purple-bordered *toga praetexta*, sit on an ivory ceremonial chair (a 'curule' chair) and be escorted by twelve attendants (lictors) bearing axes and rods (fasces), which indicated their right to inflict corporal and capital punishment.[2] There was already some degree of separation between religious and political functions. A priest known as the *rex sacrorum* took over some of the rituals and sacrifices previously performed by the king, while others were performed by the consuls or the *pontifex maximus* (chief priest), but magistrates also had religious duties. Magistrates were elected, or at least ratified, by the *comitia centuriata*, the assembly of citizens meeting in their military units, and there may have been a right of appeal (*provocatio*) against arbitrary action by a magistrate against a citizen. The early introduction of this right has been a matter of debate, but a balance between *imperium* and *provocatio* against arbitrary action was fundamental to the Roman political system, so an early date for this is not impossible.[3]

The number of annual magistrates, their titles and how they related to each other are very problematic questions, and the nature of the chief magistracy may have changed in the course of the fifth century. There seems to have been a time when Rome was ruled by a single pre-eminent magistrate, supported by one or more junior ones. Dio (quoted in Zon. 7. 12), who may have used an early source, says that Brutus, the first magistrate, ruled alone, although a colleague was quickly co-opted in case he was tempted to declare himself king. The Roman writer Festus (249) says that the most senior magistrates in the early Republic were called praetors, not consuls, and Livy (7.3) describes an archaic annual ritual in which a magistrate referred to as the *praetor maximus* drove a nail into the wall of the Capitoline temple to mark the year. This custom, known from other parts of Italy,[4] was usually the task of the most senior magistrate, suggesting that the *praetor maximus* was the most senior magistrate at Rome in the early Republic. Another magistrate who held supreme power, if only temporarily, was the dictator. The dictatorship was an office of great antiquity in Latium, and the regular chief magistracy at Lanuvium and Aricia, so it is at least possible that Rome may once have been governed by an annual dictator; but if so, this quickly changed. For most of the Republic, the dictator was an extraordinary magistrate, appointed to lead Rome in times of national emergency and holding office for only six months, although his powers were very wide-ranging.[5]

At other times, however, there were multiple magistrates (usually known as consuls or military tribunes with consular power) operating on a collegiate basis. Livy records no fewer than five consuls in the year 509, as deaths or resignations caused one or other of the consuls to be replaced on three separate occasions during the course of the year, but there were only two at any one time. In subsequent years when consuls were elected, there were always two of them, but in the years in which the supreme office was held by military tribunes with consular power ('consular tribunes' for short), they were elected in groups of between three and six per year. This confusing mix of consuls, praetors, dictators and consular tribunes suggests that forms of government in Rome in the fifth century were still very fluid. The *fasti* list two magistrates per year except in years when there were colleges of consular tribunes, but it is possible that this structure was imposed on the record by historians and antiquarians in order to bring early records into line with later practice. Even if we accept the existing record, it is a list of names that tells us little about the titles of, and the relationships between, the magistrates. The most we can say is that Rome in the fifth century was ruled by elected annual magistrates, probably in varying numbers and possibly with varying titles. Rule by two annually elected consuls of equal status was not established as the norm until the Licinio-Sextian reforms of 367.

Despite these uncertainties, the changes taking place in the early Republic established some important principles. One was the fixed time limit on terms of office, which placed restrictions on personal power. Once again, the interests of the leading Roman *gentes* were at the forefront of developments, as they sought to ensure a wider distribution of power between heads of leading families, rather than domination by a single monarch or dynasty. Another key change was the establishment, during the course of the fifth century, of a collegiate element. The practice of electing more than one person at a time to a magistracy prevented any individual from gaining sole control of the state. These two principles, of collegiality and of fixed-term tenure, became fundamental to the government of the Republic and were applied to most of the anciliary magistracies that were created later to assist the consuls. In the early fifth century these assistants consisted of two quaestors, rising to four in 421,[6] but additional magistracies – the aedile and a new form of praetor – were added during the course of the fifth and fourth centuries. It was possible to stand for election more than once, although restrictions were gradually introduced, and at no stage (with the possible exception of the first few years of the Republic) was it permissible to hold a magistracy for more than one year at a time. The net result of these changes was that power was shared out more widely within the elite, rather than being concentrated in the hands of one man for life. Access to power was, however, a bitterly divisive issue throughout the fifth and fourth centuries. During the course of the fifth century many legal, social and political rights – including the right to stand for election to the consulship – became restricted to a small elite, and one of the dominant narratives of the later fifth and early fourth centuries was the struggle by other groups within Rome to gain access to power and privilege.

If the magistracies of the early Republic are obscure, other aspects of government are even more so. The senate wielded great power in the middle and later Republic, but little is known about its membership in the fifth century. The formal collective mode of address used of senators, 'patres conscripti' (enrolled or conscripted fathers), suggests that it was an advisory council composed of the heads of the elite families, but membership may have been more selective. Festus (290L) believed that in the regal period and early Republic members were chosen by the king, and later, the consuls. 'Patres conscripti' may have been a contraction of 'patres *et* conscripti' – 'fathers and enrolled men' – implying that some members were there because they were heads of families, but others were appointed for different reasons. As Cornell points out, if the senate originated as an advisory council for the king, it is not unreasonable to expect a mixture of heads of families and other members who were invited because they had relevant knowledge or experience. The later senate was more formally constituted, and was composed of men who met various criteria of birth and wealth, and who had been successfully elected to magistracies. In the fifth century, however, the structures of government were more fluid and such strict formal criteria are unlikely.

The function of the fifth-century senate is equally obscure. It probably originated as the advisory council of the king, and retained this advisory and non-executive role after the fall of the monarchy. Although it came to play a central role in the Republic and exercised influence over all aspects of government, it never had much formal power. Its resolutions (*senatus consulta*) were merely expressions of opinion or advice, and it had no direct executive power or even the power to meet unless convened by a magistrate. At the height of its influence the weight that the senate and its opinions carried stemmed from the fact that all men who had been elected to high public office were members (unless deemed to be morally unfit by the censors) and it was therefore composed of the most eminent men in Rome. In the early Republic, in contrast, it was a smaller body with a more restricted membership, and less moral authority. The business of running Rome in the fifth century was less onerous and complex than it later became, so the need – and scope – for a strong and influential senate were less acute. One reason why we know so little about the early senate may be that it was simply not that important.

Patricians and plebeians, patrons and clients

By the fifth century the Roman elite was changing. According to Roman sources, the society of early Rome was divided into two groups – the patricians and the plebeians – but establishing the nature of these groups, and how and when they developed, is highly problematic. Both the Romans themselves and many nineteenth-century scholars saw the patricians as a primordial part of Roman society. Livy and Cicero assumed that Romulus himself had established the Patrician Order (Livy 1.4; Cic., *Rep.* 2.14). He is said to have selected a hundred men from among the heads (*patres*) of the most important families to act as an advisory council, which later developed into the senate. These families became known as patricians, and in this narrative they developed a legal, political and religious stranglehold over the Roman state, validated by Romulus' decision to entrust them with control of the senate and key priesthoods. After the establishment of the Republic, this translated into a domination of the senate and the new magistracies until challenged by an emerging and disgruntled plebeian movement from 494 onwards in a conflict known as the Struggle of the Orders.

This neat explanation for the origins of both the senate and the patricians does not stand up to close scrutiny.[7] A major problem lies in the question of when the distinction between patricians and plebeians became clearly defined. This may not have occurred until the mid-fourth century, leading some scholars (for instance, the historian Richard Mitchell, in his contribution to Raaflaub's book on the Struggle of the Orders) to doubt that access to enhanced legal status and privileges was really at the heart of the struggles of the fifth century. Even the identity of some of the patrician families is uncertain. The patricians may have included a group of nineteen families, comprising the Aemilii, Fabii, Cornelii, Cloelii, Folii, Furii, Julii, Manlii, Sulpicii, Nautii, Postumii, Quinctii, Quinctilii, Sergii, Servilii, Valerii and Veturii, along with some branches of the Claudii and Papirii, but the evidence is sometimes unclear, and the status of some prominent families in the early Republic is unknown. At least fifteen early consuls are of unknown status, and others are from families that were later classed as plebeian. Others, such as the Claudii, were divided: the Claudii Pulchri were patrician, while the Claudii Marcelli were not. This uncertainty about the status of elite families in early Rome suggests that the division between patricians and plebeians was not as clear-cut as it later became and that patricians did not have a complete monopoly on office in the early fifth century. The addition of 'conscripti' to the senate when necessary also demonstrates that public life and political power was not as closed as Livy and others suggest. The reduction in the number of magistrates from non-patrician families after *c.* 480 suggests that the Patrician Order was not a primordial part of the Roman state, dating back to Romulus, but was a social class that gained power during the course of the fifth century.

Identifying the plebeians is equally problematic. They are often defined, negatively, as citizens who did not belong to a patrician family and therefore possessed no political role other than the right to vote. The reality was considerably more complex, and it is clear that the plebeians were not just a homogeneous mass of poor Romans. Like the patricians, they were not a primordial group whose membership was set in stone, and there were many grey areas between the two orders. For instance, clients of patrician families – though well down the social scale – may have had special protection derived from their patrons, and may therefore not have counted as plebeian. The unrest of the fifth century was triggered by many different grievances, suggesting that the plebeians were composed of diverse social and economic interest groups, each with its own agenda. The rural and urban poor were angry about endemic debt and unfair distribution of land, while wealthier non-patricians were less engaged by economic issues but resented their exclusion from power. Increasingly, the plebeians as they appear in our sources were not the Roman masses but a self-selecting group of non-patricians who were ambitious and politically active. In general, they were less wealthy than patricians, at least during the fifth century, but the gradual emergence of a group of plebeians who demanded a share of political power and were wealthy and influential enough to exercise it effectively when they got it demonstrates that it was not a straightforward case of rich versus poor or aristocracy versus the people.

Thanks to the codification of Roman law that took place in the fifth century, we have invaluable insights into the structure of the Roman family (*familia*). The head of a Roman household (*paterfamilias*, defined as a free Roman male with children but no surviving forebears) had absolute control, not only over his family, but also all family property, including slaves. This right of control, or *patria potestas*, extended to the right of life and death over all members of his household, as well as the right to sell his descendants into slavery. He decided whether children born into the household should be raised or exposed and left to die, and could dispose of family property with little restriction. Even adult children had no freedom within the family, and did not own property of their own. Roman men did not attain freedom until the death of their *paterfamilias* unless they were formally emancipated from his authority. The *paterfamilias* was expected to take advice from a family council of senior relatives and friends, but there were very few restrictions on his power.

Women had fewer rights, and a woman required a male guardian to supervise her legal affairs and undertake legal or economic transactions on her behalf. In most cases this was either her father or her husband, depending on her marital status and which form of marriage she had entered into. Three different procedures – the religious ceremony of *confarreatio, usus* (marriage implied by simply living together) or *coemptio* (a symbolic sale of a women to her husband) – all had the effect of transferring a woman out of the *patria potestas* of her father and into the authority (*manus*) of her husband. Other forms of marriage left her under the authority of her father – a potentially more onerous situation, since a woman under the *manus* of her husband became independent on his death, while a woman under the *potestas* of her father was dependent until the death of her last male relative. There were legal loopholes that allowed a woman to leave the *manus* of her husband by spending a certain number of days away from him each year, but in that case she reverted to the *patria potestas* of her father. Given the extensive level of control over her by either father or husband, this may seem a rather academic distinction, but the laws of inheritance treated women differently according to whose *manus* she was under, so it could have implications for her ability to inherit her share of family property.

The relationship between the individual *familia* and the wider *gens* (clan or extended family) is difficult to determine. Although *gentes* remained an important feature of Roman society in the fifth century, for instance, by determining which order one belonged to, their structure and legal and social roles may have changed in this period. By the middle of the fifth century the Twelve Tables seem to indicate that power resided with the head of the *familia*, and that land was assumed to be held by an individual, rather than communally by the *gens*.

Early Rome was a slave-owning society, and most households included slaves. Chattel slaves (i.e., those born or sold into slavery, as opposed to those who became slaves because of unpaid debt) had no legal rights and could be bought and sold, but they could also be freed. One of the peculiarities of Roman society in the eyes of some Greeks (Dion. Hal. 4. 24) was that slaves freed by Roman citizens automatically acquired citizenship themselves. Once freed, they became freedmen or freedwomen (*liberti/ libertae*). They took the names of their former owner, who became their patron. The number of slaves in Rome in the fifth century was much lower than after the Punic wars, and the number of slaves per household varied widely, but the regulations concerning the buying, selling and ownership of slaves in the Twelve Tables demonstrate that slavery was significant in early Rome.

Patronage was central to Roman society. The patron had, as the word implies, a quasi-paternal relationship to his clients and had a moral obligation to protect them and assist them legally and financially. In return, they had an obligation to attend on him and to assist him in any way required. This may simply have entailed calling at his house to greet him (the morning *salutatio*, when clients gathered at their patron's house, was an important part of the daily routine for a high-ranking Roman), but it could also involve undertaking matters of business for him, supporting him in law cases or his political career or even fighting for him as one of his armed retainers. In later times this was a wide-ranging but ill-defined relationship, essentially based on trust and accepted social norms rather than legal requirements, although we know little about how patron–client relationships worked in the fifth century.[8] It is unclear how pervasive the patron–client relationship was at this date, and whether most Romans below the level of the elite were attached to higher-ranking patrons or whether many were excluded from this network of contacts and support. In practice, it seems likely that the system was a fairly fluid one, in which people with good connections could find themselves attached to a number of patrons, and in which many people would be both patron of those less well-off or well connected than themselves and also a client of more important families. Roman society cannot be neatly divided into a class of patrons and a class of clients; rather, the two were interdependent.

Roman religion: power and the priesthoods

The connection between religion and public life in Rome ran deep, and religion played a vital role in public affairs, both in their day-to-day conduct and in the way in which the Roman state developed. An attempt was made to separate religious and political offices in the early Republic by delegating some of the religious duties of the king to the *rex sacrorum*, one of the few priests to be forbidden to hold public office, but despite this, there was a great deal of overlap between religious and secular aspects of public life. Rome did not have a specialist priesthood or priestly class, and priests were, for the most part, men who held office as part of a public career. Many routine ritual tasks were the responsibility of the serving magistrates, not a separate priest, and one of the functions of the senate was to act as a source of religious knowledge and expertise, something noted by Cicero:

> Among the many institutions [...] created and established by our forebears under the inspiration of the gods, nothing is more famous than their decision to commit to the same men both the worship of the gods and the care of state interests; the result was that the most illustrious citizens might assure the upholding of religion by the proper administration of the state and the upholding of the state through the careful interpretation of religion.
>
> (Cicero, *De Domo Sua*, 1)

The senior magistrates carried out sacrifices on behalf of the people, took the auspices and carried out other religious duties, such as dedicating temples. Other religious duties were the responsibility of a college of priests, headed by the *pontifex maximus*,[9] who had ultimate supervisory authority over the state cult, as well as duties such as overseeing the official calendar.

A notable feature of Roman culture, and one that was remarked on by various ancient writers, is its openness to cults from other areas, including some from outside Italy. In the sixth century Rome imported the Sibylline books, a compendium of prophecies, from Cumae. Legend had it that these were handed over to the Romans by a famous prophetess, the Sybil of Cumae, and they were consulted for guidance in times of crisis such as war, plague or famine. The cults of Ceres and Diana maintained strong connections with sanctuaries of Demeter and Artemis, their Greek counterparts, and priestesses of Ceres were still recruited from Greek cities in Italy and Sicily as late as the first century (Dion. Hal. 6. 17. 2; Cic., *Balb.* 24. 55). This willingness to incorporate new elements is characteristic of Roman religious development, but it was closely controlled by the senate, the body that had overall responsibility for state religion.

The other most striking feature of Roman religion is its highly ritualised nature, with a great emphasis on continuity of tradition and on punctiliousness in the performance of rituals. It was vitally important to perform the correct rituals with absolute accuracy on the appropriate occasions (Val. Max. 2.1.1), and to consult the will of the gods via the auspices or examination of sacrificial victims. A mistake or interruption could invalidate the entire ritual and require its repetition.[10] There were many cautionary tales of disaster that could have been averted if magistrates or generals had been more careful about rituals, such as a naval defeat in 249 which Cicero uses to make the point:

> It is by failing to seek out the unpropitious signs we run into awful disasters. For example, Publius Claudius, son of Appius Caecus, and his colleague Lucius Junius, lost very large fleets by setting sail when the auguries were adverse.
>
> (Cicero, *De Divinatione* 1.29)

These two strands – conservatism and adherence to tradition on the one hand and openness to new cults on the other – may seem to contain the potential for conflict, but in fact they enabled Rome to have the best of both worlds, maintaining its traditional religious culture while still remaining open to new influences.

One of the essential features of Roman public life was divination by procedures through which men could consult the will of the gods. According to Cicero, 'no public business was ever transacted at home or abroad without first taking the auspices' (Cicero, *Div.* 1.3). Divination could be carried out in various ways. The senate kept records of events that were regarded as omens, and a range of natural phenomena such as earthquakes or violent storms, or deformed births of humans or animals, could be declared prodigies – bad omens that required expiation. Information on potential omens was gathered from all over Roman territory for consideration by the senate and referral to the magistrates, or priests for appropriate ritual action. More usually, however, augury or haruspicy were used to determine the will of the gods. These were both Etruscan practices, on which the Etruscans had an extensive body of sacred law. Consulting the auspices was undertaken by observing the behaviour of birds and animals from a specially demarcated enclosure in which the augur – sometimes a special priest and sometimes a senior magistrate – would stand to make his observations. Haruspicy was the practice of examining the entrails of sacrificial animals to see if the omens were favourable. Magistrates performing a sacrifice were assisted by a haruspex to make the examination and interpret the results. These rituals were an essential part of public life and were performed before any important action was taken, as well as at religious festivals. They preceded meetings of the senate, elections and votes on legislation. They were particularly important in time of war, and it was regarded as essential to take the auspices or consult the entrails before any military action was undertaken.

Many of these aspects of Roman religion were believed to be of ancient origin, but it is only in the later Republic that we can start building up a coherent picture of religious practice and religious offices. Even if they date back to the time of the kings, it is still unclear what the duties of many of the archaic priesthoods were, and how they were affected by the transition from monarchy to republic. At this date, however, many priesthoods seem to have been reserved for patricians, as were certain religious duties that were essential to exercising power. Religious duties and access to priesthoods were therefore closely intertwined with the periodic outbreaks of strife between patricians and plebeians, and became an additional bone of contention during this turbulent period of Roman history.

An era of austerity

Like many other areas of Italy, Rome showed signs of economic stress during the middle years of the fifth century. Both farming and craft production slowed down after *c.* 470, and from *c.* 450 the quantity of imported goods declined markedly. The development of Greek trading connections with Adria and Spina discussed in Chapter 6 fundamentally changed the pattern of Greek contact with Latium, and the large quantities of imported Attic pottery found at Rome in the sixth century decrease rapidly in the fifth. There is an equally drastic decrease in Etruscan imports, particularly luxury items such as fine pottery or bronze vessels, around the same time. This decline in imported goods was not offset by an increase in local manufacture, and pottery production in Rome itself was primarily confined to low-quality domestic vessels. The vibrant trade networks and artisan production of the archaic period largely disappeared. Instead, local trade networks within Latium became more important. The treaty between Rome and the Latins in 493 included special protection for trade and for commercial contracts between Rome and other Latin states. Alongside this, there is evidence of diminishing individual and family prosperity. A decrease in the numbers of burials and of the number and quality of grave goods at the Esquiline cemetery may point to a decline in disposable wealth. However, this is not the only explanation of these changes. Sumptuary laws limiting extravagant funerary display hint at a new culture of restraint among the elite, and greater emphasis on group solidarity.

Large-scale public building projects are a good index of social stability and economic health. They require a significant economic surplus, as well as a good supply of skilled and unskilled labour, materials and organisational skills. Building activity in the 490s and 480s was an attempt by the new Republic to celebrate and establish its political identity (fig. 23),[11] but the fact that major public works were few in number between *c.* 484 and 400 shows that there was little surplus to invest in new projects. The much lower level of temple construction at this period may also be linked to Rome's fortunes in war. Successful wars, such as those of the late sixth century, provided a good supply of labour, in the form of slaves, and wealth, in the form of booty. Since many temples were paid for out of the spoils of war and dedicated as victory offerings to the gods, this decline in activity may be directly linked to a lull in Rome's wars against its neighbours or to a lack of success in them.

Rome suffered periodic food shortages and high grain prices at this period, caused by drought or bad weather and deepened by political and social turmoil. Ten such periods of food shortage are recorded between 496 and 411, many coinciding with periods of warfare or civil unrest which exacerbated the effects of poor harvests by disrupting agricultural production and making transport of foodstuffs difficult. In the worst years grain was imported from Campania, Etruria and other areas of Latium to ease shortages, and its sale was regulated by the magistrates. In 440–439 Lucius Minucius organised a distribution of grain to alleviate a shortage of corn, an event that was honoured by a statue dedicated to him. The importance

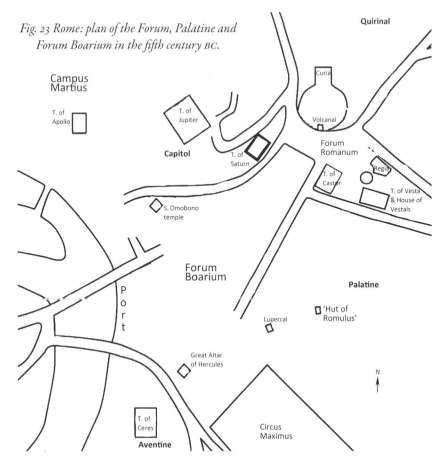

Fig. 23 Rome: plan of the Forum, Palatine and
Forum Boarium in the fifth century BC.

of this was such that it was commemorated on coinage issued by one of his descendants as late as 135. A poor harvest and outbreak of disease in 433–432 forced the magistrates to send representatives to other parts of Latium, Etruria and eventually as far afield as Sicily to buy up supplies of grain, and further distributions of cheap grain were made in 439 and 433. Such distributions were sometimes accompanied by civil unrest: Spurius Maelius, who imported and sold grain cheaply in 439, was assassinated since it was rumoured that he was doing it to gain popularity with a view to staging a coup. There is considerable anachronism in this account: distributions of free or subsidised grain in the second and first centuries were associated with populist politicians courting popularity and prestige rather than economic hardship, and later accounts may have interpreted Maelius' ill-fated grain distribution, and the response to it, in the light of these later events.[12] Nevertheless, there is archaeological evidence for economic problems throughout Italy in this period, and food shortages, and actions to deal with them, are consistent with this.

This period seems to have been one of tensions surrounding land ownership and problems with debt. Land ownership was a sensitive issue in ancient Rome because land was not just the main economic resource for most people, it also had an important social dimension. Property, defined as ownership of land, and legal status went hand in hand. Wealth classes, defined in terms of the value of landholdings, underpinned the organisation of both the Roman army and the main electoral assembly, the *comitia centuriata*. According to Cicero (*Offic.* 1.150–151), returns from land ownership were the only acceptable form of income for an upper-class Roman. The economic activities of wealthy Romans were undoubtedly more diverse than Cicero admits, but there is little doubt that there was a close link between land and social status from an early date in Rome's history. A shortage of land or an unfair distribution of land was therefore a serious cause for concern. It not only inhibited the ability of many of the Roman people to make a living but also limited social and political aspirations.

The supply of land was linked to successful military action. It became common policy, during Rome's wars against its neighbours, to confiscate a proportion of the territory of a defeated enemy. This was declared to be *ager publicus*, or publicly owned land belonging to the Roman state. It could be reallocated to Roman owners, who formed colonies in the newly acquired areas, or rented out by the state. Our understanding of *ager publicus* in the fifth and fourth centuries is limited. It is unclear how much land was involved, and how long it stayed in public hands, so the extent of the problems over land is difficult to pin down. After the defeat of the Etruscans at the battle of Aricia (505 or 504), and defeat of the Latins at the battle of Lake Regillus (probably 499), Rome's scope for wars against its immediate neighbours was limited, particularly after the Cassian treaty of 493 bound Rome to maintain peace with the Latins. Needless to say, this did not stop Rome waging war against other people, notably the Aequi, Volsci and Hernici as well as the Etruscans of Veii, but the frequency and success of military campaigns diminished for several years. As a consequence, supplies of newly acquired land became smaller and the Roman people became increasingly restive about perceived injustices in the way in which *ager publicus* was allocated. Unrest about distribution of publicly owned land, and the fairness of the allocations made, is said to have broken out during the second consulship of Spurius Cassius (486), and continued until well into the fourth century. The Licinio-Sextian laws of 367 drew something of a line under the problem, but public concern with ensuring fair allocation of land was a feature of Roman politics for well over a century.

The other intractable economic problem of the era was a rise in the number of people over-burdened by debt. Until the late fourth century Romans relied on a rudimentary form of currency,[13] *aes rude* (literally, 'rough bronze'), which were small rough-cast bronze ingots of standard weights, sometimes stamped with a weight symbol, which first appear in Italy in the eighth century.[14] Despite the absence of struck coinage, Romans were familiar with the concept of a monetary economy. Both the reforms of Servius Tullius and fifth-century Roman laws assess property, payments and fines in weights of bronze (the *as*, later a denomination of coinage, was originally a fixed weight of bronze). They were also familiar with the concepts of debt and of lending at interest. This became much more prevalent during the fifth century, as economic conditions tightened. As the number of people in debt and the rates of interest increased, an institution known as debt bondage (*nexum*) became a problem. This was a custom by which a creditor could seize the person of a debtor who had defaulted and use him as bonded labour – in effect, enslaving him – until the debt had been worked off. These debt problems surfaced regularly as a popular grievance throughout the fifth and fourth centuries, despite numerous attempts to regulate interest and repayment terms.

The Struggle of the Orders

The fifth and fourth centuries were dominated by the so-called Struggle of the Orders, a conflict between patricians and plebeians that began in 494 and lasted intermittently until 287. This long-running, although episodic, strife affected many aspects of Roman society and is difficult to evaluate precisely because it was so diverse and long-lasting. Essentially it was a struggle for power and influence between two sub-groups within the Roman aristocracy. However, it included many other issues of wider concern, such as food shortages, land shortages, a growing debt crisis and the consequent phenomenon of debt slavery, as well as demands for legal reform and political representation. The various interest groups involved pursued their grievances by methods ranging from legal and legislative action, via mass civic disobedience, to violent confrontation.

The first episode in this conflict – known as the First Secession – took place in 494 and may have been triggered by a debt crisis. Our sources present a harrowing tale of people forced into debt and then imprisoned and enslaved by their creditors. The man at the centre of the story, a war veteran who had taken out a loan at a usurious rate of interest, had been forced to surrender his property and ultimately his liberty to pay this off. Public outrage at his plight prompted sustained civil disorder and a crackdown by the consuls, who responded by issuing even harsher judgements against debtors. Eventually, the plebeians staged a secession, a tactic that was to be repeated several times between 494 and 287. This was a form of strike action that involved all or part of the plebeians withdrawing from the life of the city and physically decamping to a location outside it, an action that was particularly threatening in this instance because Rome was at war with both the Sabines and the Volscians, and this secession disrupted the military levy. The situation was eventually resolved by a respected figure, Menenius Agrippa, who persuaded the plebeians of the importance of solidarity in the face of military threat.

The settlement attributed to Agrippa had profound implications. The main plebeian grievance was not usury or the institution of *nexum per se*. It was the lack of protection from arbitrary action by the magistrates who enforced penalties for debt. The solution was the creation of a new magistracy, the *tribunus plebis* (tribune of the people), reserved exclusively for plebeians. Its function was to protect the people from arbitrary and oppressive action by other magistrates. Tribunes went on to play an important role in the history of the Republic because of the unique nature of the office and the extraordinary powers they possessed. Because their role was, in the first instance, to protect plebeians from ill-treatment, they had the right of *auxilium*, namely the right to intervene personally to protect plebeians threatened by patricians, and the power to impose legal penalties (fines, imprisonment or even death) on anyone who threatened them or challenged their authority. Their persons were sacrosanct to prevent any attempts on their lives.[15] Their most important power, however, was the power of veto (*intercessio*), which allowed them to stop any proposal or piece of legislation dead in its tracks. This became a potent political weapon during the later stages of the Struggle of the Orders, and at various points in the second and first century. In addition, they had the power to propose legislation and to convene meetings of the senate, although these may have been added later than the fifth century.

Another new magistracy, the aedileship, was created around the same time and, like the tribunate, the office was reserved for plebeians. The title *aedilis* is probably derived from *aedes*, the Latin term for a temple, and may reflect the close connection between the *aediles* and the temple of Ceres on the Aventine, which became their headquarters. From the mid-fourth century *aediles* were responsible for the infrastructure of the city, especially in respect of food supplies, maintenance of streets and buildings, organising games and upholding public order. In the fifth century their duties were ill defined, but given that food shortages were a problem linked with the Struggle of the Orders, food supply and distribution must have been one of their key roles.

Around the same time a plebeian assembly was created, in which the plebians could pass resolutions. The *concilium plebis*, as it was known, supposedly dates from 494, and was apparently open to anyone who was not a patrician; but little is known about how it operated or what it did at this date. In 471, however, the *concilium* was reorganised into an assembly with a reformed structure, including the method of electing plebeian magistrates. It elected its magistrates and voted on resolutions using a block voting system similar to that of the *comitia curiata* and *comitia centuriata* (i.e., decisions were reached by a majority of votes in each block, and then by a majority of block votes, not by the total number of individual votes), but the voting unit was the tribe (*tribus*) rather than the *curia* or century. Despite the name, the tribe had nothing to do with ethnic or kinship groups, but was the geographical area in which its members lived. The territory of Rome, and the citizens who lived there, was divided between a number of tribes (twenty-one until the conquest of Veii in 396, but increasing from that point on as Roman territory grew until they reached a maximum of thirty-five in 241), and the citizens met and voted in their tribes. Eventually, the tribes were adopted as voting units for assemblies of the whole Roman people (the *comitia populi tribute*, usually known simply as the *comitia tributa*), as well as for the *concilium plebis*.

Even after this reform, the status of the *concilium plebis* and the measures it passed remained ambiguous. Since only plebeians were eligible to attend, it was not a full assembly of the people, and its resolutions, on proposals put forward by the tribunes, were known as *plebiscita*, rather than laws (Aul. Gell., *NA* 15.27). They were binding on the plebeians, since they were eligible to vote on them, but it is much less clear whether they could be enforced on the community as a whole. A set of laws known as the Valerio-Horatian laws, passed in 449, dealt with some of these issues, but the plebeian assembly remained a *concilium*, which could pass resolutions that were at best provisional, until the Lex Hortensia of 287 finally made its decisions binding on the entire Roman people. After that point it became virtually indistinguishable from the tribal assembly of the people (the *comitia tributa*), and became Rome's most important legislative body.

The settlement that ended the First Secession effectively created a parallel organisation for plebeians within the Roman state, as well as a new political geography for Rome. During the First Secession the plebeians decamped to a hill known as the Sacred Mount, but during later secessions they withdrew to the Aventine. This became associated with plebeian politics, and with popular protest in general. The temples of Ceres and of Diana on the Aventine were particularly closely associated with plebeian magistrates and their actions. The fact that the Aventine was outside the *pomerium* and was topographically at a distance from the Capitol and Forum, the areas most closely associated with the power of the state, meant that it was a powerful symbol of rejection of established authority. The temple of Ceres was said to have been built from the spoils taken after the battle of Lake Regillus (Dion. Hal. 6.17.2–4), forming a plebeian counterpart to the temple of Castor in the Forum Romanum, which commemorated the same battle. The association with the cults of the Aventine also had practical significance. The plebeian cult at the Temple of Ceres, Liber and Libera on the Aventine was associated with the aediles and their activities and particularly with their role in food distribution, since Ceres was the Roman goddess of agriculture.[16] Anyone who threatened a tribune could have his or her property seized and dedicated to Ceres, and according to Livy (3.55.13), copies of senatorial decrees were sent to the temple, ensuring that they were displayed and stored in a location that the plebeians could access. The Aventine cults of Diana and Ceres also had strong Greek connections. The cult of Ceres may have been of Greek origin, and according to Cicero (*Balb.* 55) the rituals were Greek. The association of these cults with the plebeians may indicate a connection between liberty and popular politics and Greek political thought.[17]

Debt and the need for protection from oppressive magistrates were not the only problems that angered the plebeians. Agrarian problems and land ownership were also fraught issues in the 480s, although the nature of the problem is unclear. Ancient accounts were coloured by later, second-century, agitation about *ager publicus*, when issues may have been very different. We do not know, for instance, how long newly acquired land stayed in public ownership, or whether the issues that annoyed the Roman people in the fifth century were those of elite monopolisation of agrarian resources (as in the second century) or were connected with perceived injustices in allocation of newly conquered land. After an outbreak of agitation in the early 480s, Spurius Cassius, the consul of 486, is said to have proposed a law to redistribute land taken from the Hernici, but sources disagree on whether only Romans were eligible to benefit, or whether Latins and Hernici could also apply for a grant of land (Livy 2.41; Dion. Hal 8.69–77). In 485 Cassius was found guilty of courting popularity in order to set himself up as a tyrant and was executed. This episode is problematic because Cassius' character and career, as presented by our sources, are closely modelled on those of Tiberius Gracchus, the reforming tribune of 133, and the existence of both the Cassian land law and his apparent bid for power have been questioned. Both textual and archaeological evidence from many areas of Italy suggest that the fifth century was a period of social and economic stress, so it is plausible that land distribution was a contentious political issue at Rome, but the details of Cassius' law and supposed attempt at tyranny are too close to the career of Tiberius Gracchus to accept.

Legal reform

A further aim of the plebeians during the Struggle of the Orders was the creation of a written law code. What little we know of Roman law before the mid-fifth century suggests that it was based on custom and practice rather than codified laws. Some laws may have been systematised and written down, but much depended on memory and oral transmission. Despite survivals such as the inscription of the *Lapis Niger* (see pl. 19), inscribed with what appears to be a sacred law or ritual, there is no evidence that laws were systematically recorded and organised. With no proper corpus of written or codified law, anyone who brought a lawsuit, or found themselves having to answer one, was at the mercy of the presiding magistrate or judge and their interpretation of the law. Plaintiffs and defendants did not have access to what the law actually said

– an inflammatory issue when legal and political power was so heavily concentrated in the hands of the elite. The creation of a written law code, in contrast, forces a community to draw up a defined set of laws which can be consulted by everyone, and applied universally. In theory this enabled all citizens to have access to justice on an equal basis, although in practice this result may not be entirely clear-cut. In societies with very low levels of literacy, such as early Rome, a written law code might be exclusive in a different way, since it limited knowledge of law to those with the skills to read it. It is possible that the introduction of a written law code, far from opening access to the wider populace, made access to fair legal hearings more exclusive. On balance, however, it seems likely that codification of law and the clarification and systematisation that went with it helped even out imbalances of power and status. The very existence of a written code which could be consulted served to limit the scope for manipulating the law to patrician advantage.

Agitation for a law code began in 462 and continued for more than ten years – a fact which, in itself, indicates both a certain strength of feeling on the subject and patrician resistance to it. The creation of codified law was a common feature of many Mediterranean states in the sixth and fifth centuries, as these grew larger and developed more complex and sophisticated institutions; so this demand for a law code placed Rome in line with the broader pattern of state development.[18] During the 450s the pressure for legal reform built up, and envoys were sent on a fact-finding mission to Athens and other Greek cities to study their law codes. In 451 patricians and plebeians reached an agreement to suspend the entire constitution while a law code was drawn up (Cic., *Rep.* 2.61; Livy 3.31–55; Dion. Hal. 10.55 ff.). A commission of ten men (*Decemviri legibus scribundis*) took over the duties of the consuls for the governing of Rome, as well as responsibility for producing a set of laws. They had wide-ranging powers, as the tribunes had apparently stood down along with the consuls, and there was no appeal against the actions of the Decemvirs.

By 450 the Decemvirs produced a series of laws which were inscribed on ten bronze tablets, and displayed in the Forum in front of the Rostra. The following year a second commission of Decemvirs, this time including plebeian members, added a further two tables, as the bronze tablets were known. This second commission is described by our sources as a tyrannical regime, which indulged in some flamboyantly oppressive behaviour and created a constitutional crisis by refusing to stand down at the end of their year of office. The most striking episode, retold with great pathos by Livy, was the murder of a young woman, Verginia, by her own father to save her from being raped by Appius Claudius, the leader of the Decemvirs and the only member to have served on both commissions. The revulsion at this crime, and at the tyrannical behaviour of the commissioners in general, caused an outbreak of unrest and a further secession of the plebeians to the Aventine. The final outcome was the suicide of Appius Claudius, and the deposition of the 'Ten Tarquins', as Livy refers to the Decemvirs, in 449.

Whether or not these stories (particularly those relating to the outrageous behaviour of the second decemvirate) had any historical basis, the resulting law code, known as the law of the Twelve Tables, remained an important part of Roman law throughout the Republic.[19] Although it was much expanded and modified by later legislation, Roman schoolchildren still had to learn to recite it even in the first century BC. A significant portion of the code survives, although in fragmentary form, through excerpts quoted by later authors. Some aspects of the code are obscure, and even seem to have puzzled later Romans, but it gives us a fascinating insight into Roman society in the fifth century. It was not a comprehensive code and did not address aspects such as the powers of the magistrates. Instead, much of it concerns family law, property law and some crimes, as well as religious laws. It also regulated the legal process, determining procedures for summoning witnesses and hearing certain types of grievances. The Twelve Tables regulated the rights and duties of the *paterfamilias*; marriage, divorce and the status of women within the family; ownership and disposal of family property, and inheritance. One aspect of the sections dealing with property and inheritance is that there are very few references to the clan or *gens*. Whatever the case in the seventh century, by the mid-fifth century property was held by the individual family and controlled by the *paterfamilias*, not collectively owned by a wider clan. Relations between patron and client are briefly covered, reminding the patron that if he wrongs a client, he shall be deemed to be accursed.

Other tables contained laws on debt, boundary disputes, damage to property, personal injury etc. Most of the clauses regulating economic life are concerned with agrarian matters such as protecting land, determining boundaries, resolving disputes arising from them and dealing with rights of way or access. There is very little relating to trade or other forms of economic activity. Regulations dealing with commercial transactions are almost all concerned with purchase of land or animals. The Tables also contain measures concerning debt and the treatment of debtors, as well as regulating the purchase and manumission of slaves. Table 10 regulated funerals, imposing restrictions on lavish funerary displays; while Table 11 prohibited intermarriage between patricians and plebeians. The funerary regulations seem designed to prevent conspicuous consumption and competition between elite families, but the ban on intermarriage is baffling. It is unclear whether it was a formalisation of a long-standing custom or the imposition of a new restriction, but at the very least it represents a new hardening of barriers between the orders.[20]

In 449 the decemvirate was abolished and laws that addressed some of the other areas of tension between patricians and plebeians were proposed, possibly as a settlement to end the secession of 450–449 (Livy 3.55; Diod. 12.24). These (known as the Valerio-Horatian laws, after Valerius Potitus and Horatius Barbatus, the magistrates at the time) marked the end of the first phase of the Struggle of the Orders, although many other controversies continued throughout the fourth century. They formally recognised many of the powers gained by the plebeians, such as the sacrosanctity of plebeian magistrates, the right of appeal against the actions of magistrates (*provocatio*) and the legal validity of the resolutions of the *concilium plebis*. Some of these clauses have been questioned, as they are also addressed by earlier or later laws, but given the political volatility of the fifth century, it is probable that concepts such as *provocatio* or the validity of *plebiscita* needed to be reaffirmed more than once. Whatever the accuracy of the details preserved, the general aim of the laws was to regularise and recognise the rights and powers of the plebeian magistracies and assembly. Shortly after this, in 445, the Lex Canuleia ended the prohibition on intermarriage between patrician and plebeian families, thus breaking down one of the major social and legal barriers to integration. It is debatable how many of the plebeians would have been affected by this, but it enabled the emergence of a plebeian elite that aspired to power and status on equal terms with patricians.

During the 440s there were other changes in the way Rome was governed. Elected magistrates were reintroduced in 449, but between 444 and 367 the senior magistrates were not always consuls. In some years magistrates known as military tribunes with consular power (*tribuni militum consulari potestate*, or 'consular tribunes' for short) were elected instead. These are not to be confused with the Tribunes of the People or with the military tribunes who served as army officers; they had the same powers as the consuls, but numbers elected varied from three to six per year, although there were occasionally as many as ten. It is not clear exactly why this change took place. Livy attributes it to pressure by the plebeians for the right to stand for the consulship and sees it as a compromise hammered out by the senate. By changing the name of the office and increasing the number of office-holders in some years, the patricians could permit plebeians to stand for election without conceding the principle that the consulship itself was still a patrician preserve. But Livy goes on to report an alternative and more practical explanation offered by some of his sources, namely that the military tribunes with consular powers were first elected in a year when Rome was at war with the Volsci, Aequi and Veii simultaneously, and two consuls would have been insufficient to lead multiple campaigns. This sounds more plausible and may go some way to explain why consular tribunes did not replace consuls every year, and why the number of consular tribunes elected varied. Between 444 and 427 consular tribunes were elected on only five occasions, but between 426 and 406 consular tribunes governed Rome in fourteen years, and increased in number from three to four in some years. By the time the practice of electing consular tribunes was abolished in 367, boards of five or six were commonplace. Since this period coincides with the widening of Rome's military commitments in central Italy, it seems plausible that the need for a larger pool of senior magistrates with the legal powers to command an army, rather than just two consuls, was driven by military necessity.

The introduction of military tribunes with consular powers as periodic replacements for the consuls was only part of a more general reorganisation of government in the years after 449. A junior magistracy, the quaestorship, is dated to 446, with primary responsibility for financial administration such as overseeing the state treasury. Another very senior one, the censorship, was added in 443. Censors were chosen from the ranks of the patricians but, unlike most magistrates, were elected at intervals of several years rather than annually. Their main role was to conduct the periodic censuses of the Roman people, assessing their property status, age and rights of residence. In doing so, they also determined eligibility for military service and voting rights. They also supervised various other transactions such as the administration of *ager publicus*, which remained in the hands of the state, collection of rents from this type of property and the commissioning and allocation of contracts for major public building projects. The new offices had links with military activities – quaestors through organising supplies and dealing with allocation of booty, and censors by assessing eligibility for army service – so it is at least possible that their introduction and some of the other reforms resulted from Rome's increasing military commitments as much as from social tensions between patricians and plebeians.

The 430s were relatively quiet, but from 424 there was further agitation over land reform, triggered by successful military campaigns and the acquisition of more *ager publicus*. There were also further moves to open up the political system to the plebeians. Although senior magistracies were still the preserve of the patricians, plebeian candidates were permitted to stand for the quaestorship, from 421. In the event, the first plebeian quaestors were not elected until 409, which suggests that the pace of social and political change was slow, but by the end of the fifth century some of the grievances of the plebeians had been addressed. Rome had a published law code, the ban on intermarriage between patricians and plebeians had been abolished, the plebeian 'state within a state' had been set up and there were signs that the wider political system was beginning to open up to non-patricians. Nevertheless, many issues remained to be resolved. Debt slavery and land reform were contentious issues throughout much of the fourth century, and political power was still largely out of reach of plebeians. The Struggle of the Orders was by no means over.

The Struggle of the Orders cannot be understood as a single event or process. The issues conventionally grouped under this heading are too disparate, and it is implausible that a single struggle for power could last over two hundred years. There is little doubt that the early Republic was riven with tensions and strife on a variety of issues, but these are too diverse to stem from a conflict between two well-defined classes or interest groups, at least before the fourth century. Patrician families did not have an exclusive grip on political power at the beginning of the Republic: according to the lists of magistrates, around 21 per cent of magistrates between 509 and 483 were plebeians, including some of the famous consuls of the period, such as Lucius Junius Brutus, the first consul of the Republican era. By the late 480s the patrician ascendancy had begun, and the proportion of plebeians dropped rapidly to 8 per cent of magistrates in 482–428 and only 1 per cent in 427–401. Examples of patrician power, and strife with non-patricians such as the unrest that led to the First Secession of 494, occurred during the early years of the Republic, but these were phenomena that grew and crystallised during the course of the fifth century.

One solution is to separate the Struggle of the Orders from the civic unrest of the fifth century. During the fourth century the identity of the patricians and plebeians and the divisions between them become clearer, and some historians have proposed that the term 'Struggle of the Orders' should be confined to this later phase of political tension. However, some of the events of the fifth century suggest that there was already a perception of political as well as economic injustice. Rather than trying to confine the Struggle of the Orders to the fourth century, I believe it would be better to view it as a developing situation, in which a wide-ranging set of legal and economic grievances in the fifth century gave way to a more direct political power struggle in the fourth, as both patricians and plebeians developed stronger identities and a more clearly defined status.

Urban development

The city of Rome itself continued to develop, but at a much slower pace than previously. There are traces of destruction in some areas of the Forum, notably around the Comitium, which shows signs of burning. The burned layer is sometimes associated with the sack of Rome by the Gauls in 390, but it seems to date more plausibly to *c.* 500, and it has been conjectured that the Comitium may have been damaged by fire during civil disturbances following the ejection of the Tarquins. Apart from this, the late sixth century and the first quarter of the fifth century were relatively buoyant, but there are signs of decline and recession from *c.* 470 to 400.

There was new building in the Forum and on the Capitoline in the early fifth century, some of which may have been initiated under the last years of the monarchy. One of the first acts of the new Republic was the dedication of the Temple of Jupiter Capitolinus. This had been commissioned by the Tarquins and largely constructed during the monarchy, but its dedication by the magistrates of 509 appropriated it as a powerful symbol of the new regime and an implicit request for divine approval. Six major temples are said to have been constructed and dedicated in the first thirty years of the Republic, as symbols of the new order and a way of gaining divine approval. Some were closely linked with specific achievements. The

Temple of Castor and Pollux, dedicated in 484, commemorated Rome's victory over the Latins at the battle of Lake Regillus in 499 (see fig. 23). There was a Roman legend that the demigods had appeared on the battlefield to assist Roman forces and were later seen watering their horses at the Lacus Iuturnae, a spring in the Roman Forum, close to the site of the temple.[21] There was also a noted cult of Castor and Pollux at Lavinium, and the temple in the Forum may have been intended to harness symbolically the power of this important Latin cult for the benefit of Rome. Most of the extant remains of the temple are, of course, of much later date, but excavation of the temple and Lacus Iuturnae have revealed early fifth-century remains.

Date of Dedication	Temple
509	Capitoline Jupiter
497	Saturn
495	Mercury
493	Ceres
486	Fortuna Muliebris
484	Castor
433	Apollo

Table 6: **Fifth-century temple building in Rome, according to literary sources**

There is a complete gap in the record after 484, with the single exception of the temple of Apollo Medicus in 431, which had been vowed in 433 following an outbreak of plague. This is corroborated by the discovery of fifth-century foundations beneath the remains of the second-century temple in the Campus Martius. Overall, however, fifth-century temples in Rome are few and far between.

There is some funerary evidence to support the ancient accounts of economic recession, but this is not clear-cut. In cemetery areas at Rome, especially the Esquiline, the number of datable burials and the quality and the quantity of grave goods decline sharply from the late sixth century. This could mean a fall in the number of people able to afford a commemorated burial, and less surplus wealth to invest in grave goods, but it could also reflect social changes rather than economic decline. The fifth-century law code, the Twelve Tables (see pp. 193), contains sumptuary regulations limiting the lavishness of funerals, suggesting a cultural shift away from conspicuous consumption and towards a more restrained level of funerary display. It is worth noting that the shift to more austere grave goods begins in the late sixth century, at a time when Rome was investing heavily in public works and the elite were building lavish houses. Decline in public building and the evidence for grain distributions and debt problems suggest that the middle years of the fifth century were a period of economic difficulty, but changes in burial custom reflect a broader social and cultural change, not just a recession.

The decrease in the quantity and quality of material evidence in the fifth century is sometimes characterised as a period of 'de-Etruscanisation' following the fall of the Tarquins and the war with Lars Porsenna, but this seems very unlikely. Etruscan goods and Etruscan people are still found in Rome in the early fifth century. Trading connections and links with Etruscan craftsmen were still in place in the early years of the Republic, and there is no evidence that the deposition of Tarquin was followed by a general anti-Etruscan backlash. The real break occurs later, between 480 and 430, when Etruscan goods and artistic influences decline significantly. Tellingly, however, Greek goods and influences also disappear around the same time, and the explanation must lie in a pattern of economic decline, disruption to trade networks and social and political instability found throughout Italy. The decline in Etruscan culture at Rome was the result of these broader factors, not a systematic ejection of Etruscans after 509.

A visitor to Rome in the late fifth century would have found a rather different community from that of the sixth century. New modes of government were accompanied by political and social polarisation, and Romans were in a distinctly fractious mood. The self-confident conspicuous consumption of the aristocracy had been replaced by a more austere culture, and there was a greater emphasis on social solidarity within an increasingly tightly defined elite. Physically, the city had become more monumental in appearance, but the emphasis had shifted from celebration of aristocratic lifestyle via impressive houses and tombs to a greater emphasis on celebration of the new Republic's military successes and political identity. A visitor, particularly during the early years of the century, would have noticed more temples commemorating Roman victories and a greater politicisation of the urban landscape, with development of civic buildings in the Forum. Rome may not have been visibly in decline, but socially and economically it was a more constrained and divided society.

10

ROME ON THE MARCH: WAR IN LATIUM AND BEYOND, 500–350

Rome's turbulent domestic history at this period was matched by difficult relations with its near neighbours – and with some more distant ones. The overthrow of the monarchy was followed by a war with Lars Porsenna and the Tarquins, the details of which are far from clear, but the defeat of Porsenna at the battle of Aricia in 505 or 504 and successful campaigns against the Latins in 496 offered some respite and enabled a peace settlement with the Latins to be negotiated.[1] Ancient accounts depict the fifth century as one of continuous warfare, during which Rome was frequently under attack. Rome became embroiled in a debilitating series of wars against Veii and, at the same time, another set of inconclusive and difficult campaigns against various southern neighbours (map 3). This war on several fronts ultimately sapped Rome's military strength without yielding any great reward in terms of territory or booty. Finally, at the beginning of the fourth century, Rome was faced with a Gallic invasion that posed a serious threat to the city's very existence.

Although our sources link these wars of the late sixth and early fifth centuries to the end of the monarchy and describe them as instigated by the Tarquins, the causes were probably more complex and wide-ranging. Lars Porsenna's campaign seems to have been a serious attempt to take advantage of a period of instability in central Italy and to extend the power of his own city, Clusium. Rome was not the only city threatened by him, and his campaigns extended into Latium and even into Campania. The battle of Aricia, at which the Clusines, under the command of Arruns Porsenna, were finally defeated, was fought by a coalition of Latins and Greek forces from Cumae. It was part of a broader struggle for power in Campania between the Etruscans and other inhabitants of the region, not a purely Roman affair, and it culminated in a successful attempt by Aristodemos of Cumae to push back Etruscan power in Campania. He crafted a series of alliances with neighbours such as the Latins and with more distant Greeks such as Hieron, the tyrant of Syracuse, which allowed the Cumaeans to inflict decisive defeats on the Etruscans. Campaigns against the Etruscans, led by Cumae, continued from 524 until 474, in alliance with some Latin and Greek states. Etruscan power in Campania was decisively undermined by a naval defeat by a fleet of ships from Cumae and Syracuse in 474 BC. Loss of naval dominance in the region, combined with erosion of their control of central and northern Campania, caused Etruscan power and influence in Campania to wane rapidly.

This helped the Romans greatly. The defeat of the Clusians at Aricia in 505 or 504 removed the immediate military pressure and gave the new Roman Republic some breathing space. Over the next few years Rome confronted the Latin states that had prevailed against Porsenna and decisively defeated them at the battle of Lake Regillus in 496. This battle assumed iconic importance for later Romans, as the point at which they repulsed the threat of the Tarquins and established their power over the Latins. It acquired an accretion of heroic legend and mythology, designed to validate this power, such as the tradition that the demigods Castor and Pollux fought for Rome and reported news of the victory to the Roman people.[2] The descendants of the Roman general, Aulus Postumius Albus, still celebrated his famous victory many generations later.

In 493, after the last of the Latin resistance had been subdued, a treaty was negotiated by the consul Spurius Cassius that brought the war to an end. It was inscribed on a bronze tablet and displayed in the Forum, where it was apparently still visible even in the time of Cicero, and was regarded as the prototype for later Roman treaties. It is quoted in full by Dionysios of Halicarnassus:

These were the terms of the treaty: 'Let there be peace between Romans and all the cities of the Latins for as long as the sky and the earth shall remain in their places. And let them not make war on each other, or bring in other enemies or grant a right of passage to the enemies of either. Let them help each other, when at war, with all their strength, and let the spoils and plunder from wars fought in common be divided into equal shares for each of them. Let disputes about private contracts be decided within ten days and in the state where the contract was made. And do not let anything be added or subtracted from this treaty except by consent of Rome and all the Latins.' These terms were agreed by the Romans and the Latins and ratified by oaths and sacrifices.

(Dion. Hal., 6.95[3])

The Cassian treaty, as it became known, established an open-ended peace between Rome and the Latins, by which they agreed not to make war or to assist each other's enemies. It also put in place a mutual aid pact by which each party would assist the other if attacked by external enemies, something central to Rome's later alliances. This clause, and the inclusion of arrangements for equal sharing of booty, suggests that joint campaigns involving both Romans and Latins were envisaged, although it offers little insight into how often this happened or how these were organised.

Fragments of works by two later writers, Cato and Lucius Cincius, offer some insight into the workings of the Latin League. Cato refers to a Dictator Latinus, the nominated leader of the Latin League. Cincius describes arrangements for command of league forces, which were settled at annual meetings at the shrine of Ferentina, near Albano. He described procedures to be followed in years when a commander was to be summoned from Rome, by order of the Latins. It is, however, unclear whether the commander was always a Roman, but only summoned in years when a campaign was about to take place, or whether the command alternated on a year-by-year basis between Rome and the Latins. The important point, perhaps, is that Rome was included on an equal basis with the rest of the Latins and Roman commanders of league forces were summoned on the authority of the Latin League.

The earlier treaty between Rome and Carthage divided the Latins into two groups: some referred to as satellites or subjects of Rome, and others as communities that were not Roman subjects. If Polybios is correct, Roman control over some parts of Latium at the end of the regal period was firm enough to be seen by the Carthaginians as a form of subjection, although this runs into the difficult issue of the dating of Rome's treaties with Carthage. In the years following the expulsion of the Tarquins, however, the balance of power changed. The Latins came together to form a league (*FRHist* Cato fr 36), and were able to see off Porsenna, with the help of Cumae, and to confront the Romans at Regillus, where the Roman victory seems to have been less overwhelming than Livy believed. The Cassian treaty changed the relationship between Rome and the Latins from domination to a situation in which the two sides became equal partners in a bilateral alliance, as noted by Cincius.

During the fifth century, however, Rome's sphere of influence expanded beyond Latium proper. Wars against Veii, already a rival in the sixth century, prompted Rome to look north to Etruria and to try to extend its influence across the Tiber. To the south, Rome's Latin allies were engaged in conflicts with the smaller ethnic groups on their southern borders. Probably the best-known, thanks to Shakespeare's *Coriolanus*, is the war against the Volsci, but there were conflicts with many other peoples. Later Romans divided Latium into two parts: Latium Vetus (ancient Latium), and Latium Adiectum (adjacent Latium). Roughly speaking, the first of these corresponds to the area around Rome itself, and the second to the region south of the Alban Hills, in the valleys of the Rivers Trerus (mod. River Sacco) and Liris (River Liri) and possibly as far as the River Garigliano, on the borders of Campania. Latium Adiectum was a hilly area occupied by a number of ethnic groups – the Aurunci, Sidicini, Hernici and Volsci – who can first be clearly identified in the late sixth and early fifth centuries. The largest and best-known of these peoples – and the ones who were the greatest threat to Rome – were the Volsci. They become identifiable in the archaeological record for the first time at this period and spread during the 490s into southern Latium, placing pressure on Rome's southern neighbours. The inland borders of Rome were also under threat from the Sabines, and the cities of eastern Latium suffered from incursions by the Aequi. Rome's fifth-century wars in Latium and beyond must be seen against the background of wider developments in central Italy. The population movements, political changes and shifting patterns of power discussed in the preceding chapter created a difficult and volatile situation. Rome was able to take advantage of this by acting with its allies to challenge the Volsci for control of southern Latium and making inroads into Hernican territory, despite being hampered by domestic instability.

Rome pursued numerous campaigns around the borders of this region and by *c.* 347 had become the dominant power in the region.

There was a lull in activity after 493, as domestic tensions made it inadvisable to embark on ambitious military campaigns and the First Secession of the plebeians in 494 had temporarily deprived the city of much of its military manpower. Rome was still under pressure, however. The Aequi and Volsci had threatened an attack while the Roman army was out of action owing to the secession, and the Hernici remained restive. Spurius Cassius proposed a diplomatic solution during his third consulship in 486 by extending the treaty of 493 to include the Hernici. This placed their relationship with Rome on a similar footing to that of the Latins, meaning that they were obliged to maintain peace with Rome, engage in mutual military aid and share the spoils of joint campaigns (Dion. Hal. 8.69.2). It created an alliance that permitted joint military operations on an equal footing by Latins, Hernici and Romans, but Rome was increasingly dominant. The few details we have of how the system worked in practice show that the three groups fought in their own separate armies, but that Rome normally supplied the commanders and therefore, presumably, controlled strategic decisions.

This tripartite alliance gave all three participants some degree of protection against the incursions by Sabines, Aequi and Volsci, who threatened the Latins as well as Rome, especially the cities of Praeneste and Tibur, which were on the hilly eastern edge of Latium and were particularly vulnerable to their Aequian neighbours. Between 494 and 455, or thereabouts, Rome was involved in almost continuous warfare with at least one, if not all, of these groups, and Rome and the Latins were frequently under fierce pressure. Between 490 and 458 the Volsci and the Aequi invaded Latium on several occasions, sometimes reaching the outskirts of Rome itself. The most famous of these campaigns were those of 490–488, in which the Volscians were led by a disgruntled Roman general, Gnaeus Marcius Coriolanus, and of 458, in which the Roman general Cincinnatus was appointed dictator and succeeded in raising an army and inflicting a significant defeat on the Aequi within a period of fifteen days (Livy 3. 31–37).

Since the nineteenth century, scholars have been divided between those who dismissed Cincinnatus and Coriolanus as literary inventions and others who argued that the wars, if not the characters, are genuine. Cincinnatus was the stereotypical exemplar of early Roman virtue. He was a farmer who was ploughing his fields when he was summoned to high office, and, having fought a highly successful campaign and gained great honour in doing so, he willingly relinquished power and command and returned to his farm. Coriolanus, in contrast, is a flamboyant antihero – a patrician who was so disgusted by growing plebeian influence and his own apparent lack of recognition that he defected. He became the general of the Volscian army and led a march on Rome. As an added twist, he rejected Roman envoys who tried to negotiate with him but agreed not to press home his attack on Rome after an emotional appeal made by his mother and his wife, an episode that showcases the role of Roman matrons in influencing events. The Romans believed that the cult of Fortuna Muliebris was founded in honour of these women.

Although neither of these stories can be accepted as historical truth, the career of Coriolanus is consistent with social customs in early Italy. There are a number of examples of noblemen who changed state and citizenship, sometimes along with large numbers of clients and followers. In addition to the Claudii, Sabines who migrated to Rome in 504, there was also Vitruvius Vaccus, a leading citizen of Fundi, who moved to the nearby city of Privernum and led the Privernate army in a war against Rome in 330. The idea that a Roman aristocrat could defect and go on to lead an enemy army is perfectly plausible. Other details are clearly not historically true: some of the locations of the action are debatable, and the cult of Fortuna Muliebris, a cult dedicated to women in child-birth, probably pre-dates Coriolanus. Although they cannot be literally true, however, the stories of Cincinnatus and Coriolanus are consistent with what we know of fifth-century society, and their grip on the Roman imagination also demonstrates their importance to Rome's sense of collective identity.[4]

Although episodes such as Coriolanus' defection offer insights into the Romans' own views of their past, reconstructing the precise events of this period is almost impossible. Although there is no reason to doubt that Rome fought numerous campaigns, the historian John Rich has suggested that this may be overstated, and doubts the accuracy of much of Livy's account of almost continuous warfare.[5] As Rich points out, Rome fought relatively infrequently between 454 and 411, with only fourteen campaigns that can be regarded as historically sound, and the Aequi and Volsci seem to have threatened Roman territory directly on only eight occasions.

The main period of Roman expansion in the fifth century came towards the end of the century, with the outbreak of war with the Etruscan city of Veii, just north of the Tiber. Wars against Veii fall into three main periods of conflict, which can be conveniently labelled the first (483–474), second (437–435) and third (406–396) Veientine wars. They were fought specifically against Veii and its allies, and do not form a general ethnic conflict between Rome and the Etruscans. Veii's main support came from the neighbouring cities of Capena and Falerii, neither of which was Etruscan, while Rome received some measure of support from Etruscan Caere.

Veii was a pressing problem for Rome. It was a powerful state located on the far side of the Tiber, only 15 km (*c.* 9 miles) north of Rome. The city was well defended, and its territory was notably well organised and productive. It also controlled the intersection of two major trade routes: one, passing from north to south, led through the territories of Veii and Rome, while the other led up the Tiber valley. The proximity of such an established regional power to the ambitious and expanding community of Rome created an explosive combination. Their mutual hostility was fuelled by competition to control trade routes and by rivalry for status and power within the region.

The First Veientine war (Livy 2.42–52) was a set-back for Rome. Apart from a Roman victory in 480, 483–474 was a period of progress by Veii and retreat by Rome, culminating in the establishment of a small but symbolic Etruscan fort on the Janiculum, just across the Tiber from Rome itself. In 474 a truce was made, under which Veii established control over the strategically important settlement of Fidenae, which occupied the left bank of the Tiber and effectively prevented Rome from gaining any foothold on the Veientine side of the river. The war is notable for an episode concerning one of the leading *gentes* of Rome, the Fabii. Diodorus presents them as leading a state army, but in Livy's version they effectively declared a private war in 479 and mobilised an army of clients and retainers to occupy a small fortification on the borders of the territory of Veii. Livy describes this as retaliation for the Etruscan occupation of the Janiculum, but it seems more likely that the Fabii were protecting their own assets, since the area along the River Cremera, on the border with Veii, was registered in the tribe Fabia and probably owned by the Fabii. They were also protecting their political reputation, since the *fasti* show that they exercised considerable dominance, and one of the consuls in every year between 485 and 479 was a Fabius. Their initiative spectacularly came to grief in 477, when Veii attacked and wiped out most of the Fabii and their army, after which their influence seems to have declined until 467, when a survivor of the battle once again became consul.

During the 460s and 450s Rome was fully occupied with internal dissent and with fending off the Volsci and Aequi, but war with Veii broke out again in 437–435 (Livy 4.16–24). The cause, according to Livy, was the murder of a group of Roman envoys on the orders of Lars Tolumnius, the ruler of Veii. The ensuing battle was famous for a single combat, in which Lars Tolumnius was killed by the Roman Aulus Cornelius Cossus. Cossus was the first man since Romulus to be awarded the *spolia opima*, a special honour given only to men who killed the opposing commander in battle. It involved stripping the fallen general and dedicating his arms and armour in the temple of Jupiter Feretrius on the Capitoline. The linen corselet reputedly dedicated by Cossus was said to be still there in the time of Augustus. In 435 Rome besieged and captured Fidenae and, by doing so, cut off Veii's access to the salt beds at the mouth of the Tiber and also access to the coast. Once again, however, the war ended in a truce, and the conflict with Veii was not resolved until the third and final Veientine war broke out in 406.

On this occasion Rome launched a direct attack on Veii rather than focusing on Fidenae (Livy 4.60–5.18). Veii was relatively isolated, thanks to its position on the southern fringes of Etruria. It received assistance from the nearby cities of Falerii and Capena, possibly because they felt equally threatened by Roman expansion, but there is little sign of support from other Etruscan cities. Tarquinii was friendly to Veii at this time, but, according to Livy, Veii's appeals for help to the Etruscan League were consistently rebuffed. The city was captured after a long siege, during which the Romans performed rituals of *evocatio* and *devotio* – ceremonies designed to undermine a besieged city by calling away its protecting deities (*evocatio*) and consigning the now unprotected city to the gods of the underworld (*devotio*). Much of Livy's account may be literary embellishment, but the outcome – the capture of Veii in 396 – is not in doubt. The Roman general Camillus called on Juno, the chief deity of Veii, to desert it and assist the Romans, promising to build a new temple of Juno at Rome as a reward. After the fall of the city, Camillus made good his promise. The cult statue of Juno Regina was symbolically removed and taken to Rome, to be placed in a temple on the Aventine. The territory of Veii was annexed, and some or possibly all of its inhabitants were enslaved. Veii's allies, Capena and Falerii, were forced to submit to Rome and accept long-term truces in 395–394.

The conclusion of the Veientine war marked an important change for Rome. It had started to expand outside Latium, had taken on a major Etruscan city and won decisively, and was becoming established as a significant power in central Italy. The territory annexed from Veii represented a big enlargement of the territory controlled by Rome, and an enhancement of its economic resources. The suppression of Capena, Fidenae and Falerii opened up control of the Tiber valley, and the removal of Veii left Rome in control of an important trade route between Etruria and Latium. Already towards the end of the fifth century Rome had taken the offensive again in southern Latium. The ports of Antium, Terracina and Circeii were all captured between 408 and 393. Inland, the Aequi were forced back and Roman influence was extended towards the Trerus valley. Rome began to roll back the Aequian and Volscian advances and regain some of the lost territory, paving the way for fourth-century expansion into Campania.

At the beginning of the fourth century this period of progress ended abruptly when Rome suffered one of the most traumatic episodes in its history – the Gallic invasion. Ancient sources attribute the arrival of the Gauls to the actions of Arruns of Clusium, an Etruscan who lured them to Italy with stories of plentiful food, wine and plunder, with a view to using them against his political enemies (Pol. 2.17; Dion. Hal. 13.10–11; Livy 5.33). In fact, as discussed in Chapter 8 (pp. 167–9), Celts (as modern archaeologists tend to describe them) had been migrating across the Alps and settling peacefully in north-west Italy since the sixth century. At some point in the early fourth century, however, a substantial band of them went on the rampage, invading Etruria and central Italy. According to Livy, the Gauls were intent on acquiring land – suggesting that these were landless new arrivals rather than established settlers – and demanded this as a price for stopping their campaign of violence. After defeating several Etruscan cities they homed in on Clusium, which appealed to Rome for help in driving them off.

Livy (5.36–47) presents a dramatic account of the events of 390, in which the Romans were undone by their own arrogance. A mysterious divine voice heard uttering a warning near the temple of Vesta was ignored. The Roman envoys sent to negotiate with the Gauls exacerbated the situation by picking a fight with the Gallic ambassadors and leading an attack on them – a deeply sacrilegious act, since envoys were regarded as being under divine protection. The senate compounded the problem by underestimating the threat posed by the angry Gallic army which was heading towards Rome, and an underprepared Roman force was crushed in battle at a crossing point of the River Allia near Crustumerium. Most of the population withdrew to the Capitoline and barricaded themselves behind the walls of the citadel, although Livy says that some senators elected to stay in their homes and were slaughtered by the Gauls, who arrived within hours of the battle. The city was sacked, but the garrison on the Capitol held out until relief arrived in the form of a Latin army summoned by the exiled Camillus, who had been living at Ardea. The Gauls were driven off and left the area.

Polybios (2.18–22) presents a fundamentally different, but rather more plausible, account in which the Gauls occupied the city, apart from the Capitol, for a period of seven months before making a treaty so that they could return home to deal with an invasion of their own territory by the Veneti, rather than being annihilated by Camillus. That Rome (apart from the Capitoline) was sacked and had to be rebuilt is common to all the accounts, but it is not supported by archaeological evidence. Many of the buildings in the Forum that pre-date the fourth century show no sign of major damage or destruction at this date. There is plenty of corroborating evidence that the events happened, as they are mentioned by Aristotle and other fourth-century Greek writers, but the sack seems to have consisted of making off with portable property, not large-scale destruction of the city's fabric.

Although the effects of the sack may have been overstated, the Gallic invasion left a lasting scar on the collective psyche of the Romans. The anniversary of the battle of the Allia remained one of the blackest and most inauspicious days in the Roman calendar.[6] On a more practical level, the Romans had acquired a healthy respect for the military prowess of the Gauls. It is probably no coincidence that construction started on a new city wall in the 380s (still visible outside Termini station. This is conventionally known as the 'Servian Wall', because ancient sources believed it dated to the reign of Servius Tullius. However, the extant structure was built from tufa quarried at Veii and is unlikely to pre-date the capture of Veii, although it may have followed the course of an earlier, sixth-century, fortification. Even the mere rumour of another invasion from the north was enough to make them call up a strong army. In 225, when there was another threatened invasion, the senate demanded a full census of all available manpower from Rome's Italian allies, and contemplated a full mobilisation of all men of military age. In the end, the threat was averted, but this episode emphasises just how deeply the events of 386 had imprinted themselves on the collective memory of the Romans.

In the aftermath of the Gallic war Rome had to work hard to re-establish control over Latium. The alliance forged by the Cassian treaty had begun to unravel, and although some Latins maintained their alliance with Rome, several, including Circeii, Velitrae, Satricum and Lanuvium, made alliances with the Volscians against Rome. According to Polybios (3.24), Rome's second treaty with Carthage, usually dated to *c.* 348, distinguished between Latins who were subject to Rome and those who were not, suggesting that Roman control of the region was limited. There were wars with Praeneste (382–380) and Tibur (361) and fierce fighting in the area around Velitrae and Satricum (386–376 and 363–346). This turbulence was fuelled by increasing unease over Rome's expansionist intentions in Latium and beyond. Roman aggression became more intense in the early fourth century as it sought ever more overtly to establish domination in the region. In 381 Tusculum was effectively annexed when Roman citizenship was imposed on it, incorporating it into the Roman state, although it continued to exercise limited local self-government. A new treaty was made with the Latins in 358, but this does not seem to have included Tibur and Praeneste, which continued to pursue hostilities against Rome until 354, when they were finally forced to accept treaties with Rome. The fractious relationship between Rome and the Latins can be seen in the refusal of Latin allies to send troops to assist Rome in 349, although Rome seems to have managed reasonably well without them. In Etruria there were wars against Tarquinii (358), Falerii (357) and Caere (353), triggered by Tarquinian raids on Roman territory, which Caere and Falerii seem to have assisted. All were defeated and were forced to sign long-term truces with Rome.

Finally, in 350–349, the Gauls invaded again. The widespread recognition of Roman power can be seen in the reactions of various other peoples in Italy and beyond. The Latins refused to help Rome, and a Greek fleet (possibly from Syracuse) turned up off the coast of Latium to observe events.[7] Rome, as it happened, defeated the Gauls without assistance, and the Greek ships withdrew. However, the incident demonstrates both anxiety about Roman power and a new engagement with it by peoples far beyond central Italy, confirmed by the new treaty with Carthage in 348 (Pol. 3. 24; Diod. 16. 69). By then Rome had bounced back from the problems of the fifth century and was established as a leading power in

Italy, well able to hold its own against Capua, the Etruscan cities or even the Greeks.

Despite the turbulence of the fifth century, at least at the beginning and end of the century, the wars of this period brought many benefits to Rome. Successful wars such as that against Veii brought booty and territory. The treaties with the Latins and the Hernici consolidated Roman power, and the Foedus Cassianum (Cassian treaty) of 493 laid down principles that underpinned Rome's expansion beyond Latium in the fourth century. It was structured so that Rome had a political and military relationship with both the Latins and the Hernici, but it was not a tripartite agreement, and the Latins and the Hernici did not necessarily have any relationship with each other that would have allowed them to combine against Rome. This practice of creating a network of bilateral agreements was central to the way in which Rome dealt with other Italian states. It had the benefit of leaving Rome at the centre of a network of alliances while at the same time denying its allies any communal organisation that could challenge Roman control.

Roman territory had expanded significantly. This new territory posed problems, however. Roman leaders had to work out what to do with it, and how to do it in such a way as not to cause discontent. As discussed in the previous chapter, any hint that land was being monopolised by the patrician aristocracy was politically explosive. Another issue, which arose directly from the Cassian treaty, was how to share out land fairly when the army that took it was composed of men from many different states. Equal division of spoils of joint campaigns was written into the treaty, but while portable property or slaves were relatively easy to distribute in equal portions, land was more problematic.

One method, which may have been controversially included by Spurius Cassius in his land law of 486, was to include Latins and Hernici in his proposed distribution of publicly owned land, but this caused unrest at Rome. A more satisfactory and less contentious method of dealing with conquered territory was to found colonies on it, either by adding Roman and allied settlers to existing communities and declaring them to be colonies or by setting up entirely new communities of Roman and allied colonists. Colonies were a useful method of defending and controlling new territory and settling a permanent Roman (or Roman-friendly) presence there, and a vehicle for distributing confiscated land to Romans and their allies without the political perils associated with more general land redistribution laws. The number of colonial foundations in the fifth and early fourth centuries was high, with a total of fourteen foundations.

Colony	Date	Colony	Date
Fidenae	498	Velitrae	401
Signia	495 and 492	Vitellia	395
Velitrae	494	Circeii	393
Norba	492	Satricum	385
Antium	467	Setia	383
Ardea	442	Sutrium	382
Labici	418	Nepet	382

Table 7: **Roman colonisation, 500–380, as reported in literary sources**

These closely follow the pattern of warfare outlined in this chapter and are clearly linked to Roman strategic concerns. Apart from the strategic site of Fidenae, the foundations of the 490s were mostly in southern Latium and secured the region against the Volscians. A second wave of colonisation in this area marks the re-establishment of Roman control in the late fifth century and in the aftermath of the Gallic invasion.

The effectiveness of colonisation as a means of control was mixed, particularly if a colony included the pre-existing population, much of which may have had no reason to support Rome. Several of the colonies listed above allied with the Volsci against Rome. Colonisation was, however, about much more than defence and had important legal, administrative and cultural implications, which will be discussed in more detail in Chapter 13. Archaeological evidence from an ambitious survey of southern Latium by the University of Groningen illustrates the difficulties of identifying the effects of early colonies. This found that, although there were long-term changes to settlement patterns and land use in the area between the sixth and fourth centuries, they could not be attributed to an identifiable phase of colonisation. If ancient accounts of colonies are accurate, they must have been small in size and did not have an immediate and archaeologically noticeable impact on the region. Other studies suggest that some fourth-century colonies were marked by urban changes in the areas settled, especially the construction of new fortifications and urban layouts, but the impact of colonial settlement seems to be both variable from area to area and, in many cases, not particularly marked. Some scholars, notably

Bradley, argue that even in the fifth and fourth centuries many colonies may have been ad hoc settlements established by Roman condottieri and their war bands rather than organised state initiatives, which may account for some of the difficulties in identifying the processes involved and their impact on the regions settled.

The Roman army during this period was essentially still the citizen militia which had been established in the sixth century. Men fought as and when called up to do so, then returned to their normal occupations. The great hero Cincinnatus, an iconic example of old-fashioned Roman virtue and public service, was famously summoned from his farm work to save the day in 458, and then returned to his labours as soon as the crisis was over. As the many campaigns discussed earlier in the chapter demonstrate, warfare was becoming an annual occurrence, and this posed a problem for Rome. The backbone of the army was the heavy infantry, recruited mainly from the ranks of Rome's small farmers, and this placed a strain on Rome's agricultural economy, as military demands took men away from their farms at precisely the times of year when they were most needed. In addition, the range of operations undertaken, which involved fighting against several enemies in different areas, placed greater demands on manpower. These were by no means as heavy as they later became, but they illustrate a tension between Rome's military and economic needs.

The army usually consisted of men called up for service as the situation required, as decreed by the senate and magistrates, and commanded by senior magistrates. Although some of these displayed a notable aptitude for warfare and gained a reputation as successful generals, there was no specialist class of military commanders, and military experience was gained on the job. By the end of the fifth century, however, the military demands created by wars in Etruria and Latium necessitated some changes to the Roman army. It was probably at this time that the propertied class from which soldiers were drawn under the Servian system was subdivided into several classes. Payment (*stipendium*) for troops while on military service was introduced and was a reflection both of the need to provide financial recompense and of the economic benefits of successful campaigns, which provided enough money to cover this outlay.

The history of the fifth century illustrates the diversity of warfare in early Italy. The struggles with the Volsci and Aequi were a chaotic series of low-level raids. Livy's account of the period tries to shoehorn this into a tidier narrative of coherent campaigns and pitched battles, but in many respects it resembles endemic brigandage rather than regular warfare. The war with Veii, in contrast, placed different demands on the Roman army, requiring it to sustain sieges of Veii and Fidenae, as well as fighting a state with an army based on heavy infantry, much like that of Rome itself. Other episodes reveal a grey area between state and private action. The campaign of the Fabii in 479 was apparently a private initiative using their own clients, tenants and retainers, although not out of line with the wishes of the senate and magistrates. This is consistent with the social structure of the period, and other examples are known from the sixth and early fifth centuries of aristocrats who moved around with bands of armed followers. The Sabine nobleman Attus Clausus, soon to be assimilated and Romanised as Appius Claudius, is said to have been attended by five thousand armed men when he arrived in Rome in 504. By the end of the fifth century, however, use of private forces of this type to pursue wars on behalf of the state was probably the exception rather than the rule. The fact that the Fabii were not particularly successful may have deterred potential imitators, and most of the campaigns discussed above were clearly state-organised.

One thing we lack for this period is any idea of what sort of numbers were involved in annual warfare. The reliability of statistical information in ancient sources on such matters as the size of armies or casualty figures is a matter of much controversy, but even this imperfect information is lacking for the fifth century. Both Polybios and Livy give regular estimates of sizes of armies in their accounts of the third and second centuries, and Livy usually includes a standard rubric for the start of each year, which tells us which commanders were appointed, how many troops they were assigned and where they were permitted to recruit from. For the fifth and fourth centuries, however, this information is not given, so there is little insight into how many men were required to leave their land or other occupations and fight each year. Although warfare at this period was relatively small-scale other than in exceptional circumstances, such as the Gallic invasion, Rome fought many campaigns simultaneously, which would inevitably have increased pressure on resources.

There is no doubt that, although Rome suffered reverses during the fifth century, its resurgence in the last quarter of the century brought significant economic benefits. From 394 Rome began a practice of requiring defeated enemies to pay a war indemnity as well as confiscating part of their territory, but this did not always cover the costs of a campaign, so a new property tax (*tributum*) was introduced at Rome to offset the expense of military action. Rome's aggressive policy towards its Italian neighbours was clearly paying off in terms of territorial gain, but it required significant outlay in both money and manpower, which sometimes created problems in staffing and financing campaigns. Strategically, these wars established Rome as a major player in Italy and beyond, and it was acknowledged by Carthage, one of the pre-eminent powers of the western Mediterranean, as a force to be reckoned with. Polybios lists three treaties between Rome and Carthage, the second of which was signed in 348 and recognised Rome as the dominant city in Latium as well as one with relations and interests beyond the region. The extent to which Roman power was attracting notice beyond Italy is illustrated by the nervousness in the Greek world at the close alliance forged between Rome and Caere in the fifth century. Dionysios I, the ruler of Syracuse, was sufficiently worried by this to try to disrupt it by attacking Caere and sacking the sanctuary at Pyrgi in 384. Despite the difficulties of the fifth century, by 350 Rome's growing power in central Italy had set the scene for its dramatic rise to Italy-wide dominance in the later fourth century.

PART III

THE ROMAN
CONQUEST OF ITALY

11

THE ROAD TO
POWER: ITALY AND
ROME, 390–342

If the fifth century was a period of struggle and recession, the fourth century was a period of recovery, although not without difficulties. Long-standing problems recurred, and the changes triggered by these had far-reaching implications for the ways in which the Roman state operated, and for the fabric of Roman society. There were further changes to the ways in which Republican government operated, and a new social and political elite emerged from the old divisions between patricians and plebeians. By *c.* 350 Rome occupied an increasingly dominant position in central Italy, and the foundations were laid for dramatic expansion in the later fourth century. From 338 onwards, Rome embarked on what proved to be a meteoric rise to Italian dominance.

The social and political conflicts that dominated much of the fifth century resurfaced again in the 380s and 370s. Issues of land, debt and political exclusion rumbled on until 367, when they were partially resolved by a new and far-reaching set of reforms, but the so-called Struggle of the Orders was not finally resolved until 287. Internal divisions may have complicated Rome's response to the Gallic invasion of 390, and the disruption caused by the sack of Rome contributed to the resurgence of social and economic tensions. These are illustrated by a tradition that there was an attempted political coup in 384. Our sources narrate an incident in which Marcus Manlius Capitolinus, who had prevented the Gauls from capturing the Capitol, was accused of aiming to take sole power and establish himself as a tyrant (Livy 6.11–20). Livy names Manlius as the first patrician to champion the cause of the plebeians, gaining mass popularity by supporting agitation for debt relief and even paying some individual debts himself. He was condemned to suffer a traditional form of execution for traitors – by being thrown from the Tarpeian rock, a steep precipice on the edge of the Capitol. His house, which was also located on the Capitol, close to the temple of Juno Moneta, was demolished and the site left vacant thereafter as a reminder of his disgrace.

The authenticity of this episode is highly questionable. Manlius' career is suspiciously similar to those of Spurius Maelius, Spurius Cassius and several other politicians accused of courting popularity with a view to seizing power.[1] The circumstantial details are confused, and Livy misinterprets aspects such as the razing of Manlius' house. The area outside the temple of Juno had to be kept clear because it was the site on which the augurs took the auspices, not because of its association with a disgraced politician. This episode cannot be accepted as Livy narrates it, but it is possible that someone called Manlius was condemned and executed in or around 385, perhaps because he had tried to undermine the state in some way.[2]

Economic revival

Rome was already recovering from its economic difficulties in the last quarter of the fifth century. Successful campaigns in Latium and adjacent areas brought in land and booty, which boosted the state's wealth. This resurgence was rudely interrupted by the Gallic invasion of 390, but this – though traumatic – was a disruption rather than a long-term problem. Rome's successful military expansion, particularly from 350 onwards, involved a significant outlay in manpower and the cost of paying and supplying the army, but it brought increasing benefits in terms of land and booty confiscated from defeated enemies. It is difficult to put an accurate figure on land acquisition before the third century because the territories of defeated communities varied considerably in size, as did the proportion confiscated by Rome, but it was clearly substantial. The conquest of Veii offers some idea of the scale of change. At the time of its sack by Rome in 396, Veii controlled a territory estimated at 562 km^2 (about 217 square miles), of which between 50 and 66 per cent (*c.* 280–370 km^2, or 108–143 square miles) may have been confiscated by Rome. Although Veii was one of Rome's largest neighbours and other victories may not have yielded anything comparable to this amount of land, it gives some idea of the rate at which Rome's territory was growing. The ambitious state building projects of the fourth century (pp. 231–4) demonstrate the increasing wealth of Rome, especially changes to the city's infrastructure, which entailed huge outlay on the water supply and on new fortifications.

Inequalities in the distribution of newly acquired land was already a grievance in the fifth century, but the amount of land involved was relatively small and the issue surfaced only intermittently. In the fourth century, however, it returned with a vengeance as a cause of strife between patricians and plebeians. As the availability of land – and the opportunities for economic advantage that it represented – increased, plebeian demands for a fairer distribution of it became more strident. As for the fifth century, we do not know enough about land ownership in fourth-century Rome to be certain of the nature of the problem, as our sources are inclined to describe it anachronistically, in terms of the issues of the Gracchan period. It seems unlikely that plebeians were legally debarred from holding *ager publicus*, but in practice they may have been unable to compete with the privileged access to newly conquered land enjoyed by patricians and their clients, creating a concentration of property in the hands of a small number of wealthy families and a system of state leases controlled by the wealthiest families and their clients. Livy (6.36.7–37.12) dramatises the issues in an angry debate in which two prominent men, Gaius Licinius Stolo and Lucius Sextius Lateranus, challenged the senators to justify why they should be allowed to occupy large tracts of land when the standard allocation allotted to ordinary Romans during land distributions was a miserly 2 *iugera* (*c.* 0.5 ha or 1.2 acres). The extent of unrest about land distribution is a controversial topic. Redistribution of public land was a very fraught issue in the 130s, and some accounts of fourth-century politics look suspiciously similar to later outbreaks of unrest on this matter. On the other hand, the acquisition of the territory of Veii represented a big increase in Roman territory, and an unfair division would have been controversial.

Land distribution was not the only source of tension in fourth-century Rome. Livy returns on many occasions to debt and debt bondage (*nexum*) as a cause of unrest during this period. Debt crises featured in the insurrection of Manlius, and recurred in 380 and 378, events that Livy connects with the construction of the new city walls (see below, pp. 230–32), a project that may have relied on bonded labour by debtors for its workforce. Some aspects of the debt problems were connected to issues of land ownership. At this date Rome had only a rudimentary monetary economy using *aes rude* (small bronze ingots, issued in standard weights and with official stamps), and many of the debts that led to debt bondage were not monetary loans. They were incurred in the form of loans of equipment or seeds made by comparatively well-resourced patricians to farmers who were operating at subsistence level. The small size of most farms left the majority of the Roman peasantry vulnerable to vagaries of the weather or poor harvests, and if disaster struck, they were operating with very little margin for error. The chances that a small farmer would be unable to repay a loan given in seed plants, livestock or equipment were quite high, particularly if a steep rate of interest and the need to pay off the debt as a single sum are factored in.

Debt resurfaced as a major issue in the events of 367, which led to the passage of the Licinio-Sextian laws, a watershed in the struggle between patricians and plebeians. These laws, discussed in more detail below, represent the first introduction of serious measures to relieve debt. They included provisions for the deduction of interest paid from the sum owed, and repayment of capital in instalments (Livy 6. 35). In 357 interest rates were restricted, and in 352 a commission, whose members included patricians and plebeians, was set up to supervise bankruptcies and introduce a new system of state-organised mortgages. Terms for repayment of loans were further regulated in 347 and 344. In 342 the Lex Genucia (Livy 7. 42. 2) banned lending at interest altogether; however, perhaps unsurprisingly, the law was widely flouted throughout the Republic's duration. Appian records an instance of debt-related civic violence as late as 89. Debt bondage continued to exist until its abolition in 326 under the Lex Poetelia Papiria.

The economic upturn and the benefits of successful wars from *c.* 425 onwards had other effects, especially on the population of Rome, which grew rapidly in the fourth century. Demographic estimates for the ancient world are difficult, given the lack of accurate statistics, and absolute figures are a matter of debate between proponents of high estimates (such as Morley) and those who favour a lower figure (such as Scheidel), but there is a broad consensus that the population of Rome increased rapidly, particularly in the second half of the fourth century. At a conservative estimate, the population in *c.* 350 was something in the region of 30,000 people, and rose to 60,000 by 300. Even this was very large by fourth-century standards and some estimates are significantly higher – possibly up to 190,000 by the early third century, although this seems too large for such an early date. The steep trajectory of this increase was due to two factors: a natural growth in the population and immigration by people eager to take advantage of the opportunities of the growing city. There was a trend for the rural population to move into the city, lured by the employment offered by large-scale construction projects such as the new city walls, or just by the greater economic opportunities offered by urban growth.

An additional factor that contributed to demographic growth was the scope of Rome's wars of conquest, particularly from 340 onwards. Successful wars meant an increase in the number of slaves, as enslavement of captives was a routine by-product of ancient wars. The phase of expansion that began with the conquest of Veii in 396 resulted in a steady supply of slaves and portable wealth, as well as land. From 340 this increased dramatically as Rome's ambitions and territorial interests expanded well beyond central Italy. The economic benefits of this will be discussed in Chapter 13, but for the moment it is worth noting that a major factor in Rome's development between 340 and 264 was the increasing number of slaves, which augmented the size of the population and provided a pool of cheap labour.

The Struggle of the Orders resumed: political reform and social change

The social and economic grievances – debt and land distribution – that jointly fuelled feelings of resentment against the patricians, and periodic outbreaks of civic unrest during the 380s and 370s, came to a head in the period between 376 and 367.[3] Two tribunes, Gaius Licinius Stolo and Lucius Sextius Lateranus, put forward a wide-ranging series of proposals designed to alleviate debt, regulate land distribution and remove some of the remaining political restrictions on plebeians. Livy (6. 34–42) presents this as an epic power struggle lasting the best part of a decade, during which the patricians repeatedly rejected the reforms and the plebeians put up stern resistance, continually re-electing Licinius and Sextius as tribunes, year after year. They, for their part, used their tribunician right of veto to prevent the election of other magistrates, and went on re-introducing their proposed reforms. The impasse was resolved in 367 by the appointment of a dictator, the veteran general and statesman Marcus Furius Camillus. He was able to broker a settlement, although not without fierce resistance and the threat of another secession of the plebeians, and the legislation was eventually passed. The reality is likely to have been of shorter duration. It is highly improbable that the tribunes could have waged a ten-year campaign or held up public business for that length of time, and the five years (375–371), known as 'the anarchy', in which elections were disrupted is likely to have been a later insertion into the *Fasti Capitolini*. Diodorus' statement that the crisis lasted only one year is far more plausible, and although patrician resistance was strong, the unrest is very unlikely to have lasted for the ten years implied by Livy.

The Licinio-Sextian laws were a defining moment in the Struggle of the Orders. They were a far-reaching package of reforms that addressed several social, economic and political grievances. The first law, on debt, proposed that interest paid should be deducted from the capital sum owed. The remaining sum was to be divided into equal instalments, to be repaid over three years rather than as a single lump sum. Debtors could no longer be trapped into endless repayments by an ever-spiralling debt, and were able to repay in instalments rather than being enslaved if they did not pay the debt outright. Although the institution of *nexum* remained, there was now a legal framework for regulating the behaviour of creditors and mitigating the effects of debt.

The second law addressed long-term grievances over *ager publicus*. It established maximum limits for the amount that could be leased and farmed by a single individual, which were set at 500 *iugera* (c. 133 ha, or 328 acres). All sources agree on this basic provision, but the Greek historian Appian includes two further clauses – that individuals pasturing animals on *ager publicus* should be limited to grazing a maximum of 100 cattle or 500 smaller animals, and that farmers of *ager publicus* should not be permitted to work the land solely by slave labour but must employ a certain proportion of free labourers. Unlike the land laws of the second century, the Licinio-Sextian legislation merely fined over-occupiers rather than forcing them to surrender their surplus land.

The terms of this law are difficult to accept, and debates on its meaning and significance have been ongoing since the nineteenth century, if not earlier. As presented by our sources, the Licinio-Sextian land law is suspiciously similar to Tiberius Gracchus' land law of 133. The close parallels between the two even raise the possibility that it was entirely a second-century invention to provide a historical precedent for Gracchus' proposed reforms, as the upper limit of 500 *iugera* is more in line with the size of landholdings in the second century.

However, the existence of a pre-Gracchan law is confirmed by a fragment of a speech by Cato in 167, in which he refers to such a law, and Livy (10.13.14) refers to prosecutions for infringements of a land law in 298, so it seems probable that there was a fourth-century agrarian law that limited the size of allocations of *ager publicus*. The two key issues are whether the 500 *iugera* upper limit is plausible for the fourth century, and whether the restrictions applied only to *ager publicus* or extended to private land as well. Some scholars, notably Cornell and (most recently) John Rich, have defended the view that the 500 *iugera* limit is accurate, and plausible within the context of the fourth century.[4] Rich, however, suggests that the upper limit applied to all land, private as well as public, limiting total individual landholdings to 500 *iugera*. If this is correct, the Licinio-Sextian land law was not just (or even primarily) a socio-economic measure: it was also a sumptuary law which restricted undue concentrations of wealth.

The final law focused on the political representation of the plebeians rather than economic problems. It abolished the office of consular tribune, which had alternated with the consulship as chief magistracy for much of the previous half century, and replaced the tribunes with two annually elected consuls, one of whom had to be a plebeian. A new office of praetor was instituted, which ranked below the consuls but above the other magistrates, and which mainly involved legal and judicial duties. Two further aediles were added to the magistracy, known as curule aediles to distinguish them from the existing plebeian aediles, bringing the total number of aediles up to four. One of the important colleges of priests, the *duoviri* (or *duumviri*) *sacris faciundis* (Board of Two in charge of sacred rituals), was reformed, to expand it and open up the membership. It became a ten-member college of *decemviri sacris faciundis* (Board of Ten in charge of sacred rituals), composed of five patricians and five plebeians. Lucius Sextius Lateranus himself stood for election to the consulship and became the first plebeian consul in 366.

The ostensible purpose of this law was to establish a framework for a more equitable division of power and public office between the two orders. Plebeians gained access to the consulship and one of the main religious colleges on equal terms with patricians, while patricians were eligible for the office of aedile. However, many details are unclear. Livy is vague about whether the law stated that plebeians were permitted to become consul, or stipulated that one of the consuls must be a plebeian. If the latter, then it must have proved difficult to enforce, as there are at least six years in the period 355–43 in which both consuls were patricians. The strong resemblance between the terms of the Licinio-Sextian laws and those of the Lex Genucia of 342 has led some historians to question the reliability of Livy's account of the laws of 367. It is possible that Livy had confused plebeian access to the consulship with a compulsion to elect a plebeian, but it is also possible – and perhaps more likely – that plebeians found it more difficult to get elected in practice, even after they had won the legal right to stand for the highest office. Consuls were elected by the *comitia centuriata*, in which voters were organised by economic class, and which might have been better disposed towards wealthy and established patrician candidates than to plebeians, who would have been less well established politically.

Like the Valerio-Horatian reforms in 449, the Licinio-Sextian laws were a major turning point in the Struggle of the Orders. Although Livy's account of the passage of the laws and some of their details cannot be accepted as historical, it seems to contain a kernel of historical fact. As with the earlier legislation, they addressed socio-economic grievances in combination with political reforms that mainly benefited the leaders of the plebeian order. This may not be entirely coincidental. By 367 the plebeian organisation within the state, based around the plebeian cults of the Aventine and the political offices of *tribunus plebis* and plebeian aedile, had been established for some time. Ambitious plebeian leaders had emerged – such as Licinius and Sextius themselves – whose influence was restricted by lack of access to the higher magistracies and who were well placed to benefit from reforms that opened these up. It seems likely that there was a widening gap between the wealth and ambitions of the leading plebeians and those of the rest of the Roman people. For the mass of Romans, however, debt and economic exclusion were much more pressing issues. By combining political and economic reform into a single package, Licinius and Sextius were able to harness mass support for their proposed laws. As a consequence, the significance of the divisions between patricians and plebeians was progressively eroded, and over the course of the later fourth century a new nobility emerged.

The nature of the so-called Struggle of the Orders remains elusive, as do the very definitions of 'patrician' and 'plebeian'. Undoubtedly the ancient sources tried to impose a degree of coherence on disparate and confusing events. In doing so, they sometimes created connections between issues and events that may have been quite separate, as well as fitting over a hundred years of highly complex history into an implausibly neat framework. The relative importance of certain issues changed over time, and it is likely that the political and social divisions between patricians and plebeians hardened between 449 and 367, as competition between them intensified. Nevertheless, we can draw a number of conclusions. One is that the economic issues of debt and fair distribution of land were serious long-term problems that resurfaced many times during the fifth and fourth centuries. Whether the plebeians were the subject of formal legal discrimination (for instance, being ineligible to lease public land) is uncertain, but even if this were not the case, their economic difficulties were exacerbated by social inequalities and the dominance of a small elite. Political concerns were intertwined with these issues throughout, particularly after 449. As plebeians gained limited political rights, ambitious members of the order sought to build on these to gain full access to political power and influence. Eventually, as the significance of the difference between plebeians and patricians was eroded, a new, unified nobility based on holding of high office began to emerge.

The development of Republican government and the emergence of a new elite

The general trend between 367 and 342 was one of gradual erosion of the divisions between patricians and plebeians, and the establishment of a more complex structure of government. The consulship, held by two men per year, was now definitively established as the most senior executive power in Rome, and there were a number of more junior magistracies, such as the quaestorship and aedileship. The exception to the process of assimilation of patricians and plebeians was the office of *tribunus plebis*. This continued to be reserved for men of plebeian family and remained an important element in Roman political life because of its unique powers. The extraordinary powers of the tribunes, which included the right to convene the *comitia tributa*, propose and veto legislation, and intervene to protect other citizens from magistrates, gave them a high degree of influence. This was perhaps less evident after 367, but tribunes remained influential throughout the Republic, and played a central role in the turbulent politics of the period 133–50.

The admission of plebeians to the consulship in 367 undermined the separation of plebeian and patrician offices. From this point onwards we can trace the emergence of a new nobility based on holding of public office and the power and status that came with it, rather than on hereditary distinctions. This was not a smooth process, and the results were not a foregone conclusion. Initially, access to power was not widened by the Licinio-Sextian laws, but simply restricted in a new way. It became commonplace for some men to hold the consulship many times, sometimes in association with the same colleague. For example, there are seven instances of men who held the consulship twice in the twenty-five years between 367 and 342, three who were elected to it three times and two who held it four times. The most dominant was Gaius Sulpicius Peticus, who was consul five times between 364 and 351. This high degree of duplication, by both patricians and plebeians, demonstrates that access to the highest magistracy was still limited, but control was now exercised by political groupings and alliances drawn from both patricians and plebeians rather than from one order only. The fact that many men who held office more than once did so with the same colleague (for instance, Genucius and Servilius in 365 and 352, and Publilius Philo and Papirius Cursor in 320 and 315) reveals the potential for co-operation between individual patricians and plebeians, with the same men repeatedly standing as joint candidates.

Although the first plebeian consul, Lucius Sextius, held office in 366, the following years were dominated by uneven distribution of the consulship. In the years between 367 and 342 there were at least six years in which both consuls were patrician, flouting the spirit (and possibly also the letter) of the law. The list of plebeian consuls (eighteen in all) shows a very narrow group of men holding office several times, notably Marcus Popilius Laenas and Gaius Marcius Rutilius, who amassed seven consulships between them, possibly owing to a need for magistrates with proven military experience during a time when Rome was under pressure from the Gauls, as Forsythe has suggested. Livy, however, suggests that die-hard patricians attempted to reassert their supremacy during the 360s and 350s. Election of plebeians was disrupted, as in 357, when an interregnum was used to postpone elections (Livy 7.17.12). Set-backs such as a military defeat in 362 (Livy 7.6.5–6), or an apparent increase in bribery and corruption necessitating legistation in 358 (Livy 7.16.5) were blamed on the election of plebeian magistrates.

Another possible explanation of these developments is that for a period of twenty years or so new political alliances developed between a group of patrician families and some of the newly influential plebeians. This 'centre party' (as Cornell and others have termed it) had the effect of marginalising other established patrician families, such as the Menenii, Cloelii and Horatii, all famous names of the fifth century. Members of these families rarely hold office after 367, and the family names largely disappear from the *fasti*. Instead, the lists of consuls are dominated by a small group of patricians, the most prominent of whom are Marcus Fabius Ambustus, Gaius Sulpicius Peticus, Quintus Servilius Ahala and Lucius Aemilius Mamercinus, along with their plebeian allies. Many of the plebeians who held office during this period had already held plebeian-only offices such as the tribunate, and had established social connections with patricians. Livy's account of the Licinio-Sextian proposals presents just such a scenario. In his version of events Licinius' reforming zeal had its roots in a family dispute between his wife, a daughter of the patrician Fabius Ambustus, and her sister, who was married to the patrician Sulpicius Peticus and attempted to assert her social superiority on this account. The bad feeling within the family eventually convinced Licinius to lead a campaign for reform and further plebeian rights. Although this is unlikely to have been the motive for the reforms, it makes an interesting point: a network of contacts and family relationships between patrician and plebeian families was developing, which was bringing some members of the two groups closer together. It also demonstrates that a plebeian leadership was emerging that had enough wealth, and social or political contacts, to take advantage of this situation.

This dominance by a smallish group of individuals caused enough resentment to trigger further legislation. Laws regulating electioneering were passed in 358 (Lex Poetelia, not to be confused with the debt laws of the same name passed in 326), and in 342 a Lex Genucia was passed following a period of civic unrest.[5] The Lex Genucia tidied up some of the loose ends left by Licinius and Sextius. It returned to the debt problem and banned interest on loans outright, but most of its content was political, although there is some uncertainty about its content. In future nobody should hold more than one magistracy in the same year, and nobody could hold the same office again within ten years. The aim was apparently to prevent domination by small groups, and – in imposing a ten-year gap between consulships – to stop individuals gaining undue power. It also opened up the consulship to a wider pool of candidates. Since there were only two consuls per year, domination by a relatively small group of candidates repeatedly elected at frequent intervals limited the prospects of advancement for their peers. This is an important point, because the new unified nobility that eventually emerged was intensely competitive. The accumulation of honours and achievements, such as successful election to political office, successful military campaigns and nomination to important priesthoods became essential to establishing and maintaining social and family status, so monopolisation of the most senior magistracy by a small clique was a source of discontent.

The main difficulty lies with another clause, which stated that it was permissible for both consuls to be plebeians. This has caused much debate, and the meaning is unclear, particularly when compared with the pattern of office-holding recorded by the *fasti* between 367 and 342. As Cornell has pointed out, there are several years in this period when both consuls were patrician, despite the eligibility of plebeians having been established in 367, but from 342 at least one consul was always plebeian. The Lex Genucia may have made it obligatory for one of the two consuls to be a plebeian, reinforcing the Licinio-Sextian reforms. Livy's confusion seems to arise from the events of 173, when two plebeians were elected for the first time, and it was realised that the Lex Genucia had created a loophole allowing this to happen.

Not all the changes sought by plebeians were political in the narrow sense of demanding access to office and to the political process. Many senior priesthoods were still reserved exclusively for patricians. Reserving these for patricians prevented ambitious plebeians from holding a group of public offices that were highly prestigious and influential. This was not, however, just a matter of prestige and political advancement. The priesthoods had great symbolic value, since a claim to have a divine authority and responsibility for the religious life of the state was a key element in patrician claims to their special status. Some inroads had already been made into this when the *decemviri sacris faciundis* was opened up to equal numbers of patricians and plebeians, but a bigger step forward was made in 300. The Lex Ogulnia, passed in this year, opened up the two other major priestly colleges, the pontifices and the augurs, to both orders. Since all priests held office for life, once appointed, this was done by increasing the number of pontifices from four to eight and the number of augurs from four to nine, with the new posts in each case being filled by plebeians. When a member died, he had to be replaced by someone from the same order, thus maintaining a balanced membership. Some priesthoods did continue to be restricted to patricians, such as the Salii (priests of Mars), but these were fairly minor, and some specified posts within the college of pontifices were restricted, such as the *rex sacrorum* and *flamen Dialis* (priest of Jupiter). From 300 onwards, however, the most important and influential religious offices were open equally to both orders. Although the final emergence of a unified nobility did not take place until the third century, the Struggle of the Orders was almost at an end.

Rebuilding and continuity: Rome after the Gauls

The Gallic sack of 390 is often described as a watershed in the urban development of Rome. Ancient writers – and especially Livy – believed that the Gauls demolished the city completely, firing buildings after the Romans had retreated to the inner defences on the Capitoline. Livy presents a lengthy and dramatic debate in which the Romans – faced with rebuilding the city – discussed whether to leave the original location of Rome and re-found it on the more defensible site previously occupied by Veii, but rejected the proposal out of loyalty to their ancestral cult places. He directly attributes the unplanned layout of Rome to the enthusiastic speed with which it was rebuilt after the Gallic sack:

> The law [proposing a move to Veii] having been rejected, the rebuilding of the city commenced in several areas simultaneously. Tiles were supplied at public expense. The privilege of hewing stone and felling timber wherever each person wished was granted, security being taken that they would finish the buildings on that year. Their haste diverted

all attention from regulating the course of the streets, while, setting aside all distinction of property, they built on any part that was vacant. That is why the ancient sewers, at first conducted through the public streets, now pass under private houses in many places, and why the form of the city appears more like one taken up by individuals, than regularly allotted [by commissioners].

(Livy 5.55)

This picture is becoming increasingly untenable, as evidence emerges that most of the key buildings in the Forum/Palatine area pre-date the Gallic invasion and show little or no evidence of destruction in the early fourth century.

Livy was undeniably right on one point: Rome developed in a haphazard manner, in contrast to the regular, planned, layouts of the great cities of southern Italy and parts of Etruria, or even of its own colonies. It never acquired the regular street grid and well-defined areas of public space that we tend to associate with the 'typical' Roman city (although these are, in fact, mainly typical of colonies, and even the typicality of colonies is starting to look questionable). Where he was wrong was in attributing this to the over-enthusiastic rapidity of reconstruction after the Gallic invasion. It was partly a consequence of the local topography, with its hills and marshy, low-lying areas, which did not lend itself to the development of a regular orthogonal plan of the sort found at Paestum or Marzabotto. (Compare fig. 18, which shows a regular orthogonal city, with figs 23 and 24, which show Rome.) The organic growth of the community over a long period of time and the Roman veneration for locations and structures associated with the foundation and early history of the city further limited what could be done to regularise the city's layout. Once these locations and buildings were established, they could not be moved without divine permission and disruption to the Romans' own cultural memories. Livy presents this loyalty to ancestral cult places as the clinching argument in the decision to stay put rather than moving Rome to a more defensible position on the far side of the Tiber.

Although the pressing necessity for rebuilding in the 380s seems to be a myth, the fourth century was a period of rapid urban development. One of the most important developments, which was prompted by the growing population and the defensive needs highlighted by the Gallic invasion, was the construction of a massive new city wall. This immense

T. of Juno
Moneta

Quirinal

Campus
Martius

City wall

Curia

T. of
Apollo

T. of
Jupiter

Volcanal
& Rostra

Forum
Romanum

Regia

Capitol

T. of
Saturn

T. of
Castor

T. of Vesta
& House of
Vestals

T. of Fortuna
& Mater Matuta

Forum
Boarium

Palatine

P
o
r
t

Lupercal

'Hut of
Romulus'

Altar and T. of
Hercules Invictus

T. of
Ceres

Circus
Maximus

Aventine

*Fig. 24 Rome: plan of
the Forum, Palatine
and Forum Boarium in
the fourth century BC.*

and impressive work was 11 km (6.5 miles) in length and enclosed a total
area of *c.* 427 ha (1,055 acres).[6] By way of comparison, the urban area of
Veii, one of the largest Etruscan cities, was *c.* 194 ha (480 acres), and that
of the Greek city of Tarentum – probably the largest in Italy at this date
– is estimated at 510 ha (1,260 acres), only a little larger than Rome. Two
surviving stretches of the wall, one near Termini station and the other on
the Aventine, show that it was 4 m thick and at least 10 m high (about 13
× 32 feet). Unlike some of the early fortifications on the Palatine, it was
a stone wall, constructed of squared blocks of tufa from the quarries at
Grotta Oscura in the territory of Veii, some 12 km (7 miles) north of Rome.
Some estimates suggest that the project required the quarrying, working
and transportation of several million stone blocks. Greek letters incised
on the stone as masons' marks suggest that Greek craftsmen may have been
hired for the project, though masons' marks of this type are notoriously

difficult to interpret and the presence of Greek masons remains conjectural. According to Livy, it was begun in 378, a date that is consistent with the source of the stone used, and not completed until some time after 353, a time span that reflects the huge nature of the undertaking. A structure of this magnitude represents a major financial investment by the state and was a mark of Rome's ambitions as a city. Fortifications were not just utilitarian structures to provide protection. A wall that surrounded an entire city was the first and most highly visible structure a visitor would see on approaching the settlement. A substantial stone wall built using the latest Greek techniques did not just send out message a that this was a well-defended city but also demonstrated that it had the economic resources to invest in such a project and that it regarded itself as the equal of important states such as Tarentum, Croton or Caere. It was a statement of cultural and political confidence, demonstrating that Rome had arrived as a major player in central Italy.

Other developments bear out this impression of a city regaining its confidence and enjoying renewed prosperity. Between 400 and 375 Rome acquired at least six new temples. Four of these – the temples of Juno Regina (Aventine), Concordia (Forum Romanum), Fortuna (Forum Boarium) and Mater Matuta (also in the Forum Boarium) – are attributed to Marcus Furius Camillus, the heroic leader of the resistance to the Gauls. The others are a temple of Juno Lucina on the Cispian hill (dating to 375) and a temple of Mars built just outside the Porta Capena in 388. Some of these are known mainly from ancient sources and have left little or no archaeological trace. The site of the temple of Juno Regina has not been identified, and although the temple of Mars is believed to have stood on the left side of the Via Appia, around a mile outside the Capena Gate, the structure itself has not survived. Others have left some trace, although they are not without controversy. The temple of Concord as it survives today dates to 121, but the platform on which it was built contained stone fragments of a fourth-century building which may be the remains of the temple dedicated by Camillus, although the identification is disputed. A new temple of Apollo Medicus was constructed in 353 in the Campus Martius, replacing the building dedicated in 431. The temples of Mater Matuta and Fortuna are more securely identified, but their dating is problematic. At some point a massive new tufa platform was constructed at the archaic sanctuary of S. Omobono on which new temples were constructed, which Coarelli and Torelli associate with ancient accounts (Livy 5.19.6

and 5.23.7; Plut., *Cam.* 5) of a restoration of the temples by Camillus in the early fourth century. Recent fieldwork and studies of archival material from earlier excavations have thrown new light on the complex chronology of this sanctuary, suggesting that this podium may have developed in several phases, the earliest of which may be significantly earlier than the fourth century, possibly as early as the late sixth century.

The choice of cults and the locations of these building projects are significant. The temple of Concordia had important political connection, as the dedication is said to have been performed in 367 to mark the passage of the Licinio-Sextian laws. This dedication to a cult of concord was a symbol of reconciliation between the warring patricians and plebeians. Most temples were commissioned by victorious generals and paid for out of booty, as a thank-offering for victory. The upsurge in temple-building in the first quarter of the fourth century is not so much a response to damage by the Gauls as a reflection of Roman military success and in particular, the conquest of Veii. There was a perceptible shift in the way in which temples were vowed and built during the fourth century. Before 396 most temples were communal dedications, built by the state, but by 325 individual dedications (mostly by victorious generals) were becoming more frequent. This process, and the very direct and literal connection between war and religion, are neatly illustrated by the temple of Juno Regina. The cult of Juno Regina was the main civic cult of Veii, and after the fall of the city the Romans removed the cult statue from Veii to Rome and installed it in the new temple on the Aventine, vowed as a gift to Juno by Marcus Furius Camillus, the victorious general. In so doing, they had symbolically persuaded the goddess to abandon Veii and take up residence in Rome.

The practice of dedicating spoils, or monuments paid for from their proceeds, gathered pace in the second half of the fourth century. L. Papirius Cursor distributed captured Samnite arms to be displayed in the Forum in 310 (Livy 9.1.4.15–16), and two thousand bronze statues from Volsinii were displayed in the sanctuary of Mater Matuta in 264. Most spectacularly, a massive statue of Hercules was dedicated on the Capitoline in 305, paid for out of the spoils of the Samnite wars (Livy 9.44.15–16; Pliny, *NH* 34.43). Ziolkowski's catalogue of mid-Republican temples lists four that were vowed by generals from the booty captured by them. The centre of Rome was becoming increasingly monumentalised not just in terms of buildings, but also in statues and other civic monuments generated by the wars of conquest.

The Forum shows little sign of destruction caused by marauding Gauls, and the Regia, Comitium and Temple of Castor were unscathed, as were structures on the Capitoline. There were, however, some major developments that are unrelated to the events of 390. The Comitium was enlarged and refurbished as a circular structure with stepped seating, possibly by Gaius Maenius (consul in 338), who added the speaker's platform (Rostra) in front of it, which was used by speakers addressing the Roman people.

The Comitium was important as a symbol of the Roman state, and its rebuilding and monumentalisation at a time of political change, characterised by the emergence of a new nobility and Rome's increasing importance in Italy, were highly symbolic. Its new form was closely based on that of a Greek Ekklesiasterion, reflecting growing Greek influence on the culture of Rome. During the Samnite wars the Romans sent an embassy to Delphi, and the oracle instructed them to set up statues of the wisest and bravest of the Greeks. Accordingly, statues of Pythagoras and Alcibiades were commissioned and placed in the Comitium, reinforcing the Hellenisation of a key Roman building. The Rostra commemorated Maenius' defeat of the powerful Volscian city of Antium, a noted naval power until this point, after which Rome confiscated its fleet. The platform was constructed out of the prows (*rostra* in Latin) of Antiate ships seized by Rome and paid for out of Maenius' share of the booty. Just to underline the personal achievement, Maenius set up a victory monument in the form of a column close to the Rostra. The use of captured ships as part of the structure turned the Rostra into a striking statement of Rome's growing dominance and ambition in Italy, as well as the changing nature of Roman politics and the greater importance of engagement with the people.

The Comitium may cast some light on the complex problem of how Roman political life worked in practice. It was used for meetings of the *comitia tributa*, the assembly of the people that was responsible for passing laws,[7] and its rebuilding reflects the growing importance of the popular assemblies in the political life of Rome. However, the size (40 × 40 m, or *c.* 130 × 130 feet) is estimated to have a maximum capacity of between 3,000 and 4,000 people, which was nowhere near enough to accommodate the male Roman citizens who were entitled to attend meetings. During the second century the Rostra was symbolically turned around, allowing the speaker to address people assembled in the Forum, but before this date meetings of the *comitia tributa* were restricted to those who could turn up on the appointed day and fit into the Comitium. This suggests that, despite the role of the *comitia tributa* as the body that expressed the will of the Roman people, the number who could realistically participate in law-making was in fact only a small fraction of those eligible to do so – possibly even limited (as Jehne has suggested) to those living in the areas of the city closest to the Comitium. Nevertheless, the Comitium and the adjacent *curia*, where the senate met, had great symbolic significance as embodiments of the key elements of the *res publica*.

Much less is known about domestic architecture in Rome in the fourth century. The sixth-century houses on the north side of the Palatine remained in use throughout the fourth and third centuries. Carandini reconstructs these as prototypes of the atrium house, the most typical form of later Roman houses, but this is based on very fragmentary evidence, and many scholars, such as Wiseman, have rejected it as too speculative. The most complete house seems to have rows of rooms opening off a courtyard, but to label this as an early atrium house is pushing the evidence too far, and it may well be a courtyard house of the type found in contemporary Etruria and Latium rather than a true atrium house.

The typical atrium house consisted of a narrow entrance vestibule leading to a large central atrium with a central pool (*impluvium*) to collect water from an opening in the centre of the roof. The atrium was lined with small rooms; a *tablinum*, or office, opened off the back of it, and there were further reception rooms and dining rooms and possibly a courtyard with a garden at the rear of the house. Roman aristocratic houses were public venues as well as private residences, and the form of the atrium house was closely connected with power and social rituals. The atrium provided space in which clients or dependants and petitioners could wait during the morning *salutatio*, while the master of the house conducted his business in the *tablinum*, and more favoured visitors could be entertained in more private spaces such as the dining rooms (*triclinia*) or the garden/peristyle area. The early development of the atrium house is, however, unclear. The covered atrium with a central *impluvium* is described by the Roman architect Vitruvius as the defining characteristic of the Roman house, but some fifth- century examples have been found at Marzabotto, suggesting that Etruscan practices had influenced Roman domestic architecture. Conversely, some of the earliest houses at Pompeii and Cosa were not atrium houses but so-called 'row houses', consisting of rows of rooms arranged around an open courtyard, and some of the atria of Pompeian houses may have started out as open courtyards which were later covered over. Some aspects of the 'row house' are similar to the seventh- and sixth-century houses found at sites such as Satricum (pp. 62–3), but there are also similarities to Greek houses, which were built around a courtyard, often with a covered colonnade or peristyle. It seems likely that the atrium house developed in the fourth and third centuries as an elaboration of the courtyard/row house, and that exposure to Greek cultural influences and new Greek ideas about urbanism at this time was a contributory factor to the evolution of Roman domestic architecture.

Houses were central to the social status and public lives of Roman aristocrats, and possession of a house in the very centre of Rome seems to have been important. Prestige was derived from owning a house on the Palatine, on the Capitoline or close to the Forum. The Cornelii Scipiones, Fabii and Maenii all owned houses close to the Forum, the Appii Claudii lived on the edge of the Campus Martius, and the Claudii Centumali owned a house on the Caelian, and the value of such a location is demonstrated by the fact that aristocratic families seem to have rebuilt houses on the same site rather than moving elsewhere when houses needed enlarging or refurbishing. Proximity to the centre of public life in Rome meant that these families were always in the public eye. Senatorial houses were crucial to social status and to the ability to perform social obligations to clients and friends, but this close identification between senators and their houses could have uncomfortable consequences. Houses of iconic figures such as Valerius Poplicola were preserved as monuments, but there are examples of destruction of houses of men who incurred public wrath, such as Manlius Capitolinus or Vitruvius Vaccus, an aristocrat from Privernum whose Roman house was demolished when he led a revolt against Rome.

Atrium houses or courtyard houses, which accommodated an entire household, including slaves and sometimes an extended family, were the preserve of the well-off. Most Romans would have lived very differently, in much more cramped accommodation. In later periods most Romans lived in multi-storey *insulae*, which covered an entire block and were subdivided into apartments. No fourth-century houses or *insulae* have survived, but the population of Rome was expanding in the fourth century, and, given the pressure on space and the urban density of the city, it is likely that the living conditions of ordinary families were cramped.

The population of Rome continued to expand, and this created the need for improved infrastructure. Water supply was a major issue for a city of this size, and in 312 the censor of that year, Appius Claudius Caecus, instituted an ambitious programme of public works. The most famous of these is the eponymous Via Appia, the first of the great Roman roads, and the initial stretch of this, linking Rome with Capua, was begun in 312. No less significant, however, was his decision to build the first public aqueduct, with a capacity of *c.* 73,000 m³ (over 1.6 million gallons) per day, to bring water into the city. This is modest compared with the capacity of later aqueducts, but the need for it illustrates Rome's growth in this period. The harbour area below the Aventine, known as the Portus Tiberinus, was developed to provide greater capacity for water-borne transport. The area had undergone substantial development under the Tarquins, but little during the fifth century. In the fourth, however, the wharfside areas were expanded and the three temples of Fortuna, Mater Matuta and Portunus were rebuilt, as outlined above.

Visitors to Rome at the end of the fourth century would have found a different city from the one such a visitor would have encountered a hundred years earlier. Rome had grown and was continuing to grow rapidly, with flourishing craft production and a thriving economy. Impressive public amenities such as aqueducts had started to appear. New temples had been built and old ones refurbished or replaced. Anyone entering the city along the newly constructed Via Appia would have passed several such temples, all of them an indirect testimony to Roman military prowess as they were built with the proceeds of conquest. He or she would also have been confronted by Rome's massive new city wall, which embodied both serious defence capability and an assertion of the strength and self-confidence of the city. An arrival by river would have been no less impressive. Visitors landed at the newly refurbished port and passed the three new temples dedicated by Camillus. The Forum remained an open and undefined area accommodating buildings of various dates – some of great age, such as the Regia, and others which had changed to reflect the new political realities ushered in by the final phase of the Struggle of the Orders – while the grand houses of the Palatine still made a big statement about the wealth and power of the Roman aristocracy. Styles of architecture had not yet changed radically, but Greek influence on architectural forms and styles, and on construction techniques, was becoming more prominent. Rome in the fourth century was a city in transition, but in contrast to the difficulties of the fifth century it was very much a city on an upward trajectory.

12

'WHETHER SAMNITE OR ROMAN SHALL RULE ITALY': THE SAMNITE WARS AND THE CONQUEST OF ITALY

B etween 343 and 272 Rome fought a series of wars against the Samnites, Etruscans and Greeks, during which it conquered most of peninsular Italy, enjoying a spectacular rise from regional dominance in Latium to the status of an international power. Livy, our main source for this, presents it as conflict between two rapidly expanding powers and a defining moment in Italian history, portraying a Roman envoy as saying:

> Romans, our quarrels will not be decided by the words of envoys or the arbitration of any man, but by Mars, on the Campanian plain on which we will meet, and by arms and common strife. Then let us draw up camp against camp, between Capua and Suessula, and decide whether Samnite or Roman will rule Italy.

> (Livy 8.23.10)

Clearly this was written with a large helping of hindsight, and a lot of simplification to make the confusing events of the fourth century fit his own vision of history, in which the Romans prevailed thanks to their strength of character. There are many unknowns about what caused the conflict and how it proceeded, and Livy's shaky grasp of the geography of Italy means that his narrative of military operations is frequently very confusing. The struggle was not in fact a single event, but a series of wars spread over a period of fifty years. The earliest skirmishes – conventionally termed the first Samnite war – were a localised conflict in Campania and do not fit Livy's vision of a war for regional dominance. The second and third Samnite wars, in contrast, developed into a mighty struggle for supremacy in Apennine and southern Italy. To complicate matters further, the Samnite wars were not the only conflicts in which Rome was engaged. There was a conflict with the Latins which in some ways had even wider consequences for Roman history, and many campaigns in Etruria and Umbria. Finally, in 281–272, there was a war in southern Italy that posed a serious threat to Rome but which ultimately secured Roman control of the peninsula.

Italy beyond Rome in the fourth century:
social change and urban development

The general trends observable at Rome, such as the breaking down of an old, closed elite based on membership of a particular group of families and the emergence of new leading families, the changing patterns of property ownership and economic activity, and urban growth, can be traced in most regions of Italy. Although the fourth century was a period of economic recovery, from *c.* 350 onwards it was characterised by stress and instability, with wars between Greeks and Oscans, further Gallic invasions and, finally, the Roman conquest.

Existing cities grew larger, and new ones formed in areas that were not yet fully urbanised, such as south-east Italy. Their territories were more densely populated and more intensively farmed, and settlements show a greater level of organisation. Cities invested more heavily in urban infrastructure, in part to address practical matters – adequate water supplies, good defences and upkeep of roads and streets – but public building was not just driven by pragmatic needs. In a competitive world, cities needed to demonstrate their status by investing in eye-catching architecture and public amenities. The Greek city of Metapontum, for example, was radically rebuilt in the fourth century, with new fortifications, an extension and reorganisation of the street plan and the rebuilding of the agora, and other Greek cities, including Locri, Croton and Velia, underwent similar changes.

This trend was not confined to Greek cities, and many of the indigenous communities of south-east Italy also invested heavily in public building projects, as well as adopting aspects of Greek building types and architectural styles. Monte Sannace, in central Puglia, looks very different from a Greek city, but clearly had urban ambitions. The fortifications were substantially extended, the street plan was reorganised and large and elaborate houses were built. Elsewhere, in contrast, there are signs of stress, and many regions show mixed fortunes. Capua and Tarentum became bywords for wealth and luxury, but some Greek cities struggled to fend off threats from Syracuse and from their Italian neighbours. Northern Etruria continued to do well, but the great cities of southern Etruria – Caere, Veii, Tarquinii and Vulci – suffered from the breakdown of Etruscan power in Campania, the disruption of their trading connections with the Greek world and the expansion of Roman power.

As at Rome, there was a trend – already established in the fifth century – towards the emergence of new elites, which were less exclusive than those of the seventh and sixth centuries, and monarchy was replaced with rule by elected officials such as the Etruscan *zilath* or Oscan *meddix*. Nevertheless, these elites continued to exercise a strong grip on power. Inscriptions from Etruria show that the wealthier burials and the positions of influence were dominated by people from a relatively small number of families, such as the Cilnii at Arretium, the Caecinae at Volaterrae and the Spurinnae at Tarquinii. The epigraphic evidence is less plentiful for other areas of Italy but points in the same direction. Both Italian and Rome elites of the fourth and third centuries were preoccupatied with commemoration of family status and traditions. The François Tomb at Vulci, dating to *c.* 300, is part of a fashion throughout Etruria for large multi-chambered family tombs which served as a marker of family status and prestige. Outside the funerary sphere, a group of inscriptions from Tarquinii, dating to the first century AD and known as the Elogia Tarquiniensia, contains excerpts from the history of the Spurinna family, one of the leading families of the city, indicating that they preserved records and family chronicles of achievements.

There was an economic resurgence, accompanied by changes in land ownership and the organisation of agriculture, which can perhaps be seen most clearly in southern Italy. Archaeological surveys and excavation in the territory of the Greek city of Metapontum revealed changes to land boundaries in this period, and a marked increase in both the number of farms and the size of individual holdings. In the territory of Tarentum there is a similar pattern, with a greater number of farms, larger villages and more specialised agriculture, with an emphasis on cultivating vines and olives. At Gravina, in central Puglia, the excavators of an impressive network of villas and estates have dated their first development to the fourth century. Not all areas enjoyed the same levels of prosperity, and in some parts of Etruria the density of rural settlement and productivity of the territory declined. Agrarian production in southern Etruria was further disrupted by land confiscations and the foundation of Roman colonies at Sutrium and Nepet, but northern Etruria continued to flourish, especially the cities of Arretium, Volsinii and Clusium. An upsurge in the number of inscribed boundary stones from Etruria demonstrates that demarcating property boundaries and establishing ownership were more important at this time. These examples can only provide snapshots of evidence, but they suggest that in most areas the agrarian economy had recovered from its fifth-century problems.

Trade and craft production also flourished. The quantity of imported Greek luxury goods remained in decline, but this was offset by new forms of artisan production in many parts of Italy. New centres of pottery production developed in Etruria and in many parts of southern Italy, some producing painted pottery using Greek forms and techniques which quickly developed into distinctive local styles. Etruscan bronze-workers continued to produce high-quality objects with finely incised or moulded decorations. Bronze mirrors decorated with scenes from Greek mythology on their reverse are found in many tombs, as are cylindrical vessels (known as *cistae*, pl. 22) with similar decoration, and rings with carved seal-stones become increasingly common. Throughout Italy aristocratic tombs continued to be decorated with frescoes on their inner walls celebrating the life of the deceased (pl. 27). Tarentum, in particular, enjoyed an international reputation for its output of bronze and terracotta figurines, for its gold jewellery of great sumptuousness and for its textile industry. The purple dye extracted from the local shellfish was reckoned to be one of the finest in the world, and the woollen cloth produced there was much sought-after. In general, the middle years of the fourth century were a time of prosperity for many areas of Italy.

By *c.* 350, Lucania and Bruttium (roughly modern Basilicata and Calabria) as well as Campania were dominated by Oscan-speaking peoples who had subdivided into three distinct ethnic groups: the Campani, Lucani and Bruttii. Although they shared the same language and many other aspects of their culture, they developed some distinctive differences. Urban life had been long established in Campania and continued uninterrupted, although most cities adopted the Oscan language and, increasingly, Oscan customs. The Lucani, in contrast, developed more diverse forms of settlement. In urbanised northern Lucania city life also continued, but central and southern Lucania became a region of fortified settlements, some of considerable size and complexity, which were very different from Greek, Roman or even Etruscan cities. Most were *c.* 15–30 ha (around 38–75 acres) in size, but one of the biggest, Serra di Vaglio, occupied nearly 100 ha (247 acres). They show signs of investment in private and public building, and almost all are heavily fortified. The impressive fourth-century walls of Serra di Vaglio are built in finely worked stone blocks and were probably built by Greek masons. Many sites were associated with a sanctuary situated a short distance away, and archaeological survey has revealed a large number of farmsteads, which suggests that many people lived in small villages or on their own lands. This characteristic separation of defended settlement and cult place is more characteristic of the Apennine areas in which they originated than the more urbanised lifestyle of their Campanian neighbours.

Despite the economic resurgence, this was a period of conflict. Between *c.* 390 and 380 the Greek cities of Calabria were under threat from outside Italy. Locri, Rhegium, Croton and some of the smaller Greek centres had been invaded by Syracusan forces as part of an attempt by Dionysios I, the tyrant of Syracuse, to extend his growing Sicilian empire into Italy. As part of this, he dismantled the Italiote League, the body that provided military co-operation among the Greeks of Italy. After the failure of his occupation the balance of power in the region shifted decisively to Tarentum. The Italiote League was re-formed under Tarentine leadership, with a treasury and meeting place at the sanctuary of Demeter at Heraklea, a Tarentine colony. For some years this ensured stability, but from 360 onwards Tarentum and the other Greek cities came under increasing pressure from the Lucanians, Bruttians and others, who started to encroach on Greek territory. In 356, Metapontum, Locri and Heraklea all came under attack by their Italian neighbours. Tarentum adopted a policy of hiring mercenary armies, led by Greek or Macedonian generals, to fight on their behalf, a policy that was by no means unusual in the Greek world at this period. Tarentum, as one of the richest cities in the Greek world, could comfortably afford it, but these freelance generals proved difficult to control and frequently had their own agenda. Some were very effective. Alexander, king of Epirus and brother-in-law of Alexander the Great, pushed the Lucanians back and advanced as far north as Paestum in a series of campaigns in 333–330, causing concern to Rome in the process, but was killed in battle at Pandosia in 330. Others had less success. The Spartan prince Cleonymos turned on his Greek employers, made an alliance with the Lucanians and sacked the Greek city of Metapontum in 302. Finally, the period from 340 onwards was dominated by the Roman conquest, an event that caused seismic changes for both Rome and the rest of Italy.

Romans, Latins and Samnites, 343–338

The essential underlying problem faced by Rome by the middle of the fourth century was that it was extending its power and influence in the same direction as the Samnites: namely, the fertile Liris valley and the lower part of the Volturnus valley in Campania. Both Rome and the Samnites were dynamic powers with expanding ambitions and territorial interests, so a clash was perhaps inevitable, but the specific causes and events of this first conflict, and the patterns of alliance and enmity are difficult to pin down. In 354 a treaty between Rome and the Samnites established the River Liris, which flows from Samnium into northern Campania, as the boundary between Roman and Samnite spheres of interest, but by the late 340s Rome had developed interests and connections well south of this boundary.

The first of the three Samnite wars is controversial because it is so poorly documented. It is clear that there was a period of warfare and raids against the Samnites, but Livy's narrative is confused and includes incidents that duplicate events of later Samnite wars. According to Livy (7.29–38), there was a period of raiding in Campania in 343, during which the Samnites harassed communities of the Sidicini in the Volturnus valley, then turned on Capua. Capua appealed to Rome for help, which put Rome in an awkward position, as it already had an alliance with the Samnites. Faced with Rome's refusal to assist, the Capuans forced its hand by means of *deditio*, an act of surrender by which they, their city and their territory became Roman property. This obliged Rome to protect them, giving it an excuse to go to war with the Samnites. This episode is puzzling, as Capua was one of the most powerful cities in Italy, and it seems unlikely that it was so hard pressed by the Samnites that it felt obliged to take this drastic course of action. *Deditio* was usually performed by a defeated enemy and was an extreme step to take. It may have been inferred by Livy as a way of presenting Rome's breach of a treaty in the best possible light, but there may have been a formal supplication by Capua to enable Rome to break its treaty obligations to the Samnites.

The campaign initially went well. Rome fought several successful engagements, and both consuls were awarded a triumph for action against the Samnites. In 342, however, political unrest in Rome affected the army, and hostilities were largely suspended until this was resolved. When campaigning resumed the following year, the Samnites offered to make peace, and their treaty with Rome was renewed (Livy 8.1–5). Exactly why peace broke out in this manner is a bit of a mystery. On Rome's part it may reflect an outbreak of political instability and strife between patricians and plebeians. The passage of the Lex Genucia, which placed further restrictions on patrician political power, took place in 342, and one of the two versions offered by Livy suggests that the civic unrest that accompanied this legislation may have spread to the army. However, it may also reflect growing tensions between Rome and the Latins, which flared up into open warfare around the same time and made it advisable to cut back on other commitments.

The Latin war, which followed almost immediately, was in many ways an extension of this first Samnite war. The end of the conflict with the Samnites resulted in a complete *volte-face*, which demonstrates the fluidity and short-term nature of alliances in this period. Rome was once again in alliance with the Samnites. Ranged against it was an alliance of Latins, Volscians, Campanians and Sidicini, driven to revolt by concern about the growth in Roman power and the extent to which Rome had begun to encroach on the territory of its neighbours. Even if Livy is anachronistic in suggesting that the Latins resented being treated as subjects rather than allies, the fact that the peoples of southern Latium and northern

Campania joined the revolt hints at a widespread anxiety about Rome's rise to regional dominance.

The war lasted from 341 to 338, and involved some fierce – although intermittent – fighting. During an intense campaign in 341–40 Roman armies defeated the Volscian city of Privernum and inflicted two major defeats on the Latin and Campanian forces. One of these, at an unknown location named as Veseris, was the scene of a famous incident in which one of the Roman consuls, Publius Decius Mus, performed an act of *devotio* (dedication), dedicating himself and the enemy forces to the gods of the underworld, and then charging the enemy. He was killed, while leading the Romans to victory. His sacrifice was so famous that his son, also Publius Decius Mus, who commanded the Roman army at the battle of Sentinum in 295, was said to have been inspired to emulate him.[1] Rome's victories successfully suppressed the revolt, and in 340 Rome rewarded the Latins who had not revolted and punished those who had. Some Capuan aristocrats were given honorary Roman citizenship, and the city of Lavinium was given honours and privileges. Despite this, the Latins attacked again the following year but were suppressed by 338.

This war fundamentally changed Rome's relationship with the Latins. It also had a wider significance, as the settlement imposed by Rome formed the entire basis of its later mechanisms for controlling Italy – something to which we will return in more detail in Chapter 13. Livy's account of the peace settlement corresponds to what we know about the status of Latin and Campanian cities in later times:

> The Lanuvians were given citizenship and their sacred places were given back to them, on condition that the grove of Juno Sospita should be common to the citizens of Lanuvium and the people of Rome. The people of Aricia, Nomentum and Pedum were granted citizenship on the same basis as the Lanuvians. The Tusculans retained their existing citizenship, and the crime of rebellion was levelled at a few instigators, without harming the state. The people of Velitrae, long Roman citizens, were severely punished because they had often rebelled: their walls were demolished and the senate was removed and ordered to live on the other side of the Tiber, on the condition that if anyone was caught across the Tiber, the ransom would be 1,000 pounds in bronze, nor could the person who had captured him release him from chains before it was paid. Colonists were sent out to the

senatorial lands [i.e., those confiscated from the senators of Velitrae], and having been enrolled, Velitrae regained its old appearance of populousness. A new colony was sent to Antium, on the condition that the people of Antium were allowed to enrol themselves as colonists if they wanted to; their warships were impounded and the Antiates were forbidden to go to sea, and they were given citizenship. The people of Tibur and Praeneste had territory confiscated, not only because of the recent allegation of rebellion along with the rest of the Latins, but because they had once joined in arms with the Gauls, a savage people, out of distaste at Roman power. The rest of the Latin peoples were denied rights of trade, intermarriage and common assembly between themselves. The Campanians (in honour of their cavalry, because they had not rebelled with the Latins) and the people of Fundi and Formiae (because they had always allowed a safe passage through their territory) were given citizenship without the vote. It was decided to give the people of Cumae and Suessula the same rights and terms as the people of Capua.

(Livy 8.14)

The essence of this settlement was that, with the Latin League dissolved, the right to hold common meetings suspended and pre-existing agreements between Latin states declared null and void, any communal organisation that could provide a focus for collective Latin activity was broken up. In future, Rome was to be at the centre of a web of bilateral agreements in which each state had a relationship only with Rome, not with other former members of the league. It effectively broke up the communal identity of the Latin states and replaced it with Roman domination. Additional punishments dealt with specific problems, such as the need to neutralise the naval power of Antium, which was deprived of its fleet of warships and settled by Roman colonists to neutralise its naval power and punish the ringleaders of the revolt. Velitrae incurred heavier penalties because it already had Roman citizenship, and its rebellion was seen as particularly heinous because of this.

This peace settlement included a number of innovative features. One was the extension of Roman citizenship to a broader group of communities than previously. The second was the breaking of the connection between Latinity as a legal status and Latinity as an ethnic origin. From this point onwards it was possible to be a Latin by virtue of being granted a package of legal rights and obligations by Rome (discussed further below, pp. 267–9), or coming from a community which had such rights, without being born in Latium or descended from Latin parents. Finally, it extended the parallel principle (already established in Rome) that Roman citizenship was a transferrable legal status, not a matter of birth or ethnicity. One could be born a Roman citizen, but one could also acquire citizenship by various means. This became an important element in Roman dealings with other peoples, both within Italy and beyond.

From this point onwards Rome organised its defeated enemies, and also states that entered into alliance voluntarily, broadly into three categories: those who became Roman citizens, those who were given Latin status and those who were given treaties of alliance. By doing this, Rome was able to extend control by building up a network of alliances, voluntary or imposed, and thus side-stepped the need to make alternative administrative arrangements. The vast majority of communities continued to be self-governing at a local level. It also meant that, in many cases, Rome avoided the highly contentious task of imposing change and limiting autonomy. This arm's-length approach allowed Rome to gain kudos from apparent magnanimity and to maintain the convenient fiction of being merely first among equals in the emerging power block. As we shall see, the implications for the Italians were profound.

The second Samnite war

The Latin war was followed by several years of low-level military action as Rome suppressed the last of the resistance in southern Latium and northern Campania. Fundi and Privernum were defeated after a short war in 330–29, as were several other communities. Rome also founded a number of colonies in this region, one of which was to prove a major bone of contention.[2] The colony of Fregellae was established in the Liris valley in 328. This was a strategically significant area where the Samnites had established a presence and consequently saw the colony as a threat. Unpicking exactly what happened and why is difficult. Livy pins the blame for the outbreak of war on the Samnites and depicts the war itself as a straightforward bout of ethnic conflict, but even the internal logic of his own narrative fails to support this

According to Livy (8.22.7–29.5) the war started after the Samnites encouraged the Greek city of Naples to make a series of raids on Roman settlers in the Ager Falernus in 327–326. After Rome declared war, Naples received support from Campanian and Samnite troops sent from Nola, and a promise of assistance from Tarentum.[3] The campaign itself was short and sharp. The Roman commander, Quintus Publilius Philo, opened operations with raids on Neapolitan territory and laid siege to the city. This effectively produced a stalemate. Naples was not easy to besiege since its harbour allowed it to be supplied by sea, but it was hampered by internal instability. The expected reinforcements from Tarentum failed to arrive, and the Samnite and Campanian troops within the city made themselves unpopular in some quarters. Early in 326 a group of disaffected Neapolitans, led by the Greek Charilaus and the Oscan Nympsius, staged a coup and opened the city gates to the Roman forces. The city, under its new pro-Roman regime, was rewarded for its timely change of heart by a treaty of exceptionally favourable terms. No details of the document have been preserved, but it went down as a byword in Roman history: Livy and Cicero refer to it as a *foedus aequissimum* ('most equal/favourable treaty'). Despite what Livy says, it is clear that a substantial faction within Naples favoured the Samnites and that it was moving against Rome quite independently of external influence.

Between 325 and 320 there is little evidence that the Samnites were attacking Roman territory, or even that of Roman allies, but there were several Roman incursions into Samnite territory, including an invasion of Samnium in 325 and an attack on the Vestini, allies of the Samnites, in the same year. The *Fasti Triumphales* record triumphs for victory over the Samnites in 325 and twice in 322. This first stage of the war came to an abrupt end, however, in 321, when Rome suffered a major disaster. The Roman army, including both consuls, was trapped in a mountain valley known as the Caudine Forks and was forced to surrender (Livy 9.1–12).[4] This was a major humiliation, which became a byword for failure and disaster. Livy suggests that the consuls were lured into a trap by Samnite trickery, from which they could not escape without risking the annihilation of the entire army, but according to other sources, the Roman army was defeated and forced to surrender. Whatever the details, the outcome was utter humiliation. The Romans were forced to make a truce, and before they were allowed to retreat back to Rome the entire army was stripped of its weapons and armour. All the troops were required to pass, half-naked, underneath an arch of spears which denoted an improvised yoke – passing under a yoke being a ritual denoting subjugation and disgrace. Rome also had to withdraw its colonies at Cales and Fregellae.

What happened next is a matter of some conjecture. Livy states that the truce was not a regular peace treaty but a *sponsio*, a solemn oath to which the oath-takers acted as guarantors. Such agreements were provisional suspensions of hostilities made by battlefield commanders and had to be ratified by the rulers of the states concerned if they were to become binding. The senate, appalled by the humiliation, tore up the agreement and handed the consuls, who had acted as sponsors, over to the Samnites to face their wrath. They then assembled an army and went on the warpath in 320–318 to avenge the disgrace, inflicting defeats on Samnite forces in northern Apulia, freeing Roman prisoners and forcing 7,000 captured Samnites to undergo the ritual humiliation of the yoke ceremony. The plausibility of this account has been vigorously contested by modern historians, many of whom believe that Roman historical tradition had invented it to gloss over the disgrace of the Caudine Forks, and that the peace (concluded by means of a treaty rather than a *sponsio*) held good until 316. Others point out that this version represents a rather odd exercise in face-saving, as it depicts the Romans as oath-breakers – in itself a disgraceful act and something that annoyed the gods, since oath-making was a religious ritual – and that a triumph recorded in the *fasti* for 319/318 for victories in Samnium and Apulia provides some corroborative evidence for Roman campaigns in the region.

Ultimately, there is no way of recovering what actually happened in 320–318, but it seems that there was a genuine lull in hostilities with the Samnites, possibly as the result of a truce, between 318 and 316. This does not mean that the Romans were at peace, however. They continued to campaign in Lucania and Apulia, bringing a number of communities in these areas into alliance, and renewing relations with some that had been in contact with Rome in 326. In doing so, they extended Roman influence to the south of the Samnites as well as to the west, and seem to have had a deliberate policy of isolating them. There are also signs that they were consolidating Roman interests in Campania. Two new voting tribes (Oufentina and Falerna) were created, and the Roman settlers and colonists in Campania were enrolled in these, integrating these communities more firmly into the Roman state.

The years 315–312 were crucial to the struggle with the Samnites. Hostilities recommenced in 316 with the Roman siege of Saticula, and in 315 the Samnites staged their only known act of aggression during the war, crossing the Liris to defeat Rome in a battle near Terracina and raid far into Latium, possibly with the assistance of the Aurunci, who rebelled against Rome. In 314, however, this force was defeated and Rome severely punished the Aurunci, systematically sacking their hill forts and settlements. In Campania, Fregellae, which may have been lost or ceded to the Samnites in 321, was retaken and a string of new colonies were established at Interamna Lirenas, Saticula and Suessa Aurunca, consolidating Roman control of the area. In 312 this control was enhanced when the censor Appius Claudius began construction of the Via Appia from Rome to Capua (later extended to Tarentum and then Brundisium). In Apulia, Luceria was captured and a colony was founded there in 314. These developments hemmed in the Samnites, pushing them back from Campania and Apulia. Rome also attacked far into the Samnite heartland for the first time, raiding Bovianum, the principal settlement of the Pentri, who were themselves the largest of the Samnite states.

After 312 the Samnite war ceased to be the main focus of Roman activity, but annual campaigns were still waged against the Samnites until 304, although our main narratives, those of Livy and Diodorus, are frequently confused and contradictory. The main outline of events is that after an important Roman victory in 310 there were a series of minor operations until the Samnites attacked in 307 and 306, invading Roman-held areas of Campania. This provoked a Roman invasion of Samnium in 306–304, which culminated in the capture of Bovianum, Sora and Aquinum and a heavy defeat of the Samnite army. The Hernici and Aequi, some of whom had rebelled against Rome, were defeated and the communities that had revolted were suppressed with great savagery. Some communities that had legal privileges conferred by Rome in 338 had these removed. In 304 the Samnites made peace and their treaty with Rome was reinstated, drawing the second Samnite war to a close.

Etruria and Umbria and the third Samnite war

From 311, the point at which the tide began to turn against the Samnites, Rome became embroiled in another set of conflicts. The main targets of these were the Etruscans, the Umbrians and the peoples of the central Apennines, but they intermittently involved hostilities against the Gauls.

Plate 15. Terracotta statue of Apollo from the sanctuary of Apollo at Portonaccio, Veii, late sixth century.

Plate 16. Lanuvium: painted terracotta architectural decoration (antefix), c. 520–470 BC.

Plate 17. Cerveteri: street of 'terraced' tombs, sixth century BC.

Plate 18. Tomb of the Triclinium, Tarquinii, sixth century BC.

*Plate 19. Rome: cast of the Forum inscription, an inscribed stone pillar
(cippus) found in a shrine beneath the Black Stone (Lapis Niger) in the
Comitium. The inscription is probably a sacred law. Sixth century BC.*

Plate 20. Roman cast-copper currency bar, c. 280–250 BC.

*Plate 21. Roman silver coin (269–266 BC), showing head of Hercules
on the obverse and she-wolf and twins on the reverse.*

Plate 22. Ficoroni cista, *Praeneste. Fourth century* BC.

Plate 23. Rome, Largo Argentina. Third-century BC *temples.*

Plate 24. Terracotta vase in the shape of a cockerel inscribed with the Etruscan alphabet, possibly an inkwell. South Etruscan, c. 650–600 BC.

Plate 25. Canopic cinerary urn, from Clusium (Chiusi), sixth century BC.

Plate 26. Bronze and ivory chariot, found in tumulus burial near Monteleone di Spoleto. Etruscan, c. 575–550 BC. The bronze cladding (mounted on a modern sub-structure) depicts scenes from the life of Achilles.

Plate 27. Paestum, tomb painting from Andriuolo cemetery, Tomb 58 (fourth century BC), showing a Samnite warrior.

Plate 28. Tomb of the Diver, Paestum, fifth century BC. Fresco depicting a symposium (drinking party).

As with the Samnites, Livy and others tend to refer to these people, unhelpfully, by their ethnic names, so it is unclear exactly which Etruscan cities Rome was fighting and why. The southern and coastal cities of Caere, Vulci and Tarquinii were relatively unaffected, and campaigning corresponds to the territories of the more northerly cities, such as Clusium, Perusia, Arretium, Volsinii. These communities were at the height of their power in this period, and therefore potential rivals for Rome. Their proximity to Umbria explains why the conquest of the two areas was so closely intertwined. What is less clear is whether they fought as individual cities or as a federal Etruscan army. Livy makes reference to a council of Etruscan cities which met at the sanctuary of Fanum Voltumnae near Volsinii and which did on occasion make joint decisions about diplomatic and military matters, but it is not clear whether military co-operation was the exception or the rule.

As with his narrative of the Samnite wars, Livy is keen to establish that the wars in Etruria were all the fault of the Etruscans. He tells us that in 311 the Etruscans attacked Sutrium, a Latin colony *c.* 50 km (31 miles) north of Rome, although he does not say why they did this. The following year Rome drove off the besieging forces and advanced into Etruria. After battles at Lake Vadimon and Perusia, Clusium, Arretium and Perusia made peace and signed thirty-year truces with Rome.[5] This campaign was notable for a bold move on the part of the Roman commander, Quintus Fabius Maximus Rullianus. His brother, who spoke fluent Etruscan,[6] was sent on a scouting mission and found his way through the impenetrable Ciminian forest into Umbria. There he travelled as far as the Umbrian community of Camerinum and persuaded it to become a Roman ally, thus giving Rome an important toehold in Umbria. Both the date and the location of this story are open to question (Camerinum is a long way from the Ciminian forest), and the role of the Fabii may have been exaggerated for reasons of family prestige by their descendant the historian Fabius Pictor. However, the treaty with Camerinum was a famous one, as it had unusually favourable terms and was well known to later Romans, so the alliance itself can be accepted, although the heroic mission by Fabius may be fictional.

The successes of 310 were followed up with further military and diplomatic advances in 309, including successful military actions, the renewal of a long-term truce with Tarquinii and an alliance with Umbrian Ocriculum. In 308 many Etruscans and Umbrians united to form a large army, aiming to march on Rome. One of the Roman consuls, Publius Decius Mus, was forced to return to defend the city, and the other, Quintus Fabius Maximus, who was campaigning in Samnium, headed to Umbria to confront the invaders. Fabius defeated the Umbrian and Etruscan army near Mevania, and some of the Umbrians were forced into alliance with Rome. As with other incidents, the specific details are confused, but this brought about some sort of resolution of matters in Umbria, as no further campaigns against the Umbrians are known until 303. In 306–298, however, Rome's focus shifted again, to the peoples of the central Apennines. The Aequi were defeated in 304 and their hilltop settlements were destroyed, after which the other peoples of the region – the Paeligni, Marsi, Marrucini and Frentani – rapidly made alliances with Rome.

The effect of these wars was to extend Roman control up the Tiber valley. As in Campania, this was underpinned by the foundation of substantial numbers of Roman colonies. In Umbria, where pre-Roman levels of urbanisation were low, there was a lot of scope for parcelling land out to new settlers. Colonies were also founded in the Apennines, at Carseoli and Alba Fucens, while a number of communities in southern Latium, including Arpinum, Frusino and Trebula Suffenas, were given a limited form of Roman citizenship (*civitas sine suffragio*, which did not include the right to vote) which tied them closely to Rome. Colonies of this period fell into two categories – colonies of Roman citizens (*coloniae civium romanorum*) and Latin colonies – that were very different in size, function and legal status. The colonies of Apulia, Umbria and the Apennines in the late fourth and third centuries were predominantly Latin colonies, which were substantially larger than colonies of Roman citizens. This programme of settlement was instrumental in breaking the connection between Latin status as a legal status and Latin language or ethnicity. The differences between these types of settlement are discussed in more detail in Chapter 13.

In 298 the two strands of Roman expansion, against the Samnites and against the peoples of central Italy, converged. Rome had continued fighting in Etruria and Umbria on an annual basis since 302, but in 298 the conflict known as the third Samnite war broke out. The reason was a Roman alliance with the Lucanians, who had been attacked by the Samnites and therefore requested Roman protection (Livy 10.11–12; Dion. Hal. 17/18.1.1–3). Rome seems to have had some immediate success, as Gnaeus Fulvius Centumalus, one of the consuls, is credited by both the *fasti* and Livy with a triumph for action against the Samnites and Etruscans

(Livy 10.12–13). This, however, presents an intriguing historical puzzle which illustrates the difficulty in assessing and reconciling conflicting evidence. A funerary inscription for Lucius Cornelius Scipio Barbatus, the other consul of 298, claims that he had subdued Lucania and captured two towns in Samnium, despite the fact that Livy says he was campaigning in Etruria at the time. It is possible that claims in Barbatus' funerary elogium may refer to action in a different year, but given that Livy's account of the third Samnite war is confused in many places, it seems more probable that Scipio was responsible for at least some campaigning in Samnium.

Fighting continued in 297 and 296, during which Roman armies raided Samnium extensively, but at the end of 296 an ominous new development took place. An anti-Roman coalition of Samnites, Etruscans, Umbrians and even some Gauls was formed, and in 295 a Roman army and the new coalition met at Sentinum, in Umbria (Livy 10. 24–31). Livy's account of the Sentinum campaign is, like much of his narrative of the war, very confused. He recounts military actions in Umbria, including a Roman defeat at either Clusium or Camerinum, followed by a confrontation at Sentinum. It is unclear whether Rome faced a combined force of Etruscans, Umbrians, Samnites and Gauls, or whether the Etruscans and Umbrians were absent, but the *Fasti Triumphales* lists Fabius Maximus Rullianus' triumph as being awarded for victory over the Etruscans, Samnites and Gauls, which suggests that it was a unified force. Sentinum was celebrated in Antiquity for the unusual size of the armies involved. The figures quoted by some Greek historians are unlikely,[7] but Cornell estimates that the Roman army may have been in the region of 36,000 men – large by the standards of the time – and sources say that the enemy forces were significantly larger. Nevertheless, the Romans, under the command of Publius Decius Mus and Quintus Fabius Maximus, prevailed, and this proved to be the turning point of the war. There was fierce fighting throughout Etruria, Umbria and Samnium for the next two years, but in 293 the Samnite army was finally and decisively defeated at Aquilonia (Livy 10.32–45). The final years of the war are less easy to reconstruct because Livy's work for this period survives only as short summaries of each book. What is clear, however, is that Rome overran large areas of Samnium, and in 290 the Samnites were forced to make peace.

Conflict continued elsewhere during the period between 290 and 264. In 290 the consul Manius Curius Dentatus conquered the Sabines and Praetuttii, and there were ongoing operations in Etruria and Umbria and against the Gauls throughout the 280s and 270s, culminating in the defeat of Vulci (280), Caere (273) and finally Volsinii (264). The Gauls were decisively defeated at the battle of Lake Vadimon in 283. Most Etruscan and Umbrian cities became Roman allies, although some were treated harshly. Caere lost most of its land and was given the status of Roman citizenship without the vote (*civitas sine suffragio* – discussed further below, pp. 264–7) in 273. The Sabines and Praetuttii were given limited Roman citizenship without the right to vote and had a large amount of territory confiscated, extending Roman territory right across peninsular Italy. This acquisition of a large amount of new territory gave Rome the opportunity for extensive new colonisation to pacify and control the newly conquered areas and to reward the Roman people with grants of land. Colonies were founded at Venusia (291), Minturnae and Sinuessa in northern Campania (296) and at various locations in Umbria (for a full list, see Tables 7 and 8, pages 211 and 276). The resolution of the conflicts in Samnium and central Italy did not, however, mark the end of Rome's wars of conquest.

The Pyrrhic war: Rome takes on the Greeks

In 281 Rome was drawn into a conflict in southern Italy that was to prove a watershed in several respects. It was the event that prompted Rome's conquest of the last areas of Italy that remained outside of its control, namely the Greek-controlled areas of Bruttium, southern Lucania and Apulia. From the end of the war, Rome was a truly international power, controlling the entire Italian peninsula. It also brought Rome into conflict with the Greeks for the first time, and tested the Roman army against Hellenistic Greek military might and, more specifically, against one of the foremost generals of the day, Pyrrhus, the king of Epirus. He led a force composed of professional mercenary soldiers as well as citizen militias of the Greek cities of Italy, so his presence confronted Rome for the first time with a state-of-the-art Hellenistic army, complete with weapons such as fighting elephants. Although our sources present a positive view of Roman conduct during the war, it is quite clear that it contained moments of considerable danger. It proved to be a long and difficult conflict, during which Pyrrhus inflicted several heavy defeats on Rome without quite having the resources to land a knock-out blow. It is also clear that Rome must bear quite a lot of responsibility for the outbreak of war in the first place, despite representations of the Tarentines as the villains of the piece.

Rome had already developed strategic interests in northern Apulia as part of the wars against the Samnites. Alliances with some states in the region were developed in 326, and the area was in the forefront of conflict between Rome and the Samnites in 320–317 (Livy 9.14.1–9, 9.26.3; Dion. Hal. 17.5.2). Further alliances were formed with (or imposed on) Arpi, Teate, Canusium and Forentum during this period, as an attempt to secure Roman domination along the border between Apulia and Samnium. There had been considerable Oscan migration into parts of the region, notably around Teate, during the course of the fourth century, so the Samnites had a certain amount of support there, while the Romans were attempting to outflank the main Samnite armies by opening up a second front. Another factor in the outbreak of the conflict is the unstable nature of southern Italy in this period. The attempt by Dionysios of Syracuse to extend Syracusan rule into Calabria had destabilised the Greek cities of the area and handed leadership of the Italian Greeks to Tarentum from c. 350 onwards, but Tarentine leadership was not popular and some Tarentine strategies caused as many problems as they solved. By the later fourth century the use of mercenary troops was widespread throughout the Greek world, and the Tarentines attempted to solve the problem of pressure from their Italian neighbours by hiring Greek generals who fought largely as freelance mercenaries. Some had considerable success, but they were difficult to control and could be as much of a menace to the Greek cities they were hired to protect as to the Lucanians and Bruttians they were supposed to be fighting.

The situation in the 280s, therefore, was that Tarentum was the dominant state in this area of Italy, but Rome had serious strategic ambitions in Apulia and commitments to allies in southern Italy. This almost inevitably led to a clash of interests, which duly happened in 285. Thurii, which resented Tarentine domination, sent a delegation to Rome asking for protection against its overbearing neighbour, as well as the encroaching Bruttians and Lucanians. Rome agreed and dispatched troops to garrison the city, but these were ejected by the irate Tarentines in 282. In 281, however, there was a more serious crisis when a squadron of Roman ships appeared off Tarentum and were attacked by the Tarentine fleet, which sank half of them (App., *Samn.* 7.1–2). When Roman envoys arrived to protest, the Tarentines rejected their objections.[8] After a short period of political tension between leaders who favoured further negotiation and those who were more hard-line, they declared war. They then – in line with their usual practice in the fourth century – called on a foreign general to assist them.

What was the Roman fleet up to? According to Appian, it was on a reconnaissance mission and had infringed a long-standing treaty which stipulated that Roman ships should not sail beyond Cape Lacinium and into the Gulf of Tarentum, but nothing further is known of this treaty, or of its date or context. The incident is particularly odd because up to this date Rome had little interest in sea power. Two officials, the *duoviri navales*, had been appointed for the first time in 311 to oversee Rome's small and rudimentary fleet, but Rome still lacked any significant naval capabilities even at the outbreak of the First Punic War in 264. The implication is that Rome had engaged in deliberate provocation, unwisely since Tarentum was one of the foremost naval powers of the Mediterranean. If Rome was on morally and diplomatically shaky ground, this may explain why ancient writers took pains to smear the Tarentines.

The Tarentine invitation to Pyrrhus was in line with previous Greek policy for dealing with external threats, but it was clear from an early stage that this would be a much larger conflict. Their choice of Pyrrhus was a good one in many respects. He was a nephew of Alexander the Great and is one of the more exotic characters of Greek history, catching the imagination of many later biographers and historians. He was one of the foremost generals of his day, and described by Plutarch as being of fierce and forbidding appearance but of noble character, brave in battle, honourable in his negotiations with the Romans and willing to make generous gestures such as releasing prisoners without ransom (Plut., *Pyrr.* 3). Many anecdotes about Pyrrhus and his chief political adviser, the wise and virtuous Cineas, have passed into literary tradition, but it is difficult nevertheless to piece together a coherent picture of the progress of the war. Even Pyrrhus' motivation is uncertain. It is claimed that he wished to conquer an empire in the west to emulate his uncle, but he was also the son-in-law of Agathocles, the tyrant of Syracuse, and may have had his eye on the opportunity to succeed him (Plut., *Pyrr.* 14.2–7; Diod. 40.4). Whatever his motives, he presented a powerful threat to Rome, since he came with a large amount of financial and military support from both Italy and the east. Antiochus, king of Syria, and Ptolemy of Egypt made financial donations to his campaign, while Tarentum supplied troops and money, as well as transporting his army of 20,000 infantry, 2,000 cavalry and 20 elephants to Italy. Pyrrhus and the Tarentines between them managed to put together a formidable anti-Roman coalition within Italy by making common cause with the Samnites and some Etruscan cities, forcing Rome to fight a war in several areas at the same time. Support among the Greeks of Italy, paradoxically, was less clear-cut. Some, principally Croton, Locri and Rhegium, elected to support Rome, seeing this as a way to escape Tarentine domination.

The first months of the war were fairly quiet. The Romans sent an army commanded by Lucius Aemilius Barbula with instructions to devastate the territory of Tarentum but not to join battle, in the hope that Tarentum would choose to make peace. Tarentum, meanwhile, continued preparations for war. Pyrrhus put the city on a war footing, banning theatrical performances, introducing universal conscription of men of military age and demanding financial contributions from other citizens.[9] The main Roman forces, under Aemilius, remained at Venusia to contain the Samnites, but the other consul, Valerius Laevinus, began to advance on Pyrrhus, finally encountering him near Heraklea. The Roman army substantially outnumbered that of Pyrrhus, who proposed arbitration of the dispute between the Tarentines and Romans, a normal feature of Hellenistic diplomacy. Laevinus rejected the move and attacked, but the ensuing battle was won by Pyrrhus, and the Romans were forced to retreat to Venusia. The battle of Heraklea was the original Pyrrhic victory, however, because Pyrrhus' losses were so heavy that he was unable to capitalise on it. Nevertheless, the battle was notable enough to be commemorated by victory dedications at the temple of Zeus at Tarentum and at the sanctuaries of Zeus at Dodona, and of Athena at Athens and Lindos.

The battle of Heraklea was a costly victory in terms of manpower, but it tipped the political balance temporarily in favour of Pyrrhus and his allies. Croton and Locri ejected their Roman garrisons and joined him, along with much of the Oscan population of southern Italy. Rhegium may have attempted to do likewise, but it was prevented by a garrison sent by Rome to protect the city (App., *Samn.* 9.1–3, 12.1). This force, which consisted of Campanian allies rather than Roman troops, took matters into its own hands by slaughtering the Greek elite and taking over the city for their own benefit.

The Romans were now very much on the defensive. Pyrrhus and his allies made a rapid march north into Campania, perhaps aiming to reach Naples, but were forestalled by Laevinus. Pyrrhus then marched on as far as Anagnia, 60 km (37 miles) south of Rome, with a view to besieging Rome or linking up with Rome's Etruscan enemies. This nearly led him into a trap as Rome had just made peace with the Etruscans, and Pyrrhus ran the risk of being caught between two Roman armies. He abandoned his advance, retreated to Tarentum and tried to negotiate peace, an episode that is problematic, as our accounts of it focus on moralistic anecdotes about Pyrrhus and Cineas, his chief adviser (Plut., *Pyrr.* 16). The main demands seem to have been a guarantee of freedom and autonomy for the Italiotes, an alliance between Rome and Pyrrhus himself, and the return of all land taken from the Samnites, Lucanians and Bruttians by Rome. The strength of Pyrrhus' position at this point can be gauged by the fact that the senate was initially inclined to accept these terms. However, vociferous opposition to peace was led by Appius Claudius Caecus, the builder of the Via Appia.[10] His intervention against the proposed treaty was decisive, and the war resumed.

After the failure of these negotiations Pyrrhus began to raise money and troops from the Italiote cities to mount another campaign,[11] and in 279 he moved into Apulia, pushing northwards towards Samnium. His way was blocked by Roman armies led by Sulpicius Saverrio and Decius Mus, who were based at Venusia, and a further battle was fought at Ausculum. Like the battle of Heraklea, this was also a 'Pyrrhic victory', in which Pyrrhus sustained losses that prevented him from following up his advantage and forced him to retreat once again to Tarentum. At this point several external factors came into play. Macedon, the powerful neighbour of Epirus, descended into civil war, leaving Pyrrhus with potential instability at home, and there was much unrest among Tarentum's Italiote allies. The situation was resolved, for Pyrrhus if not for the Italiotes, when Syracuse invited him to lead a war against the Carthaginians of western Sicily. Agathocles, the tyrant of Syracuse, had died in 289, so he declared his own son (Agathocles' grandson) tyrant of Syracuse and departed for Sicily, leaving a garrison at Tarentum.

During 278–276 the Romans gradually made encroachments on the territory controlled by Pyrrhus, winning victories over the Lucanians, Bruttians, Samnites and Greeks. In 276 Pyrrhus returned to take charge of the situation, but during the crossing back to Italy he was attacked by a Carthaginian fleet and suffered severe losses (Plut., *Pyrr.* 22; App., *Samn.* 12.1–2). He landed at Locri, which still supported him, and attempted to take Rhegium, but without success, and caused bad feeling by seizing the temple treasure from the temple of Persephone at Locri. Support from both Oscans and Greeks was waning considerably, but Pyrrhus mounted a last campaign, marching north through Lucania. In 275 he encountered the army of Manius Curius Dentatus at Malventum (later Beneventum), where he suffered a decisive defeat. After this he withdrew to Tarentum and shortly afterwards returned to Epirus, leaving a garrison under his son, Helenus, and Milo, his second-in-command. Helenus was ordered back to Macedon in 274–273, although Milo remained for a few months longer. Tarentum continued to hold out against Rome until 272, when it was finally taken.

Rome in control: Italy in 270

By the end of the Pyrrhic war most of peninsular Italy was under Roman control. It took several years to finish mopping up resistance in the far south of Apulia, and the *Fasti Triumphales*, the official list of Roman triumphs, list four triumphs awarded for campaigns against the Sallentini, as Rome called the people of the region, in 267–265. After this point, however, Roman control was established and was not challenged again until the mass rebellions in southern Italy during the Hannibalic war.

Little is known about what happened to Rome's Italian opponents at the end of the war, as Livy's history only survives in short summaries for these years, and all other accounts are similarly fragmentary. Tarentum, and presumably its allies, surrendered in 272, and probably became Roman allies. The *Epitome* of Livy simply says that Tarentum was taken and that peace was made, but there is no mention of what happened to the other Greek cities. The Byzantine historian Zonaras (8.6) tells us that the city walls of Tarentum were demolished and a payment of tribute imposed, but this may be a conflation of the events of 272 with those of 209, when Tarentum was heavily penalised for rebelling during the Hannibalic war. The political consequences may have involved the exile of anti-Roman politicians and the installation of pro-Roman governments. Locri went out of its way to make a public statement of loyalty to Rome, issuing a series of coins showing Nike crowning the goddess Roma and bearing the legend Pistis (faith). Quite apart from settlements with the hostile Greek states, Rome also had to deal with its ally Rhegium. The Campanian garrison sent by Rome to protect it at the beginning of the war had run amok, slaughtering many of the Greek ruling elite and taking control of the city. The ringleader, Decius Vibellius, was killed by a Rhegine plot, but Rhegium remained under Campanian control throughout the Pyrrhic war. Rome finally ejected the renegade garrison in 265, made reparations to the citizens and executed the remaining Campanians. The fate of the Italiote League is completely unknown. There is no record of its being dissolved, but equally no certain evidence that it survived. A few details from the years between 272 and 218 give an indication that the peace terms were not too onerous. The Italiotes retained their military capacity, both in land forces and ships, as they supplied ships and troops to assist Rome on various occasions in the third and second centuries, most notably helping to transport the Roman army to Sicily at the outbreak of the First Punic War in 264.

The new territory acquired by Rome as a result of these wars was controlled by a network of alliances of the types discussed in the following chapter. This was underpinned by an extensive programme of colonisation which placed groups of Roman settlers of various sizes at strategic points in the conquered areas. There was an extensive programme of Roman settlement in Umbria and Picenum, where Roman citizen colonies were founded at Sena Gallica (283), Castrum Novum (early 280s) and Aesis (247); and larger Latin colonies were founded at Narnia (299), Interamna Nahars (date unknown but probably early third century), Ariminum (268) and Spoletium (241). In the south, new settlements, all of which were Latin colonies, were founded at Luceria (314), Venusia (291), Paestum (273), Beneventum (268) and Brundisium (244), establishing Roman control over key strategic points in Samnium and northern Apulia, and over a major port at Brundisium. This was an ambitious programme, involving the relocation of several thousand colonists, dwarfing the indigenous populations of the regions where they settled and fundamentally changing the culture, demography and ownership of land and property in the communities affected.[12]

The late fourth and early third centuries were also the period of the first great road-building programmes, which were closely linked to colonisation programmes. The two earliest initiatives, the first stage of the Via Appia, linking Rome and Capua, and the Via Valeria, linking Tibur with Cerfennia, date to 312 and 307 respectively and were clearly part of a move to improve connections with Campania and the Apennine areas. The Via Appia was extended to Venusia in 285, shortly after the foundation of the colony there, and another road, the Via Caecilia, linking Cures Sabini with Castrum Novum in 283, coincides with a period of colonial settlement in Umbria. In addition, two roads called the Via Clodia were built in the 280s, although there is uncertainty about their route. These six projects may seem small-scale, but they were the beginning of Rome's impressive network of roads which permitted the rapid transmission of troops and – just as importantly – information around Italy, and which proved to be a powerful instrument of Roman control. These two features – colonisation and road-building – also had a transformative effect on Italy. Colonies changed the social, cultural and demographic character of an area or community, while proximity to (and conversely, distance from) the road system could enhance or undermine a community's economic performance and political and administrative status. By the end of the Pyrrhic war, Rome had not just achieved military dominance but was beginning to transform Italy in much more profound ways.

13

Co-operation
or conquest?
Alliances,
citizenship and
colonisation

Rome's conquest of large areas of Italy posed a major, and growing, logistical problem: how could a city-state with limited administrative resources exercise effective control over its satellites? The problem had become apparent as early as the late fifth century, but now became pressing. By the onset of the third century finding an effective solution was imperative.

The answer lay in an innovative system of arm's-length relationships, which allowed Rome to dominate without the need for responsibility for the day-to-day administration of new territories. Some conquered areas were directly incorporated into the Roman state by a variety of means, or were colonised by Roman settlers, but others retained a considerable amount of freedom. This neat solution allowed Rome to dominate in practice without incurring the resentment that might have arisen from attempts to exercise a closer degree of control. It proved a remarkably strong and stable system for exercising Roman domination in Italy and provided the basis for expansion further afield. It lasted for well over two hundred years, despite being compromised by increasingly heavy-handed Roman behaviour and corresponding Italian discontent during the second century. The so-called Social War (the war against the *socii*, or allies), which broke out in 91, when many Italians revolted, forced Rome to accede to Italian demands for greater equality and to extend Roman citizenship to all Italians.

These are not just dry administrative matters. They raise some profound questions about social, economic and cultural relationships between Italy and Rome, and about the essential nature of Roman expansion. Rome's system of control fundamentally shaped the cultural and political development of Italy, and poses interesting questions about the impact of the wars of expansion on both Rome and on the areas conquered. The relationship between Rome and the rest of Italy was fundamental to Rome's later development as an imperial power, and casts light on what Roman rule may have meant in real terms to the inhabitants of Italy.

Controlling Italy: citizens, Latins, colonists and allies

In the earliest stages of Rome's expansion, conquered territory was incorporated directly into that of Rome, the *ager romanus*, but as Roman territorial interests grew wider, this quickly became impossible. By the fifth century a new pattern started to emerge. Instead of annexing defeated enemies, Rome made peace treaties with them and left them to carry on ruling themselves, although some treaties came with conditions attached. Rome sometimes confiscated a portion of the territory of a defeated enemy and settled small groups of Roman colonists on it. In other cases – particularly in dealing with the Etruscan states and the Faliscans – Rome did not bother to make a treaty but simply negotiated truces (*indutiae*), which suspended hostilities for a fixed term but did not create any permanent relationship between the various parties involved. The duration of these truces varied from short ceasefires, intended to give Rome a breathing space from hostilities, to long-term arrangements. For instance, a truce of only a year was made with a group of Etruscan states in 308, but truces of twenty years with Veii and Volsinii (433 and 390), thirty years with Perusia, Cortona and Arretium (310), and of a hundred years with Caere (353) are known.[1]

263

By the middle of the fourth century these arrangements began to crystallise into something more systematic. The catalyst was the Latin War of 340–338. The settlement imposed on the rebellious Latins and Campanians was undoubtedly framed to make an example of them, but it also provided a stronger and more lasting arrangement to secure stable and peaceful relations with Rome's nearest neighbours. The post-war settlement, outlined in the previous chapter, introduced several new features. It created a new form of Latinity and formally made Roman citizenship a legal, transferrable status. All other Italians were linked to Rome by a complex web of treaties and alliances.

Roman citizenship and the Italians

The smallest of the categories into which the settlement of 338 divided the area subject to Rome was that of Roman citizens. The core of this group were the people of the city of Rome itself – people who were Romans by virtue of birth and ethnic origin. As discussed in earlier chapters, however, the Romans had a relatively open, but also highly legalistic, attitude to citizenship. Citizenship was not defined in terms of place of origin but was a specified status in Roman law, which could be conferred (or in extreme cases, withdrawn) by act of the state.

From 338 there were two types of Roman citizenship. Full citizenship (*civitas optimo iure*) conferred the civil and political rights of a Roman, including the right to vote on laws, elect magistrates and stand for political office at Rome, but the settlement of 338 created a new category of citizenship (*civitas sine suffragio*), in addition to this. It offered the civil rights of a Roman but none of the political rights. People with this status could claim the protection of Roman law and had the status of Roman citizens, but it imposed many of the obligations of citizenship, including military service and (possibly) taxation, while not permitting them to vote at Rome or stand for political office there. It removed the independence and autonomy of communities with this status while denying them   and particularly their ruling classes – the compensation of access to influence at Rome. This restricted citizenship was probably intended as a way of exercising closer Roman control without offering many benefits, and was specific to the late fourth and third centuries. No new *cives sine suffragio* are known to have been created after the middle of the third century, and it is likely that most of the communities with this status were quietly upgraded to full Roman citizenship during the early second century.[2]

There were a number of means by which citizenship could be obtained. Individuals or small groups could be enfranchised as a reward for services rendered to Rome. In 340, for example, Campanian aristocrats who had remained loyal to Rome during the Latin war were rewarded with Roman citizenship. By the second century it was possible for Italians to obtain some of the rights of Roman citizens by establishing long-term residence in Rome, but it is unclear how early this practice began. It was a matter of concern to the senate by the 180s, but we have little evidence for this practice before *c.* 200. Individual grants of Roman citizenship, or acquisition by migration to Rome, was relatively small-scale, and much the most common and most widespread method of disseminating Roman citizenship was through colonisation programmes and/or grants of citizenship *en bloc* to whole communities.

The impact of a grant of citizenship on a community could be considerable. Absorption into the Roman state involved a fundamental loss of independence. From the point at which Roman citizenship was granted, a community became part of the Roman state, thus curtailing freedom of action in many respects. These *municipia*, as communities of full or partial Roman citizens were known, were viewed by Rome in terms of *munera* – obligations – defined in terms of taxation and military service, and were obliged to follow Rome's lead in their dealings with other communities. Military service, in particular, was central to the duties of a Roman citizen. The Roman army at this date was a citizen militia, in which adult male citizens under the age of forty-five were required to serve on request, and annual levies of troops were carried out to select men for service. Men of military age from other Italian states who gained Roman citizenship were required to serve in the Roman army on the same basis, giving Rome access to additional military manpower. In military matters, and also in relations with other states, a grant of Roman citizenship could impose significant changes and limitations.

Despite this loss of autonomy, *municipia* remained locally self-governing communities, responsible for their own internal administration, although this involved considerable reorganisation. It is probable that newly enfranchised communities were expected to abandon local forms of law in favour of Roman law. The inhabitants had to register as citizens at the next Roman census, and were allotted to a voting tribe so that they could exercise their rights to vote at Rome.[3] Pre-Roman forms of government were adapted so that they resembled those of Rome itself. Most citizen communities were governed by two annually elected senior magistrates (known as *duoviri*), supported by junior magistrates and a local council drawn from the elite of the city – a system broadly equivalent to the Roman consuls, lesser magistrates and senate. These were responsible for running the community in day-to-day terms, dealing with aspects such as maintaining order, passing local laws, dealing with legal cases, overseeing public finances and maintaining the fabric of the city.

Residents of cities with full Roman citizen status were, in theory, entitled to vote in Roman elections and participate in the Roman lawmaking process. In practice, the extent to which Roman citizens living outside Rome were able to exercise these rights may have been limited. Although the initial registration of citizens and the periodic censuses of Roman citizens were undertaken locally and submitted to Rome in writing, there was no mechanism for submitting written votes from a distance. In order to exercise political rights, an individual had to be present in Rome at an election, or on the day on which the assembly of the people voted on legislation. Some of the Latin cities that gained citizenship in 338 were close enough to Rome to make it possible to travel into the city to attend an election or a vote. Tusculum, Lanuvium and Lavinum, for instance, are all within 20–30 km (*c.* 12–18 miles) of Rome, which was judged to be one day's travel by Roman standards, but participation in the legislative or electoral process by Romans from outside Rome is likely to have been limited by social class. We hear of many Italian aristocrats who owned houses in Rome and regularly spent time there, networking with their Roman counterparts. No doubt they were able to exercise their political rights if they came from states with Roman citizenship, but participation by less wealthy Romans from beyond the city is much less likely.

This raises the question of how the inhabitants of the communities enfranchised by Rome might have felt about becoming Roman citizens, and about the day-to-day changes involved. Most of our sources, looking at this from a Roman perspective, put a positive spin on it, presenting grants of Roman citizenship as an honour which increased a community's status and prestige. On the other hand, attitudes changed considerably over time. The majority of our sources were written at a period when being a Roman citizen conferred many benefits. With the acquisition of a Mediterranean-wide empire, the disparity of status between Romans and non-Romans widened, causing citizenship to become much sought-after, just at the point at which the senate became increasingly reluctant to extend it more widely. During the fourth and third centuries, however, the situation was very different. The benefits of being a Roman were less obvious, and the loss of independence inherent in accepting the citizenship of another state (or having it imposed) was perceived as a loss of status. At this date Roman citizenship may have seemed less of a privilege and more of an imposition and punishment. The extent to which loss of self-determination and the demolition of collective identity were regarded with distaste is illustrated by the protests of some communities faced with incorporation as *civitates sine suffragio*. In 304, for example, Livy says that the Aequi complained bitterly that they did not wish to become Roman citizens and feared having this imposed on them. The Hernici, they said, had tried to resist this but had been forced to become Roman citizens as a punishment. The imposition of *civitas sine suffragio* on Latins and Campanians in 338 is also presented as a punishment, and the threat of it was certainly felt as such by communities on the receiving end. Autonomy within the framework of an alliance with Rome was valued. Roman citizenship, particularly *civitas sine suffragio*, which carried no political rights to compensate for the loss of independence, was seen as an intrusion into the civic life of another state and, as such, could be very much resented.

Roman citizenship was undoubtedly beneficial in the long run, particularly for the ruling elites, who were well placed to take advantage of the economic and political opportunities it offered. Communities with citizenship undeniably found themselves in a privileged position in the second century, when the benefits of being Roman citizens became much greater, but in the fourth and third centuries many Italians were ambivalent about exchanging independence for Roman status, and it could be viewed by both Romans and Italians as a punishment rather than a favour.

Latins and Latin status

Another innovative feature of the settlement of 338 was the creation of Latin status as a package of legal and civic rights. From this point onwards being a Latin was not a matter of place of origin or ethnic identity but a collection of legal rights which could be conferred by the state. This new legalistic definition did, of course, include many people and communities who were ethnic Latins, and most of the earliest grants of Latin status were made to communities that were actually in Latium, but nevertheless it uncoupled Latin status from Latin ethnicity. Unlike Roman citizenship, Latin status was rarely conferred individually before the first century AD, and was primarily disseminated by means of colonisation. (On Latin and Roman colonies, and the difference between them, see below, pp. 275–8.)

Essentially, the new status was a collection of legal rights and obligations in relation to Rome. Latins had the right of intermarriage (*conubium*) with Roman citizens, meaning that the children of such a marriage would be legitimate and inherit their father's status, and wills or dealings with family property would be protected by Roman law. They also had rights of trade with Romans (*commercium*), which gave them legal protection in economic dealings with Romans. Finally, they had – or came to acquire at some point during the third century – the right to migrate to Rome, live there and acquire Roman citizenship by virtue of establishing long-term residence. The extent to which Latins exercised this right of migration to Rome (the so-called *ius migrationis*) before the Punic wars is unclear. We do not hear of it being perceived as a problem, but whether this was because it was not taking place or because the senate was not worried by it is unclear. In the second century, in contrast, the number of Latins settled in Rome increased, and it became a highly charged issue.

The principal obligation of a community with Latin status was to support Rome with military force, as and when requested to do so. Since they were not Roman citizens, Latins fought not as part of the Roman army but in their own local units, commanded by their own officers. Nevertheless, we have plentiful evidence that Latins were an important military resource for Rome. Livy's history is structured as a year-by-year chronicle, and he frequently introduces his account of each year with a list of information such as the consuls for the year, assignments by the senate of military commands and provinces, and how many troops each general was allowed to recruit.[4] These almost always give figures of troops as a breakdown into specified numbers of Romans, Latins and Italians, revealing that a significant number of Latin troops were required to assist Roman forces every year.

Unlike communities with Roman citizenship, which were part of the Roman state and had limited autonomy, Latin colonies remained fully independent and self-governing states, although they were expected to adopt forms of government and civic organisation that were closely based on those of Rome. They were governed by elected boards of annual mag-istrates (mostly *quattuorviri*, or boards of four magistrates), supported by a council of leading men. Latin was adopted as the language of public business, even where it was not the native language of the community.[5] We do not know of any legal compulsion to do so, and as far as we can tell this seems to have been voluntary, although it may have been encouraged by Rome.

The new Latin cities and colonies were fundamental to Roman control of Italy, because of their close political, social and cultural ties with Rome. Their troops became a key element of Rome's fighting strength, something graphically demonstrated in 209, at the height of the war against Hannibal: when twelve Latin states declared that they no longer had the resources to help Rome, this caused consternation in the senate, not just because of the military loss but also because it was feared that the loyalty of Rome's closest allies and supporters might be wavering. The colonies concerned were Nepet, Sutrium, Ardea, Cales, Alba, Carseoli, Sora, Suessa, Setia, Circeii, Narnia and Interamna Lirenas, many of which were located rela-tively close to Rome. Fortunately, the other twenty-three Latin states did not follow suit, but the episode starkly illustrates the significance of the Latin element in Rome's military power. The senate's outrage is underlined by the penalties imposed on them in retaliation. In 205, when Rome had begun to re-establish control over Italy, the dissenting colonies had their annual military quotas doubled and their troops were also sent to serve overseas, prolonging the length of service required.

Looking beyond military matters, the legal rights inherent in being Latin helped to forge closer social and economic links between Rome and the Latins than was the case with the rest of Italy. Particularly at the elite level of society legal protection for trade and commercial contracts facilitated economic interaction, and the recognition of the legitimacy of offspring from intermarriage helped maintain kinship links between Rome and the Latin communities. Latin cities and colonies also played an important role in the dissemination of many other aspects of Roman culture – such as Roman-style forms of government, the use of the Latin language and Roman forms of urban life – which will be considered in more detail below.

Allies and alliances

The remaining Italian states that were conquered by Rome, or which nego-tiated voluntary alliances, remained independent. Relations with Rome were governed by treaties. These were bilateral agreements, which created a web of alliances with Rome firmly at the centre. Rome undermined mul-tilateral federations, such as the Samnite League or the Latin League, by insisting on dealing individually with each member. Networks of informal contacts and alliances between groups of Italians did, of course, exist and sometimes caused complex clashes of interests, as the needs of one treaty cut across the demands of another. Rome, however, did not recognise these and maintained the initiative by virtue of being the one common point of contact between all Italians.

As far as we can tell, the terms of the treaties that underpinned this structure were very formulaic and also very general. The only surviving evidence is Dionysios of Halicarnassus' version of the Cassian treaty of 493, discussed above (pp. 200–201), which stipulated that the Romans and Latins should maintain peace and friendship and provide mutual military help in the event of being attacked by another state. These terms are consistent with other information about treaties between Rome and Italian states in the fourth and third centuries. At the conclusion of the Pyrrhic war in 270, for instance, Tarentum became a Roman ally but was permitted to retain its own independence (Livy, *Per.* 15).[6] However, most of our evidence for treaties relates to a later period. Livy (27.21.8, 29.21.8) describes some Italian communities that fought for Hannibal in the Second Punic War having their autonomy and their own laws recognised by Rome as part of a peace treaty. Inscriptions recording the terms of a number of treaties between Rome and various allies have survived, but these date to the second century and refer to alliances with the Greek world, not other Italians.[7] Nevertheless, the terms of these are very similar to those of the Foedus Cassianum. The principal differences lie in the omission of the clauses concerning contracts, which may have been specific to the circumstances of fifth-century Latium, and the provision for the terms of the treaty to be altered. Overall, it seems likely that the terms of treaties between Rome and its Italian allies followed the same pattern as those of the Foedus Cassianum and the second-century treaties.

The central duty of a Roman ally was to support Rome in time of war, either by supplying troops to the Roman army or by denying assistance to

Rome's enemies. Strictly speaking, treaties were mutual defensive pacts, by which Rome agreed to assist any ally that was attacked by a third party, and in return the allies agreed to assist Rome if it was attacked. This was based on the Roman idea of *bellum iustum* – a 'just war', undertaken for self-protection when attacked. A war of aggression, in which Rome made the first attack, was by definition not *iustum*, and therefore allies were not, strictly speaking, obliged to help. Needless to say, as Rome's power grew, the defensive nature of these alliances came to be honoured more in the breach than the observance. Roman demands for troops from allies and Latins became an annual event as Rome's wide-ranging strategic commitments made annual campaigns, and eventually a standing army, a necessity. The principle that, if one of Rome's allies was threatened, Rome could call on the whole alliance to support it was rapidly established. The growing network of allies presented ever-increasing opportunities to interfere in support of those allies' interests. In theory, these treaties were alliances between equals, but the growing disparity between the power of Rome and that of any other individual ally from the third century onwards ensured that Rome quickly became the dominant partner. At the same time, the notion that only a 'just' or defensive war could be sanctioned by religious custom began to disappear, and by the second century, when Rome was expanding into both the east and west Mediterranean, Italian allies were being increasingly called on to support overt wars of conquest.

In other respects, allies were self-determining independent states. Before the end of the third century there seems to have been little Roman interference in the internal affairs of her allies except when there was a threat to Roman interests or to the loyalty of a particular ally, but where there was, punishment could be severe. In 314, for instance, the Apulian city of Luceria revolted against Rome. When the revolt had been suppressed, the leaders of the rebellion were executed and a Latin colony was established there. This arm's-length relationship changed somewhat in the second century, a period during which Rome's policy towards the allies became more interventionist and heavy-handed, but before 200 there is relatively little evidence that Rome took a close interest in the internal affairs of its allies. They retained their own laws and forms of government and were free to act as they wished – always providing that they did not do anything that went against Rome's wishes or interests. They retained their own languages and cultures, although the dominance of Rome and the practical need to be able to communicate and interact with Romans

– both officials and others – meant that some aspects of Roman culture were gradually adopted throughout Italy.

The nature of Roman control in Italy

As will be apparent by now, Rome's control of Italy was primarily a military alliance. It secured domination by loosely tying Rome to the rest of Italy via a network of treaties whose principal purpose was to safeguard Rome from attack and allow it to draw on Italian military manpower. The main duty of other Italians – whether allied, Latins or Roman citizens – was to provide troops to give military support to Rome as and when required. This could in itself extend Roman administrative control by indirect means. Polybios describes an invasion of Gauls into northern Italy in 225 that alarmed the senate to such an extent that it sent messengers to all the allies requesting a census of their total military manpower. In the event, the incursion was defeated on the battlefield, and a full muster of all available Italian troops was not needed, but Polybios' descriptions of this, and other military levies, gives us valuable information about relations between Rome and its allies:

> At any rate, I must proceed to describe the levy and the number of troops available to them at that time. Each consul commanded four legions of Roman citizens, composed of 5,200 infantry and 300 cavalry each. The allied troops in each consular army totalled 30,000 infantry and 2,000 cavalry. The Sabines and Etruscans, who had temporarily come to Rome's aid, had 4,000 cavalry and more than 50,000 infantry. The Romans gathered these troops and stationed them on the border of Etruria, commanded by a praetor. The levy of the Umbrians and Sarsinates, who lived in the Apennines, totalled around 20,000, and there were 20,000 Veneti and Cenomani. [...] The list of men able to fight that were sent back were as follows: Latins, 80,000 infantry and 5,000 cavalry; Samnites, 70,000 infantry and 7,000 cavalry; Iapygians and Messapians, 50,000 infantry and 16,000 cavalry; Lucanians, 30,000 infantry and 3,000 cavalry; Marsi, Marrucini, Frentani and Vestini, 20,000 infantry and 4,000 cavalry.
>
> (Pol. 2.24)

The figures for military manpower given by Greek and Roman historians are debatable, but Polybios' figures do not seem entirely unlikely.[8] They give a vivid sense of the enormous reserves of military manpower available to the Romans by the late third century, and this was an important factor in Rome's ability to withstand the wars against Pyrrhus (281–270) and Hannibal (218–200), as well as conquering a Mediterranean-wide empire. They also indicate that Rome was willing to demand a full census of adult male citizens from its allies, and that the allies were able to supply it. This in itself demonstrates that Roman conquest imposed a certain level of administrative accountability on Italian states and required them to adopt some means of listing and registering their citizens.

The mechanisms by which Rome put the terms of the treaties into practice are obscure. Some sources refer to something called the *formula togatorum* – literally, the list of those who wear the toga – in connection with military levies. It seems to have been a list of allied and Latin states that had a duty to supply troops to Rome, but it may also have been more detailed – possibly a register of how many soldiers Rome was entitled to ask for, or an estimate of each state's maximum manpower of the sort described by Polybios. Either way, it seems that Rome kept some form of record of allied manpower and how much it was entitled to demand if the military need arose.

Polybios provides a detailed description of how a Roman army was assembled each year, drawn up in its units and wealth classes, with the allied troops selected for that year assembled in similar fashion, but this is idealised and probably does not reflect actual practice. In his books covering the second century Livy says that the senate allotted troops to each commander at the beginning of the year, specifying maximum numbers of infantry and cavalry levied from Roman citizens, Latins and allies, but rarely any restriction on where they were to come from. The numbers provided by each ally seem to have been left to the individual general. The occasions when the senate did intervene over the obligations of a particular state were usually the result of exceptional circumstances: for instance, the doubling of the obligations of some Latin colonies in 205 as a punishment.

The lack of a central administration for Italy seems to have resulted in ad hoc arrangements for regulating the allies' behaviour and enforcing their military obligations. Nevertheless, Rome's military demands did have wider implications. Allies needed to have the administrative capabilities to produce regular and accurate censuses of their citizens in order to meet Roman military demands. There is considerable evidence that shared military service in the third and second centuries helped to break down barriers between Romans and other Italians, and also to disseminate some key aspects of Roman culture, notably the use of Latin. Although allied troops served in their own local units, their officers still needed to be able to communicate with their Roman counterparts. By the end of the third century Italy was still highly regionalised and a long way from being culturally Romanised, but the demands of military alliance and military service certainly helped to spread some aspects of Romanisation.

Roman colonisation

The practice of founding colonies in territory confiscated from conquered enemies was regarded in Antiquity as central to Rome's success as a major power. Cicero refers to colonies as being 'bulwarks of empire', and Livy believed they enhanced Roman strength by increasing the number of citizens. This connection between colonisation and Roman power is corroborated by a letter of King Philip V of Macedon to the city of Larissa in Thessaly, written in 217. In it he says that 'the Romans, [...] when they free their slaves, admit them to citizenship and grant them a share in their magistracies, and in this manner, they have not only increased the size of their own country, but have also been able to send colonies to nearly 70 places' (*SIG* 543).[9]

Clearly colonisation was an important means of spreading both Roman power and Roman culture. It transformed the way Italian communities were organised, as they were forced to adopt forms of law and government based more closely on those of Rome. We have a number of detailed accounts of how colonies were founded, and a growing body of epigraphic and archaeological evidence for their impact on the regions colonised. By 241 it is estimated that around 30 per cent of the total area of Italy was classed as *ager romanus* – territory directly owned and ruled by Rome (fig. 25). At least nineteen Latin colonies and ten Roman colonies were founded between 338 and 241, involving resettlement of an estimated 71,300 adult males (i.e., more than 150,000 people) and more than 7,000 km² (over 2,700 square miles) of territory for the Latin colonies alone. Colonisation was a process with a transformative effect on a large amount of Italy and many aspects of Italian life. Recent scholarship on colonisation has, however, questioned many earlier assumptions about how colonies were founded, aspects of their urban development and how they interacted with the local populations.[10]

Romans traditionally divided colonies into two groups – Latin and Roman – which had different administrative and legal relationships with the Roman state. Roman colonies were, as the name suggests, colonies of Roman citizens. They were formally part of the Roman state, with only limited local autonomy. Their territory counted as *ager romanus* – territory of the city of Rome – and their inhabitants had Roman citizenship. Latin colonies, in contrast, were much larger, and were independent and self-governing states.

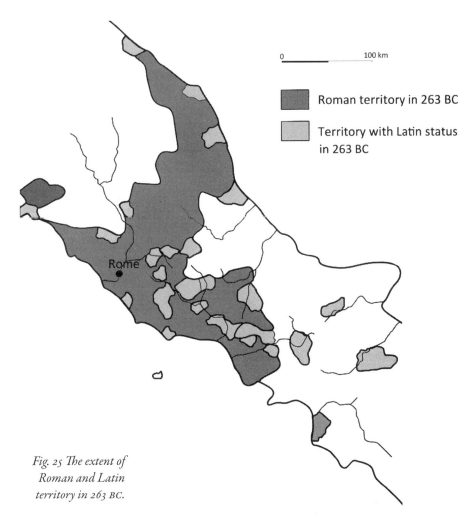

Fig. 25 The extent of Roman and Latin territory in 263 BC.

Date	Colony	Region/Territory
338	Antium	Volsci
329	Tarracina	Volsci
318	Privernum	Latium
296	Minturnae	Aurunci
296	Sinuessa	Aurunci
290–286	Castrum Novum	Picenum or Etruria
283	Sena Gallica	Umbria
247	Aesis	Umbria
247	Alsium	Etruria
245	Fregenae	Etruria

Table 8: **Roman colonies, 338–245**

There were other important distinctions, aside from the fundamental differences in their legal status and relationship to Rome. Most Roman colonies were too small to be independent self-governing communities, which is why they remained part of the Roman state and retained Roman citizenship. Livy, where he gives figures, says they consisted of between two and three hundred settlers, who were usually settled in an existing community, rather than forming a new one. Each colonist was allotted a modest plot of land (typically *c.* 5–10 *iugera,* roughly corresponding to 2.5–5 ha, or 6–12 acres) confiscated from the community, or from anti-Roman elements within it, as a consequence of defeat by Rome. Latin colonies, in contrast, could be much larger, and were often – although not always – new cities, again founded on land confiscated from Rome's enemies. They seem to have typically consisted of *c.* 2,500–6,000 colonists, although some second-century colonies were larger.

The smaller Roman colonies seem to have been used to establish a permanent Roman presence in areas that were perceived as militarily vulnerable or particularly troublesome and were within the existing *ager romanus*. In the fourth century, Roman colonies were founded in a number of coastal settlements, such as Antium, Minturnae and Tarracina, which were vulnerable to attack from the sea. These were designated as *coloniae maritimae* (maritime colonies), and, unusually, the colonists were exempted from serving in the Roman army. These colonies acted as resident garrisons to keep an eye on the local population and to protect

Date	Colony	Region	Settlers (adult males)	Territory (km²)
334	Cales	Campania	2,500	100
328	Fregellae	Latium	4,000	305
314	Luceria	Apulia	2,500	790
313	Saticula	Samnium	2,500	195
313	Suessa Aurunca	Latium	2,500	180
313	Pontiae islands	(Latium)	300	10
312	Interamna Lirenas	Latium	4,000	265
303	Sora	Latium	4,000	230
303	Alba Fucens	Central Apennines	6,000	420
299	Narnia	Umbria	2,500	185
298	Carseoli	Central Apennines	4,000	285
291	Venusia	Apulia	6,000	800
289	Hadria	Central Apennines	4,000	380
273	Paestum	Lucania	4,000	540
273	Cosa	Etruria	2,500	340
268	Ariminum	Umbria	6,000	650
268	Beneventum	Samnium	6,000	575
264	Firmum	Picenum	4,000	400
263	Aesernia	Samnium	4,000	485
Total			71,300	7,135

Table 9: **Latin colonies, 334–263** (after Brunt 1971, based on figures from Livy)

them from attack. Where large settlements were established in strategic areas outside the *ager romanus*, they were given Latin status and were independent, self-governing communities. In many cases these were regions with low levels of urbanisation, and one effect of Latin colonisation was to spread Roman-style urban settlement. Recent studies (notably by Pelgrom and Stek) suggest that the status of colonies in the early and mid- Republic was far more fluid than previously believed, and that there may have been much more flexibility in the legal relationship and military obligations between colonies and Rome. Decisions about founding a colony, its status and its location seem to have been driven by short-term pressures of various types, whether strategic demands or the political agendas of factions and individuals, rather than the result of a coherent strategy of expansion.

Given that Latin colonies were relatively large, they pose the question of where the colonists came from, and how Rome managed to send substantial groups of settlers without depleting its own population. Many were Roman citizens who gave up their citizenship in exchange for land, becoming citizens of the new community, and therefore holding Latin status, instead. As Philip V's letter (page 274) notes, manumitted slaves provided a pool of potential colonists, as did landless urban Romans, but these groups are too small to account for all the colonists sent out in the fourth and third centuries. Other colonists were probably allies. After a successful campaign, the spoils (land as well as movable booty) were divided between the Roman and allied troops that had taken part. Land could be allocated as individual allotments, but it was often used to found a colony, and since allies were entitled to a share of confiscated land, it seems likely that they were eligible to join new colonies. Latin colonies were, therefore, probably a mixture of Romans and allies, all of whom gave up their original citizenship to become citizens of the colony, although with Latin rights, conferred by the Latin status of the new community. If we assume that settlers in Latin colonies included allies as well as Romans, it helps to explain how Rome was able to send out so many large colonies, and also underlines the role of colonies as an important mode of integration between Romans and other Italians.

Ancient writers describe the foundation of a colony as a structured process which took place according to prescribed rituals. The Roman writer Aulus Gellius (Aul. Gell., *NA* 16.13) goes so far as to describe a colony as a mini-Rome, replicating many of the important features of the city itself. At first glance, the evidence seems to bear this out. Colonisation is often presented as a state-driven process which was the product of conscious decision-making and which was highly organised. First, the senate authorised the foundation of a colony, setting out where it should be founded, what sort of colony it should be and how many colonists should be sent there. Commissioners to oversee the foundation were appointed, usually as a board of three men (*tresviri*), who were in charge of recruiting colonists, distributing land and drawing up a colonial charter to establish laws and government of the colony. Where the colony was a new settlement, the auspices were taken by a magistrate and a ritual boundary was established to separate the urban centre from its territory. Key cults were founded, the land was surveyed and distributed to the colonists and new forms of civic administration were established. The civic organisation of colonies was based, like that of Rome, on a local senate and annually elected magistrates, usually a board of two *duoviri* (or sometimes of four *quattuorviri*), although details differed from place to place. Some adopted internal subdivisions named after areas of Rome, such as the 'vicus Esquilinus' mentioned in an inscription from Cales. Overall, the impression is of a highly organised process deliberately designed to replicate aspects of Rome itself.

However, none of this is straightforward. Most sources for foundation rituals, and for other forms of colonial organisation, date to the first century or later. They often conflate foundation rituals from different contexts and periods, or represent later practices. Additionally, investigations of colonial sites raise important questions about whether they really were as organised and structured in their earliest phases as they sometimes appear to be. Many only acquire their characteristic regular urban plan and key Roman buildings some considerable time after their foundation, possibly, as Sewell has suggested, as a result of Rome's widening Mediterranean connections, driven by the influence of Greek urban planning rather than a desire to replicate Rome or convey any ideal of *romanitas*. On current evidence, it is questionable whether colonisation was quite such a highly organised and state-sponsored act as was previously believed. Early colonies, founded between the sixth and early fourth centuries, may have been the result of individuals settling bands of their own supporters, clients or troops – all-male groups which then intermarried into the local population – in a much more ad hoc manner. The arrival of clans such as the Appii Claudii in Rome in the fifth century demonstrates that it was possible at this date for groups of people simply to migrate to a new state. The process of founding a colony undoubtedly did become more systematic, and most colonies adopted many Rome-like features in their organisation and physical appearance, but this may have been a long-term process, reflecting changes in ideas about colonial and urban form during the third and second centuries, rather than as a result of a specific Roman 'blueprint' of how to found a colony.

The impact of Roman settlement on the communities colonised varied hugely, according to the location and circumstances. Thanks to the archaeological and epigraphic evidence now available, it is possible to trace the development of some colonies in considerable detail. Colonisation could alter the social structure of a community profoundly. Many Italian city-states were small, and even a small group of several hundred colonists would make an impact on a community of this size, and the introduction of several thousand settlers – mostly from a different ethnic background and speaking a different language – would have meant change and disruption. One of the better-documented colonies – Pompeii – was founded in the 80s and is outside the scope of this volume, but it is worth noting that Pompeian electoral inscriptions show that the colonists came to occupy most positions of political power very quickly. The elite of the pre-colonial period were rapidly supplanted. Although we do not have equivalent evidence for earlier colonies, there is no reason to suppose that colonists were any less effective in imposing themselves as a new social and political elite. At Antium, colonists and pre-colonial inhabitants initially seem to have formed parallel communities with separate administrations, and we know of other cases where the colonists had a status that was different from – and more privileged than – the indigenous population.

Colonies undoubtedly assisted the dissemination of Roman culture and Roman forms of urban life, but this was a complex process and there seems to have been wide variation between different regions and even between the experiences of different colonies. Colonies adopted Latin as an official language, and many constructed specifically Roman types of public building, although the extent to which they happened systematically and from the earliest phase of settlement is increasingly doubtful. The work of Pelgrom and Stek has cast doubt on whether fourth- and third-century colonies were even organised as fully fledged cities in their early stages of existence. Town centres were too small to accommodate all the colonies, and many seem to have lived in dispersed settlements in the area settled, using the 'urban' area as a meeting place and administrative centre. Certainly, many key buildings that have previously been regarded as characteristic of Roman colonies were not added until a later state of development.

Capitolia (temples of Jupiter Capitolinus), for instance, are often assumed to have been constructed shortly after foundation as a symbol of Roman rule, since this was the central cult of the Roman state. Recent studies, however, show that in many colonies this was a later development, taking place well after the establishment of the colony, and in some cases not at all. In other cases the capitoline cult co-existed with other cults with strong local roots. At Alba Fucens, the important local cult of Hercules was worshipped alongside that of Jupiter, suggesting that religious continuity was at least as important, if not more so, than accommodation of Roman gods and practices. *Curia* and *comitia* – buildings that housed political gatherings and meetings of the local senate – were constructed in many colonies, and most were organised around the regular street grid and rectangular forum that are instantly familiar as the cultural archetype of a planned Roman city. One problem with this argument, however, is that Rome itself had an extremely irregular and unplanned development, very different from the layout of colonies, and excavation of Fregellae, Alba Fucens, Cosa and Paestum has shown that they were less uniformly planned than previously believed. Rather than spreading clones of the city of Rome, colonisation disseminated a form of urban life that was, in fact, very different from the way in which Rome itself developed, and which may reflect growing Greek influence on ideas about urbanism, in both Rome and Italy.

In order to give a sense of the impact of a colony, we can examine two contemporary but contrasting examples. Cosa and Paestum were both Latin colonies founded in 273, but their circumstances were very different. Cosa, founded on the Etruscan coast, was a new settlement. Paestum, in contrast, had a long previous history, having been founded by Greek settlers in the early sixth century, and at the time of the Roman colonisation it was a flourishing community with a mixed Greek and Lucanian population.

Although Paestum (fig. 26) was a well-established city, with all the buildings, amenities and organisation that this implies, the impact of the Roman colony was immediate and drastic.[11] Third-century inscriptions refer to the magistrates as *quattuorviri*, a Roman title, indicating that the civic administration had been reorganised on Roman lines. Both the languages of pre-Roman Paestum – Greek and Oscan – disappeared rapidly, and Latin was used for all public inscriptions. There were also many changes to the fabric of the city. The agora – the Greek equivalent of a forum or market-place, which was the centre of public life in the earlier period – was abandoned, and a circular building (Ekklesiasterion) used for meetings of the council and people of the city was demolished. Instead, a large rectangular area next to it was cleared, and a new forum was constructed. This contained two Roman-style temples, of which one may have been dedicated to Jupiter Capitolinus, and the other dedicated to the Roman cult of Mens Bona. Other additions were a Curia/Comitium

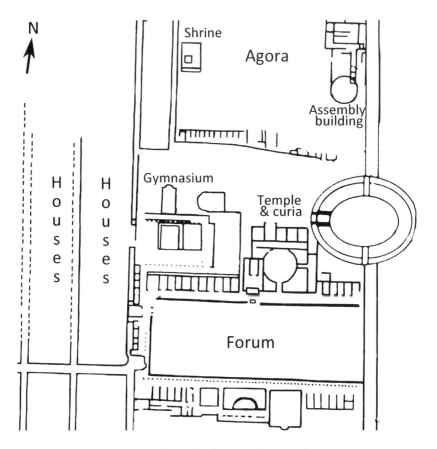

N

Shrine

Agora

Assembly
building

Houses

Houses

Gymnasium

Temple
& curia

Forum

Fig. 26 Paestum: plan of the forum and surrounding area.

to house political assemblies and meetings of the new colonial senate, baths and a gymnasium. The entire area was surrounded with shops and porticoes. Altogether it makes a powerful statement about the new political order, and marginalises the Graeco-Oscan city centre both literally and symbolically. The new order is visible in other aspects of civic life. New Roman cults were established, and although some pre-Roman cult places continued in use, they show changes in religious practice. At the sanctuary of Hera, for instance, many worshippers now offered votive figurines of mothers and children – which suggests the establishment of a new fertility cult – rather than the traditional statuettes of Hera. Other cults show more continuity, but votive inscriptions change from Oscan to Latin, suggesting that the worshippers were colonists rather than locals.

Cosa, 140 km (86 miles) north-east of Rome, was a rather different case. It was a new city founded on a hilltop overlooking the coast and a small harbour (fig. 27). Although close to the site of a small Etruscan town, there are few signs of any pre-Roman settlement on the site of the colony itself. It consisted of *c.* 2,500 settlers, and the traces of the land survey grid suggests that they were each given small plots of land of 6 Roman *iugera* (*c.*1.5 ha, or 3 acres). As it was a new town, the colony's founders had more freedom to plan it as they pleased, although the steep terrain imposed limits to this.

Like many Roman colonies, it had a regular plan based around a street grid dividing the city into roughly equal square plots. Because of the steepness of the site, the forum is placed on one side of the city rather than in the centre, as is more usual. The city was surrounded by a wall 1.5 km (just under 1 mile) long, with four gateways, enclosing an area of 13.25 ha (32 acres). In addition to its obvious function as a fortification and a boundary between city and countryside, this served as an imposing statement of Roman power and control to anyone approaching Cosa. There was also a second internal wall surrounding the highest point in the city, serving as an additional fortification surrounding the main temple of Cosa, which was located on the hilltop.

The earliest structure on the citadel was not a temple but a square enclosure. This is significant, as one of the key rituals performed when

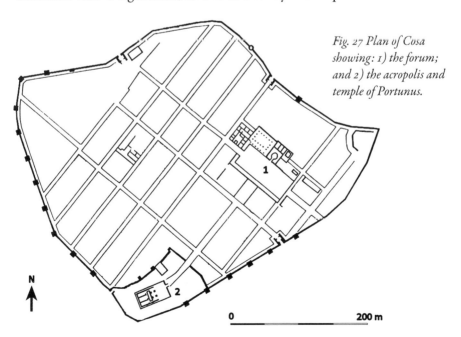

Fig. 27 Plan of Cosa showing: 1) the forum; and 2) the acropolis and temple of Portunus.

N

0   200 m

a colony was founded was the taking of the auspices, which required the augur to stand in just such an enclosure on the highest point of a site. Most of the earliest public building centred on the forum and focused on structures concerned with the government of the new colony. An important complex of buildings on the north-east side of the forum included a circular Comitium to house meetings of the local senate and possibly public assemblies of the colonists. Unlike many colonies, Cosa did not have a temple in the forum but there was an open-air precinct to one side of the Comitium which contained an altar. There was also another small shrine in the south-east corner of the forum, and a small structure which may have been a prison.

One of the major problems in understanding the development of Cosa is that there is remarkably little archaeological evidence for the third-century colony. Although Frank Brown, the original excavator, viewed it as a 'typical' Roman colony, more recent investigation by Fentress, Bodel and others has revealed that only the walls, the Comitium and its associated enclosure, and the prison, can be dated to the third century; all other structures, including housing, relate to the arrival of a second group of colonists in 197. The investigators conclude from this that there is little evidence to support the presence of a substantial colony between 273 and 197, and that the third-century settlement was either very much smaller than our sources suggest or was unsuccessful and rapidly abandoned by most of the first group of settlers.

At Paestum we can see that the priority for the new colony was to establish the Roman identity of the city and, if necessary, to overshadow important symbols of the previous community. Roman cults were set up; public buildings that were intimately connected with Roman ways of government were constructed to house the colonial administration; and public space was organised in ways that reflected Roman ideas about urban life. Roman forms of government were adopted, and the Latin language became the norm for public business. Colonies were not clones of Rome in the literal sense of replicating the exact layout of Rome itself, but they had an important role in disseminating Roman language and culture and the Roman way of life. However, the slow development of Cosa demonstrates that there was a wide variation in colonial development, and that it is impossible to construct a single universal model of how they grew and interacted with the local population.

This brings us to one of the most difficult issues in recent scholarship on ancient Rome and its relations with the peoples it conquered, namely the diffusion of Roman culture and its interaction with the cultures of the people it came to rule. This topic – the process traditionally termed 'Romanisation' – has generated enormous controversy in recent years, to the point where 'Romanisation' is no longer an acceptable term to describe it in the eyes of many historians. To a large extent this is justified: the term was all too often used to describe a top-down, one-way process in which a well-defined collection of cultural practices, ranging from urban life and Roman-style buildings and architecture, Roman inscriptions, the use of Latin and adoption of Roman-style names to personal styles, such as wearing the toga, were disseminated by more advanced Romans and progressively adopted by less sophisticated (and sometimes downright barbarian) Italians and provincials.[12]

A key problem in dealing with the concept of 'Romanisation' is that it is largely descriptive rather than analytical. Another is that it assumes a largely passive population of non-Romans, uncritically consuming Roman culture and customs. More recent and nuanced approaches, such as those of Wallace-Hadrill, Mattingley, Roth and Witcher, give greater agency to the peoples with whom Rome interacted, emphasising selectiveness in what aspects of Roman culture they adopted and how they used them. They explore how, and why, people might have switched between local and Roman cultural behaviours which continued to co-exist, and examine the development of hybrid Roman/local cultures. It is difficult to create an overarching model for explaining and understanding the interactions of Roman and non-Roman cultures in all circumstances in ancient Italy. However, a key point is that we should regard such interactions, and changes arising from them, as a cultural dialogue between Romans and others, in which Roman customs were selectively adopted and often adapted into hybrid forms, and in which Roman and non-Roman cultures co-existed. It is also not a linear or one-way process. Being (or becoming) Roman covers a range of different scenarios – ethnic identity, legal status or adoption of Roman material culture and Roman ways of life – and is not static. Roman culture itself changes during the period covered by this volume, as a result of social and economic developments, and of contact with other cultures such as those of the Greeks, Etruscans and Campanians, as do those of other Italian peoples.

The cultures of Rome and other Italian states were starting to converge in some respects in the third century, but regional languages and cultures were still flourishing. Contact with Romans and with Roman government varied considerably according to geographical location and social status. Members of the ruling elites of Italian states had far more contact with their Roman counterparts than the ordinary Italian peasant or craftsman, and had shared interests and concerns, such as the need to protect and enhance family properties and economic interests, and maintain their social status, particularly in comparison to their peers. Noble families regularly intermarried, creating networks of family connections and social obligations between the aristocracies of different states. Pacuvius Calavius, a leading Capuan aristocrat, married into the Claudii and was well connected in both Capua and Rome (although this did not stop him leading a Capuan revolt against Rome in 215). This web of social connections of various types, whether family relationships, guest-friendships or other contacts, helped to maintain contacts not just between Romans and Italians but between Italians from different states and regions and to break down cultural boundaries between them. Below the level of the elites, contact between Italians and Romans may have been fairly limited beyond the areas within easy travelling distance of Rome. Within a certain radius, however, there was regular movement of people and goods between Rome and neighbouring states within Latium, southern Etruria and Sabine territory.

From the third century onwards army service played an important role in disseminating Roman culture. Roman armies increasingly consisted not only of Romans themselves but also of contingents of allies summoned by Rome to assist in its wars. The misbehaving 'Roman' garrison that went rogue and took over Rhegium in 285, for instance, was not actually Roman but a contingent of allied troops from Campania. These fought in their own units, commanded by their own officers, but inevitably there must have been a fair amount of contact between Roman and Italian troops during the course of a campaign and, in particular, between Roman and Italian commanders. This became a particularly powerful force for contact and integration between units from all over Italy during the second century, when campaigns often lasted for years on end, but even in the third century, when they tended to be shorter, it was significant. By 218, when Hannibal invaded Italy, historians such as Polybios and Livy were able to draw a contrast between the Carthaginian army, which they described as a motley collection of Carthaginians and allies of different origins who lacked a common language or identity, and the Roman army, in which both Romans and Italians had a sense of shared kinship that overcame their linguistic and ethnic differences.[13] There was clearly a sense of shared kinship between all Italians, including Romans, when faced with a foreign threat, but Italian regions and individual communities retained many elements of their own culture until well into the second and first centuries.

Although the system of control described in this chapter may seem cumbersome, and developed in an ad hoc manner as Rome sought answers to administrative problems posed by rapid expansion, it was remarkably stable and successful. It also gave Italy a unique place in the Roman world. Roman conquests outside Italy, beginning with Sicily in the mid-third century, were invariably turned into provinces under the direct supervision of the senate. They had a Roman governor and administration, and often had a Roman army based there as well. Italy, in contrast, remained as a loosely knit collection of allies and colonies until the Italian revolt of 91–89 forced Rome to extend its citizenship to the whole peninsula.

The flexibility of the alliance was one of the key aspects that made it so effective. The treaties with other Italians committed Rome to very little other than to provide military protection in return for similar assistance when required. However, this was in itself something that helped drive Roman expansionism, and the extension of Roman influence through a network of alliances that were mutual defence agreements led to a self-perpetuating cycle of wars. The larger the number of allies, the greater the chance at any given time that either Rome's interests and security or those of one of its allies would be threatened by some outsider, and the greater the likelihood that Rome would call out an army and go to war. As a result, Rome became embroiled in wars at an ever-increasing distance from the city, and acquired an ever-increasing set of alliances, entanglements and obligations as a result. At the same time, the military nature of the alliances gave Rome access to a vast reserve of Italian manpower, permitting Roman forces to take on ever greater challenges. This process culminated in Rome's first venture outside Italy in 264, when an alliance with Messana (modern Messina) in Sicily led to the First Punic War, and the acquisition of the island as Rome's first overseas protectorate. The Second Punic War, fought mainly in Italy, put Roman control under unprecedented strain as Hannibal inflicted major defeats and sought to undermine Rome's alliances with the Italians. In the meantime, it is worth noting that, despite its complex and peculiar nature, Rome's web of alliances and colonies in Italy proved remarkably stable and a firm basis for the establishment of its empire.

PART IV

FROM CITY-STATE TO
ITALIAN DOMINANCE

14

THE IMPACT
OF CONQUEST:
ROME, 340–264

The fifth-century government of Rome was an exercise in experimentation, but during the fourth and third centuries we can see it starting to develop further towards the form that it took in the middle and late Republic. The Licinio-Sextian laws definitively established the consulship as the most senior magistracy, while the Lex Genucia of 342 limited the number of times and frequency with which men could hold the highest offices, but it seems to have been some time before these measures had much impact on public life. Between 366 and 291 fifty-four of the 142 consulships (38 per cent) were held by just fourteen individuals, most of whom held office many times. Despite the restrictions imposed by the Lex Genucia, it was not until the 290s that this began to change. After this point, however, it became very rare to hold the consulship more than once. High office and the power, prestige and status that went with it were shared among a much wider group of Roman nobles. By the middle of the third century Roman life was no longer dominated by a narrow hereditary nobility. It was still controlled by an oligarchy, but one drawn from a wider group of families, whose power was increasingly linked to the growing influence of the senate.

The development of the influence of the senate was not a foregone conclusion. The years between 312 and 291 were a period of turmoil and political experimentation, during which senatorial dominance was challenged by a group of influential men who attempted to rule via engagement with the popular assemblies, but after 291 the senate increasing established itself as the dominant force in Rome. The best-known of these challengers to senatorial power is Appius Claudius Caecus, whose unusual career is documented in an honorific inscription restored in the Augustan period:

> Appius Claudius Caecus, son of Gaius, censor, consul twice, dictator, *interrex* three times, praetor twice, curule aedile twice, quaestor, military tribune three times. He captured a number of towns from the Samnites, and defeated an army of Sabines and Etruscans. He prevented peace being made with King Pyrrhus. During his censorship, he paved the Via Appia and built an aqueduct for Rome, and built a temple of Bellona.
>
> (*CIL* 6.40943)

If the inscription is correct about the order of these offices (it gives no indication of the dates at which he held them), it seems that, although he held a number of magistracies that were usually held before the consulship, Appius does not appear to have followed them up by election as consul. Instead, he became censor in 312, a senior office that was later reserved for those who had already held the consulship. One of the key duties of the censor was to scrutinise and revise membership of the senate. Another was responsibility for supervising the leasing of *ager publicus* and issuing contracts for construction of major public works. Despite having held important military commands, he was never awarded a triumph, and his main claims to fame were his censorship, a number of wide-ranging reforms and a high-profile, and expensive, programme of public works, including the construction of the Via Appia and the Aqua Appia, the first of Rome's major roads and aqueducts. In many respects they were much needed, as Rome's military campaigns in the south required roads for moving troops, and the city of Rome was growing rapidly and in need of better infrastructure, but they were costly and were said to have drained the state treasury of cash.

Surviving accounts of Appius' reforming activities are contradictory, and their political significance is not always clear. They are also coloured by a literary tradition that portrayed members of the patrician Claudii as arrogant, reactionary and very defensive of patrician status and privilege. As presented by Livy (who acknowledges that there were multiple differing accounts of his actions), he was an uneasy combination of reactionary and radical populist, whose political reforms were contentious. When revising the senate, he was accused of passing over suitably qualified men of good character on spurious and politically partisan grounds. Some of the men who were admitted to membership were regarded as unworthy, compared to those who were omitted. His colleague as censor, Gaius Plautius, resigned in disgust, leaving Appius Claudius as sole censor until 308. His revised senate was rejected by the consuls for 311, who continued to summon it using the pre-312 membership lists, and his attempted overhaul of senatorial membership ultimately failed.

Controversially, Appius followed this with an attempt to reorganise the voting tribes of the *comitia tributa* and *comitia centuriata*. By this date Roman citizens were divided into thirty-one tribes, membership of which was determined by which area of the city or of Roman territory an individual came from. New colonies or newly enfranchised citizens were enrolled by region, and the areas of Italy that were legally Roman territory were carved up into a patchwork of different voting tribes. Not all tribes were equal, however. Four were designated 'urban tribes', and the remaining divisions, which reached a final total of thirty-one in 241, were known as 'rural tribes'. The original division was a distinction between those citizens from the city of Rome itself and those who lived in the various territories belonging to Rome, but it rapidly became a social distinction. Most landowners were registered in rural tribes, according to where they held their estates, while some social groups of low status – freed slaves, for instance, or those who owned no land – were restricted to the urban tribes. The outcome of an election or a vote on legislation was determined by a block vote – the number of tribes for or against, not the number of individuals – so the twenty-seven (later thirty-one) rural tribes wielded far more legislative and electoral power than the four urban tribes, which could always be outvoted. It seems that Appius Claudius' reform tried to redistribute landless city dwellers, many of whom may have been freedmen or their descendants, throughout all the tribes rather than confining them to the less influential urban tribes. Livy presents this as divisive, commenting that 'from that time onwards the citizen body was divided into two parts: the sensible people, who supported and

upheld the good, took one view, while the "Forum faction" took another'
(9.46.13), although this division is anachronistic, reflecting the political
thought of the first century BC.

Unlike the reform of the senate, however, these changes seem to have
been implemented and remained in force until 304, when they were challenged and overturned. The event that prompted this reversal was the
election of one Gnaeus Flavius as curule aedile for 304. Flavius was the son
of a freedman, who had started out as a scribe, and was the first descendant
of a slave to be elected to a curule magistracy. He carried out important
legal reforms to make public business more accessible to the people, pub-
lishing a calendar indicating the days on which public business could be
conducted (*dies fasti*) and also a document setting out legal procedures.
Neither of these acts was particularly well received by the traditional
Roman aristocracy, but Flavius' real problem was his family background,
which caused some people to refuse him the honours and courtesy usually
due to a magistrate. His election prompted a challenge to the reform of the
tribes, and the censors overturned them and re-established the practice of
confining the landless, descendants of slaves and other social undesirables
to the four urban tribes. Livy knew of several versions of events, one of
which connected Flavius with Appius Claudius. According to this, Flavius
had been Appius Claudius' secretary before his rise to public office, and
he was enrolled as a senator during Claudius' censorship, causing outrage
because of his humble origins.

Appius belatedly went on to become consul in 307, stood for a second
consulship in 297 and caused another political storm by challenging the
result of the election. If conducted strictly according to the laws enforcing
the election of one patrician and one plebeian consul, the outcome would
have been the election of Appius and the plebeian Lucius Volumnius
Flamma. However, there was a strong popular demand for the re-election
of Quintus Fabius Rullianus as the second consul, which was impossible on two counts. He was unable to be a candidate as he was one of
the current consuls and therefore presiding over the elections, and he was
also a patrician, making a joint consulship with Appius illegal. According
to Livy, Appius proposed that the law forbidding two patrician consuls
should be waived to allow the election of Fabius Rullianus as his colleague,
but he was unsuccessful in this.

Appius Claudius' censorship seems to show more radical than reactionary elements. His proposed reforms of the senate and assemblies

reasserted the importance of the assemblies and seems to have encouraged political participation by a wider cross-section of the Roman people, while his public works would have primarily benefited the people of Rome, providing employment and enhanced amenities. It would also have had the effect of enhancing his own reputation and increasing his body of clients. His later career, which included an attempt to overturn the ban on electing two patrician consuls in the same year and his opposition to the Lex Ogulnia, which opened up the priestly colleges to plebeian members, is much more problematic. Most of these measures are reactionary and protective of patrician privilege, a stance that contradicts much of his earlier career. This has led some scholars (notably Wiseman) to reject the authenticity of the sources on Appius Claudius entirely, and Forsythe has argued that many of the changes attributed to him are suspiciously similar to the reforms of Sulla in the 80s. This is too extreme, and his earlier career is both plausible and (in respect of offices held and public works undertaken) is corroborated from other sources; but it is far more difficult to accept the accounts given of his later career. Cornell makes a persuasive case for Appius Claudius as a charismatic politician who tried to appeal to the wider Roman people and challenged the increasing influence of the senate, but most accounts of his later career must be rejected. What emerges most strongly from these episodes is that the late fourth century was a time of transition, in which there were many unresolved debates about the shape of the Roman state and the role of the senate and people.

In the early 280s (probably *c.* 287) there was another outbreak of social and political unrest which resulted in a measure, the Lex Hortensia, that is often regarded as the final resolution in the Struggle of the Orders. Despite this, relatively little is known about it.[1] It is said to have arisen out of economic stress and widespread debt, which triggered a plebeian secession. A plebeian leader called Quintus Hortensius was appointed dictator and resolved the crisis by passing laws that finally gave the full force of law to the decisions of the popular assemblies. He is also said to have tackled the debt problem (Dio frag. 37), but this is very unclear, as it is uncertain whether this fragment of Dio refers to Hortensius or not.

Like so many episodes in the so-called Struggle of the Orders, the crisis of *c.* 287 is a mixture of economic problems and political issues. The background of debt, unrest and secession looks suspiciously similar to incidents in the fifth and fourth centuries, and some of the measures proposed are similar to earlier laws.[2] Nevertheless, references to the Lex Hortensia in later Roman sources and compendia of Roman law make it difficult to dismiss as an historical error, though some details are difficult to accept at face value. The civic unrest may have been caused by a series of crop failures rather than a debt crisis of the type found in the early Republic. There are records of several famines, crop failures and epidemics of disease in the early third century, which might support this explanation. Nevertheless, the content of the law remains a problem. Given the political volatility of the early third century, the plebeians may have felt they needed to reiterate the principle of the legislative power of the assembly even if technically it already existed, but this does not entirely explain away the difficulties. Writing some seven centuries later, the antiquarian Macrobius suggests that the Lex Hortensia may have contained additional clauses, including a stipulation that the law courts had to be open for business on market days, perhaps to facilitate access to law for people living at a distance from Rome, who were likely to visit the city only to sell their produce.[3] If so, the Lex Hortensia may have been intended to reassert the authority of the assembly and to make it easier for people to exercise their political rights.

Whatever its exact content, the Lex Hortensia seems to have effectively drawn a line under the turbulence of the early Republic. From this point onwards we can see the emergence of a form of Republican government that more or less corresponds to that of the second and first centuries. The consulship was now established as the principal magistracy; the consuls wielded the principal executive power in the state, and the office was shared more widely within the elite, with few men holding it more than once in a lifetime. The office of dictator largely fell out of use, and the few dictatorships known in the third century were the result of military emergencies. The *cursus honorum*, which dictated the order in which offices should be held during a political career, was not regularised until the Lex Villia Annalis in 180, but the sequence in which offices were held was becoming more established by the middle of the third century. The office of praetor, introduced in 367, was subordinate to the consuls and had a mainly judicial role.[4] Much of the praetor's time was taken up by hearing lawsuits and supervising the law courts. However, both consuls and praetors possessed *imperium*, or the right of command, and were therefore entitled to command an army. A second praetorship was created in 246 BC, and the numbers were increased further in 227 to meet the need for men to govern territory conquered in Sicily and Sardinia during the First Punic War. It developed into a college of senior magistrates, subordinate only to the consuls in power, whose duties included commanding armies, acting as envoys to foreign powers and (after 264) governing provinces, as well as supervising Rome's law courts. When the office was first established, the praetor enjoyed very high prestige, possibly because only one was elected each year. It was monopolised by patrician families until 337/6, when Quintus Publilius Philo became the first plebeian praetor. The aediles increased from two to four, thanks to the creation of the post of curule aedile which was open to patricians (the aedileship had previously been a plebeian office), but this distinction between curule and plebeian aediles quickly disappeared as the restrictions on plebeians were eroded, leaving a college of four annually elected aediles who were responsible for the day-to-day running of Rome – the maintenance of buildings and streets, supervision of markets and shops, conduct of games and festivals, and maintenance of law and order. Below these were the quaestors, the most junior magistrates, who were primarily financial officials. By the end of the fourth century, Rome was developing a career structure or *cursus* of magistracies (quaestorship, aedileship or tribunate, praetorship, consulship) held by men pursuing a political career.

The assemblies of the Roman people remained the bodies in which the people voted on proposed laws (*comitia tributa*) or elected their magistrates (*comitia centuriata*), but their importance declined during the third and second centuries. Despite their apparent supremacy, and the Lex Hortensia, which reiterated the principle that the *comitia* was the principal law-making body, their role in the political process was essentially passive. They could not meet on their own initiative but only when summoned by a senior magistrate – a consul, a praetor or a tribune. They could only listen to the speeches of the summoning magistrate and accept or reject the proposals (or candidates for office) presented to them, but had no power to debate proposals, make amendments or counter-proposals, or nominate candidates for office. Although measures could not become law without being approved by the popular assembly, giving the people the final say in legislation or elections, they had no power to take the initiative and no input into political debate.

The growth of Roman territory and the changes in the Roman state that took place during the conquest of Italy had a fundamental impact on the assemblies. Most people with land or significant social status were registered in rural tribes, leaving the landless and the lower-status (particularly the urban population of Rome) concentrated into the four urban tribes. This reduced their electoral and voting influence, as they could easily be outvoted by the much greater number of rural tribes. Roman territory was now extensive, and many Roman citizens lived well away from Rome, which limited political participation. Votes and elections had to be completed in a single day, so anyone wishing to vote on a proposal, or in an election, had to arrange to be in Rome on the day on which the *comitia* met. In a world without any easy means of communication or transport, this effectively restricted participation to those who could afford to travel to Rome frequently, or remain there for longer visits – in other words, the well-off and well-connected. Although the Lex Hortensia and other similar laws established the principle of the primacy of the popular assembly, in practice its influence was limited.

A key development of the third century was the emergence of the senate as a new and influential force in the Roman state. Most of our sources date to periods in which the senate had a high degree of influence, and they accord it a similar degree of prominence in early Roman history, but this may not have been the case. As discussed in Chapters 7 and 9, it probably originated as the king's advisory council, later transformed into an advisory body for the consuls. Senators had high personal status – as demonstrated by tales of the way the invading Gauls in 390 were impressed by the dignity with which the senators met them – but we know very little for certain about how they were selected or the role of the senate.

By the later fourth century this was changing. The reforms that admitted plebeians to the senior magistracies and which merged the plebeian 'state within a state' and the patrician institutions into a single system, inevitably had a major effect. The key change was the Lex Ovinia, passed sometime in the late fourth century and certainly by 318. This transferred responsibility for determining membership of the senate to the censors, meaning that senators were no longer dependent on the goodwill of magistrates for their continued membership. Although censors were permitted to nominate anyone of good character (and could reject or remove members on grounds of immorality), in practice the senate was largely composed of ex-magistrates. An important effect of the opening up of senior magistracies to plebeians was the introduction of plebeians into the senate in increasing numbers.

The role of the senate was to debate matters of state and advise the consuls and other senior magistrates, but it had no executive power and its decisions, known as *senatus consulta*, did not have the force of law – passing laws was the prerogative of the *comitia tributa*. Despite this lack of formal powers, the senate had great moral authority and political influence. Once attained, membership of the senate was usually lifelong, and senators were no longer dependent on the patronage or approval of magistrates. As a result the senate as a body acquired greater independence. Most senators were appointed because they had already held a magistracy, and the senate as a whole therefore benefited from the cumulative expertise and also the accumulated moral authority of these ex-magistrates. Its decisions were influential and difficult for either magistrates or assembly to ignore. Our knowledge of how it operated, and how it related to assemblies and magistrates in the third century, is still imperfect, but its power seems to have grown during this period, acquiring control over military and foreign policy, receiving foreign embassies and envoys, determining the size and composition of armies to be levied in any given year and allocating duties and military forces to the consuls. It made decisions about land distributions and foundation of colonies, controlled state finances, maintained public order and exercised control over religious affairs. By the second century, according to the contemporary account of Roman institutions composed by the Greek historian Polybios (Pol. 6.11), the senate was the most powerful and influential element of the Roman state.

One reason for the development of the senate as a dominant element in Roman public life was the practical demands of an increasingly complex state. Rome's growing size and expanding territorial and military interests created a need for a pool of military and administrative expertise. It was no longer possible for the two consuls and their junior magistrates to conduct multiple military campaigns and undertake the complex administrative tasks required to run the expanding state. The practice of extending a magistrate's powers for a fixed period after his year of office, in order to provide military or administrative continuity in a particular task, was introduced. It became routine for an ex-consul or ex-praetor to have *imperium* extended in this way and to be required to take on governorship of a province or some similar task. By detaching possession of *imperium* from the office of consul or praetor, and making it possible for a proconsul or propraetor (as ex-magistrates with *imperium* were known) to exercise some of their powers after their year of office had ended, Rome created a wider pool of men who had the power, authority and experience to conduct military campaigns or govern Rome's expanding empire. The first example of this type of extension of power beyond the year of office (*prorogatio*) occurred in 326, when Quintus Publilius Philo had his military command during the war against Naples extended after his year of office had ended, becoming the first proconsul. On this occasion the powers were awarded by a vote of the popular assembly, although the right to confer them, determine the task allotted and to terminate such a command later became the prerogative of the senate. By the later third century the senate exercised collective power over the careers of individuals as well as being a source of expertise and moral authority, although the absence of Livy's narrative for the early third century makes it difficult to date this development. The result of these changes was that by the mid-third century the senate became established as an important body in Roman government.

Priestly colleges and the development of state religion

The colleges of priests were already long established, but for the fourth and third centuries we have more evidence for how members were selected and how they operated. The three main colleges, the colleges of the pontifices, augurs and *viri sacris faciundis* (Board for Sacred Matters, originally two in number, but increased to ten in 367), each had different roles and methods of selection. Members were drawn from the senatorial class and served for life. In addition, there were other religious colleges and brotherhoods, such as the Salii (priests of Mars) and the Fratres Arvales, or Arval brotherhood, and colleges with more specialised roles such as the *fetiales*, who were in charge of declaring peace and war, and the haruspices, who were responsible for divination. Priesthoods were highly prestigious and influential positions, and membership of the priestly colleges became a privilege that was much sought-after. The collegiate structure preserved the principle of collective responsibility which underpinned many aspects of the Roman state. Since members served for life, priestly colleges built up religious expertise which could be consulted by the senate and magistrates. The college of augurs, for instance, was composed of nine men who advised on the taking of auspices, and the *decemviri sacris faciundis* were a board in charge of caring for the Sibylline books and other sacred objects.[5]

The most important of the three colleges, the college of pontifices, had the most complex structure. Membership was probably restricted to patricians in the first instance, but after 300 it had equal numbers of patricians and plebeians. It was led by the *pontifex maximus* (chief priest), and included the *rex sacrorum* (who took over some of the religious duties of the king), vestal virgins, and the *flamines* (priests of specific cults, the most important of whom was the *flamen Dialis*, the priest of Jupiter).[6] It had a powerful role, advising on a wide range of aspects of sacred law, including many aspects of family law. When a member died, giving rise to a vacancy, the surviving members of the college were responsible for nominating his or (in the case of the vestals) her successor, giving them control over membership. The opening up of the priestly colleges and religious brotherhoods to plebeians gave men of plebeian background access to important new sources of power, prestige and influence after 300.

Rome had no concept of a dedicated priesthood separate from the rest of society.[7] State religion was closely intertwined with the life of the state, a matter of ritual observance rather than belief, and membership of priestly colleges had a political as well as a religious dimension. Holding a priesthood was not a matter of religious vocation or initiation (although some, such as the augurs, had to acquire specialist knowledge in order to fulfil their duties) but an important part of a public career, on a par with being elected to a magistracy or celebrating a triumph. Honorific inscriptions and epitaphs list priesthoods alongside magistracies and other honours and achievements. Rituals such as libations and sacrifices were frequently the responsibility of a senior magistrate (or, in the case of an army in the field, the general) rather than a priest.

The *auspicium*, the power to consult the will of the gods by taking the auspices, offers an insight into both the nature of priesthood and the close links between rituals and political power. Only the higher magistrates – the consuls and praetors – could take the auspices, and they were obliged to do this, and interpret the results, before significant political or military acts. This conferred considerable power, as the will of the gods could be – and in some cases was – interpreted to the advantage of the presiding magistrate. It is significant that the patricians fought bitterly to retain their control of the right to take the auspices, and plebeian membership of the pontifical colleges was not granted until long after their right to hold the consulship had been established. The many interregna and dictatorships that characterised the period between 367 and 342 may have been an attempt to disrupt the normal magistracies to prevent plebeian magistrates from exercising the right to take the auspices.

Religious festivals and games had become established as an important part of Roman life by the third century, although we know little for certain about whether these were celebrated at earlier periods of Roman history and if so, what they consisted of. The practice of holding *ludi* may have originated as one-off events linked to triumphal celebrations, vowed by a victorious general as a gift to the gods, but this is far from certain. The establishment of the *ludi romani* was attributed either to Tarquinius Priscus or to the victory celebrations after the battle of Lake Regillus (Livy 1.35. 9, 7. 71; Cic., *Div.* 1.26), although this cannot be corroborated. The earliest evidence for the *ludi* is a description by Dionysios of Halicarnassus (Dion. Hal. 7. 72) which he claims to have based on Fabius Pictor, and the *ludi plebeii* have sometimes been connected with the First Secession, but there is no secure evidence for such an early origin. By the third century, however, *ludi* were established as annual occasions rather than single events. The *ludi romani*, dedicated to Jupiter, took place in mid-September and lasted several days. They consisted of a procession, in which images of the gods were carried, chariot and foot races, and dramatic performances (Livy 24. 43. 7). By the end of the third century, several other games were celebrated, including the *ludi plebeii, ludi cereales* (honouring Ceres), *ludi apollinares* (honouring Apollo) and *ludi megalenses* (honouring the Magna Mater), although most of these, with the possible exception of the *ludi plebeii*, dates to the period of the Punic wars.

The Roman army

Warfare remained endemic in the fourth and third centuries, and the demands this placed on Roman military organisation necessitated some changes. Campaigns took place in most years, covering an increasingly wide geographical area. By the middle of the fourth century Rome often had to maintain several armies in different areas of Italy, usually commanded by a consul, though praetors also had the necessary authority. Although Italian allies were obliged to provide military assistance on request, allowing Rome to shift some of the military burden onto other states, the core of the army remained Roman, and by the end of the fourth century it was clear that even two legions were no longer adequate to meet the demands of wide-ranging campaigns. The experience of facing enemies with different tactics and styles of fighting exposed the limitations of Rome's reliance on heavily armoured infantry fighting as a single phalanx. This was effective against most other Italians, who had similar weapons and tactics, but the Roman army struggled when faced with the Gauls, whose troops operated in smaller and more mobile units.

These problems were addressed by structural reforms and the adoption of new armour and weapons. Heavy bronze body armour was replaced by a lighter mail tunic or bronze breastplate; the archaic round shield was abandoned in favour of an oblong or oval shield, giving greater protection; and spears designed for fighting at close quarters were replaced by javelins and throwing spears. In 311 the army was reorganised. The number of legions raised annually was increased from two to four, and military tribunes were elected by the assembly to assist the consuls commanding these forces. This increased the size of the Roman infantry from *c.* 4,000 to *c.* 6,000 men, and the cavalry, previously a very small unit, was expanded to 1,800 men. A daily rate of pay (*stipendium*) was introduced to compensate each soldier for loss of earnings and income while he was on military service, and each cavalryman was supplied with a horse at public expense – a reform that recognised the economic strain imposed on Romans of military age by increasingly lengthy campaigns. Each legion was subdivided into units of 120 men known as maniples, allowing troops to be deployed more quickly and flexibly, and giving commanders a greater range of tactical options. Troops raised from Italian allies were not incorporated into the legions. They served alongside Roman troops and under the ultimate control of Roman generals but fought in their own units and were commanded by their own officers.

At the same time, a commission of two men (*duoviri navales*) was created to command Rome's small navy. Roman power was based on the heavy infantry of the legions, supplemented by smaller units of cavalry and light support troops. Its naval interests were more limited, although not non-existent. The fourth-century philosopher Theophrastus (*Historia plantarum* 5.8.1–2) believed that the Romans sent a fleet of twenty-five ships to found a colony on Corsica, although he offers no date or context for this, and Rome had certainly acquired a navy by the late fourth century. The Volscian city of Antium owned a strong fleet of ships and, like many of the coastal Etruscan cities, had a formidable reputation as a naval power. After Rome's conquest of Antium and foundation of a colony there in 338, its fleet was confiscated and became the basis of Rome's navy.[8] This was still a small fleet, amounting to only two squadrons of ships, supervised and commanded by the new *duoviri*. It seems to have been used mainly to deter piracy and protect the coast of Latium from any sea-borne raiders, although it sometimes went further afield. One of the causes of the Pyrrhic war was an exploratory mission by a squadron of Roman ships which unwisely sailed into the Gulf of Tarentum in contravention of a treaty and was promptly driven off, with significant losses, by the more powerful Tarentine fleet. The co-option of the Antiate ships and the creation of commissioners for supervising naval forces demonstrate that Rome was aware of the need to develop a fleet, but its naval capabilities remained relatively small-scale, and, despite Theophrastus' reference to a strategic interest in Corsica, it was not in a position to challenge the much greater naval power of the likes of Tarentum, Syracuse or Carthage. The situation changed rapidly after the outbreak of the First Punic War in 264. This was fought mainly in Sicily, and, embarrassingly, Rome was forced to beg and borrow ships from its Greek allies in southern Italy to transport its army across to the island. Rome had no quinqueremes, the state-of-the-art warships of the third century, until the prospect of having to take on the powerful Carthaginian fleet after 264 forced it to initiate a rapid programme of ship-building. Until then Roman attention was focused on expanding and reforming the organisation of the army.

Social change: the emergence of a new nobility

As the distinctions between patricians and plebeians became eroded, a new Roman elite class began to emerge, based on attainment of high office rather than on birth or membership of a particular social order. The highest social and political rank was no longer dependent on belonging to a patrician family, or even one of the leading plebeian families. Instead, it depended on acquiring noble status. The status of being *nobilis* (noble) was arrived at by holding the highest public office – that of consul – or being descended from someone who had done so. This meant that the nobility became a matter of achievement rather than birth, and in theory any Roman qualified to stand for public office – i.e., any free-born male citizen – could attain noble status. In practice, however, it operated as an oligarchy to which relatively few outsiders gained access, and the hereditary principle did not disappear from Roman society and politics. Prestige, *auctoritas* (moral and political authority, as opposed to the powers derived from a specific office) and status were cumulative over the generations, and being a member of an established noble family with a long history of membership of the senate was a huge advantage for anyone hoping to pursue a political career. 'New Men', as men without senatorial antecedents were called, could and did achieve the consulship. Titus Coruncanius, Manius Curius and Gaius Fabricius were all 'New Men' who held six consulships between them in this era (Cic., *Am.* 18, 39, *Sen.* 43, *Nat. Deor.* 2.165), but as the importance of the senate grew, the power and influence of established senatorial families increased along with it. Pursuit of public office at Rome required both wealth (and, in particular, land ownership) and a network of connections. There was no formal wealth qualification for membership of the senatorial class at this date, although one was later introduced, but a political career required extensive private means. There was no payment for holding office, and important men were expected to show generosity to the people. Men who built new public amenities at private expense were not just showing their munificence but promoting their own reputations. Magistrates who were in charge of any of the regular religious festivals were in a strong position because these often involved public celebrations or games. Being exceptionally lavish with public entertainments at private expense was a way to ensure popularity.

The Roman nobility placed a great deal of emphasis on consolidating and displaying their status. An impressive house in a prominent location, in which to entertain friends and allies and receive clients and dependants, was an important symbol of prestige and social identity. Recognition of achievement was essential, preferably in a form that acted as a lasting commemoration of it. A general celebrating a triumph was the centre of an impressive occasion on the day, leading his troops, accompanied by their captives and spoils, along a special route from the Campus Martius to the Capitol to undertake celebratory sacrifices to the gods, but commemorating the occasion was equally important. Many successful generals invested their booty in building temples or other monuments, to serve as reminders of their achievements, and there was a marked shift away from temples built by the state towards temples dedicated and paid for by individuals (mostly victorious generals, but sometimes magistrates or priests). This may have acted as a form of social safety valve. A general with *imperium* had sole control over the booty taken in his campaigns, and the value of such booty had increased rapidly during the wars of the early third century. Dedicating and financing a new temple was an acceptable use for these funds. It provided a convenient form of self-memorialisation for the donor, but it was also a public amenity, and a type of activity that was unlikely to stir up envy or unrest among the people. There is a sharp contrast between the third century, during which many generals used their booty to pay for temples and other monuments, and the second century, when far less was used for public works, but was retained for private use.

Social prestige was cumulative, and it was important to display the achievements of ancestors as well as the present generation. Noble families kept wax portrait masks of their forebears on display in their houses, and on the occasion of funerals these were paraded in the funeral procession, worn by their family members. The illustrious past of the family was there for all to see, and previous generations were symbolically present to witness the achievements of their descendants. Polybios (Pol. 6.53) gives a vivid description of an aristocratic funeral, an event that showcased the eminence of the family over generations, as well as mourning the dead. It involved a procession featuring the masks of the ancestors, a eulogy which presented the achievements of the dead, cremation and interment of the ashes in an impressive tomb, placed in a prominent location. Although this relates to practices of the second century, there is no reason to believe that it was a new custom at that date. It became increasingly common to add an inscribed epitaph listing offices held and honours won. These elogia and records of family genealogies and traditions were important as a means of establishing family status but were regarded as open to embellishment and to accretion of fictitious elements. Livy notes that they were not a reliable source of information.

As in archaic Rome, political alliances and social connections were often a family affair. Adoptions – even of adult children – and intermarriage between noble families were common. Women, although debarred from any public role except that of priestess, were important to the family ethos of the Roman nobility, and the Roman matron was an important figure. She was expected to conform to norms of Roman female virtue, running her household, inculcating Roman values in her children and supporting the interests of the family wherever possible. As a member of a powerful family, she occupied an influential position, and there are many anecdotes from the early history of Rome that feature women behaving with forcefulness and initiative. Whether these are historically true is beside the point: they illustrate what was expected of a noble Roman woman, namely loyalty to Rome and using her influence in support of her family.

The new nobility that emerged from the Struggle of the Orders was more open in the sense that it was based on wealth and achievement rather than on membership of a particular group of families. New Men could – and did – achieve noble status, but this became an increasingly rare occurrence. The cumulative nature of status over generations and the Roman reverence for ancestors and tradition meant that families with senatorial rank tended to form a dominant oligarchy to which it was difficult to gain entry. The outcome of the so-called Struggle of the Orders was the development of an elite that included both patrician and plebeian families, the influence of which was based on wealth and senatorial rank.

Economic and social change

Between 340 and 264 Rome began to reap the economic rewards of its conquest of Italy. The Samnite and Pyrrhic wars involved considerable financial outlay, but they brought enormous economic gains. State and personal wealth increased dramatically, thanks to the booty, land and slaves accruing from them. The extensive programme of public building, discussed in the next section, was funded mainly from the proceeds of war booty, and is a testament to the financial benefits of the wars of the period, while the increasing personal wealth of the elite is demonstrated by their investment in prominent houses and tombs, as well as public works.

The size of the *ager romanus,* the territory owned by Rome, was increased dramatically by the territory confiscated from defeated enemies. Modern estimates suggest that between 338 and 264 it increased from 5,525 km² (2,133 square miles) to 26,805 km² (10,349 square miles). Some of this land remained in state ownership as *ager publicus*, but much of it was redistributed to Roman citizens and allies as part of extensive colonisation programmes, providing a basic allocation of land to *c.* 70–80,000 adult males and their dependants. For the elite, land was also the most prestigious and respectable form of wealth in which to invest, and fines levied in 298 for infringements of the Licinio-Sextian land laws suggest that wealthy Romans were already keen to build up their landholdings. Archaeological evidence demonstrates that in most areas of Italy the shift from farms and estates providing crops for household consumption to villa-based agriculture producing cash crops for the market did not take place until the first century. Despite this, there is evidence that patterns of landholding were changing, and that larger farms and estates were developing as early as the later fourth century. These larger farms and estates were modest in size compared with later villas, but they were a valuable form of investment.

Despite the agrarian opportunities offered by the new land, it is clear that Rome had outstripped its ability to support itself. Between 338 and 264 the population of the *ager romanus* grew from just under 350,000 to somewhere in the region of 900,000. Estimates of the population of the city of Rome range from 90,000 to 190,000, but, whatever the absolute figure, it is generally accepted that the population roughly tripled during the hundred years from the middle of the fourth century. A population this size required substantial quantities of food to sustain it, and estimates suggest that up to 11,000 tonnes of grain per year may have been imported.

Trade and craft production were also on the increase. Rome produced a range of goods, such as pottery in a high-quality black-glazed fabric, some which can be attributed to specific workshops and manufacturers. One, identified as the Atelier des Petites Estampilles because most of its output was decorated with small stamped motifs, was particularly prolific. As well as tableware, Roman potters also produced a form of cup known as a *pocolum deorum* (goblet of the gods) because it is most frequently found inscribed with the name of a god and deposited as a votive offering. Evidence for production of metal items is more limited, but still persuasive. The main evidence is a cylindrical bronze vessel of a type known as a *cista* (pl. 22) found in a tomb at Praeneste and dating to *c.* 315. Praeneste was particularly noted as a centre for the production of *cistae* (sometimes known as Praenestine cists), but the so-called Ficoroni *cista* is unusual because it carries an inscription that states that it was made not at Praeneste but at Rome, by a craftsman called Novius Plautius. Bronze mirrors and *cistae*, decorated with incised decoration and elaborately moulded handles, were widely produced in central Italy at this date.[9] The styles and techniques were Etruscan, but the decorative scenes were frequently drawn from a mixture of local and Greek myths. They illustrate the extent to which artistic styles, techniques and craftsmen crossed state and regional boundaries, as well as the development of a central Italian visual culture that was shared by Latins, Etruscans, Romans and Faliscans, but which had absorbed significant Greek influence. Unlike the tombs of Praeneste and many parts of Etruria, those of Rome contained very few luxury bronze items such as mirrors and cists, and there is no way of knowing whether Novius Plautius was a single craftsman or the sole surviving evidence of a flourishing Roman bronze industry. Ancient references to the manufacture of large bronze statues at this date, such as the statues of Pythagoras and Alcibiades in the Comitium, and a bronze statue of Jupiter to replace an older terracotta one on the roof of the Capitoline temple (Livy 10.23.10–11), suggest that a Roman bronze-working industry had indeed developed.

The distribution of these goods suggests that Rome was part of an economic network of central Italian cities. Some ceramics, such as terracotta figurines and small votive altars, are only found in Rome and neighbouring areas, suggesting that the cities of Campania, Latium and Etruria were important trading partners. Other items, such as black-glaze pottery, were exported throughout the western Mediterranean, to Sicily, southern France, eastern Spain and north Africa, providing evidence of a far more wide-ranging network of economic and commercial contacts. Rome was a net consumer of large quantities of imported goods – both agricultural produce and manufactured items – and acted as a magnet for goods and services, but was also exporting goods across a substantial area.

Rome was already a monetary economy, using bronze currency bars of standard weights (pl. 20), but the third century saw the first minted Roman coinage. The earliest Roman coins are silver, with the Greek legend *Romaion* ('of the Romans'), minted in Naples some time around 326. They used the same weight standard as Neapolitan coins, and circulated mainly in Campania. A second issue of coinage, *c.* 310, this time with the Latin legend *ROMANO* (sometimes abbreviated to *ROMA*), was also minted and circulated in Campania and Magna Graecia. Cast-bronze discs in a number of weights, known as *aes grave*, circulated in parallel with these coins until the middle of the third century, when they were reformed into a specifically Roman currency system with its own weights and denominations based on the Roman pound. New coin symbols were adopted, and the legend *ROMA* became a standard mark of identification. In the mid-third century, Rome set up its own mint and began to issue coinage minted in Rome itself. One possible date is 269, a year in which a large number of silver coins were minted with a new design featuring Hercules, a god closely associated with Rome, on the obverse and the she-wolf and twins on the reverse (pl. 21).

The adoption of struck coinage was not primarily driven by economic need, as Rome already had a form of monetary system using currency bars. Coin issues were made when the state needed to make large-scale transactions such as paying for major public works or paying troops. The development of coinage was a reflection of an increased supply of bullion with which to produce them, a rising level of investment in major projects and the need to pay troops on a regular basis. Coins also served as a form of self-promotion, and by issuing its own coins Rome was making a statement about its place in the world. It is no accident that the first Roman coinage was issued in 326, possibly to commemorate the treaty with Naples, an influential Greek ally, or that the first coins to be minted at Rome carried the image of the she-wolf, which would become the iconic symbol of Roman power and identity.

One of the transformative social and economic changes of the third century, along with the land and portable wealth accruing from the wars of 340–270 BC, was the vastly increased number of slaves at Rome. Ancient Rome had been a slave-owning society from an early date, and laws governing slavery were included in the Twelve Tables.[10] As discussed elsewhere, there were two legally distinct forms of slavery in early Rome. Debt bondage (*nexum*) occurred when a debtor was forced to work as tied labour in lieu of payment, and was abolished in 326. Chattel slaves were either born into slavery or enslaved by other means and were owned outright, with no legal rights or freedoms. The increase in this type of slavery in the fourth and third centuries was driven by Rome's conquest of Italy and the practice of enslaving captives seized in war. The number of prisoners of war enslaved during the Samnite and Etruscan wars ran into tens of thousands. Estimates for slaves taken during the third Samnite war of 297–293 alone come to more than 66,000 people, and it is possible that slaves may have accounted for around 15 per cent of the total population of Rome by the mid-third century. Even allowing for the approximate nature of figures given by ancient authors, the slave population had increased enormously between *c.* 350 and 264.

This created a pool of cheap labour which transformed Rome's economy and society. Agricultural slave labour boosted economic production by enabling more intensive cultivation of land and the development of larger farms and estates. Availability of cheap labour also facilitated large-scale public works, such as the construction of the fourth-century city wall of Rome, the so-called 'Servian Wall' – a massive undertaking that required the quarrying, transportation and laying of several million large tufa blocks – and the programmes of public building described later in this chapter.

Date	People and places	Number of slaves taken
297	Cimetra	2,900
296	Murgantia	2,100
296	Romulea	6,000
296	Samnites	1,500
296	Etruscans	2,120
296	Samnites	2,500
295	Samnites and Gauls	8,000
295	Samnites	2,700
294	Milionia	4,700
294	Rusellae	*c.* 2,000
293	Amiternum	4,270
293	Duronia	Fewer than 4,270
293	Aquilonia	3,870
293	Cominium	11,400
293	Velia, Herculaneum and Palambinum	*c.* 5,000
291	Saepinum	Fewer than 3,000
Total		*c.* 66,330

Table 10: **Enslavement of prisoners of war in the third Samnite war** (after Harris 1979)

Slaves were not just heavy labour, however. Many became domestic servants, and it is estimated that most Roman families, other than the very poorest, could have expected to own a small number of slaves, while noble households would have been staffed by a much greater number, including skilled slaves to act as scribes, teachers and administrators and in many other roles. They were essential to many aspects of the running of private households, and of the Roman state. The influx of slaves not only increased the population of Rome and transformed its economic potential; it also had an impact on its cultural and ethnic diversity, as most of these slaves came from the Greek or Oscan areas of Italy.

Paradoxically, given that slaves had no legal rights, this slave population had a large impact on the citizen body. Not all slaves remained so for the rest of their lives, and many were freed by an act of manumission which granted them not just freedom but a limited form of Roman citizenship.

Slaves could obtain manumission in a number of ways: as a reward for good service; by saving enough from the small allowances their owners paid them to buy their freedom; others were freed on the death of their owner. It was not unusual for a person to free a proportion of their slaves in their will. Slaves employed in heavy manual work may not have survived to enjoy the benefits of manumission, but the introduction of a 5 per cent tax on manumissions in 357 suggests that there was a large enough number of manumissions to generate a significant amount of revenue.

Manumission conferred not just freedom but also Roman citizen-ship, although freed slaves retained some legal disabilities, such as being debarred from holding public office. They were not entirely liberated from their former owners but remained tied to them as clients and adopted the owner's name as a sign that they retained a connection to the household.[11] In the case of a large household this had the useful effect of creating a substantial pool of clients who would be expected to be helpful to, and supportive of, their patron in his private business and public career. The Romans' treatment of freed slaves was regarded by the Greeks as both notable and slightly peculiar. Philip V's letter to the city of Larisa (page 274) mentions the ability to increase the citizen body by freeing slaves as an important source of Roman strength. Dionysios of Halicarnassus, in contrast, was horrified that Roman citizenship was open to former slaves but was not automatically extended to a distinguished and learned Greek such as himself. Roman anxieties about manumitted slaves focused on perceptions of social and political influence – for example, when Gnaeus Flavius, the son of a freeman, was elected as aedile in 304 – rather than an absolute objection to enfranchising freedmen.

Urban development: the city of Rome in the third century

The effects of Rome's expanding horizons and booming economy can be seen in the transformation of its urban infrastructure. Demographic growth had profound implications, providing a large pool of labour (both free and slave) that contributed to the economic well-being of Rome but posing many logistical problems. Supplying a city of between 100,000 and 200,000 people with food was problematic, requiring regular imports of foodstuffs, and placed a strain on the water supply. Rome was well supplied with natural springs, such as the lacus Iuturnae, but these were nowhere near sufficient. The pressing need for investment in infrastructure is demonstrated by the road and aqueduct commissioned by Appius Claudius Caecus in 312, and by the need for an additional aqueduct within forty years, the massive Aqua Anio Vetus built by Manius Curius Dentatus in 272. These appear to have run mainly underground, but part of the Aqua Appia was carried on an arched arcade, like many of the later aqueducts. They were high-profile public projects, paid for from the booty taken in the Samnite and Pyrrhic wars, and were a striking demonstration of the prestige and power of Rome and its growing status as a city, as well as serving a practical function.[12]

More docks and warehouses were required to deal with a greater volume

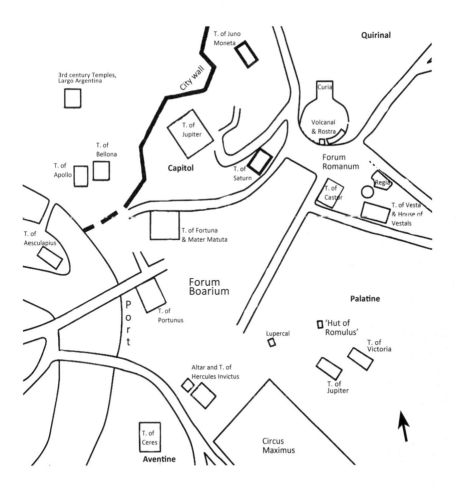

Fig. 28 Rome: plan of the Forum, Palatine and Forum Boarium c. 264 BC.

of imported goods and foodstuffs (fig. 28). Land transport was slow and expensive, so the Tiber was a vital artery for moving goods into the city. The development of Ostia as the main port of Rome was a later phenomenon, and any goods arriving by sea there had to be shipped upriver to Rome. Ancient sources describe an expansion of the old harbour area, the Portus Tiberinus, near the Forum Boarium. Few remains of this survive, but the construction of the temple of Portunus, the patron god of the harbour, at this period is a demonstration of the importance of the Portus Tiberinus and corroborates the literary sources. Most of the extant temple dates to the first century, but it is built on foundations of the late fourth or early third century. In the late third century construction began on a new harbour area, known as the Emporium and located on the stretch of the Tiber below the Aventine hill. This offered more room for expansion than the Portus Tiberinus, and during the period of the Punic wars and the early second century it developed into an area with extensive wharves and warehouses.

The wars of conquest funded an upsurge in other construction projects, particularly temples. At least fourteen can be dated to the third century with some certainly, but there may well have been more than this – possibly as many as thirty-two.[13] Some are known from archaeological evidence, but much of our information about temple-building comes from Livy and since there are major gaps in his history of the third century it is quite likely that our list of new or refurbished temples is incomplete. It can be augmented by some known only from archaeological evidence, such as the early phases of the Temples of Portunus and Hercules Invictus, near the Forum Boarium and port, the temples of Spes and Juno in the Forum Holitorium and a group of small temples found in the Largo Argentina, on the site of the ancient Campus Martius.

Many of the temples known from archaeological evidence, particularly the victory temples, were fairly small structures, built of local tufa with terracotta decorations. Marble was not widely used for building in Rome until the following century. Their form was common in central Italy, and consisted of a podium with steps leading to a small temple with a columned porch and a single interior room. Temples A and C in the Largo Argentina (pl. 23) are fairly typical. However, other temples could be larger, such as the temple of Jupiter Stator (c. 290 BC), which was big enough to accommodate meetings of the senate. Some of the temples were impressively decorated. The Temple of Salus was famous for its paintings

Date	Temple	Location
Late fourth/early third century	Temple of Portunus	Portus Tiberinus
Late fourth/early third century	Temple of Hercules Invictus	Portus Tiberinus (?)
302	Temple of Salus	Quirinal
Early third century	Temple C, Largo Argentina	Campus Martius
296	Temple of Bellona Victrix	Campus Martius
295	Temple of Jupiter Victor Temple of Venus Obsequens	Quirinal (?) Circus Maximus
294	Temple of Victoria Temple of Jupiter Stator	Palatine Palatine
293	Temple of Quirinus Temple of Fors Fortuna	Quirinal Right bank of the Tiber
291	Temple of Aesculapius	Tiber Island
278	Temple of Summanus	Circus Maximus
272	Temple of Consus	Aventine
268	Temple of Tellus	Esquiline
267	Temple of Pales	Not known
264	Temple of Vertumnus	Aventine
Mid-third century	Temple of Spes	Forum Holitorium
Mid-third century	Temple of Janus	Forum Holitorium
Mid-third century	Temple A, Largo Argentina	Campus Martius

Table 11: **Temple-building at Rome in the third century**

(Val. Max. 8.14.6), and the Ogulnius brothers paid for silver bowls to be placed in the temple of Jupiter Capitolinus, as well as a new bronze statue of Jupiter to replace a terracotta one on the temple roof (Livy 10.23).

Temple-building was intimately connected with conquest and with the personal prestige of the person who dedicated the building. Most temples were thank-offerings to the gods for a successful military campaign, paid for out of the booty taken. It is no accident that many of these temples are dedicated to gods connected with war and conquest (Victoria, Hercules Invictus, Jupiter Victor, Bellona Victrix) or to gods closely connected with Rome's identity and legendary past (Consus, Pales, Quirinus), or that many of them are close to the processional route followed by generals and armies celebrating a triumph. At this date the booty taken in a campaign was the property of the victorious general, to dispose of as he wished. By using some, or all, of it to build a temple as a thank-offering for victory, he both honoured the gods and promoted his prestige and public image. Temples of this type acted as a permanent reminder of military achievement and triumphs celebrated. The most striking example of how a victory temple could become a dynastic monument is the temple of Bellona, vowed by Appius Claudius Caecus, who decorated it with shields and portraits of his ancestors (Ovid, *Fast.* 6.201–8; Pliny, *NH* 35.19).

The landscape of the city was further transformed by the addition of spoils of war, and impressive bronze statues to public spaces. These included items taken from defeated enemies, such as the statues from Volsinii displayed in the temple of Mater Matuta and the spoils taken from the Samnites, which were displayed in the forum in 310/09 and 293, but many were newly manufactured. Some honoured gods, such as the colossal statues of Hercules and Jupiter set up on the Capitoline, while others honoured individuals, such as the equestrian statue dedicated to Quintus Marcius Tremulus, the consul of 306 (Pliny, *NH* 34.23). They reflect not just the monumentalisation of temples and public spaces but also the immense amount of captured bronze required as raw materials for producing these items.

The social and political ambitions of the Roman elite, and the need to display these to demonstrate family status, influenced the urban development of Rome profoundly. Few remains of private houses of this date have survived, but, as discussed in Chapter 11, ancient accounts suggest that a large and impressive house in a prestigious location was important to the self-image and political and social status of a noble family. There is stronger evidence of significant investment in new and imposing family tombs by aristocratic families. These contained space for burials of several generations in underground or semi-underground tomb chambers, but with a visible superstructure to make the tomb an eye-catching monument for passers-by, and thus a prominent reminder of the importance of its owners. The two best-preserved examples, belonging to the Fabii and the Scipios, both span the third–second centuries and therefore lie partly outside the chronological range of this volume, but they offer valuable insights into the world-view of the aristocracy of mid-Republican Rome.

The tomb of the Fabii is not well preserved. The remains of this and another tomb of similar date were found under the church of S. Eusebio on the Esquiline, and little of the external structures has survived. Internally, they had a single burial chamber, decorated with frescoes (some of the earliest surviving tomb paintings from Rome), and are believed to date to the third century.[14] Although the frescoes only survive in fragments, they depict historical episodes, possibly from the Samnite wars, including scenes from a siege and a scene of surrender, although there is no consensus on their precise meaning. A caption next to one of the figures identifies him as one of the Fabii, possibly Quintus Fabius Rullianus, one of the leading Roman generals during the second Samnite war. One possibility is that the tomb was a publicly funded burial place in recognition for his achievements.[15]

The better-known, and better-preserved, Tomb of the Scipios demonstrates just how much effort the aristocracy of this period invested in competitive self-promotion. This was located on the Via Appia, and was part of a more general relocation of Rome's cemeteries. The Esquiline cemetery was now little used, and most burial now took place outside the city gates and, in particular, along the roads leading out of Rome. Tombs of noble families such as the Scipios would have been passed by anyone entering or leaving Rome on the new highway heading south to Campania and would have been eye-catching monuments. The visible portion consisted of a high podium supporting a superstructure, although the decoration with columns and niches dates to the mid-second century. Beneath it was a large rectangular chamber tomb with niches to accommodate urns and sarcophagi and space for around thirty burials, accessed by a passageway under the podium. The earliest part of the tomb was constructed in the early third century, the first burial being that of Scipio Barbatus, who was consul in 298 and died some time around 280. It remained in use until the late second century and was extended and refurbished in *c.* 150, when the façade was remodelled to include Greek-style columns and statues. Most of the burials were inhumations in large stone sarcophagi, which have epitaphs recording details of the careers and achievements of the deceased. These give a vivid insight into the aristocratic values and world-view of the nobility of mid-Republican Rome and provide an intense demonstration of family achievement and prestige. The earliest epitaph, that of Scipio Barbatus, reads:

Cornelius Lucius Scipio Barbatus, descended from his father Gnaeus,
a man strong and wise, whose appearance was most in keeping with his

virtue, who was consul, censor, and aedile among you – He captured Taurasia, Cisauna, Samnium – he subdued the whole of Lucania and led off hostages.

(CIL 6.1284)

This makes explicit the qualities that were central to the identity of the emerging nobility of Rome in the third century and from which they drew their prestige and status: family continuity, moral qualities, an impressive and cumulative list of public offices held and a distinguished and successful military record. Tombs such as those of the Scipios and the Fabii were public monuments to family status and showcased the record of civic and military achievement, over many generations, from which the nobility drew their social and political status. The emergence of a new nobility at Rome, based on the holding of public office and cumulative achievement over generations, created a need for monuments that celebrated such long-term achievement.

The culture of third-century Rome

There is no doubt that Roman expansion and the socio-political changes of the late fourth and early third centuries fuelled rapid growth and a building boom within the city and had a wide-ranging impact on Roman culture more generally. Michel Humm has suggested that the prevalence of victory dedications in the fourth and third centuries – whether temples, victory monuments or statues paid for from booty or captured arms, booty and art works displayed in Rome – was driven by increasing Hellenisation and a desire to imitate Greek ways of commemorating victories. However, this is debatable. Greek cultural practices undoubtedly had a profound impact on Rome at this date, but these practices seem to have their roots in Roman elite competition, particular in military matters, and the increasing Roman conquests of the period rather than in the adoption of Greek customs.

However, Greek influence on the culture of Rome can be identified in many other areas. Ancient sources describe Greek practices such as chariot-racing and the setting up of monumental statues to honour eminent people. The Greek practice of dedicating temples and cults to abstract virtues such as the temples to Salus (Health) and Victoria (Victory) was adopted, and the Greek healing cult of Aesculapius, to whom a temple was constructed on the Tiber Island, was established in 291. Roman envoys were also sent to consult Greek oracles on a number of occasions, demonstrating that Rome was engaging with the diplomatic and religious practices of the Greek world. Even Greek influence on personal habits becomes apparent. Some eminent Romans adopted Greek cognomina, notably Quintus Marcius Philippus, who held the consulship in 281. Varro and Pliny (Varro, *RR* 2.11; Pliny, *NH* VII.59) claim that the fashion for being clean-shaven among Roman men, which caught on in the third century, was due to an influx of Greek barbers from Sicily. The extent of the impact of Hellenism is demonstrated by Plutarch's observation (Plut., *Cam.* 22) that the fourth-century philosopher Herakleides Ponticus described Rome as a Greek city. This may be a reference to the Greek foundation legends associated with it rather than an informed comment on contemporary culture, but Greek influence on the intellectual culture of Rome was considerable. Greek political thought may lie behind the actions of some politicians who favoured a greater role for the Roman *comitia*, most notably Appius Claudius and Quintus Publilius Philo, and Appius Claudius is also said to have written books of anecdotes and moral homilies, in the contemporary Greek manner. There was considerable interest in Greek philosophy, particularly Pythagoreanism, something that Humm traces to the conquest of Tarentum, where Pythagorean philosophy had had a resurgence in the fourth century.

Archaeological evidence corroborates the impact of Hellenism on material culture. Greek artistic styles and techniques are apparent in the frescoes of the Tomb of the Fabii and the sarcophagi found in the Tomb of the Scipios, while the decoration of objects such as the Ficoroni *cista* (pl. 22) imply that there was both a knowledge of, and an appreciation of, Greek mythology in Rome, as well as a market for items decorated with Greek subjects. The architecture of some third-century temples, such as those of Temples A and C in Largo Argentina, also shows signs of Greek influence although they are traditionally Italian in form.

These cultural changes are a reflection of two broader trends. The first is that Greek artistic styles and intellectual culture were influential throughout central Italy at this date. Sculpture, painting and bronzes from Etruria and from other areas of Latium adopted both Hellenised styles and Greek subject matter, which was absorbed into local traditions. The decorative schemes of Etruscan and Praenestine mirrors and *cistae* are drawn from a mixture of Greek myths and local myths and traditions, sometimes blended to form a distinctive local form of Greek mythology and tradition. A fourth-century *cista*, for instance, is decorated with a scene combining a number of characters from Homeric legend – Helen, Achilles, Chryseis, Orestes and Tyndareus, accompanied by someone labelled Seci Lucus, apparently a Latin or Italic name, whose identity is unknown. On another example, a figure appearing with Ajax and Agamemnon is labelled Soresios, possibly indicating a native of Sora, on the border between Latium and Samnite territory. The meaning of these scenes is unclear, but they demonstrate that knowledge of Greek literature and mythology was widespread in central Italy, and that it was integrated with indigenous traditions and myths to form a distinctive hybrid of Greek and local elements. Since Rome was embedded in the cultural milieu of central Italy, it was undoubtedly influenced by Greek culture meditated through the cultures of Etruria and Oscan Italy. The second trend is that from the late fourth century onwards Rome had an increasing level of direct contact with the Greek world. By the end of the Pyrrhic war, Magna Graecia was under Roman control, and relations with Campania, and especially the Greek cities of Naples and Cumae, were even longer established. Rome had begun to actively involve itself in the wider Greek world, sending diplomatic missions to Greek states and establishing religious connections with major Greek sanctuaries.

The manner in which the Romans responded to these influences, and what they did with them, offer some important insights. The earliest coinage provides a good illustration of the complexity of the problem. The first silver coins undoubtedly owe a debt to Rome's connections with Greek Campania, and, in particular, with Naples. They used Greek weights, Greek designs and, in the case of the very first issue, a Greek inscription. In many ways they can be seen as using Greek technology and Greek conventions, but doing so to present the distinctive identity of Rome. However, they were mainly minted for circulation outside Rome, and do not seem to have been used within the city. By the time coins were minted for circulation in Rome, they were much more clearly Roman, using a Roman weight standard and Roman denominations and carrying the distinctive Roman symbol of the she-wolf. Greek influence on Roman culture was a matter not just of adoption but of adaptation to serve Rome's own political and cultural agenda and to add to a distinctively Roman identity.

As Macmullen has recently argued, there was a strong strand of conservatism in Roman culture and a deep attachment to traditional Roman customs and values, but this went hand in hand with a willingness to innovate, adapt and embrace new influences. There can be little doubt that Romans adopted the aspects of Hellenism that they found useful or congenial, or that Greek influences on Roman culture increased in the fourth and third centuries, but they were discriminating in what they took on. The development of coinage, discussed above, demonstrates that they were not passive consumers of Greek culture and ideas, but were willing to adopt some aspects, reject others and adapt yet others to Roman norms and customs. Third-century Rome still shared the social and cultural norms of central Italy and was selective about adopting Greek customs, goods and culture, but this does not imply isolationism or lack of engagement – simply a strong sense of, and attachment to, traditional Roman culture. Hellenism was an increasingly visible aspect of Roman life; it was only one element in the culture of third-century Rome.

15

EPILOGUE: ROME, ITALY AND THE BEGINNINGS OF EMPIRE IN 264

✦❈✦

At the beginning of this book Italy was a region of many different ethnic groups and cultures, many of them in the process of urbanising. Rome was a scatter of settlements on the south bank of the Tiber, only one among many developing communities and overshadowed by more powerful and better-resourced neighbours north of the river. Throughout the eighth to sixth centuries the Etruscans were the most dynamic economic and cultural force in central Italy, while the Greek colonies flourished in the south. Other regions were richer in natural resources and better connected to the wider Mediterranean world, and yet by 264 Rome was an imposing city with broad international interests and unchallenged dominance of Italy, and was poised on the brink of becoming a world power.

Throughout Italy we can trace the development of proto-urban communities in the ninth and eighth centuries and their development into increasingly complex city-states during the course of the seventh and sixth centuries, accompanied by cultural changes that saw the transformation of an Iron-Age warrior elite into a wealthy princely class in the orientalising period and then into a more open nobility exercising power through a mixture of birth, wealth and elected office. This was accompanied by changing patterns of economic and cultural contacts, reflected in the orientalised elites of the seventh century, the influence of Etruscan culture on Italy in the sixth and fifth centuries, and the increasing Hellenism of the Italian elites from the fourth century onwards.

The development of Rome closely follows these broader Italian trends. It developed into a proto-urban settlement and then into a city-state, possibly dominated by the heads of its leading families, during the eighth and seventh centuries. During the period associated with the Tarquin kings it established itself as a regional power within Latium. The turbulence caused by the ejection of the kings could have brought this process to a halt, but the embryonic and rather experimental system of elective government introduced in the aftermath of Tarquin's exile grew into something more complex. Republican government settled down into a more stable elective system, and Rome's ruling elite was transformed from one based on hereditary patrician privilege to an oligarchic nobility based on wealth and achievement as well as birth. The volatility of the fifth and fourth centuries gave rise, first, to a period of experimentation characterised by greater popular involvement, but then to a system of government dominated by the senatorial order, an oligarchic group of leading families. This was accompanied by an apparently ruthless and inexorable rise to power beyond Latium. Even allowing for a strand of triumphalism in Roman sources, and a tendency to gloss over any lulls and set-backs, it was a remarkable achievement.

One of the enduring problems of Roman history in this period is that, since most of our detailed evidence, and all of our historical narrative, either concerns Rome or comes from Roman sources, it is difficult to reach any conclusions about whether Rome's development was typical of most Italian states or not. Was it simply more successful than its neighbours and rivals in coping with the challenges of economic recession and social and political changes in fifth and fourth centuries? Or were there significant differences between the development of Rome and – for instance – similar states in Campania and Etruria? Recent research has highlighted the extent to which developments (for instance, changes in land use and the rise of larger estates in the fourth and third centuries or the changing settlement patterns of Apennine Italy) that were once thought to be the result of Roman conquest and 'Romanisation' were independent trends that can be perceived throughout central and southern Italy. However, there are some areas in which Rome appears to be unique.

Openness to outsiders was built into Rome's very foundation legend through Romulus' creation of an asylum and kidnap of the Sabine women. Willingness to admit outsiders as citizens was by no means unusual in Italy, and there are examples of Etruscan states doing the same thing, but most of these examples were aristocrats and their followers, whose transition to citizenship of a new state was smoothed by existing social ties. Where Rome was different, at least after the Latin war of 340–338, was in extending Roman citizenship on a larger scale. After this point it was not unusual for groups of people – often whole communities – to be absorbed into the Roman state. This ability to expand their community of citizens at will and the extra manpower this created were already noted in the ancient world as factors in Rome's success.

Rome's strategies for handling its growing territory and dealing with conquered areas created a unique relationship with the rest of Italy. Other Italian states developed inter-state co-operation based on localised leagues, which had limited political and military impact. Rome's complex network of alliances, colonies and direct rule, in contrast, gave it unrivalled influence and control. By the end of the fourth century it had ruthlessly broken up any alternative power structures and made sure that all Italian states were now linked, first and foremost, to Rome. The benefits of this embryonic empire soon became clear. Rome now had access to an unequalled pool of military manpower, thanks to treaties that obliged Italians to assist in Rome's wars. The practice of confiscating land from defeated enemies had extended Roman territory until it included a large part of central Italy, creating an important economic resource. The foundation of colonies or the extension of Roman citizenship created a permanent connection to Rome in many areas, and colonial settlement provided land for many poorer citizens. For the rich it offered opportunities to invest in land and building up substantial estates. The influx of slaves transformed the demography of Rome and provided a pool of cheap labour, and the portable wealth acquired during the wars of conquest enabled ambitious public works, as well as enriching the elite.

This rapid rise to power poses the question of just why Rome expanded so aggressively, and from an early date. Many elements in Roman culture and society predisposed it to expand vigorously. The Roman aristocracy was intensely competitive, and military success was an important factor in gaining and maintaining prestige. Members of the nobility were under constant pressure to equal or exceed the achievements of both ancestors and contemporaries. A successful general could expect public acclaim and honours such as a triumph, which enhanced his reputation, and his electability if he planned to stand for future office. Wars brought booty, which translated into personal wealth, and opportunities to amass estates, fine houses and a lavish lifestyle, as well as the ability to pay for eye-catching public works to further establish personal and family importance. Many of the temples of Republican Rome were dedications by generals, paid for out of spoils of war to thank the gods and advertise personal achievement. It is clear that the Roman elite benefited hugely from the wars of conquest, in land and wealth as well as prestige. On a collective level, the fourth-century wars of conquest brought territory and booty which enriched the Roman state beyond anything which could have been imagined in an earlier period, and benefited the entire citizen body. Rome was able to pay its troops and, in 264, when it became necessary, build and man a navy. State investment in public building transformed the cityscape, and landless citizens benefited from a mass colonisation programme.

The nature of the Roman alliance in Italy provided the means to carry on expanding, since it ensured that Rome had access to a vast pool of military manpower, but the extent of its territorial involvement meant that by 270 it also had extensive interests to protect. Since war required divine approval, only wars undertaken in self-defence were divinely sanctioned (*bellum iustum*, or 'just war'), so wars undertaken by Rome were – in the eyes of the Romans themselves – inherently defensive, to protect its interests and those of its allies. As Rome's territorial interests and network of alliances grew, so did the scope for Rome to become embroiled in further conflict, and so did Roman fear of losing control of its allies, creating a self-perpetuating cycle of wars. The motives that drove the Roman acquisition of Italian, and ultimately Mediterranean, empire were a complex mixture of aggression, opportunism and defensiveness.

As a city, Rome had come a very long way. A hypothetical visitor in the eighth century would have found a community composed of separate clusters of thatched wood-and-daub cottages separated by areas for collective religious activity and demarcated by a rudimentary wall. By the sixth century, visitors would have encountered a fortified city with a drained and paved forum and monumental temples. Modest dwellings co-existed with large and opulent houses built by the aristocracy, stretching along the prestigious Sacra Via and the edge of the forum. The city had grown rapidly, and buildings were on an altogether larger scale, decorated with brightly painted terracotta mouldings. It had developed into a flourishing cosmopolitan community, bringing in craftsmen and imports from Etruria and from the Greek world, and attracting the attention of other regional powers, such as Carthage.

By the middle of the fifth century the political topography of Rome was taking shape. The forum developed further, and new temples were constructed, including some, such as the temples of Diana and of Ceres, Liber and Libera on the Aventine, which had specific social and political affiliations. Despite this, the economic downturn and cultural realignments of the period meant that Rome did not grow as dramatically as it had in the sixth century. The culture of the elite was now more austere, and wealth was less obviously flaunted. It was still an impressive city, but one periodically plagued by food shortages and social strife.

The development of Rome between 342 and 264 is a story of increasing wealth and power as the benefits of conquest became apparent. At the same time the reforms of the mid-fourth century and the declining importance of the patrician/plebeian divide ushered in a period of significant social and political change. The senate, which had previously played a rather ill-defined role, began to assert a much greater degree of influence, and a new unified nobility emerged, based on attainment of high office rather than hereditary membership of a closed elite, and developed new ways of asserting its power and status. Public events such as games and military triumphs, as well as family rituals such as funerals, became opportunities to showcase the grandeur of important individuals and their families. The impact of the conquest of Italy became apparent in many ways. Rome now had access to a vast pool of manpower, which placed it head and shoulders above other Italian states in its military capability. The rapid expansion of Roman territory conferred obvious economic benefits, as did the plunder accruing from many years of successful warfare, but it also initiated demographic changes that had an important impact on both Rome and the rest of Italy. Acquisition of land and booty made Rome and its elite suddenly much richer; greater contact with the Greek world and with Carthage opened Rome up to a greater range of cultural influences from beyond Italy; and the influx of new population into Rome transformed the demography of the city.

By the third century Rome was profoundly transformed. It had grown to be one of the largest communities in Italy, boasting a state-of-the-art city wall, numerous monumental temples and public buildings, and impressive private houses, along with civic amenities such as drainage, roads and aqueducts. The population was more varied, with immigrants from many other areas of Italy and beyond. It was still fundamentally a central Italian city, and its strongest economic and cultural connections were with its immediate neighbours, but the influence of Greek culture – both visual and intellectual – was becoming increasingly apparent. It could not yet compete with the grandeur of contemporary cities in the Greek world, such as Athens, Ephesos or Alexandria, or even a small number of other Italian cities, such as Tarentum and Capua, and even in the second century the statesman Scipio Aemilianus, a noted philhellene, is said to have been thoroughly ashamed at how provincial Rome looked by comparison. Nevertheless, Rome had absorbed cultural influences from across Italy and the Mediterranean, and its leaders were busily investing the proceeds of its newly acquired territories in enhancing both the city and the interests of their own families.

Further afield, the growth of Roman power and ambition was increasingly bringing it into contact and potential conflict with a more established power in the western Mediterranean – Carthage. An alliance with Messana (modern Messina) gave Rome a toehold in Sicily but was instrumental in dragging Rome into a complex and long-established struggle between Greeks and Carthaginians for domination of the island. It presented Rome with a new series of challenges – how to confront the foremost naval power of the western Mediterranean, how to wage war beyond Italy and, ultimately, how to govern its first overseas province. These questions are beyond the scope of this book, and are the theme of the next volume in this series, but the outbreak of the First Punic War in 264, the first stage in an epic struggle with Carthage for domination of the western Mediterranean, placed Rome on the path to conquest of a world empire.

APPENDIX

ROMAN DATES AND CHRONOLOGY

O ne of the more complex and difficult aspects of early Roman history is its chronology or, to be more accurate, its multiple and competing chronologies. In common with most modern works on Roman history, the dates used in this volume are those of the so-called Varronian chronology. Many of these will be familiar to modern readers: on this system the foundation was in 753, the first year of the Republic in 509, the Gallic sack in 390 and the first plebeian consul in 366. However, there are many other chronologies, all of which pose their own problems. Readers should be aware that these are only one possible scheme for assigning a calendrical date to the years of office of each consul.

The Romans dated events by the names of the eponymous magistrates of the year, usually the consuls. Thus events might be identified as happening 'in the consulship of Gaius Caesar and Lucius Aemilius Paulus', which corresponds to AD 1. In order to determine the dates of events by modern chronology, we need a reliable list of consuls which allows us to count back from AD 1 to determine the date BC. The chronological scheme developed by the antiquarians Atticus and Varro in the mid-first century BC was adopted by the senate as its official method of dating, calculated from Varro's date for the foundation of Rome. It was also used by the *Fasti Capitolini*, Augustus' codification of Rome's lists of consuls, which provided the basis for Roman dates. However, there are problems with some of the dates assigned by Varro to specific consular years, as well as many problems with the *Fasti Capitolini*.

From *c.* 300 BC the consular *fasti* contain a full and accurate list of consuls (or consular tribunes, in years where these were elected instead), allowing us to correlate Roman consular dates with modern dates BC fairly accurately. The *fasti* for the period between 390 and 300, however, show signs of having been distorted by the addition of so-called 'dictator years' (333, 324, 309 and 301), in which dictators rather than consuls are listed as the eponymous magistrate, and a five-year period referred to as 'the anarchy' (375–371), in which political strife is said to have prevented elections from taking place. Both of these are widely regarded by scholars as later inventions, which inserted fictitious 'dictator years' and expanded a single electoral crisis into a five-year 'anarchy'.

The reason for this lies in the discrepancy between Greek and Roman chronologies for a key event of the fourth century, the Gallic sack of Rome. Polybios (1.6.2), probably basing this on dates given by Greek historians of the fourth and third centuries, dated it in the same year as a well-known event of Greek history, the Peace of Antalcidas, which was negotiated in 386 BC. The problem was that, according to the *fasti*, the consular tribunes in whose year the Gallic sack took place were those of 381, not 386. The additional years may have been inserted in an attempt to harmonise the *fasti* into line with the date of the Peace of Antalcidas. Unfortunately, by inserting both the 'dictator years' and expanding a probable electoral crisis in one year into a five-year 'anarchy', the revisions over-compensated, leaving the *fasti* and the Varronian chronology, which now placed the Gallic sack in 390, four years out of step with other sources for much of the fourth century.

Many other ancient writers used chronologies that differ from that of Varro. Livy, for instance, uses a different chronology which omits the 'dictator years' but expands the 'anarchy'. Greek historians had their own dating system, which was based on Olympiads, the four-yearly cycle of the Olympic Games, which used the first Olympiad (776 BC) as a baseline and calculated dates from this point. Some, such as Dionysios of Halicarnassus, developed a careful and complex dating system that attempted to correlate the *fasti* with Olympic dates and also with dates derived from lists of Athenian eponymous magistrates (*archons*). All, however, record the consuls for each year, which allows us to harmonise their dates with each other, with Varro's dates, and with the *fasti*.

TIMELINE

Date	Key events in Rome	Key events in Italy
9th century	Settlements on the Palatine and other hills around Rome. Burials in the area of the later Forum Romanum.	Italian Iron Age: complex settlements develop in Etruria, Latium, Campania and southern Italy.
8th century	Settlements on the Palatine and Capitoline become more complex. Forum cemetery replaced by burial area on the Esquiline.	Proto-urban settlements develop in Etruria and elsewhere in Italy. Greek settlement in Campania and southern Italy.
7th century	Settlements on Palatine and other hills develop into a single nucleated urban settlement. Traditional dates of the early kings (Numa-Ancus Marcius).	Urban development in Etruria; increasing orientalising influence on Italic culture. Further Greek settlement and expansion in southern Italy.
c. 615–530	Tarquin dynasty rules Rome; expansion and monumentalisation of the city; reforms of Servius Tullius.	Expansion of Etruscan power in northern Italy and in Campania. Beginnings of Celtic migration in northern Italy.
525		Etruscans defeated by Cumae.
510–509	Fall of the monarchy at Rome: exile of the Tarqins and establishment of the Republic. War between Rome and Clusium. First treaty between Rome and Carthage.	Exile of the Pythagoreans and civil unrest in Greek Italy.
c. 505	Battle of Aricia: Clusine army defeated by Cumae and the Latins.	
496	Battle of Lake Regillus: Rome defeats the Latins.	

Date	Key events in Rome	Key events in Italy
c. 493	Peace between Rome and the Latins: signing of the 'Cassian treaty'. First Secession of the plebeians and the beginning of the Struggle of the Orders: creation of the tribunate.	Migration of Volsci, Aequi, Hernici and Sabines in Latium. War between Rome and the Volscians
486	Consulship of Spurius Cassius: civil unrest over land and debt.	
483–474		War between Rome and Veii.
474–473		Etruscan fleet defeated by Cumae and Syracuse: end of Etruscan power in Campania. Beginning of Samnite migration into Campania. War between Greeks and Italians in southern Italy.
452	Roman delegation to Athens to consult about law codes.	
451–449	The decemvirate and the publication of the Twelve Tables; Valerio-Horatian laws.	
445	Lex Canuleia: marriage between patricians and plebeians legalised.	
440–432	Repeated famine and food shortages. Assassination of Spurius Maelius.	Samnite takeover of Capua and the rest of Campania. Further war between Rome and Veii.
408–393		Rome conquers Veii and establishes control of Latium. Samnites expand into Lucania and Bruttium.
390–386	Gallic invasion and sack of Rome.	
386–346	Civil unrest in Rome over debt and land distribution; laws (367 BC) and laws regulating debt.	Rome at war with Etruscans and Latins: conquest of Tarquinii, Falerii, Caere, Tibur and Praeneste.
350–348		Further Gallic invasion. Second treaty between Rome and Carthage.

Date	Key events in Rome	Key events in Italy
343–338		First Samnite war with Rome; war with the Latins. Peace settlement of 338 establishes basis for Roman control of Italy.
327–304		War with Naples and second Samnite war: Rome defeated at the Caudine Forks (321); Roman defeat of Samnites (304) and conquest of Etruria.
298–290		Third Samnite war. Gallic invasion and defeat at battle of Sentinum.
287	Lex Hortensia: end of the Struggle of the Orders.	
281–270		Pyrrhic war: Roman conquest of southern Italy.
264		Beginning of the First Punic War.

A NOTE ON SOURCES

1. *Archaeology*

Most of what we know about the non-Roman cultures of Italy, and the earliest history of Rome itself, comes from archaeological evidence. The ever-growing quantity of data offers us a rich body of information, but one that has its limitations. The chief of these is the fact that our knowledge of early Italy is dependent on the vagaries of survival and discovery of particular sites. In areas such as Etruria, where systematic investigation began in the nineteenth century, this leads to major distortions. The overwhelming preoccupation was with finding burials containing high-quality art objects, and, as a result, excavation of cemeteries was prioritised over that of settlements. Material culture was studied as art history, not for its broader social and cultural significance. In the past thirty to forty years, however, our understanding of Etruscan cities, how they formed and how Etruscans lived in them has been transformed by a shift from excavation of cemeteries to field surveys and excavation focused on settlement. As a result, previously unknown and quite sizeable Etruscan settlements, such as Doganella, have come to light, and our understanding of those which were previously known has been transformed. This pattern is also true for the rest of Italy, although some sites in the south – notably some of the Greek settlements that were abandoned in Late Antiquity – offer more scope for extensive excavation and survey.[1]

The challenges are particularly acute for sites such as Rome, which have been continuously occupied since Antiquity. The depth and richness of the archaeological record at Rome is in itself difficult for anyone primarily interested in the earliest centuries of its history. Roman remains are buried under many metres of later building and in many cases only come to light during programmes of renovation and urban development. The extension of the Rome metro system, for instance, has greatly increased our knowledge of the ancient city, but only as snapshots along the route of the new line. A comprehensive view of the archaeology of Rome is nearly impossible. Excavation between later Roman remains and later buildings has, however, enabled us to build up a far more coherent picture of early Rome than was previously possible. Andrea Carandini's excavations on the Palatine, which have revealed much previously unsuspected information about eighth- and seventh-century Rome, is a case in point. However, we must recognise that all archaeological evidence has its limitations, and we cannot expect it to answer the same questions as written records (and vice versa). Archaeology permits us to examine economic and social behaviour. It can, for example, tell us about the whereabouts of farms and what was grown, and therefore much

335

about the economy of a region, but not who owned the land, on what basis or whether it was worked by tenants, slaves or free farmers. It is also very much open to interpretation and can be radically changed by new discoveries. The difficulties over the chronology of Iron-Age Latium and Rome, the revision of our understanding of urban development in Etruria and the new light on Rome cast by the Palatine excavations are cases in point. Archaeology can tell us a lot about broad social or cultural trends, but it cannot prove or disprove specific events or provide insight into individual actions and motivations. For that, we are reliant on the ancient sources, which pose their own challenges.

2. Sources and their dates

Our surviving accounts of the history of early Rome were all written long after the event. Earlier Greek historians, many of whom had a keen interest in other cultures, commented on events in Italy and aspects of the peoples of Italy, including the Romans, which offers some contemporary information from the fifth century onwards but it is sporadic and limited. However, these accounts were written from the standpoint of an external observer, not from within the cultures that they describe. We have, for instance, no account of Etruscan history written by an Etruscan, even if such a thing existed[2] – only the observations of Greeks and Romans, who had an imperfect understanding of Etruscan culture and history, and their own agenda in how they wished to represent it. Inscriptions are the only direct form of written record to survive from early Italian history and offer insights into archaic Italy, but they are relatively few in number before the third century.[3] The extent to which alternative traditions may have been lost is illustrated by the fact that we know of over a hundred Roman historians whose works have been lost or survive only in fragments and short quotations. Even more strikingly, a speech by the emperor Claudius, which survives in an inscribed version, makes reference to an otherwise unknown Etruscan tradition about early Rome (discussed on pp. 129–31) that is rather different from the Roman one.

Oral tradition may have played an important part in shaping Roman myths and traditions about their earliest history. Cato and Varro both believed that there was an ancient tradition of performances of songs about famous men and their deeds at banquets, although the implication is that this was no longer current even in Cato's day (Cic., *Tusc.* 4.3). Plays and dramatic performances may also have transmitted stories about early Rome. Drama as a literary form developed in the years after the First Punic War (probably *c.* 240), but Livy (7.2) suggests that the custom of staging dramatic performances had developed by 364, and so-called *fabulae praetextae*, plays based on themes drawn from early Roman history and mythology, were performed in the second and first centuries. These represent myths and popular traditions, rather than history, but they offer some insight into how Roman traditions may have been shaped and transmitted.

Our earliest account of Rome, that of Polybios, written in the mid-second century, is the work of a Greek, writing specifically with the aim of explaining Rome for a Greek audience. Although it is an invaluable account of the Punic and Macedonian wars of the late third and second century, its coverage of earlier Roman history is limited. The earliest surviving narrative accounts of early Rome (although with some gaps) are those of Livy and Dionysios of Halicarnassus, both writing in the late first century BC. These can be supplemented by more specific material included in the works of Polybios, Cicero, Varro and many others, as well as historians, antiquarians and biographers of the first and second centuries AD, but all of these were writing long after the events described, and any evaluation of their content must take into account what (if any) their source material might have been, as well as how they used it. The questions they pose are: what were their sources of information, and how reliable were they? How close were these to the history of regal Rome or the early Republic? And how did these sources shape what the historians wrote?

3. Records and their nature

One particularly contentious area is whether the early Roman state (or individuals) kept archives or records, and if so, when did these start, how reliable were they, and how many survived? These are points on which ancient evidence is contradictory and modern historians are deeply divided.

It seems likely that some records did exist, though they were rudimentary by modern standards, but the date at which they began is difficult to establish. Systematic record-keeping was limited, and the content and publication of those records which were kept is difficult to establish. Religious records, known as the *annales maximi*, were kept by the *pontifex maximus*, but they were very specific in content.[4] They listed the significant events of the year, such as famines, natural events such as eclipses (with a particular emphasis on anything that might have religious significance) and probably also the names of the year's magistrates. Cato and Cicero (Cato, *FRHist*5 F80; Cic., *Or.* 2. 52) comment on their limited content. They were displayed on whitened boards in the Forum, outside either the Regia or the Domus Publica. When the boards were full, the information was stored in an archive, although we know little for certain about the form in which they were stored. Roman sources imply that the earliest *annales* dated back to the beginning of the Republic, although some modern historians have argued that systematic record-keeping did not begin until the fourth century at the earliest. The end-point of these records is easier to establish. They were maintained until the 120s BC, when they were discontinued by the *pontifex* Mucius Scaevola. The contents were apparently published either by Mucius Scaevola or later, in the reign of Augustus. The *annales* were said to have been published in eighty books, a length that implies either a more substantial set of records than other sources suggest or the addition of extra material at the time of publication, possibly not entirely reliable.

Romans kept other official records, although we have few details about how systematic these were. The fifth-century law code, the Twelve Tables, was a matter of public record, and Cicero, Polybios and Dionysios of Halicarnassus all indicate that some treaties and laws of the sixth and fifth centuries were preserved. Dionysios of Halicarnassus (Dion. Hal. 6.95) says that a copy of the Cassian treaty of 493 BC was still extant, and Polybios (Pol. 3.22) claims to have read an early treaty between Rome and Carthage, which he dates to 509 and describes as being written in difficult and archaic language. Official calendars of religious festivals and days for public business in the assemblies and law courts were maintained, as were the *fasti*, annual lists of magistrates and of triumphs celebrated, although we know little about how they were originally recorded. The *fasti* are preserved in an inscription set up by the emperor Augustus in 12 BC,[5] and the form in which they are presented probably represents a reorganisation and systematisation of the original material to fit later assumptions about magistracies of the early Republic. There are differing views on how reliable they are as a record for the magistrates of the fifth century. The survival of fragmentary magistrate lists such as the *fasti Antiates*, an inscription of the mid-first century BC found at Antium, demonstrate that the Roman *fasti* are unlikely to be an Augustan invention. Oakley and Smith make strong arguments that they should be accepted as containing some genuine historical information about the early Republic, although their listing of magistrates as two consuls per year may be an attempt to impose the framework of Rome's later constitution onto an earlier and messier reality. It is possible that they contain inaccurate records, inserted by later magistrates to enhance the reputation of their families. However, as Oakley points out, records of offices held were central to family status and identity, and the Roman nobility was unlikely to tolerate any serious tampering with them. It seems likely that the *fasti* do contain historical information, although probably reordered to fit the preconceptions of the Augustan era.

In addition to state documents, noble families throughout Italy took steps to preserve their own records and family histories. Family status relied on cumulative inherited kudos from the eminence and achievements of earlier generations, so there was a strong incentive to record achievements of ancestors, although it is not clear what forms these took. They are likely to have included genealogies and funerary eulogies, preserved either in writing or as oral traditions. A group of inscriptions from Tarquinii, known as the Elogia Tarquiniensia, may be based on a family history of the Spurinna family, one of the leading families of Tarquinii, and the Fabii are said to have maintained family histories. The reliability of family traditions is open to question. Oral transmission is inherently open to distortion, and there is a limit to the time over which genuine memories and traditions can be transmitted without serious loss of accuracy. Even written records of this type pose problems. Given that their purpose was to preserve memories of family reputation and achievement, there is a clear incentive for exaggeration and the creation of fictive traditions to enhance family status and importance. Livy clearly knew about, and used, such histories, but he took a sceptical view of them, saying that family histories included much invented material (Livy 8.40.4, 22.31.11).

One contentious aspect is how far records survived and whether they could be consulted, other than by restricted groups such as members of the priestly colleges. Some ancient authors (cf. Livy 6.1.2; Plut., *Numa* 1.1) believed that few public and private documents survived the Gallic sack of the early fourth century, which, if true, would mean that even the earliest historians had no access to genuinely early information, and that all traditions about Rome before this date should be rejected as invented. This is problematic on two counts. The first of these is that there is little archaeological evidence of widespread burning or destruction at Rome in the period of the Gallic invasion, casting doubt on whether the city had suffered widespread damage. Wiseman has argued that this destruction was a hypothesis invented by ancient writers to explain the non-existence of records earlier than the beginning of the fourth century, but the testimony of the writers listed above suggests that some documentary evidence did exist. Early records are likely to have been extremely limited in number, and restricted in the scope of what they recorded, but we are not justified in assuming that none existed. The approach adopted in this book is that some records were kept from the fifth century, but that these were limited in content.

The accessibility of records to any of our surviving sources, or to earlier writers, is difficult to judge. It is unclear whether the publication of the *annales maximi* was intended to allow wider access to the records or was simply a systematisation of the records into a single publication in the archives of the *pontifex maximus*, for use by the pontifical college. Publication of records could be a matter of controversy, as access to them was bound up with political power. The lengthy agitation over a written law code in the fifth century is a vivid demonstration of this, as was the controversy caused by Gnaeus Flavius' publication of the calendar and legal documents in 304 BC (Livy 9. 46). Flavius' actions, and the publication of the *annales* by Mucius Scaevola, demonstrate that there were attempts to make legal and religious records more accessible, but the fuss caused by Flavius' actions also shows that it was a controversial area.

Nevertheless, there is persuasive evidence not only for the existence of documentary evidence from the beginning of the Republic but also for its use by some of our surviving sources. Dionysios of Halicarnassus and Polybios both quote what they claim to be original texts of treaties, and Livy regularly prefaces the historical account of each year with factual information which may be derived from official records.[6] Although material derived from these sources may have been reworked and reinterpreted in the light of later assumptions, there is no persuasive reason to doubt that at least some pre-fourth-century records existed or that later authors could make use of them.

4. The earliest historians of Rome

Although the surviving narratives of early Rome date to the late first century BC or later, there were earlier histories which have not survived except in fragmentary form. However, the earliest of these were written in the late third century, a long time after the regal period and the early Republic. The first histories of Rome were written in Greek and were influenced by contemporary Greek approaches to writing history, but the Romans quickly developed their own conventions. Earlier Greek historians such as Herodotos and Thucydides focused on contemporary history, sometimes with digressions on the past or on non-Greek peoples where required by the narrative. Roman historians, in contrast, had a very close focus on the history of Rome and mostly included a substantial outline of early Roman history before they engaged with more contemporary history.

The first Roman historian, Quintus Fabius Pictor, composed his work in the late third century and set the pattern for most of the early Roman writers of the genre. He was a senator who had served in the Gallic war of 225 and was part of a Roman delegation that travelled to Delphi in 216. His history was probably written in annalistic form, recounting events year by year. It survives only in quotations and references in other writers, but the contents of its earliest sections were listed in an inscription found in the public library of Tauromenion in Sicily. It covered the foundation of Rome, an outline of its early history and a history of the period from 264 to 217, covering the First Punic War and its aftermath (Dion. Hal. 1.6. 2; Pol. 1.14. 1; App., *Hann.* 116). This structure, combining the foundation and early history of Rome with contemporary history, drew on both Hellenistic Greek historiographical convention and a Roman tradition of annalistic records. The later books of Pictor's history covered events of which he had personal knowledge, or were within living memory, but we do not know what (if any) sources he had for the earlier books. His structure, and possibly his style, may have been modelled on the pontifical *annales*, but there is no proof that he actually consulted these.

The form and style of Fabius Pictor's history set the pattern for most of his third and second-century successors, such as Lucius Cincius Alimentus, and Aulus Postumius Albinus. Like him, they were men of senatorial rank, who had pursued public careers. As far as we can tell, they wrote histories of their own period, using an annalistic structure, but included a narrative of Rome's foundation and earlier history. Like Fabius Pictor, they appear to have written in Greek, the accepted literary language of the day and also (as demonstrated by the possession of Fabius' work by the library at Tauromenion) a way of ensuring a Greek readership. A possible motive for his decision to write a history of Rome was a desire to make Roman history accessible to a Greek audience.

The work of Fabius Pictor was probably translated into Latin, but the first historian to write in Latin as his first choice of language was Cato the Elder, one of the leading public figures of the early to mid-second century. He was an eminent general and statesman, and a prolific author with wide-ranging cultural and intellectual interests. As well as his historical writings, he composed technical treatises on farming, law and military strategy, books of aphorisms on a wide range of subjects, and over 150 speeches. Only his farming handbook, *De Agri Cultura*, survives. His historical work, *Origines*, some fragments of which are preserved, was innovative. Apart from his decision to write it in Latin rather than Greek, he was the first Roman to write extensively on Italy as well as Rome. There are many uncertainties about the content and organisation of this work, but the first three books seem to have covered the origins and foundations not just of Rome but of other Italian peoples and communities, while the later books were a history from the Punic wars to his own time. Unlike most other Roman historians, he seems to have organised his work on thematic rather than annalistic principles.

Other historians of the second and first centuries BC, such as Cassius Hemina, Calpurnius Piso, Licinius Macer, Valerius Antias and others, follow very much the same pattern as Fabius Pictor in both their careers and their approach to history. They were men of senatorial rank who pursued public careers, and their work, as far as we can tell from surviving fragments, was annalistic in structure, starting with descriptions of Rome's foundation and early history as a prelude to more detailed histories of contemporary events. Increasingly, these works were written in Latin, although some, such as Cato's contemporary Gaius Acilius, continued to write in Greek.

One final figure who must be considered, although he was not strictly speaking a Roman historian, is Polybios. Polybios was a Greek, the son of Lycortas, one of the leaders of the Achaean League, who came to Rome as a hostage during the Roman conquest of Greece but stayed for much of his life, as a friend of the prominent statesman Scipio Aemilianus. His history, which focused on the Hannibalic war and the subsequent wars in the eastern Mediterranean, aimed to explain Roman culture and Rome's rise to power to a Greek readership. Although his work focuses on a later period, it contains many comments on the earlier history of Italy. Polybios' reputation for diligent research and historical inquiry, and his familiarity with key figures of second-century Rome, means that information included by him – for instance, his information about the early treaty with Carthage – is a valuable resource.

5. Sources of sources

Although we can identify possible sources, ranging from documentary evidence to earlier historians, it is not always entirely clear how far, and in what ways, Livy, Dionysios of Halicarnassus and others used them. Dionysios, a Greek from Halicarnassus who lived in Rome for much of his life and was an enthusiastic supporter of the Classical revival in Augustan Rome, quotes copiously from earlier material. His principal surviving work, the *Antiquitates Romanae*, was a history of Rome from its foundation to 264 BC. One of his purposes in writing the book was to prove that Rome was in fact Greek in origin, and to highlight elements of Roman culture that he believed were similar to those of the Greeks. In the early books of his work, dealing with the foundation of Rome and the regal period, he uses a wide range of sources, listing the earlier Roman historians consulted, and citing both these and a considerable number of Greek authors, amounting to fifty authors in all just in Book One alone. Many of these citations concern early Roman rituals, festivals and institutions, and his emphasis on antiquarian material suggests that he may have used Varro's work extensively as well as his cited sources. On several occasions he gives alternative versions of famous events drawn from different sources, using them to make a moral point. His references to early records suggest that he believed that Roman history had started with local records which were eventually expanded to form the basis of the first histories of Rome. He occasionally claimed to quote from original documents, such as the Cassian treaty of 493 BC. He seems to have made extensive and sophisticated use of earlier sources, but mainly to try to explain aspects of the foundation of Rome and its earliest history. His later books, covering the fifth century, cite very few earlier historians.

Livy, who was roughly contemporary with Dionysios of Halicarnassus, wrote a history of Rome, published in 142 books, covering the history of the city from its foundation to 9 BC. It survives as short summaries of the full work and the entire texts of books 1–10 and 21–45. The work was organised on the annalistic principles adopted by Fabius Pictor and his successors, alternating accounts of domestic and foreign affairs for each year. Livy begins coverage of each year with factual information such as magistrates elected, commands allocated by the senate and religious matters such as omens and prodigies observed. Much of this may have come from archival sources such as the *annales maximi* or the *fasti*. Subject matter of this type, including similar items such as records of colonial foundations, troops levied and items of senatorial business, are usually reported in a conspicuously plain style which may echo the language of the documents from which the information came. He made use of a number of earlier Roman historians for his early books, including Fabius Pictor. For the period after 218 he made extensive use of Polybios in preference to other Roman accounts, as can be established by comparing the two texts. He cites Polybios in complimentary terms, but took a critical approach to some of his other sources. Valerius Antias is often mentioned only to be rejected in favour of an alternative, and he is sceptical of the tendency of Antias and Licinius Macer to prefer traditions that gave credit to their own forebears. It is clear that both he and Dionysios of Halicarnassus made critical use of a range of earlier historians, and of state records as well.

Other historians whose work includes the history of Rome before the Punic wars adopted a wide-ranging 'world history' approach, basing their work on that of earlier historians. Diodorus Siculus, a Greek from Agyrium in Sicily (mid-first century), composed a history of the world in forty books, parts of which survive intact, including those dealing with the period from 482 to 302, which contain occasional references to Roman events. He had a keen interest in mythology and ethnography, and he preserves much information about myths, legends and unusual customs. For his Roman history he relied on two principal sources, of unknown identity, although one seems to have been a writer of narrative history and the other to have been a chronographer from whom Diodorus derived lists of dates and magistrates, and his chronology differs significantly from that of many other authors.

Comments on early Rome can be found in Roman historians of the early empire, such as Tacitus and Velleius Paterculus, and there is a substantial amount of material in the works of two further Greek historians, Appian and Dio Cassius. Appian (early second century AD) wrote a history of Rome from the foundation down to his own day, organising it geographically rather than annalistically. He relied on a number of earlier authors but rarely cites these and, like many Greek writers of the era, may have had limited knowledge of Latin sources. His narrative of the Samnite and Pyrrhic wars survives only in fragments but is valuable, given that Livy's narrative for the Pyrrhic war only survives as a short summary. Dio Cassius (third century AD) wrote a history of the Roman world in eighty books organised annalistically, though the books covering the early history of Rome exist only in fragments and in summaries by the Byzantine historian Zonaras. Although he does not name his sources, there are a number of points (notably the passages relating to the early consulship) where he differs from Livy and Dionysios of Halicarnassus and may have been following a different, and possibly early, source.

History was a literary genre, and all historians writing about early Rome have their own agendas and their own approaches to writing history, which colour their presentation of events. The style of the earliest Roman historians may have been modelled on the brief and plain factual style of the *annales*, but authors such as Polybios, Dionysios, Diodorus and Livy were writing in a Hellenistic tradition, the conventions of which required them to present a compelling narrative, adding another layer of complexity to how we must approach their work. They had contrasting approaches and aims: Polybios placed great emphasis on personal inquiry and aimed to explain Roman power to a Greek audience; Dionysios wrote to promote an Atticising style and the view that Romans and Greek shared a common origin; and Livy sought to chart and justify Rome's rise to power. For Livy character (both individual and collective) was central to everything, and Rome only prevailed when it was true to its ancient moral virtues. His narrative of early Rome is shaped to emphasise the characters of both the individuals and the Roman people, and to illustrate the perils of departing from ancestral virtues, and many of the events he includes, and the interpretation placed on them, were designed to illustrate this. He and most other historians present the early history of Rome in terms of the politics, society and culture of their own time, injecting many levels of anachronism and retrojection. Descriptions of early Rome assume that it had a structured government with a prominent and influential senate, as it did in the late Republic, while narratives of the social unrest of the fifth and fourth centuries are shaped by the political and social struggles, and described in the political language, of the late Republic. This does not mean that these events did not take place, but we cannot accept the details of the narrative, and the actions and motivations attributed.

6. Antiquarians and others

Information about early Rome is not confined to writers of narrative history. Grammarians, biographers, antiquarians and even poets preserved useful information about early Rome. There was particular interest in early Rome in the first century BC and first century AD. Cicero comments on many aspects of early Rome in his works, particularly in his treatises on law and government (*De Legibus, De Republica*). His contemporary Varro was a prolific and highly influential figure who took a keen interest in the history of early Rome and was influential in the development of its foundation myths and chronology, although only his works on the Latin language and on agriculture survive intact. The Greek geographer Strabo (late first century BC) preserves information about the topography, foundation myths, cults and customs of ancient Italy, derived from his own travels and experiences and the works of earlier Greek geographers. Verrius Flaccus, an Augustan scholar and antiquarian, wrote extensively on early Roman ritual and culture, including matters relating to augury and Etruscan ritual. His work survives principally as a summary compiled by the grammarian Festus (second century AD), which is a mine of information on aspects of early Rome, and of Roman beliefs about it. All of these preserve valuable information about early Rome, and especially about aspects such as ritual and chronology, which was unknown to or ignored by historians.

Two grammarians, the Roman Aulus Gellius (second century AD) and the Greek Athenaeus (second century AD), wrote compilations of anecdotes, quotations, notes and short essays on a wide variety of topics and preserve quotations and fragments of works that would otherwise be lost, including some on Roman and Italian history and cultures. The Roman polymath Pliny the Elder (first century AD), composed a thirty-seven-volume encyclopaedia covering everything from art, geography and ethnography to many areas of natural science. The *Natural History* is an invaluable source of information on Italian cities and peoples. The Greek biographer and essayist Plutarch (second century AD) included biographies of a number of figures from early Roman history in his *Parallel Lives*, including Romulus, Numa, Valerius Publicola, Coriolanus, Camillus and Pyrrhus. The life of Pyrrhus is a useful resource for a period for which other narratives, such as those of Livy, Dio and Appian, are fragmentary or lost, and may have drawn on a wide range of earlier Greek and Roman historians.

Finally, although poetry may not seem an obvious source for a history of early Rome, Roman poets took a close interest in historical myths and traditions, and offer an insight into how these developed. The most obvious case is Virgil, whose *Aeneid* is the best-known version of the Aeneas myth, but Ovid's *Fasti*, which is structured round the Roman ritual calendar, gives further insights into the development of Roman myths and traditions about the past in the Augustan period. Fragments of some of the earliest Roman poets, most of whom came from outside Rome, contain some interesting information. Quintus Ennius, a native of Rudiae in south-east Italy who migrated to Rome and claimed that he had *tria corda* (literally 'three hearts', but in this context probably three languages – Latin, Greek and his native Oscan), wrote an epic poem, entitled *Annales*, on the history of Rome from its foundation. Although this was epic, not history, his account of the Pyrrhic war was written from an almost contemporary perspective and from local knowledge of the region affected, and it seems to have shaped Roman traditions about this and earlier eras. He and his near contemporary Naevius, a native of Campania, were at the forefront of the development of Roman literature and were writing at the time when Roman traditions about their past were being reshaped by new literary and cultural influences.

The importance of non-narrative sources, such as grammarians, antiquarians and poets, for Roman history, particularly in preserving variants that did not make it into mainstream history, can be seen particularly clearly in the development of the mythological tradition about the foundation of Rome. Writers of this type preserve over sixty different versions of Rome's foundation, some of which are completely different from the familiar stories of Aeneas and Romulus that became the central foundation myths of Rome.

7. Approaches to ancient sources

There is a range of scholarly opinion on whether ancient accounts of the early centuries of Rome's history are usable as historical evidence. Some historians, most recently Cornell, Oakley and Forsythe, take the view that ancient authors had access to genuine information about the archaic period (sixth to fourth centuries), and that this can be separated out from the accretion of myth. Others, such as Wiseman, believe that even the earliest historians such as Fabius Pictor could have had no genuine knowledge of any history earlier than the fourth century, and see the ancient sources as a collection of myths and traditions, which have relevance to the Romans' own view of themselves, their identity and their history, but little value as historical evidence.

At the other extreme, Carandini has proposed that the myths of the foundation and early kings can be treated as historical, and can be combined with the archaeological evidence to reconstruct the Rome of Romulus and his successors. This poses a number of methodological problems, perhaps most seriously the construction of a circular argument in which archaeological and mythological evidence are used to validate each other. In trying to reconstruct the history of early Italy, it is essential to engage with both archaeological and written evidence – we cannot hope to gain an insight into archaic Italy or Rome otherwise, and some chapters of this book are largely reliant on archaeological material – but it is important to approach each type of evidence on its own terms. Only then can we evaluate whether and, if so, how they might be integrated. Carandini's approach also assumes that the mythological traditions were both very ancient and relatively static. As noted above, Roman traditions about the remote past of the city were not static, and there were many different variants, not all of which involved Romulus. It is possible – even likely – that the mythological tradition did contain ancient material, as Greek historians make reference to versions of it as early as the fifth century, but the earliest possible evidence from Italy is no earlier than the sixth century, and the earliest secure evidence dates to the fourth century. The myths also evolved and changed considerably, particularly in the fourth century, when aspects of the myth such as Remus' role either appear for the first time or gain new prominence, and in the first century BC, when the stories which are now the best-known and most widely accepted versions of the myth were established by antiquarians such as Varro. Against this background it is difficult to accept an archaeological reconstruction based on the foundation of Rome by Romulus.

The principal underlying problem is that we cannot know for certain whether the earliest histories were based on any evidence other than myths, memories and oral traditions, all of which are highly unreliable. Wiseman's assumption that no records existed from the early Republic, and that the story of the city's destruction by the Gauls was invented by the Romans to explain this gap, is difficult to accept. There are enough references to early Roman history, though admittedly few and far between, in contemporary Greek history from the fifth century onwards to suggest that the Roman annalistic tradition was not entirely made up, and to give us some information about the peoples of Italy (in particular, the Etruscans) with which the Greeks came into contact. There are also lost sources that may lie behind some aspects of Roman history of the sixth and fifth centuries. Many historians believe that a Cumaean source was the basis for most of our information on Aristodemos of Cumae and, thanks to their connections with Aristodemos, for the later history of the Tarquin family.

The crux of the problem, however, is whether public records such as the *annales* and *fasti* are believed to have existed, to have been reasonably reliable and to have been used as a source of basic information by Livy and others. As indicated above, this volume shares the position of Oakley, Smith and Cornell, that some records did exist in the early Republic, although probably not earlier, but that they did not necessarily correspond to the later, published forms of the Augustan era, which significantly reshaped them to fit later assumptions about the development of the Republic. It would be unwise to assume that these were anything other than rudimentary, but they may have provided a basis for some of the basic information – names and dates of magistrates, names and dates of laws and treaties, dates of colonies and numbers of settlers, triumphs awarded, rituals celebrated and other information of this type.

In dealing with such a long period, it is difficult to arrive at a single satisfactory approach to these problems. Ancient traditions about the foundation of Rome and the early kings are clearly best approached as myths representing Rome's collective identity, not history. For the sixth to fourth centuries, however, there is some corroborating evidence from Greek sources, and accounts of Rome's development are sufficiently compatible with the archaeological evidence to suggest that they contain some historical material. The years covered by the final chapters of this book are within two generations of the first histories of Rome – a period from which memories and oral testimonies would have survived. Accounts of personalities and motivations must be treated as literature or mythology rather than history, and many aspects of our surviving narratives must be discounted, but the trajectory of the development of Rome that they present is consistent, at many points, with the picture presented by material evidence. The ancient sources have been summarised and discussed, highlighting the extent to which they can be useful in understanding Roman history throughout this volume, but the general approach adopted for the fifth century onwards is that of Oakley,[7] which accepts that the general outline presented by Livy and others may be broadly correct, but that most of the detailed narrative of specific events, characters and motivations are literary invention.

NOTES

Chapter 1: Introducing early Rome

1. Unless otherwise specified, all dates in this volume are dates BC. A discussion of Roman dates and chronology can be found in the Appendix.

2. Greek historians, for instance, offer corroboration of some dates and events, such as the expulsion of Tarquin (Pol. 3.22.1), and comments on some contemporary Italian cultures and events. The earliest Roman historian, Fabius Pictor, wrote in the late third century.

3. Thucydides (Thuc. 7.77) defines cities entirely in terms of people, while Plato (Laws 788–9) and Aristotle (Arist., *Pol.* 1330b) mention both population and form. In contrast, the second-century AD writer Pausanias (Paus. 10.4.1) dismissed the small city of Panopaeus in Greece as barely worth the name because of its lack of amenities, and Romans such as Tacitus (*Agricola* 21, *Germania* 16) see cities in terms of possession of particular sets of buildings and a specific legal status.

4. Although his main focus was a history of the Persian wars, Herodotos' work contains much information about the rest of the Mediterranean, including the west. He had a particular interest in ethnic origins and includes a lot of foundation myths.

5. Some earlier Greek writers reserve the term *Italike* (Italy) for small parts of southern Italy. It is only in the fourth century BC that *Italia* (Latin) and *Italike* (Greek) come to be used consistently for the whole peninsula.

6. There is a divergence between archaeologists and historians in naming conventions for the Celts. Although 'Celt' is preferred by archaeologists, and many (although not all) ancient historians refer to them as 'Gauls', they are in fact the same people. The divergence arises from a difference between the name ascribed by the Greeks (*Keltoi*) and that by the Romans (*Galli*). In some quarters even the concept of Celt as an identity is controversial and regarded as a modern construction, although this is a rather extreme view. For the sake of simplicity, this book will use the term 'Celt' to describe this population.

Chapter 2: Setting the scene: Iron-Age Italy

1. The earliest inscription found so far is a graffito on a pottery vessel from Osteria dell'Osa (fig. 3)and has been dated to *c.* 770 BC. Some Greek and Etruscan inscriptions date to the later eighth century, but these are few in number.

2. The fibula is an important object in Italian archaeology. It was in essence a safety-pin shape, with an arched back and a catch-plate to secure the pin in place, but there were many different variants. The arch of the brooch could be plain or decorated, wide or narrow, straight or twisted into decorative shapes, and the catch-plate could be short or long. They were most commonly made of bronze, but silver or even gold examples are found in elite burials. Fibulae (for an example, see pl. 2) were used as brooches and to fasten dresses, tunics and cloaks, and are among the most frequent objects found in burials, either as grave gifts or pins to secure the burial shroud. Their ubiquity is what makes them so useful to the archaeologist. The various types can often be dated, at least relative to each other, so they can be used to establish a chronology. Different types are often associated with different sections of society – for instance, men and women might wear different fibulae, as might adults and children – so they can sometimes be used to determine the gender or age of a person associated with them.

3. These were of a local form of pottery known as impasto, which was made from coarse clay, usually worked by hand and fired to a medium hardness. The name of the vessel comes from its shape, which resembles a smaller cone inverted on top of a larger one.

4. There are instances in which graves with weapons (or, in later and richer periods, chariots) have been subsequently proved to be female burials, suggesting that these items were generic status symbols rather than specific markers of gender.

5. The association between elite status and horse ownership is pervasive in early Italy (and elsewhere in Iron-Age Europe, as discussed in Cornell, *The Beginnings of Rome*, p. 250). Horse harnesses are restricted to wealthy burials, and in the seventh and sixth centuries princely tombs contained lavishly decorated chariots and even the skeletons of horses. Horses and chariots are depicted in Italian art as symbols of power and status in the seventh to fifth centuries.

6. Hansen's criterion, developed as part of the Copenhagen Polis Project, is that cities require a minimum distance of 30 km (*c.* 18–19 miles) between them for a full independent existence to be assumed.

7. Examples of this settlement pattern are found at Tarquinii, Orvieto, Caere, Volterra and Populonia, as well as Nepi and Veii.

8. The extent to which these activities cut across social divisions is illustrated by a bronze rattle found near Bologna (fig. 13), which shows a high-ranking woman and her servants weaving.

9. The Greeks habitually drank their wine mixed with varying proportions of water, and drinking sets usually included a krater, a large, deep vessel used for mixing the drink, as well as drinking cups, and serving vessels such as jugs and amphorae. The Greek symposion was a highly ritualised all-male social occasion which was specific to Greek society, but Italian societies developed banqueting cultures of their own (in many cases of mixed gender, rather than segregated male parties), at which Greek drinking sets were used.

10. In one strand of Roman mythology Alba Longa was founded by the son of Aeneas, and ruled by his descendants until the coup in which the legitimate king was overthrown and his daughter's infant sons, Romulus and Remus, were abandoned. The intricacies of these traditions and their possible relationship to the history of early Rome are discussed in the following chapter. Romans believed Alba Longa to have been in the Alban Hills, near the mountain known as Mons Albanus, but there is little evidence for this, or any to support its association with a later Roman town, now Albano Laziale. Archaeological evidence from the Alban Hills demonstrates that there were small villages in the area in the Final Bronze Age and early Iron Age, but these failed to develop into larger settlements and are certainly unlikely to have founded Rome.

11. The essential problem is a mismatch between dendrochronology and dating based on artefacts. In the last twenty years dates of timbers from late Bronze-Age sites in northern Italy and central Europe have suggested that this period was up to fifty years earlier than previously suspected, and that dates of the final Bronze-Age cultures of Italy should be revised to keep them aligned with those of the rest of western and central Europe. This creates a major problem for the dating of the early Iron Age in Italy, as it conflicts with dating based on pottery. The chronology of the pottery in question – Greek protogeometric cups, which were exported to many areas of the Mediterranean – has also been revised, and these objects were produced over a long period between *c.* 900 and 750. At the moment there is no easy way of resolving the conflict.

12. Surveys of the lakeside suggest that there were many villages around its shores, and at least one other area of burials.

13. The precise date is uncertain, but it seems to be between 770 and 750.

14. Studies of comparative data from various African and Mesoamerican societies suggests that an area of 4.5–10 m^2 (*c.* 48–107 square feet) can accommodate a single person, while *c.* 17 m^2 (*c.* 183 square feet) could accommodate a couple and *c.* 30 m^2 (*c.* 322 square feet) – the size of the largest Satricum huts – would be sufficient for a small nuclear family. The model of huts with specialised functions and an open area for communal activities is based on a comparison with use of space by the Bamangwato people of Botswana.

15. Regions are usually referred to by their ancient names (Latium, Samnium etc.) throughout, but when referring to south-east Italy, the modern name, Puglia, is used when dealing with the pre-Roman period, and the Roman name, Apulia, when discussing the period of Roman conquest and rule. The reason is that most Roman authors use 'Apulia' to refer to the whole region, whereas Greek writers make a distinction between the Salento (Iapygia or Messapia), central Puglia (Peucetia) and northern Puglia (Daunia and/or Apulia).

16. The term 'Sikel' is strictly applied to the indigenous population of central and eastern Sicily, but some ancient writers used it as a more general term for all the native Sicilians. Thucydides is drawing a very specific distinction between Phoenician behaviour – settling on offshore islands, principally for the purposes of trade – and that of the Greeks, who settled on the mainland of Italy and Sicily.

17. The reference is to the description of Nestor's cup in Homer, 'a cup of rare workmanship which the old man had brought with him from home, studded with bosses of gold; it had four handles, on each of which there were two golden doves feeding, and it had two

feet to stand on. Anyone else would hardly have been able to lift it from the table when it was full, but Nestor could do so quite easily' (*Iliad* 11.616).

18. This type of burial, known as *entrychismos*, in which the body of a child was placed in a large amphora, is not uncommon as a form of infant burial in the ancient world.

19. The equation of particular types of objects with the ethnicity of their owners is highly problematic. It assumes that one group could not have adopted the fashions of the other, either from necessity, because their preferred types of goods were unavailable, or from choice. It also presupposes that objects always move about with their owners, whereas they could just as easily be transferred between people and communities by means of trade or as gifts. However, given the wider evidence for the multicultural nature of Pithecusae, it is not implausible that the presence of Italic-style grave goods could mean that there were Italic people living there.

20. In later Greek history Achaea was an underdeveloped area of the north-west Peloponnese. However, 'Achaean' is used by Homer as the collective ethnic name for the Greeks, and it is possible that when the sources for colonisation refer to 'Achaeans' they simply mean Greeks, not people from the Peloponnese.

Chapter 3: Trojans, Latins, Sabines and rogues: Romulus, Aeneas and the 'foundation' of Rome

1. Later historians were unable to agree on a precise date. Dionysios of Halicarnassus, for example, gives a range of alternative dates in the mid-eighth century (Dion. Hal. 1.73–4). The 'traditional' date of 753, which is cited by most modern scholars, was first fixed by antiquarians (principally Atticus and Varro) in the later first century. For a discussion of Varronian dating and the reasons for this chronological imprecision, see the 'Appendix: Roman dates and chronology'.

2. Carandini's thesis is presented in a short translated version in *Rome: Day One* (Princeton, 2011) and at greater length in *La Nascita di Roma*.

3. The extent of these is, however, open to question. Until relatively recently it was assumed that much of the area occupied by the later Campus Martius, just outside the northern limits of the Republican city, and that occupied by the Forum were marshy until the drainage of the Forum area in the sixth century, a work attributed to one of the Tarquin dynasty. New geological studies have raised doubts about the extent of the marshy areas under the later Forum, suggesting that these may have been much smaller than previously believed, and that the problem may have been seasonal flooding of a stream rather than extensive areas of marshland.

4. All the Palatine huts are very similar in type to those found at some other Latin sites, notably the hut found at Fidenae. Possible uses of domestic space by the people of Iron-Age Latium are discussed on pp. 23–4.

5. Some archaeologists regard the group of smaller huts as contemporary, while others argue that they were consecutive phases of a single hut which was rebuilt several times.

6. The principal sources are Livy 1.1–7, Dion. Hal. 1.76–88 and Plut. *Rom.* 1–11. Other accounts are discussed by J. Bremmer in Bremmer and Horsfall (eds), *Roman Myth and Mythography* (1987), and by Wiseman, *Remus: A Roman Myth* (1995). Both names are

closely related to that of Rome itself. Romulus literally means 'the Roman', and in Greek versions of the story Remus' name is given as Romos. An alternative version apparently existed in which the twins were rescued by a prostitute (*lupa*, the Latin word for a she-wolf, was also a common Roman term for a prostitute).

7. Roman antiquarians such as Festus, and Verrius Flaccus, believed that *Roma Quadrata* ('square Rome') was both a sacred boundary and an actual structure on the Palatine, near the later temple of Apollo. The exact meaning of the term is difficult to unravel, as it was obscure even to later Romans.

8. The dramatic sub-plot of Aeneas' marriage to Dido, queen of Carthage, introduced in Books 1 and 4, almost subverts this destiny until the gods intervene to force him to leave Carthage for Italy. The story of Dido and Aeneas is clearly coloured by Rome's wars against Carthage in the third century BC. Virgil presents Carthage as a potential rival to Rome, and hints that there is a danger that Aeneas' attraction to Dido might cause him to found the wrong imperial city.

9. On the so-called Struggle of the Orders between patricians and plebeians, see below, pp. 186–96.

10. According to Dionysios of Halicarnassus (1.45.5–48.1), there was much uncertainty over what the foundation legend of Rome actually consisted of. Remus appears in some versions but not others; the identity of Aeneas' son, from whom Romulus and the kings of Alba Longa were descended, is disputed; and there were many other discrepancies.

11. The ancient accounts of the Septimontium are wildly contradictory, and each names a different set of hills and regions of Rome that were said to participate. The Palatine and the Cermalus are included as two separate communities, suggesting that it may indeed date back to a proto-urban era in which this was the case, and may have originated as a shared festival celebrated by the people of the various settlements at Rome. The significance of the twenty-seven sacred locations visited by the procession during the festivals of the Argei is likewise obscure.

12. The location of the House of Romulus has been identified by archaeologists with a rectangular enclosure in the precinct of the later temple of Victory, on the south-west side of the Palatine and close to the site of the eighth-century huts.

Chapter 4: The rise of the international aristocracy: Italy and the orientalising revolution

1. A small number of the metal and pottery vessels are inscribed with the phrase 'mi larthia' ('I belong to Larthi', or possibly 'I belong to Larth'). Whether this was the name of the deceased or the name of the person who donated these particular objects is a matter of debate. It is also unclear whether the dedicator/dedicatee named was a man (Larth) or a woman (Larthi). In early Etruscan, Larthia could be genitive of either the female name Larthi or the male name, Larth.

2. The types of items found at Murlo are not found beyond the locality, implying that it was producing goods for local needs rather than for wider export.

3. Most evidence for the cult comes from Roman sources, and from a temple of Mater Matuta at Rome, where she was associated with Fortuna, the goddess of good fortune. In other areas of Italy similar cults were linked with goddesses of dawn, and of childbirth.

4. Sometimes referred to by the Latin term *gens*, although I have restricted this usage to the discussion of extended families in Rome, since it may have had specific significance in Roman law.

5. Other regions of Italy do not have enough epigraphic evidence dating to the eighth and early seventh centuries to permit any conclusions to be drawn.

6. This style is known as situla art, named after the predominant form of vessel with this type of decoration. The situla was a large bucket-shaped bronze vessel, probably used to mix and serve wine, which is the most frequent object decorated in this style, but the general style of decoration is also found on a range of other bronze vessels. Items decorated in this style were produced from *c.* 650 to 550, and most came from workshops at Felsina (mod. Bologna).

7. Roman society seems to have been conservative in this respect. In many areas of northern and central Italy, such as Etruria and the Veneto, women were given personal names as well as family names, at least by the sixth century, but Roman women continued to be known only by a female form of the clan name. Even in much later periods additional names, used to differentiate between daughters of a family (e.g., 'number' names such as Prima, Secunda, Tertia or diminutives) were only used as an informal addition, not as a true given name.

8. Diod. 5.40; Dion. Hal. 2.44.7. Ancient descriptions of Etruscan society as polarised between the upper classes and slaves or serfs use Greek or Roman terms, and it is difficult to assess whether these reflect Etruscan customs or later Greek and Roman assumptions. Some Etruscan inscriptions refer to some people as *lautni*, which seems to mean either a freed slave or someone with only limited legal rights, but these are all much later than the seventh century. Roman sources offer a vivid account of the social tensions caused by domination of both land ownership and political power by an overbearing elite, but this also relates to the fifth and fourth centuries, leaving us with a lack of evidence for the orientalising period.

9. Etrusco-Corinthian was a form of pottery that was locally produced in Etruria but which based its shapes and forms of decoration on those of Greek pottery from Corinth.

10. All of these were found in tombs at Caere and had been dedicated as funerary gifts, or were buried as prize possessions of the deceased.

11. The tomb, Circolo degli Avori Tomb 67, was a chamber tomb beneath a large tumulus and held two burials, one male and one female. The writing tablet seems to be associated with the female deposition.

12. Opinions are divided on this, with Fausto Zevi arguing that he was a historical figure while David Ridgway sees him as an archetype who illustrates social and economic trends rather than a real person. The narrative as it survives is coloured by later Greek ideas. A stray Bacchiad turning up in Etruria is entirely plausible, but his exclusion from citizenship, despite marrying into the local elite, is clearly based on Greek, not Etruscan or Roman, views of citizenship.

13. There are about a hundred Campanian inscriptions dating from *c.* 650–400, most of which date to *c.* 550–400, and all but a small handful are written in the Etruscan

alphabet. It can be difficult to identify the language securely, because most of these are short texts identifying the owner of the item on which they are written, but where it can be identified, the language is usually Etruscan. There is only a small number of non-Etruscan names or language (about eighteen, according to Crawford's corpus of Italic inscriptions).

Chapter 5: Orientalising Rome and the early kings

1. The principal narratives of the reigns of the early kings can be found in Livy, Book 1, Dion. Hal., Books 1–3, and Plutarch's lives of Romulus and Numa.

2. All the kings were described as adults and old enough to be experienced military and political leaders when they gained power, which makes average reigns of more than thirty years unlikely. Moreover, of the seven reigns only two (those of Numa Pompilius and Ancus Marcius) ended with the natural death of the king. A man who became king in his twenties might have enjoyed a long reign, but the probabilities of a series of seven consecutive kings surviving this long would have been low.

3. This building, known as the Villa Auditorio because it was found during the construction of a new auditorium and concert hall, was large and similar in form to a group of archaic houses found on the Palatine.

4. As major families subdivided into separate branches, some acquired extra family names to show which branch they belonged to. Personal names were often abbreviated, the most common being Lucius (L.), Marcus (M.), Sextus (Sex.), Gaius (C.), Publius (P.), Quintus (Q.) and Manius (M.).

5. The significance and historicity of these tribes is unknown, and the idea that the three tribes were distinct ethnic groups has no support in the ancient sources. The popularity of this explanation in the nineteenth and twentieth centuries may owe more to the ethnic and nationalist politics of the time than to a plausible reconstruction of early Rome.

6. The term *curia* is believed to derive from *co-viria* – men who meet together – and therefore to have a geographical element. It may also be the origin of the term *Quirites* (derived from *co-virites*), an archaic term for the citizens of Rome.

7. The ceremonies of the Lupercalia and the Argei may have been concerned with ritual purification of the community as well as demarcating boundaries.

8. The purpose of having a standardised and written calendar may have been as much political as religious. An orally transmitted list of festivals and rituals left open the possibility of manipulation of religious observance by priests or other members of the elite, but this codification removed the possibility.

9. As the author acknowledges, these are inferences based on a combination of changes to the location of cemeteries at Rome and comparison with the development of other Latin communities, such as Gabii and Lavinium.

10. The ancient sources, notably Dionysios of Halicarnassus, describe the Volcanal as a sacred enclosure containing a cypress tree and a lotus plant.

11. The priestesses of Vesta were one of the most important religious orders in Rome. In later Roman history, girls from noble families were selected at a young age (typically

between six and ten) to join the priesthood. They served for a period of thirty years, after which they were free to leave and to marry. During their period of service they were obliged to live in the House of the Vestals and maintain a strict vow of chastity. The cult of Vesta was central to the well-being of the Roman state, as the fire of Vesta was symbolic of the well-being of the Roman household. The Domus Publica was located next to the House of the Vestals and was the official residence of the *pontifex maximus* (the chief priest, whose role is discussed further on pp. 300–302).

12. Ovid *Fasti* 6.263; Tacitus *Annales* 15.41; Plutarch *Numa* 14; Festus 346–348. Most of the kings were believed to have had houses elsewehere in Rome; the Regia was a location for official duties, not a full-time residence. On the possible identification of the house of Tarquinius Priscus, see below, pp. 145–6.

13. Carandini, who suggested this scenario, associated the move from the original Domus Regia to the Domus Publica with Tarquinius Priscus.

14. Francesca Fulminante's recent study of the urbanisation of Rome compares this sacred geography of the area around Rome with the archaeological evidence and concludes that it is likely that the territorial boundary of Rome in the seventh and early sixth centuries was larger, possibly as much as a radius of *c.* 9 km (5–6 miles) outside the city, but the territory of Rome on this estimate (*c.* 320 km², or 123 square miles) seems too large for the seventh century.

15. Fulminante's work contains a comprehensive set of tables setting out the various population estimates and a discussion of the various ways of weighting this data.

16. This roughly coincides with the traditional dates for the reign of Tarquinius Priscus (*c.* 616–579), named by Livy and other writers as an enthusiastic builder. As noted in the previous chapter, we cannot attribute the changes to Tarquinius (or even infer that he definitely existed), but it is another instance in which the archaeological evidence and Roman traditions about their past are broadly in agreement. The problem is that the traditional chronology of the Tarquin dynasty is demonstrably erroneous, as discused in Chapter 7.

Chapter 6: The urban revolution: city and state in sixth-century Italy

1. Populations are estimated on the basis of the size of urban area, size of territory (and how many people its produce might have supported) and density of occupation. Comparative figures from medieval and early modern Italy can sometimes be used for comparative purposes.

2. Claire Joncheray argues convincingly that the Etruscan cities of the Po valley did not simply copy Hippodamean models but developed their own forms of urban organisation based on both Greek and Etruscan practices.

3. Much of the evidence for this, however, comes from the Roman empire or later. Records exist of disputes between nomadic shepherds and the communities through which they passed in the second and third centuries AD – in particular, a letter from a member of the imperial household instructing the magistrates of the city of Saepinum not to impede the progress of flocks belonging to the emperor. The most detailed information is not ancient but comes from the medieval Dogana, tax and administrative records

covering the long-distance seasonal movements of flocks around the Apennines. The problem lies in determining in whether these record long-term customs can be traced back to Antiquity or whether they are a medieval innovation.

4. The sacrifices and other ceremonies at the sanctuary of Hera, for instance, would have taken place at the altar in front of the two massive temples, not inside them. The temples were the house of the god, and housed the cult statue, offerings made by worshippers and the sanctuary treasury.

5. The Iguvine tables are a set of seven bronze tablets inscribed in Umbrian with detailed protocols for rituals to be carried out on behalf of the Umbrian city of Iguvium. They are the most complete document we have for the ritual life of an Italian community but pose many linguistic problems and are a chronological minefield. The surviving texts were inscribed over a long period, between the third and first centuries BC, and may well also preserve earlier material or be copies of earlier documents.

6. The texts are written in ink on linen, a common practice in Etruria, but the book survived because it was torn into strips and reused as wrappings for a mummy, making the text very difficult to reconstruct.

7. There may, however, be other explanations for changes in burial practice. We know, for instance, that in Rome sumptuary laws were passed at various points in the fifth and fourth centuries, limiting the sizes of tombs and the cost of funerals.

8. Theopompus, who wrote in the fourth century, seems to have had a strong moral bias. His work, which survives only in fragments, was influential and may have been used as a source by others, notably Diodorus.

9. The sanctuary of Reitia at Baratella, just outside Este, was the most important cult place in the region and provides a fascinating insight into the role of women. A very high proportion of votives depict, or were offered by, women, and a series of bronze plaques incised with images of women dressed in the costume of high-status Veneti and ceremonial head-dresses depict priestesses and/or female worshippers.

10. A third-century Etruscan inscription from Cortona concerning a sale or lease of land between one Petru Sceva and the Cusu brothers mentions Sceva's wife as a party to the agreement, but its meaning is ambiguous and it cannot be taken as clear proof of female property ownership.

11. In particular, they suggested a possible surplus wine production of *c.* 1,250 litres (274 gallons) per year, once the estimated consumption of the household had been allowed for.

12. The skeletal evidence can indicate various vitamin and mineral deficiencies. Dental examination showed that many adults had extensive wear on their teeth, suggesting that the diet of archaic Italy was based on bread, fruit and vegetables, all of which needed extensive chewing.

13. Greek cities had their own standards of weights and denominations, but the most common were the stater (*c.* 8 g or around ¼ oz), drachm (5–6 g) or multiples of the drachm, such as the 16–17 g (½ oz) tetrachrachm. Smaller denominations were also produced. Other Italian communities all had their own standards of weights and measures and (once they started producing coins or currency bars) their own monetary systems.

14. The exceptions to this were a small number of fifth-century coins minted by Vulci and Populonia, but this seems to have been a short-term and limited development.

15. The shrine is usually known by its Latin name, Fanum Voltumnae, but it was a sanctuary of the Etruscan deity Veltha, a chthonic god associated with the underworld and (according to Varro) the chief god of the Etruscans.

16. The priesthood could apparently only be won by killing the incumbent, so the priest had to constantly be ready to fight off challengers, until such time as one of them finally succeeded in killing him and assumed the post himself.

17. Figures are taken from Crawford's corpus of Italic inscriptions and from an unpublished database of Etruscan inscriptions compiled by the present author. See p. 350 n. 13 for the problems of identifying languages from such short inscriptions. Most of the 'non-Etruscan' inscriptions are written in the Etruscan alphabet but contain personal names that are of Oscan, Latin or Greek origin. The use of the Oscan language and the development of a distinctive local alphabet do not occur until the late fifth century.

18. It is, however, worth bearing in mind that many Greek traditions about the Etruscans are about establishing their 'otherness' and barbarism. A fragment of a work by the Greek author Callimachus, for instance, implies that they practised human sacrifice of prisoners of war, but there is little supporting evidence. Assertions about their savagery and tendency towards piracy should be treated with caution, although there is enough historical evidence for their activities in the western Mediterranean to suggest that some Etruscan cities were formidable naval powers.

19. The agreement between Thefarie Velianas and Carthage is recorded on a set of gold tablets found in the sanctuary at Pyrgi. Polybios describes an ancient treaty between Rome and Carthage, probably of a similar date.

Chapter 7: Tyrants and wicked women: Rome, the Tarquin dynasty and the fall of the monarchy

1. Discussed on p. 80. His son is said to have been debarred from high office at Tarquinii because of his father's foreign origins.

2. The family tree of the Tarquinii, shown in fig. 20, represents a reconstruction of the family as presented by the ancient sources.

3. Claudius was noted for his knowledge of Etruscan history and religion. He may have had information from Etruscan sources, although the reliability of these is impossible to judge.

4. The scene runs across two adjoining walls of the tomb, and Gneve Tarchunies and Marce Camitlnas are positioned on the second wall but appear to be part of the same scene as the other figures. Bruun offers a radical reinterpretation, suggesting that the Tarchunies/Camitlnas scene is not part of the Mcstrna scene, and associating Marce Camitlnas with the fourth-century Roman Marcus Furius Camillus. This is, in my view, problematic, as it shares the same format – combat between naked captives and armed warriors – as the rest of the fresco. The identification of Gneve Tarchunies as a member of the Tarquin family is not clear-cut, as all known members used the *praenomina* Sextus or Lucius, not Gnaeus, but it is not impossible.

5. As well as Claudius himself, Tacitus (*Ann.* 4.65) and Varro (*LL* 5.46) claim that the Caelian was named after Caelius Vibenna. In Roman literature, the antiquarians Varro and Verrius Flaccus (who had considerable knowledge of, and interest in, the Etruscans) both wrote about the Vibennas, although only fragments of their comments survive.

6. Two that appear to be later are the Clustumina and the Claudia; the former took its name from Crustumerium, which was not conquered by Rome until the 490s, and the latter was named after the Claudian family, which is said to have migrated to Rome at the beginning of the Republic (trad. 504 BC).

7. This voting system existed in the Middle Republic, and was current until the later third century, when it was modified to reduce the imbalance.

8. Identifying early Roman colonies is particularly tricky. Later colonies involved well-defined legal and administrative changes to colonied areas, and typical patterns of reorganisation of both urban centres and surrounding countryside which can be recognised in epigraphic and archaeological evidence. Early colonies, on the other hand, leave few such traces. The nature of Roman colonisation is described in Chapter 13.

9. Polybios mentions three treaties in all, giving no date for the second and dating the third to the Pyrrhic war. Further evidence is provided by Livy and Diodorus (Livy 7.27.2; Diod. 16.19.1), who record a fourth-century treaty, which they date to 348, without mentioning any earlier ones, but both accounts are confused. Given that Polybios claims to have actually seen three treaties, one of which was written in archaic language, it seems likely that there was an earlier treaty, although the precise date cannot be corroborated.

10. This is a difficult issue. Communal ownership of land by the *gens* is frequently hypothesised by modern scholars, but there is little ancient evidence for it.

11. Portunus was a very ancient deity who appears in the earliest known Roman calendar (the Romans believed this to have been instituted by Numa Pompilius). As his name suggests, he seems to have had a particular association with ports and harbours.

12. In the Republic temples to Fortuna and Mater Matuta were established on the same site (Livy 24.47.15), but they probably date from the fourth century. Livy and Dionysios disagree on whether the earlier temple was dedicated to Fortuna (Dion. Hal.) or Mater Matuta (Livy).

13. There are many confusions in the sources over whether particular monuments or building projects should be attributed to Tarquinius Priscus or Tarquinius Superbus, with some being erroneously attributed to both. Pliny and others (Dion. Hal. 4.61; Livy 1.55–56.1) suggest that the Capitoline temple was begun by Tarquinius Priscus but completed by Tarquinius Superbus, but this would require a very long period of construction.

14. Under the Republic, the word *rex* ('king') became a huge insult in Roman public life. Allegations that a particular politician was aiming at kingship could be particularly damaging. Julius Caesar arranged to be offered the crown just so that he could be seen to refuse it publicly and deflect rumours that he intended to declare himself king. His nephew Octavian made a point of adopting titles with a Republican precedent – *princeps* (leader), *imperator* (general) and ultimately Augustus, which had religious connotations. *Rex* remained unacceptable even in the age of imperial rule.

15. Livy 2.6–15; Dion. Hal. 5.21–35; Pliny, *NH* 34.139; Tac., *Hist.* 3.72. Tacitus describes the burning of the temple of Jupiter Capitolinus in AD 69 as worse than the surrender

of Rome to Porsenna or the Gauls, and Pliny makes reference to the terms of a peace treaty imposed by Porsenna. Both references seem to imply that a Roman surrender to the Etruscans was a well-known historical tradition.

Chapter 8: The 'fifth-century crisis' and the changing face of Italy

1. Pausanias, a Greek travel writer of the second century AD and the author of a guidebook to Greece, describes these as two groups of bronze statues. One consisted of statues of bronze horses and captive women dedicated to commemorate victory over the Messapians (Pausanias, *Description of Greece*, 10.10.6). The other, which was a complex sculpture showing the defeat of Opis, king of the Peucetians, commemorated a victory over the Peucetians and Messapians (Pausanias, *Description of Greece*, 13.10).

2. The career of Aristodemos, Rome's war with Clusium and the Tarquin connection with Cumae are narrated in Dion. Hal. 7.3–11 and Livy 2.1–21.

3. Around 80–85 per cent of Etruscan inscriptions found in Campania date to *c.* 550–450 BC, and only a small number can be securely dated to the late fifth or fourth centuries.

4. The date and purpose of this visit, recorded by Timaeus and echoed by Lycophron, are much disputed. The most obvious context, the Athenian expedition against Syracuse in 415, is too late to fit the numismatic evidence for the adoption of Athenian coin types. Of the other possible dates put forward, *c.* 470 and *c.* 450, the latter looks more plausible, although numismatic data could support either. However, a date some time in the 450s BC is fairly close to the date of the foundation of Thurii and thus falls into a period when Athens was known to have had interests in the west.

5. Pythagoras of Samos had moved to Croton in southern Italy *c.* 530 BC and spent the rest of his life there. His teachings were very influential in southern Italy, but it is not entirely clear what the political beliefs of the 'Pythagoreans' described by Polybios (2.39) were, and how far they were related to the philosopher's teachings.

6. The relationship of Oscan to Latin is roughly similar to that between Welsh or Breton and Irish. Oscan had a slightly different set of vowels and used *p* where Latin used *q*, and *f* where Latin used *p*. The Latin pronoun *qui* transforms into *pus*, for instance, and the Oscan name for the goddess Persephone was Futrei, while the Oscan place-names of Pompeii and Nola were Pumpaii and Nuvla. There are also differences in grammatical forms.

7. Some of the more southerly Oscan-speaking communities, principally those of Lucania and Bruttium, used an adapted form of the Greek alphabet as an alternative.

8. The *touto* (and its Umbrian and Venetic equivalent *teuter*) is found in inscriptions from various regions of Italy. Many of these post-date the Roman conquest, but there are sufficient attestations in inscriptions of the fifth, fourth and third centuries to indicate that the *touto* was a pre-Roman institution.

9. Hallstatt and La Tène are the names given by archaeologists to the earlier and later Iron-Age cultures of northern and western Europe. Hallstatt C and Hallstatt D (*c.* 700–600 and 600–475 BC) correspond to the early Iron Age in these regions, and La Tène culture corresponds to the later Iron Age (*c.* 475–415 BC in north-west Italy).

Chapter 9: A difficult transition: the early Roman Republic

1. The arguments for and against acceptance of the *fasti* as evidence for the fifth century are reviewed in detail in C. Smith, 'The magistrates of the early Roman republic', in Beck, Jehne and Pina Polo (eds), *Consuls and the res publica*, 19–40. One of the arguments put forward for rejecting the early entries is the belief by some Romans that few documents survived the Gallic sack of Rome in the early fourth century, but the archaeological evidence, discussed later in this chapter, does not support the idea that the city was badly damaged.

2. Many of these symbols of office such as the purple-bordered toga, ivory chair and fasces, originally derived from the Etruscans.

3. According to Livy, Valerius Poplicola was forced by popular agitation to introduce such a right of appeal as early as 509, although many modern scholars believe that this measure is fictitious, arguing that Livy has anachronistically created a precursor for a better-documented right of *provocatio* (appeal, or intercession) in 300 BC.

4. Livy says that the Etruscans kept count of year by hammering nails into the wall of a temple of the goddess Nortia, and the ceremony of hammering a nail is illustrated on a fourth-century Etruscan mirror. However, it should be noted that Livy's description of the practice at Rome refers to a revival of the ceremony in 364–363, not to the early Republic.

5. Dictators were mostly appointed in times of military crisis that posed a severe threat to Rome, and their role was to act as a military leader. For instance, Quintus Fabius Maximus was appointed dictator in 216, when Rome was in the aftermath of a crushing defeat by Hannibal and faced imminent annihilation. The office was an extraordinary measure to deal with a crisis, not a regular part of the government of Rome.

6. This may have been a revival of a post that already existed under the kings (Tac., *Ann.* 11.22), and Tacitus suggests that they were originally assistants appointed by the consuls, only becoming elected magistrates later in the fifth century.

7. There are many possible alternative interpretations of the definition and rights of the patricians and their relationship to the senate. Some scholars believe that they were of ancient origin but that their monopoly of power dates to the fourth century; others suggest that their importance was legal and religious rather than political. A good selection of contrasting views can be found in Raaflaub's volume on the subject.

8. The earliest Roman law code (discussed further below) includes the rather startling statement that any patron who was proved to have wronged a client was to be accursed, but does not impose any legal penalty. Forsythe, however, argues that this means not only that a misbehaving patron lacked divine protection but also that he had no legal protection and could be killed with impunity.

9. Priestly authority at Rome was divided between various colleges, each with different responsibilities. These principal colleges were the college of pontifices (which included *flamines*, the *rex sacrorum* and the Vestal Virgins), the college of augurs and the *duumuiri sacris faciundis*, augmented by a number of minor colleges (principally the Salii, *fetiales* and Arvales). Since much of the evidence for their composition and activities is of later date, they will be discussed in more detail in Chapters 11 and 14.

10. Examples given by Valerius Maximus (1.1.5) include a priest who accidentally invalidated a sacrifice because his cap of office fell off during the rites and invalidation of a ritual because it was interrupted by a squeaking mouse, although these are extreme cases.

11. This burst of activity early in the Republic may also be a reflection of Rome's successes in the last years of the monarchy. The Capitoline temple was dedicated in 509, as a symbolic act by the first consuls of the new Republic, but the building was commissioned by the Tarquins.

12. Maelius and Minucius are discussed in Livy 4.12–14. Grain shortages are mentioned by both Livy and Dionysios of Halicarnassus. According to Cato (*FRHist* 5 F80), grain shortages were a matter of official record, written up in the daily information posted up by the *pontifex maximus* in the Forum, although we do not know how early this practice began. Livy's recurring theme of opportunistic tribunes using food distributions to whip up popular support with a view to seizing power is suspiciously similar to the turbulent behaviour of tribunes in the second and first centuries, but even if we reject much of this circumstantial detail, recurrent food shortages – and the political and social tensions they caused – are entirely plausible.

13. The Romans must have been familiar with coinage, as the Greek areas of Campania had been minting their own coins since the early fifth century and the Greeks of southern Italy had done so from *c.* 530. A small number of Etruscan coins of fifth-century date are also known, probably minted at Populonia, but most Etruscan states – like Rome – did not mint their own coins until the late fourth or early third century. The Greek cities of Cumae and Naples, in contrast, minted their own coinage from *c.* 470 and *c.* 450 BC respectively.

14. From the sixth century more regularly shaped rectangular ingots were also in circulation as currency. The value of both these and *aes rude* (and also that of ancient coinage) depended on their weight and bronze content.

15. *Sacrosanctitas* was a powerful notion as it conferred divine protection on the tribunes during their year of office and permitted anyone to kill a person who harmed a tribune.

16. All three of these deities were associated with agriculture and fertility. Ceres was particularly associated with corn, and Liber and Libera with grapes and wine production.

17. The Aventine cult of Diana seems to have had connections with the famous Artemis cult at Ephesos. Later images (mostly on coins) depicting the Aventine cult statue show it as similar to that of Ephesos. The cult of Ceres, Liber and Libera was a Roman equivalent of the Greek cult of Demeter, Kore and Dionysos, which was particularly strong in Greek areas of southern Italy, and some of its priestesses at Rome were recruited from the Greek cities of Elea in Italy and Eryx in Sicily. Demeter was often worshipped as Demeter Thesmophoros – Demeter the Law-Bringer, which made her particularly appropriate as a patron deity for a group seeking greater legal recognition. The term *libertas* may, in itself, be derived from the cult of Liber and Libera.

18. The law codes of Zaleukos at Locri and of Charondas at Katane are two examples of early Greek law codes in Italy and Sicily, but the most famous examples are probably the law codes attributed to the Athenian law-givers Drakon (seventh century) and Solon (sixth century).

19. The surviving fragments of the law are published, with translation and commentary, in M. H. Crawford, *Roman Statutes*, 555–72.

20. Cornell (*The Beginnings of Rome*, 292) points out that the Decemvirate included both patricians and plebeians, so the prohibition must have served the interests of both groups, by protecting both patrician privilege and the separate identity of the leaders of the plebeian movement.
21. The spring, which was believed to have healing properties, was later enclosed in a stone basin, and statues of Castor and Pollux were added in 168 BC.

Chapter 10: Rome on the march: War in Latium and Beyond, 500–350

1. Ancient writers offer several alternative chronologies for this period, and some of these date the battle of Lake Regillus to 499 (Livy 2.21.3–4).
2. Cf. pp. 196–7 for the connection between this legend and the establishment of a temple to Castor and Pollux, and for the political significance of this cult.
3. There must be some doubt over whether he had consulted it in person or could have understood the archaic Latin in which it was no doubt written, but it is usually accepted as evidence for the treaty terms. The fact that it still existed and that the terms were so well known makes it unlikely that Dionysios had entirely invented or misrepresented it.
4. The history of this debate, and the arguments for and against the historical value of these stories, are usefully summarised by both Forsythe and Cornell.
5. The *Fasti Capitolini* are incomplete for this period, although the surviving portions record several triumphs awarded for victories over the Aequi and Volsci.
6. Ovid, in his seduction poem the *Ars Amatoria*, makes the irreverent suggestion that a thrifty suitor should arrange his dates on inauspicious days such as the anniversary of the Allia, since the shops would all be closed and he would not have to buy a gift for his girlfriend.
7. Livy does not specify where this Greek fleet came from, but Syracuse attempted to expand its power into southern Italy during the early fourth century and raided some areas of Etruria, notably in 384, when a Syracusan fleet sacked Pyrgi. Large numbers of Gallic mercenaries were employed by Syracuse, and it is possible that many of the Gallic incursions into central Italy were instigated by Syracuse in an attempt to undermine Caere as a commercial rival in the western Mediterranean, or were groups of Gauls making their way south to seek employment in Syracuse.

Chapter 11: The road to power: Italy and Rome, 390–342

1. Forsythe and Oakley discuss these similarities with other stories of demagogues and would-be tyrants in detail, including more recent parallels with the character of Catiline, whose attempt to overthrow the government was forestalled by Cicero in 63 BC.
2. As has been widely noted, the tradition that Manlius' disgrace was marked by a decision that no further Manlius should be called by his name (Marcus) is borne out, as no further Marcus Manlius is known from this date onwards.

3. The events of 376–367 are further confused by chronological difficulties posed by both Livy's account and the *Fasti*, as discussed in the appendix on 'Roman dates and chronology'.

4. A review of the arguments can be found in Cornell (*The Beginnings of Rome*, pp. 328–9) and, more recently, in J. W. Rich, '*Lex Licinia, Lex Sempronia*: B. G. Niebuhr and the Limitation of Landholding in the Roman Republic', in L. de Ligt and S. Northwood (eds), *People, Land and Politics: Demographic Developments and the Transformation of Roman Italy 300 BC–AD 14* (Leiden, 2008), 519–72.

5. Livy (7.38.5–41.8, 7.42.3–6) gives two separate accounts of the events of 343–342 BC. One describes civic unrest at Rome which was ended by negotiation with the consuls, and the other describes unrest in the army, then on campaign in Campania, which spread to Rome. As Forsythe points out, both versions show the influence of later Roman history, and neither can be accepted in detail.

6. Stones that seem to belong to an earlier defensive wall have been found along the line of parts of the 'Servian Wall', suggesting that there was an earlier fortification which pre-dated it. However, the narratives of the Gallic sack imply that the Romans had to retreat to the Capitoline in order to make their stand against the Gauls, suggesting that this was still the only strongly fortified part of the city.

7. The *comitia centuriata*, in contrast, was strictly speaking a military assembly since the classes into which it was organised were the basis of military recruitment, and meeting within the city boundaries would have contravened laws against military assemblies inside Rome. Instead, it assembled in the Campus Martius, which now underlies the area around the Pantheon and Piazza Navona. This region was originally the exercise ground on which the Roman army assembled and trained and was therefore a suitable venue for meetings of the *comitia centuriata*.

Chapter 12: 'Whether Samnite or Roman shall rule Italy': the Samnite wars and the conquest of Italy

1. The duplication of these incidents has caused some scholars to doubt Livy's account of them.

2. Cales, founded in 334 BC, was also a substantial and strategically important colony. The colonies established at Antium (338), Terracina (329) and Privernum (318) were smaller, but Antium and Terracina played a vital role in guarding the coast of Latium.

3. Dionysios of Halicarnassus (Dion. Hal. 15.5.2–6.5) takes a more balanced view, and some scholars have suggested that he had access to Campanian or Neapolitan accounts of the conflict with Rome. Like Livy, he takes the view that the Samnites were supporting the Neapolitans but is less inclined to blame them for stirring up the initial conflict.

4. The whereabouts of this is uncertain. Livy locates it between Caudium and Calatia, but this area does not match his description. Some modern scholars identify it as a valley between Arpaia and Arienzo, but there is no certainty about this.

5. One of the peculiarities of Roman involvement in Etruria at this period was that peace was made by agreement to a fixed-term truce rather than the open-ended treaties that

were the basis of Roman relations with most other areas of Italy. The significance of this is examined in Chapter 13.

6. He is said to have been sent to Caere to be educated in the household of a guest-friend of the Fabii and to have been able both to speak and to read Etruscan (Livy 9.36.3). Livy adds that in the fourth century it was not uncommon for young Roman nobles to be sent to Etruria for their education.

7. A figure of 650,000 men is quoted for the total of both armies, which is implausibly large, as is the assertion of the Greek historian Duris of Samos that 100,000 men were killed. Livy puts the casualty figures at 33,700 (8,700 of which were Roman dead).

8. The Tarentines' rejection of the Roman embassy is depicted in ancient accounts as a drunken riot during which the envoys were grotesquely insulted by the Greek mob, and their invitation to Pyrrhus to assist them is ascribed to weakness and cowardice. This is clearly an attempt to denigrate the Tarentines, whose military strength at this date was considerable, and to put an unflattering interpretation on the Tarentine policy of hiring in mercenary generals and their armies to assist them.

9. Symbols associated with Pyrrhus, including the spearhead emblem of the Epirote royal house and the eagle and thunderbolt of Zeus, appear as images on Tarentine coins of this date. Pyrrhus also exploited other cultural symbolism, claiming that since the Epirote royal house was descended from Achilles, he was the natural heir of the Homeric Greeks, destined to conquer the Roman descendants of the Trojans.

10. Appius Claudius' opposition to Pyrrhus is mentioned in an inscription in his honour found at Arretium in Etruria which boasts that 'he prevented peace being made with King Pyrrhus'. However, the inscription is of Augustan date and is suspiciously similar to the wording of an inscription associated with a statue of Appius in the Forum of Augustus at Rome, so there must be considerable doubt about whether it was a copy of a third-century original or a later Augustan text.

11. Tarentine coins of this period are reduced in weight, a feature that suggests financial stress. Inscriptions recording the accounts of the sanctuary of Zeus Olympios at Locri show substantial payments from the temple treasury, probably to Pyrrhus. The sums involved add up to approximately 295 tonnes of silver, with the largest single payment of 2,685 talents (*c.* 69.5 tonnes).

12. Estimates vary, but some scholars, notably Cornell, have suggested that as many as 70,000 Roman colonists may have been resettled in the areas colonised between 290 and 264 BC, although others regard this figure as too high. Whatever the absolute figures, however, it is clear that population movements imposed by Rome were large-scale and disruptive.

Chapter 13: Co-operation or conquest? Alliances, citizenship and colonisation

1. These longer truces may have been intended to free up Roman armies to deal with incursions into Roman territory by the Samnites. A truce of a hundred years may imply that Rome envisaged a more permanent peace, although without committing to a more formal peace deal, although in practice it did not last that long.

2. Livy mentions that Fundi, Formiae and Cumae gained full citizenship in 188 BC.

3. The registration of those enfranchised in 338 took place at the census of 332 BC. The registration process may have taken place locally, via census rolls compiled by local officials and then sent to Rome.

4. There are relatively few lists of this type in Livy's coverage of the fourth century, but he includes them increasingly frequently for the third and second centuries, and the consistent format suggests that they must ultimately have been obtained from some form of official record. It seems probable that Livy derived them from an earlier historian (possibly Valerius Antias), who transcribed them from official records.

5. The spread of Latin in Italy was undoubtedly encouraged by the Roman reorganisation. States that had full Roman citizenship and those with Latin status were expected to use Latin for public business, although oddly this does not seem to have applied to those with *civitas sine suffragio*. Official inscriptions in Oscan from Cumae and Capua demonstrate that this was still the language of government in the third century, and Cumae's upgrade to full citizenship in 188 BC was, according to Livy, accompanied by a request for permission to adopt Latin as the official language of the city.

6. References to Livy, *Per.,* refer to *Periochae*, short summaries of each book of his work. These are the only surviving versions of books 11–19 and books 46 onwards.

7. Inscriptions preserve the texts of treaties between Rome and Callatis, Astypalaia and Mytilene, among others, and the terms of these are consistent with what we know of treaties between Rome and various Italian states, but we have no direct epigraphic evidence of these.

8. The most comprehensive discussion of this issue for Roman Republican history, including the Polybios figures quoted here, is that of Peter Brunt.

9. Greek views of Roman concepts of citizenship, and especially the granting of citizenship to freed slaves, were ambivalent (cf. Dion. Hal. 4.24). Philip's letter, however, seems to be making the point that the increase in the number of citizens (largely through slave manumission) provided the Romans with the manpower necessary to send out colonies, thereby increasing Roman power. Whether manumitted slaves could become magistrates is much less clear. They were debarred from doing so in the later Republic, but it is unclear whether this was the case in the third century.

10. A collection of the most recent contributions to this debate can be found in T. D. Stek and J. Pelgrom (eds), *Roman Republican Colonization: New Perspectives from Archaeology and Ancient History* (Rome, 2014).

11. The Lucanian takeover in the late fifth century, in contrast, seems to have been much less traumatic, despite the tendency of Greek writers to depict it as a violent event. Greek, as well as Oscan, continued to be spoken, Greek cults continued to be worshipped, and wealthy burials in both Greek and Lucanian styles suggest that the ruling elite of the city became ethnically and culturally mixed.

12. The concept of Romanisation was developed by Francis Haverfield in the early twentieth century as a theoretical model to explain the impact of Roman culture in the provinces, rather than Italy and it carries heavy overtones of bringing civilisation to barbarian cultures.

13. Both Livy (28.12.2–4) and Polybios (2.19.1–4) praise Hannibal's achievement in holding together such a disparate army, but they implicitly draw an unfavourable contrast with the Roman and Italian forces.

Chapter 14: *The impact of conquest: Rome, 340–264*

1. The sources for this law are particularly problematic, as only summaries of Livy and fragments of Dio Cassius survive.
2. There are close parallels with parts of the Valerio-Horatian laws of 449 and the Lex Publilia of 339 BC.
3. Macrobius' principal surviving work, *Saturnalia*, written in the fifth century AD, is a collection of information about Roman festivals and religion.
4. Also discussed on pp. 223–4.
5. The name changed to reflect this, from *duoviri* (board of two) to *decemviri* (board of ten) and, later still, to *quindecemviri* (board of fifteen).
6. Like the college in charge of sacred objects, the college of pontifices was expanded from nine to fifteen members in the first century BC, to reflect the greater demands on it.
7. The nearest equivalent was the Vestal Virgins, who vowed to remain chaste and devoted to the service of the goddess Vesta for a period of thirty years, living in a special house next to the temple of Vesta. But after this was over, they were free to leave and rejoin their families or to marry.
8. The bronze-clad prows of some of the Antiate ships also had a symbolic function. They were taken to Rome as trophies and used to decorate the speaker's platform in the Forum, which became known as the rostra, after the Latin word for a prow.
9. Many of these luxury goods are found in female burials and may have been given as gifts on coming-of-age or marriage.
10. Slave numbers increased hugely after the end of the Hannibalic war, but there is persuasive evidence that they were already growing in the fourth and third centuries.
11. Typically, a freed slave would take the owner's *praenomen* and *nomen* and retain his or her own name as a *cognomen*. For example, the third-century poet Livius Andronicus, a Tarentine captive enslaved (possibly during the capture of the city in 272) and later freed, took his former owner's name, Livius, in addition to his Greek birth-name Andronicus. Epitaphs of freemen and freewomen can be identified by the use of the abbreviation l (*liberti* = 'freedman/-woman of') instead of the usual *f* (*fili* = 'son/daughter of').
12. Rome's aqueducts became a symbol of Rome's power and civic pride, and were renowned throughout the ancient world. Julius Frontinus, an imperial administrator in charge of the water supply in AD 97 who wrote a treatise on aqueducts, claimed that they were a greater achievement even than the pyramids (Front., *Aq.*, 16, 87–8).
13. The interpretation of this difficult data is discussed by Ziolkowski in *The Temples of Mid-Republican Rome*. Some estimates include eighteen further temples probably dating to the period between 293 and 218 BC, in addition to those listed in Table 11.
14. The Tomb of the Fabii and its frescoes may date to the era of the Samnite wars, but some scholars now believe that they are later, and cannot be earlier than the second century. However, there is no conclusive evidence as to the date of these images.
15. Cicero implies (Cic., *Phil.* 9.13) that public tombs could be set up on the Esquiline.

A Note on Sources

1. Large-scale field survey projects, such as the South Etruria survey and more recently the Tiber Valley project, both conducted by the British School at Rome, have transformed our understanding of substantial areas of central Italy, along with major Dutch surveys of the Pontine area and parts of south-east Italy, and long-term US and Italian survey projects in Magna Graecia.

2. Cornell, in an article titled 'Etruscan historiography' (*Annali di Scuola Normale di Pisa* 6, 1976), has argued that the Etruscans may well have written works of history, and had family records and chronicles.

3. Most inscriptions are brief – often written on tombstones, votive objects or personal possessions and in languages that we do not fully understand – but they can provide us with a wealth of information about languages spoken, deities worshipped and family structures and relationships. A few longer inscriptions record documents such as laws and treaties, demonstrating that the practice of keeping written records was not confined to Rome. Surviving non-Roman inscriptions from much of Italy are collected in Crawford, *Imagines Italicae*.

4. The surviving portions of the *annales maximi* and a discussion of what they may have contained can be found in John Rich's entry in Cornell's edition of the fragmentary Roman historians. Both Rich and Oakley's commentary on Livy include lengthy discussion of the *annales maximi* in their introductions.

5. The surviving portions of the *Fasti Triumphales* and *Fasti Capitolini* are on display in the Capitoline Museum in Rome. Oakley (*A Commentary on Livy, Books VI–X*, vol. 1) and Smith (in Beck et al. (eds), *Consuls and the Res Publica*) present convincing cases for accepting the evidence of the *fasti* as historical.

6. Oakley (*A Commentary on Livy, Books VI–X*, vol. 1) includes a lengthy discussion of the points at which Livy may have made use of documentary evidence. Polybios' extensive criticism of Timaeus and his working methods takes up much of the surviving fragments of Book 11 of his work.

7. Discussed in S. Oakley, *A Commentary on Livy Books VI–X*, vol. 1.

FURTHER READING

The bibliography on early Rome and on pre-Roman and Roman Italy is enormous and ever-expanding. The selection given below is by no means comprehensive, but is intended to be a starting-point for anyone interested in exploring the subject further.

Chapter 1: Introducing early Rome

Ancient Sources: Ancient sources for the geography and ethnic groups of Italy are very diverse, and include brief comments by many Greek and Roman writers, but few extended descriptions. Strabo, *Geography*, books 5 and 6, give an outline of Italian geography and ethnography, although this is written from a later, Augustan, perspective. Pliny, *Natural History*, book 3, also gives a survey of peoples and places. T. J. Cornell, *The Fragments of the Roman Historians* (Oxford, 2013), includes the surviving fragments of Cato, *Origines*, the earliest ethnography of Italy written by a Roman.

Modern Literature: A good introduction to the ethnic and cultural geography of ancient Italy can be found in G. J. Bradley, E. Isayev and C. Riva (eds), *Ancient Italy: Regions without Boundaries* (Exeter, 2009), which contains chapters on most of the key cultures and ethnic groups of ancient Italy, and a new volume on the subject, G. J. Bradley and G. Farney (eds), *A Handbook on the Ancient Italic Group*s, is in preparation. Brief outlines can be found in K. Lomas, *Roman Italy, 338–AD 200: A Sourcebook* (London, 1996), 1–16, and K. Lomas, 'Italy beyond Rome', in A. Erskine (ed.), *A Companion to Ancient History* (Chichester, 2009). For fuller discussions see E. T. Salmon, *The Making of Roman Italy* (London, 1982), J.-M. David, *The Roman Conquest of Italy* (Oxford, 1996) and M. Pallottino, *A History of Earliest Italy* (London, 1991). There are excellent discussions of the state of scholarship on Etruscan origins by G. Bagnasco Gianni (modern perspectives), D. Briquel (ancient sources) and G. Kron (DNA evidence) in J. M. Turfa (ed.), *The Etruscan World* (London, 2013).

Chapter 2: Setting the scene: Iron-Age Italy

Ancient Sources: Most of the sources for this period of Italian history are archaeological. However, accounts of the earliest Greek colonies can be found in: Hdt. 1.163–65, 8.62;

Thuc. 6.2–5; Strabo, *Geog.*, books 5 and 6; Livy 8.22.5–7; Diod. 8.21–3. On the origins of the Etruscans: Hdt. 1.93–6; Dion. Hal. 1.30; Strabo, *Geog.* 5.2.2–4; the earliest inscriptions from the west are published in R. Arena (ed.), *Iscrizioni greche arcaiche di Sicilia e Magna Grecia*, 5 vols (Pisa, 1988–96), and G. Bagnasco Gianni, *Oggetti iscritti di epoca orientalizzante in Etruria* (Florence, 1996).

Modern Literature: English-language introductions to the culture of the Etruscans and their Villanovan antecedents include G. Barker and T. Rasmussen, *The Etruscans* (Oxford, 1998), and S. Haynes, *Etruscan Civilization: A Cultural History* (London, 2000). A good summary of the Villanovan culture can be found in the contributions by G. Bartoloni to M. Torelli (ed.), *The Etruscans* (London, 2000), and J. Turfa (ed.), *The Etruscan World* (London, 2014). The volumes of thematic essays edited by Torelli and Turfa are a mine of information about all aspects of Etruscan life and culture, as is S. Bell and A. Carcopino (eds), *A Companion to the Etruscans* (Chichester, 2016). The chapters by Ridgway, Salmon and Asheri in the *Cambridge Ancient History*, vol. 4: *Persia, Greece and the Western Mediterranean, c. 525 to 479* (Cambridge, 1988), also provide good overviews of the topics covered in this chapter. Introductions to the Latial Iron Age can be found in R. R. Holloway, *The Archaeology of Early Rome and Latium* (London and New York, 1994), and C. J. Smith, 'Latium and the Latins', in G. J. Bradley, E. Isayev and C. Riva (eds), *Ancient Italy: Regions without Boundaries* (Exeter, 2009), 161–78. On Greek colonisation, D. R. Ridgway, *The First Western Greeks* (Cambridge, 1992), examines the settlement at Pithecusae, while the chapter on colonisation in R. Osborne, *Greece in the Making, 1200–479* (London, 1998), introduces the recent debate on the nature of colonisation. More detailed discussion on the nature of colonisation can be found in G. Bradley and J.-P. Wilson (eds), *Greek and Roman Colonization: Origins, Ideologies, Interactions* (Swansea, 2006), and L. Donnellan, V. Nizzo and G. J. Burgers (eds), *Conceptualising Early Colonisation* (Brussels, 2016). J. Boardman, *The Greeks Overseas: Their Early Colonies and Trade*, 4th edn (London, 1990), is still a good overview of the Greek relations with the archaic Mediterranean. Finally, a ground-breaking study of one of the key Iron-Age sites can be found in A. M. Bietti Sestieri, *The Iron Age Community of Osteria dell'Osa* (Cambridge, 1992).

Chapter 3: Trojans, Latins, Sabines and rogues: Romulus, Aeneas and the 'foundation' of Rome

Ancient Sources: Ennius, *Annals* 77–96; Cic., *Rep.* 2.2–10, *Offic.* 3.40–41; Livy 1.1–17; Dion. Hal., 2.1–56; Plut. *Rom.*; Ovid, *Fast.* 4.807–858; Propertius 4.4.73–4; Virg., *Aen.*, esp. book 8; Augustine, *City of God*, 3.6 and 15.5.

Modern Literature: Probably the best discussions of the literary traditions and archaeological evidence for early Rome available in English are T. J. Cornell, *The Beginnings of Rome* (London, 1995), and G. Forsythe, *A Critical History of Early Rome* (Berkeley, 2005). P. Wiseman, *The Myths of Rome* (Exeter, 2004) and *Unwritten Rome* (Exeter, 2008), offer an alternative perspective on the traditions on the foundation of Rome. Useful overviews of the archaeology and summaries of recent archaeological discoveries can be found in C. J. Smith, 'Early and archaic Rome', in J. Coulston and H. Dodge (eds), *Ancient Rome:*

The Archaeology of the Eternal City (Oxford, 2000), and 'The beginnings of urbanisation in Rome', in B. Cunliffe and R. Osborne (eds), *Mediterranean Urbanization, 800–600* (London, 2005), 91–112, and by I. Edlund Berry, 'Early Rome and the making of "Roman" identity through architecture and town planning', in J. D. Evans (ed.), *A Companion to the Archaeology of the Roman Republic* (Malden, MA, 2013). C. J. Smith, *Early Rome and Latium* (Oxford 1996), F. Fulminante, *The Urbanisation of Rome and Latium Vetus: From the Bronze Age to the Archaic Era* (Cambridge 2014) and R. R. Holloway, *The Archaeology of Early Rome and Latium* (London and New York, 1994), provide more detailed discussion of Rome and Latium. Fulminante provides an excellent summary of the current state of archaeological research on early Rome. Carandini's fullest exposition of his ideas, *La Nascita di Roma* (Florence, 1997), is available only in Italian, but a more recent summary, A. Carandini, *Rome: Day One* (Princeton, NJ, 2011), has been translated. Critiques of Carandini's views can be found in many of the items listed above, but the fullest and most comprehensive discussion of the difficulties with his approach is by Carmine Ampolo in 'Il problema delle origini di Roma rivisitato: concordismo, ipertradizionalismo acritico, contesti', in *Annali della Scuola Normale Superiore di Pisa, Classe di Lettere e Filosofia* 5.1 (2013). A shorter but no less incisive critique is offered by E. Fentress and A. Guidi. The mythology of early Rome has been discussed at length by Peter Wiseman. See especially: *Remus: A Roman Myth* (Cambridge, 1995) and *The Myths of Rome* (Exeter, 2004). E. Dench, *Romulus' Asylum: Roman Identities from the Age of Alexander to the Age of Hadrian* (Oxford, 2005), is a detailed study of the development of Roman cultural identities and the role of the foundation myths in this process. Introductions to the sources for early Rome can be found in: R. M. Ogilvie and A. Drummond, 'The sources for early Roman history', in *Cambridge Ancient History*, 2nd edn (Cambridge, 1988), VII: 1–29; T. J. Cornell, *The Beginnings of Rome: Italy and Rome from the Bronze Age to the Punic Wars* (London, 1995); and G. Forsythe, *A Critical History of Early Rome* (Berkeley, CA, 2005). The volume of essays edited by James Richardson and Federico Santangelo, *The Roman Historical Tradition: Regal and Republican Rome* (Oxford, 2014) brings together essays by many leading scholars and is a good way into the debate on the sources for early Rome. The *Lupa Capitolina Electronica* web site (http://lupacap.fltr.ucl.ac.be) is a mine of information about sources for the foundation of Rome.

Chapter 4: *The rise of the international aristocracy: Italy and the orientalising revolution*

Ancient Sources: Dion. Hal. 2.44; Pol. 6.2.10; Livy 1.33–4; Hesiod, *Works and Days* 38–9, 220–21.

Modern Literature: A brief overview of the orientalising phases of Rome and central Italy can be found in T. J. Cornell, *The Beginnings of Rome*, Chapter 2, and a wider area of Italy is reviewed in M. Pallotino, *A History of Earliest Italy* (London, 1991). C. Riva, *The Urbanization of Etruria* (Cambridge, 2010), presents a densely argued discussion of this period in Etruria and of the interpretative problems posed by the evidence. Other useful works on the Etruscans include Haynes, *Etruscan Civilization,* and Barker and Rasmussen, *The*

Etruscans, as well as Torelli, *The Etruscans*, and Turfa, *The Etruscan World*. An introduction to Campania can be found in M. Cuozzo, 'Ancient Campania', in G. J. Bradley, E. Isayev and C. Riva (eds), *Ancient Italy: Regions without Boundaries* (Exeter, 2009), 224–67, while C. J. Smith's chapter in the same book reviews the evidence for Latium. Regular updates on the important excavations at Murlo, and lists of publications, can be found at http://poggiocivitate.classics.umass.edu/index.asp.

Chapter 5: Orientalising Rome and the early kings

Ancient Sources: Livy 1.16–34; Dion. Hal. 2.57–3.43; Plut. *Numa*; Varro, *LL* 5.55, 5.142–59, 7.9–10; Cic., *Div.* 1.3.

Modern Literature: Discussions of Rome in the orientalising period can be found in: Cornell, *The Beginnings of Rome,* Chapter 4; Forsythe, *A Critical History of Early Rome*, Chapter 4; C. J. Smith, *Early Rome and Latium* (Oxford, 1996), and his contribution to J. Coulston and H. Dodge (eds), *Ancient Rome: The Archaeology of the Eternal City* (Oxford, 2000), 16–41; and in F. Fulminante, *The Urbanisation of Rome and Latium Vetus: From the Bronze Age to the Archaic Era*. The publications by Carafa on the Comitium, Volcanal and house of Vesta present recent archaeological research but are also heavily influenced by the controversial interpretations of Carandini. A critique of approaches to the urbanisation of Rome is offered by N. Terrenato in his contribution to Barchiesi and Scheidel, *The Oxford Handbook of Roman Studies*. The current state of scholarship on S. Omobono can be found in D. Diffendale, P. Brocato, N. Terrenato and A. Brock, 'Sant'Omobono: an interim *status quaestionis*', *Journal of Roman Archaeology* 29 (2016), 7–14. The web site of the S. Omobono project (http://sites.lsa.umich.edu/omobono/) has information on recent excavations and publications.

Chapter 6: The urban revolution: city and state in sixth-century Italy

Ancient Sources: Athen., *Deip.* 12.517 d–f; Dion. Hal. 3.61, 4.49, 7.5–8; Strabo, *Geog.* 5.4.3, 6.1.1–5, 6.1.12–14; Hdt. 7.170; Pol. 12.5–7; Diod. 12.9–12.

Modern Literature: The development of sixth-century society, and in particular family/clan organisation, is the subject of a detailed study by C. J. Smith, *The Roman Clan* (Oxford, 2006). An alternative view is offered by N. Terrenato in his contribution to Terrenato and D. Haggis (eds), *State Formation in Italy and Greece* (Oxford, 2011). On the Etruscans, see Barker and Rasmussen, *The Etruscans* (Oxford, 1998), and Haynes, *Etruscan Civilization: A Cultural History* (London, 2000). An accessible region-by-region discussion of the spread of Etruscan power is given by G. Camporeale (ed.), *The Etruscans outside Etruria* (Los Angeles, CA, 2004). M. Torelli (ed.), *The Etruscans* (London, 2000), J. Turfa, *The Etruscan World* (London, 2013), and S. Bell and A. Carpino, *A Companion to the Etruscans* (Chichester, 2016), contain articles on many aspects of Etruscan culture and society. The classic account of the Greek colonies in this period, T. J. Dunbabin, *The Western Greeks* (Oxford, 1948), is now rather old. Shorter but more recent discussions can be found in R. Osborne, *The Making of*

Greece, and K. Lomas, *Rome and the Western Greeks*. G. Pugliese Carratelli (ed.), *The Western Greeks* (London, 1996), and L. Cerchiai, L. Jannelli, and F. Longo (eds) *The Greek Cities of Italy and Sicily* (Los Angeles, 2002), are good sources of archaeological information.

Chapter 7: Tyrants and wicked women: Rome, the Tarquin dynasty and the fall of the monarchy

Ancient Sources: Livy 1.35–60; Dion. Hal. 3.56–4.86; Pol. 3.22.11–12.

Modern Literature: The bibliography on sixth-century Rome is vast, and much of the archaeological material is published only in Italian. Of the material available in English, T. J. Cornell, *The Beginnings of Rome: Italy and Rome from the Bronze Age to the Punic Wars (c. 1000–264 BC)* (London, 1995), C. J. Smith, *Early Rome and Latium* (Oxford, 1996), and G. Forsythe, *A Critical History of Early Rome* (2005), are excellent discussions of the historical and archaeological evidence, and of the problems of interpreting it, while J. H. Richardson and F. Santangelo (eds), *The Roman Historical Tradition: Regal and Republican Rome* (Oxford, 2014), offers a collection of classic essays on the subject. For a more recent discussion, see G. Bradley, *Early Italy and Rome* (Edinburgh, forthcoming). A highly readable critique of the interpretations and reconstructions of early Rome is offered in T. P. Wiseman, *The Myths of Rome* (Exeter, 2004) and *Unwritten Rome* (Exeter, 2008). Introductions to the archaeological evidence can be found in C. J. Smith, 'Early and Archaic Rome', in J. Coulston and H. Dodge (eds), *Ancient Rome: The Archaeology of the Eternal City* (Oxford, 2000), 16–41, while Fulminante, *The Urbanisation of Rome*, and the various studies by Gabriele Cifani (listed in the bibliography) offer a more in-depth analysis of the material evidence for the period.

Chapter 8: The 'fifth-century crisis' and the changing face of Italy

Ancient Sources: Hdt. 6.23; Thuc. 6.44, 6.103; Livy 4.24–37, 5.33–6, 9.13.7; Pol. 2.14–20, 2.39; Diod. 11.51–3, 12.8–12, 12.76; Athen., *Deip.* 12.522d, 14.632a; Paus. 10.10, 13.10.

Modern Literature: A good overview of the changes of the fifth century is presented in M. Pallottino, *A History of Earliest Italy* (London, 1991). E. T. Salmon, *Samnium and the Samnites* (Cambridge, 1967), is a comprehensive study of the Samnites but is archaeologically rather dated. The most recent full-length study in English is E. Dench, *From New Men to Barbarians: Greek, Roman, and Modern Perceptions of Peoples from the Central Apennines* (Oxford, 1995). A shorter introduction to the Samnites can be found in E. Bispham, 'The Samnites', in G. J. Bradley, E. Isayev and C. Riva (eds), *Ancient Italy: Regions without Boundaries* (Exeter, 2009). The same volume also contains useful chapters on Campania (by M. Cuozzo), Lucania (E. Isayev) and Celtic Italy (R. Häussler). The Lucanians are covered in more detail in E. Isayev, *Inside Ancient Lucania: Dialogues in History and Archaeology* (London, 2007). For a comprehensive new edition of Oscan, Umbrian and early Latin inscriptions, with commentary and discussion, see M. H. Crawford (ed.), *Imagines Italicae: A Corpus of Italic Inscriptions* (London, 2011).

Chapter 9: A difficult transition: the early Roman Republic

Ancient Sources: Livy books 2–5; Dion. Hal. books 5–8; Cic., *Rep.* 2.61; Tac., *Hist.* 3.72; Pliny, *NH* 34.139; Aul. Gell., *NA* 15.27; Crawford, *Roman Statutes*, no. 40 (the Twelve Tables).

Modern Literature: Cornell, *The Beginnings of Rome,* Chapter 10, and Forsythe, *A Critical History of Early Rome*, Chapters 6–7, both provide an excellent overview of the early Republic and the Struggle of the Orders. The *Cambridge Ancient History*, vol 7.2, covers much of the same ground in some depth. A challenging and detailed critique of Roman social development in the early Republic, and especially the problems surrounding patricians and plebeians, can be found in C. J. Smith, *The Roman Clan*, Chapter 8. On the Struggle of the Orders, K. Raaflaub, *Social Struggles in Archaic Rome: New Perspectives on the Conflict of the Orders*, contains an excellent collection of essays on various aspects of the struggle. The chapters by Mitchell, Eder and Raaflaub are especially useful. The volume of essays edited by Beck, Dupla, Jehne and Pina Polo offer new insights into the development of the early Republic and its institutions.

Chapter 10: Rome on the march: War in Latium and Beyond, 500–350

Ancient sources: Livy, books 2–5; Dion. Hal. 6.95 and books 15–20; Diod. 11.51–3.

Modern Literature: An accessible account of the early expansion of Rome can be found in T. J. Cornell, 'Rome and Latium', in *Cambridge Ancient History* (Cambridge, 1989), vol. 7.2, 309–50, and in *The Beginnings of Rome*. The archaeological evidence for early colonisation and its impact is assessed in P. Attema (ed.), *Centralization, Early Urbanization and Colonization in First Millennium Italy and Greece* (Leuven, 2004), and Termeer, 'Early colonies in Latium (ca 534–338 BC): a reconsideration of current images and the archaeological evidence', *BABESCH* 85 (2010), 43–5.

Chapter 11: The road to power: Italy and Rome, 390–342

Ancient Sources: Livy, books 5–7.

Modern Literature: The later stages of the Struggle of the Orders is discussed by Cornell, *The Beginnings of Rome,* Chapter 13, Forsythe, *A Critical History of Early Rome*, Chapters 8–9, and R. Develin, 'The integration of plebeians into the political order after 366', in K. Raaflaub (ed.), *Social Struggles in Archaic Rome* (Berkeley, CA, 1986), 327–52. On the development of the city of Rome, see T. J. Cornell in J. C. Coulson and H. Dodge (eds), *Ancient Rome: The Archaeology of the Eternal City* (Oxford, 2000), and I. Edlund Berry, 'Early Rome and the making of "Roman" identity through architecture and town planning', in J. D. Evans (ed.), *A Companion to the Archaeology of the Roman Republic* (Malden, MA, 2013), 406–25. Information on individual buildings and areas of Rome can be found in M. Steinby (ed.,) *Lexicon Topographicum Urbis Romae* (Rome, 1993–2000).

Chapter 12: 'Whether Samnite or Roman shall rule Italy': the Samnite wars and the conquest of Italy

Ancient Sources: Livy, books 9–10; Diod. 10.104; Dion. Hal. books 15–20; Plut. *Pyrrhus*; App., *Samn.*7–12; Dio 9.39–41; Pol. 3.24.

Modern Literature: Excellent accounts of the Samnite wars and Pyrrhic war can be found in the *Cambridge Ancient History* (vol. 7.2) and T. J. Cornell, *The Beginnings of Rome*, Chapter 14. E. T. Salmon, *Samnium and the Samnites*, also contains an extensive discussion of the Samnite wars, although this is now somewhat dated, particularly in its coverage of the archaeological evidence. On Rome's conquest of Etruria and Umbria, see W. V. Harris, *Rome in Etruria and Umbria*, and, more recently, G. J. Bradley, *Ancient Umbria*; and on the Pyrrhic war and relations with southern Italy, see K. Lomas, *Rome and the Western Greeks, 350–AD 200: Conquest and Acculturation in Southern Italy*. S. Oakley, 'The Roman conquest of Italy', in J. Rich and G. Shipley (eds), *War and Society in the Roman World* (London, 1993), gives a good overview of the conquest and its impact on Rome and the Italians. M. P. Fronda, *Between Rome and Carthage* (Cambridge, 2010), Chapter 1, argues that the conquest of Italy was less firmly established in the third century than most modern accounts. H. Jones (ed.), *Samnium: Settlement and Cultural Change*, contains a series of articles about aspects of Samnium. For anyone with an interest in the detail of Livy's account of the wars, Oakley's massive commentary on Livy (S. Oakley, *A Commentary on Livy Books VI–X*, Oxford, 1998–2005) is a mine of information.

Chapter 13: Co-operation or conquest? Alliances, citizenship and colonisation

Ancient Sources: Livy 8.11–15, 9.41–5; Vell. Pat. 1.14–15; Dion. Hal 6.95; Pol. 2.23, 6.12–26; Cic., *Balb.*; Cic. *Leg. Agr.* 6.23.

Modern Literature: The standard work on the administrative organisation of Italy is still A. N. Sherwin-White, *The Roman Citizenship*, 2nd edn (Oxford, 1980). A more recent work, although with an emphasis on the second century onwards, is E. Bispham, *From Asculum to Actium: The Municipalisation of Italy from the Social War to Augustus* (Oxford, 2007). More general overviews of the subject in the context of the conquest of Italy can be found in E. T. Salmon, *The Making of Roman Italy* (London, 1982), T. J. Cornell, *The Beginnings of Rome* (London, 1995), and J.-M. David, *The Roman Conquest of Italy* (Oxford, 1996). Finally, for a collection of translated sources (with discussion), see K. Lomas, *Roman Italy, 338–AD 200: A Sourcebook* (London, 1996). A good (although somewhat dated) starting-point on Roman colonisation is E. T. Salmon, *Roman Colonisation under the Republic* (London, 1969), and the recent debates on the nature of colonisation are discussed in G. J. Bradley, 'Colonisation and identity in Roman Italy', and E. Bispham, '*Coloniam deducere*: How Roman was Roman colonisation in the Middle Republic', both in G. J. Bradley and J. P. Wilson (eds), *Greek and Roman Colonisation: Origins, Ideologies and Interactions* (Swansea, 1996). The most recent discussions of colonisation can be found in J. Pelgrom and T. Stek (eds), *Roman Republican Colonization: New Perspectives from Archaeology and Ancient History* (Rome, 2014). The excavations at Paestum are published in a major series of excavation reports issued by the École Française de Rome, but a more manageable English-language account of the city's history can be found in J. G. Pedley, *Paestum: Greeks and Romans in Southern Italy* (London, 1990). A good introduction to Cosa can be found in F. E. Brown, *Cosa: The Making of a Roman Town* (Ann Arbor, MI, 1980), and a more comprehensive and up-to-date description in F. E. Brown, E. H. Richardson and L. Richardson, *Cosa III, The Buildings of the Forum: Colony, Municipium, and Village* (University Park, PA, 1993). More recent approaches can be found in E. Fentress and J. P. Bodel, *Cosa V: An Intermittent Town, Excavations 1991–1997* (Ann Arbor, MI, 2003).

Chapter 14: The impact of conquest: Rome, 340–264

Ancient Sources: Livy book 10 and summaries of books 11–15; Dion. Hal. books 15–20.

Modern Literature: The transitions of the late fourth and third centuries are discussed by Cornell (Chapter 15), Forsythe (Chapters 9–10) and Staveley ('Italy and Rome in the early third century', in *Cambridge Ancient History*, vol. 7.2). Summaries of military developments can be found in the contributions by J. Rich and L. Rawlings to P. Erdkamp, *A Companion to the Roman Army* (Oxford, 2007). On the Hellenisation of Rome, see the exhibition catalogue *Roma medio-Repubblicana: Aspetti culturali di Roma e del Lazio nei secoli IV e III a.C.* (Rome, 1973), and R. W. Wallace, 'Hellenization and Roman society in the late fourth century: a methodological critique', in W. Eder (ed.), *Staat und Staatlichkeit in der frühen römischen Republik* (Stuttgart, 1990). For discussion of the changing nature of the city of Rome, see T. J. Cornell's contribution to J. C. Coulson and H. Dodge (eds), *Ancient Rome: The Archaeology of the Eternal City* (Oxford, 2000), and I. Edlund Berry, 'Early Rome and the making of "Roman" identity through architecture and town planning', in J. D. Evans (ed.), *A Companion to the Archaeology of the Roman Republic* (Malden, MA, 2013), 406–25. For individual buildings, see M. Steinby (ed.), *Lexicon Topographicum Urbis Romae* (Rome, 1993–2000).

Chapter 15: Epilogue: Rome, Italy and the beginnings of empire in 264

Modern Literature: A good discussion of the nature of Roman imperialism and the possible explanations for it can be found in W. V. Harris, *War and Imperialism in Republican Rome, 327–70 B.C.* (Oxford, 1979), and in A. Erskine, *Roman Imperialism* (Edinburgh, 2010). Harris is challenged by J. Rich in Rich and Shipley (eds), *War and Society in the Roman World*, Chapter 2.

GUIDE TO SITES, MUSEUMS AND ONLINE RESOURCES

❦

The remains of early Italy, and especially of early Rome, are much less well preserved than those of the late Republic or the Roman empire. Nevertheless, there are many interesting sites and museum collections that include early material. This guide is not intended to be comprehensive, but provides an introduction to the important sites and collections. Many smaller museums and more remote sites and monuments have limited opening hours, especially during the winter, so checking online for latest information is advisable.

Web sites for many Italian museums and archaeological sites are run not by individual museums but by the state archaeological service for each region. Web addresses change frequently, but there are a number of sites that provide information about museums and links to their web sites, including: www.beniculturali.it (see under *Luoghi della Cultura*); http://www.musei.it/ and http://www.museionline.it.

Other useful web sites include Fasti Online (http://fastionline.org/), a database of the latest excavations in Italy, the Gnomon Bibliographic Database (http://www.gnomon-online.de/) and VRoma (http://www.vroma.org/), an online resource dedicated to the city of Rome. The Perseus Digital Library (http://www.perseus.tufts.edu/hopper/), Lacus Curtius (http://penelope.uchicago.edu/Thayer/E/Roman/home.html) and Livius (http://www.livius.org/) are excellent resources for images, articles and translated texts on ancient Rome.

Lombardy/Piedmont/Liguria

There are relatively few visible remains of the early history of this region still in situ, although some can be seen at the Area Archeologica Monsorino di Golasecca. There are a number of museums with extensive collections of material from the Golasecca, Celtic and early Roman periods. The Museo Civico in Como holds an extensive collection of pre-Roman artefacts, as do the Museo del Paesaggio at Verbania, the Museo di Archeologia Ligure in Genoa and two museums in Milan (the Museo Archeologico contains finds from the Roman period, while the prehistoric collection is housed in the Castello Sforzesco). Smaller local museums include those at Sesto Calende, Golasecca and Mergozzo.

Veneto/Alto Adige

The two most significant museum collections are those of the Museo Nazionale Atestino in Este and the Musei Civici agli Eremitani in Padua. Both house extensive collections of Venetic finds. Further afield, the Museo Archeologico at Adria, the Museo Civico at Rovigo and Museo di Altino at Quarto d'Altino have smaller but significant collections of Greek, Etruscan and Venetic objects, as do the Museo Archeologico at Montebelluna and Museo Civico at Vicenza. Finally, a fascinating collection of Venetic objects from the northern Veneto can be found in the Museo Archeologico Cadorino, located in the Town Hall of Pieve di Cadore. Very few archaeological sites are open to visitors, but two excavated areas can be visited at Quarto d'Altino, and there are plans to open the Venetic cemetery at the Casa di Ricovero, Este.

Emilia Romagna/Marche

The Etruscan site of Marzabotto, near Bologna, is one of the best-preserved Etruscan cities, and one of the few where the centre of the city has been comprehensively excavated. The Museo Archeologico in Bologna houses a major collection of artefacts from Marzabotto and from the earlier Etruscan settlement of Felsina. The Museo Archeologico Nazionale delle Marche in Ancona has an impressive collection of material from the region, including both prehistoric and Roman items, and the Museo Civico Archeologico at Verucchio has a rich collection of Etruscan and other pre-Roman artefacts.

Tuscany

Some of the remains of the northern Etruscan cities can be explored in extensive archaeological parks, such as those at Roselle and Fiesole. Cosa, near Orbetello, is one of the best-preserved and best-excavated Roman colonies in Italy. There are also excellent museum collections in Chiusi, Arezzo, Florence and Fiesole. A significant number of the finds from southern Etruria are held in museum collections in Rome, especially those of the Villa Giulia and the Museo Gregoriano Etrusco. Most main Etruscan centres also have their own museums, however, although some are in the nearest town rather than attached to archaeological sites.

Umbria

The largest museums in the region are the archaeological museums at Perugia, Orvieto and Spoleto, all of which house extensive collections of Umbrian and Roman artefacts. The famous Iguvine Tables are located in the Museo Civico at Gubbio. The sites of Carsulae,

Otricoli, Orvieto, Corciano and Perugia can be explored, although in some cases most of the visible remains belong to the late Republic or empire.

Lazio and Rome

The northern part of Lazio – an area of Etruscan settlement in Antiquity – is rich in Etruscan remains. The most spectacular Etruscan are the cemeteries of Caere (mod. Cerveteri), Volsinii (mod. Orvieto – see under Umbria) and Tarquinii (mod. Tarquinia) and the archaeological parks at Vulci and Veii, which include areas of the ancient cities. Many of the tombs are open and can be explored by visitors, although some of those in a less stable condition can only be visited by appointment. Smaller sites that can be visited include Castel d'Asso, Norchia, San Giovenale and Ferento. Important museum collections include those of the Museo Archeologico at Viterbo, the Museo Etrusco (Barbarano Romano), the Museo Archeologico dell'Agro Falisco e Forte Sangallo (Civita Castellana) and the Museo territoriale del Lago di Bolsena (Bolsena), as well as museums at Cerveteri, Tarquinii and Vulci. The Sabine culture to the north-east of Rome can be explored in the Museo Archeologico di Trebula Mutuesca (Monteleone Sabino) and the Museo Archeologico at Fara in Sabina. The sites of the sanctuaries of Hercules (Tivoli) and Fortuna Primigenia (Palestrina) can both be visited, as can the Museo Archeologico Nazionale di Palestrina (Palestrina).

Relatively few of the early remains of Rome itself are now visible. The Forum Romanum and Palatine are both easily accessible, but most of the extant buildings are of later date. However, the Capitoline Museum has an excellent display area in the basement including the foundations of the temple of Jupiter Capitolinus, part of which dates to the sixth century. The gallery houses finds from archaic Rome and a reconstruction of some archaic temple sculptures. Extensive collections of Etruscan objects are held by the Museo Gregoriano Etrusco, which forms part of the Vatican Museums, and by the Museo Nazionale Etrusco di Villa Giulia. A smaller collection of Etruscan and Italic objects can be found in the Museo delle Antichità Etrusche ed Italiche. The main collections of material from protohistoric Rome are held by the Museo Nazionale Romano in the Baths of Diocletian, and the Museo Nazionale Preistorico Etnografico 'Luigi Pigorini'.

Two of the very few extant buildings relating to early Rome can be seen at Fidenae and Gabii, both in the suburbs of Rome. Recent excavations at Gabii have unearthed a sixth-century building, while the unique preservation conditions of an eighth-century house at Fidenae have allowed archaeologists to reconstruct it. The sacred grave at Lucus Feroniae (Capena) can also be visited, as can the sanctuary of Minerva and the so-called tomb of Aeneas at Lavinium (Pomezia), where there is also an archaeological museum. There are also museums at Pratica di Mare (Satricum), Anzio, Artena and Lanuvio that contain objects from the early history of Latium.

In southern Latium, the Museo archeologico di Fregellae at Ceprano contains material from an early Roman colony, and the archaeological areas at Minturnae and Priverno preserve extensive physical remains of ancient settlements. Civic museums at Alatri, Cori, Cassino, Arpino, Formia and Fondi all contain collections of pre-Roman and Roman finds from the region.

Abruzzi/Molise

These regions are particularly rich in both Roman and pre-Roman archaeological sites. The sites of the ancient settlements of Amiternum, Peltuinum and Alba Fucens (all close to L'Aquila) can all be visited, as can the settlement of Iuvanum near Montenerodomo, south of Chieti, and the sanctuaries at Schiavi d'Abruzzo and Sulmona. The Samnite sanctuary site of Pietrabbondante, near Isernia, the hill fort of Monte Vairano (at Busso, near Campobasso) and the Samnite and Roman settlement of Saepinum (now Sepino) can all be visited. The Museo Archeologico Nazionale d'Abruzzo and the Museo Archeologico La Civitella, both at Chieti, house important collections of pre-Roman finds. Other important museums include the Museo Civico Aufidenate (Alfedena), the Museo Lapidario Marsicano (Avezzano), which specialises in epigraphy from the region, the Museo Nazionale d'Abruzzo at L'Aquila and the Museo Archeologico at Sulmona. In Molise there are important museums at Campobasso (Museo Sannitico), Sepino (Museo Archeologico di Saepinum-Altilia) and Venafro (Museo Archeologico).

Campania

Relatively few ancient remains have survived at Naples, but sections of the ancient theatre can be seen close to the Duomo, and there are fascinating remains of the Roman city beneath the church of San Lorenzo Maggiore. There are much more extensive remains of the other three Greek colonies of Campania at Cuma (Cumae), Paestum (Poseidonia/Paestum) and Velia (Elea). Further inland, the Samnite and Campanian sites of Aequum Tuticum (Ariano Irpino), Compsa (Conza in Campania) and Aeclanum (Mirabella Eclano) and the Roman colony of Cales (Calvi Risorta) can all be visited. The Parco archeologico urbano dell'antica Picentia at Pontecagnano preserves remains of the pre-Roman and pre-Samnite culture of the region, and the remains of the Roman colony of Sinuessa (mod. Mondragone) is also open to the public. The Museo Nazionale in Naples is one of the leading collections of antiquities in Italy. Other important collections include the museums at Paestum, Cumae, Velia, the Museo Irpino at Avellino, the Museo del Sannio at Benevento, the Museo Archeologico Nazionale del Sannio Caudino at Monesarchio and the Museo Archeologico dell'antica Capua at Santa Maria Capua Vetere, as well as museums at Nola, Mondragone, Nocera and Allife. The Museo Archeologico di Pithecusae at Lacco Ameno, on Ischia, houses a fascinating collection of objects from the earliest Greek colony in Italy, although no visible remains are preserved.

Basilicata

The main Greek sites of the area, those of Metapontum and Herakleia (mod. Metaponto and Policoro), have been extensively excavated and can be visited. The museums of Metaponto and Policoro display finds from the sites. Further inland, the Lucanian sites of Serra di Vaglio and Rossano di Vaglio (both near Vaglio di Basilicata) can also be visited, as can part of the third-century Roman colony of Venusia (Venosa). The Museo Archeologico Nazionale della Basilicata (Potenza) has extensive displays of finds from the region. At Grumento, most of the visible remains on the archaeological site are those of the later Roman city, but the Museo Archeologico Nazionale dell'Alta Val d'Agri contains material from the earlier history of the settlement.

Puglia

Relatively few traces of the ancient city of Taranto are visible. However, the Museo Nazionale in Taranto houses one of the most important collections of antiquities in Italy. The Messapic settlement of ancient Gnathia (mod. Egnazia) is well worth visiting, as is the archaeological park of Monte Sannace, one of the largest of the Peucetian settlements. The caves of Grotta Porcinara, near Marina di Leuca, and Grotta della Poesia, 20 km outside Otranto (both ancient cult sites), are also open to the public. There are a large number of museums with interesting collections of pre-Roman and early Roman finds, which are well worth visiting. The larger collections are those of the Museo Storico Archeologico of the Universita del Salento (Lecce) and the Museo Archeologico Provinciale Francesco Ribezzo (Brindisi), but others, including the civic museums at Alezio, Mesagne, Oria, Ugento, Ostuni, Gravina di Puglia and Gioia del Colle, also hold interesting collections of objects from the region.

Calabria

The Museo Nazionale in Reggio di Calabria houses a major collection of antiquities from Greek and Roman Reggio, including the famous Riace bronzes, and there are other museums dedicated to the Greek settlements of the region at Vibo Valentia, Crotone and Sibari. The Museo dei Brettii e degli Enotri at Catanzaro is a vast collection of material from non-Greek sites in Calabria. The sites of the ancient colonies of Locri, Croton and Sybaris and the smaller Greek settlement (and later Roman colony) of Scolacium have been extensively excavated and can all be visited.

BIBLIOGRAPHY

Adam, R. and Briquel, D., 'Le miroir prénestin de l'Antiquario Comunale de Rome et la légende des jumeaux divins en milieu latin à la fin du IVe siècle avant J.-C.', *Mélanges de l'École française de Rome–Antiquité (MEFRA)* 94 (1982), 33–65

Alföldi, A., *Early Rome and the Latins* (Ann Arbor, MI, 1965)

Ammerman, A. J., 'On the origins of the Forum Romanum', *AJA* 94 (1990), 427–45

Ammerman, A. J., 'The Comitium in Rome from the Beginning', *AJA* 100 (1996), 121–36

Ampolo, C., 'Analogie e rapporti fra Atene e Roma arcaica. Osservazioni sulla Regia, sul rex sacrorum e sul culto di Vesta', *La Parola del Passato* 26 (1971), 443–60

Ampolo, C., 'Servius rex primus signavit aes', *La Parola del Passato* 29 (1974), 382–8

Ampolo, C., 'Demarato. Osservazioni sulla mobilità sociale arcaica', *Dialoghi d'Archeologia* 9–10 (1976), 333–45

Ampolo, C. (ed.), *Italia omnium terrarum parens: la civiltà degli Enotri, Choni, Ausoni, Sanniti, Lucani, Brettii, Sicani, Siculi, Elimi* (Milan, 1989)

Ampolo, C., 'Il problema delle origini di Roma rivisitato: concordismo, ipertradizionalismo acritico, contesti', *Annali della Scuola Normale Superiore di Pisa, Classe di Lettere e Filosofia* 5.1 (2013), 218–84

Asheri, D., 'Carthaginians and Greeks', *Cambridge Ancient History*, vol. 4: *Persia, Greece and the Western Mediterranean, c.525 to 479* (Cambridge, 1988), 739–90

Attema, P. (ed.), *Centralization, Early Urbanization and Colonization in First Millennium Italy and Greece* (Leuven, 2004)

Aubet, M. E., *The Phoenicians in the West: Politics, Colonies and Trade,* 2nd edn (Cambridge, 2002)

Badian, E., 'The Early Historians', in T. A. Dorey (ed.), *Latin Historians* (London, 1966)

Bagnasco Gianni, G., *Oggetti iscritti di epoca orientalizzante in Etruria* (Florence, 1996)

Barker, G. (ed.), *A Mediterranean Valley: Landscape, Archaeology and 'Annales' History in the Biferno Valley* (Leicester, 1995)

Barker, G., and Rasmussen, T., *The Etruscans* (Oxford, 1998)

Bartoloni, G., 'The origins and diffusion of Villanovan culture', in M. Torelli (ed.), *The Etruscans* (London, 2000)

Beard, M., North, J. A., and Price, S. R. F., *Religions of Rome*, 2 vols (Cambridge, 1998)

Beck, H., 'The early Roman tradition', in J. Marincola (ed.), *A Companion to Greek and Roman Historiography* (Malden, MA, 2007)

Beck, H., 'From Poplicola to Augustus: senatorial houses in Roman political culture', *Phoenix* 63 (2009), 361–86

Beck, H., Duplà, A., Jehne, M., and Pina Polo, F. (eds), *Consuls and the 'Res Publica': Holding High Office in the Roman Republic* (Cambridge, 2011)

Bell, S., and Carcopino, A. (eds), *A Companion to the Etruscans* (Chichester, 2016)

Beloch, K. J., *Der italische Bund unter Roms Hegemonie: staatsrechtliche und statistische Forschungen* (Leipzig, 1880)

Berger, S., *Revolution and Society in Greek Sicily and Southern Italy* (Stuttgart, 1992)

Bernard, S. G., 'Continuing the debate on Rome's earliest circuit walls', *Papers of the British School at Rome* 80 (2012), 1–44

Bickermann, E., 'Origines gentium', *Classical Philology* 47 (1952), 65–81

Bietti Sestieri, A. M., *The Iron Age Community of Osteria dell'Osa* (Cambridge, 1992)

Bietti Sestieri, A. M., *L'Italia nell'età del bronzo e del ferro: dalle palafitte a Romolo (2200–700 a.C.)* (Rome, 2010)

Bispham, E., 'The Samnites', in G. J. Bradley, E. Isayev and C. Riva (eds), *Ancient Italy: Regions without boundaries* (Exeter, 2009)

Boardman, J., *The Greeks Overseas*: *Their Early Colonies and Trade,* 4th edn (London, 1990)

Bordenache Battaglia, G., and Emiliozzi, A., *Le ciste prenestine* (Rome, 1990)

Bourdin, S., *Les peuples de l'Italie préromaine: identités, territoires et relations inter-ethniques en Italie centrale et septentrionale (VIIIe–1er s. av. J.-C.)* (Rome, 2012)

Bradley, G., 'Colonization and identity in Republican Italy', in G. Bradley and J.-P. Wilson (eds), *Greek and Roman Colonization: Origins, Ideologies, Interactions* (Swansea, 2006), 161–188

Bradley, G. J., *Ancient Umbria* (Oxford, 2000)

Bradley, G. J., Isayev, E., and Riva, C. (eds), *Ancient Italy: Regions without Boundaries* (Exeter, 2009)

Bradley, G. J., and Farney, G. A. (eds), *A Handbook on the Ancient Italic Group*s (Amsterdam, forthcoming)

Bremmer, J., 'The Suodales of Poplios Valesios', *ZPE* 47 (1982), 133–47

Bremmer, J., 'Romulus, Remus and the foundation of Rome', in J. Bremmer and N. Horsfall (eds), *Roman Myth and Mythography* (London, 1987), 25–48

Briquel, D., 'Le système onomastique féminin dans les épigraphies de l'Italie préromaine, II', in S. Gély (ed.), *Sens et pouvoirs de la nomination dans les cultures hellénique et romaine,* II: *Le nom et la métamorphose* (Montpellier, 1992), 25–35

Briquel, D., *Mythe et révolution: la fabrication d'un récit: la naissance de la république à Rome* (Brussels, 2007)

Brown, F. E., *Cosa: The Making of a Roman Town* (Ann Arbor, MI, 1980)

Brown, F. E., Richardson, E. H., and Richardson, L., *Cosa III, The Buildings of the Forum: Colony, Municipium, and Village* (University Park, PA, 1993)

Brunt, P. A., *Italian Manpower 225 BC–AD 14* (Oxford, 1971)

Bruun, C., ' " What every man in the street used to know": M. Furius Camillus, Italic legends and Roman historiography', in C. Bruun (ed.), *The Roman Middle Republic: Politics, Religion and Historiography. c. 400–133 BC* (Rome, 2000), 41–68

Buchner, G., *Pithekoussai.* 3 vols (Rome, 1993)

Burnett, A. M., 'The beginnings of Roman coinage', *Annali dell'Istituto Italiano di Numismatica* 36 (1989), 33–64

Camporeale, G. (ed.), *The Etruscans outside Etruria* (Los Angeles, CA, 2004)

Capuis, L., *I Veneti* (Milan, 1993)

Carafa, P., *Il Comizio di Roma dalle origini all'età di Augusto* (Rome, 1998)

Carandini, A., *La nascita di Roma*, 2 vols (Turin, 2003)

Carandini, A., *Rome: Day One* (Princeton, NJ, 2011)

Carter, J. C., *The Chora of Metaponto: The Necropoleis* (Austin, TX, 1998)

Cascino, R., Di Giuseppe, H., and Patterson, H. L. (eds), *Veii, The Historical Topography of the Ancient City: A Restudy of John Ward-Perkins's Survey* (London, 2012)

Cazenove, O.,'Pre-Roman Italy, before and under the Romans', in J. Rüpke (ed.), *A Companion to Roman Religion* (Oxford, 2007), 43–57

Cerchiai, L., *I Campani* (Milan, 1995)

Cerchiai, L., *Gli antichi popoli della Campania: archeologia e storia* (Rome, 2007)

Cerchiai, L., Jannelli, L., and Longo, F., *The Greek Cities of Italy and Sicily* (Los Angeles, CA, 2002)

Cifani, G., 'La documentazione archeologica delle mure archaiche a Roma', *Mitteilung des Deutschen Archäologischen Instituts: Römishe Abteilung* 105 (1998), 359–89

Cifani, G. *Architettura romana arcaica: edilizia e società tra monarchia e repubblica* (Rome, 2008)

Cifani, G., 'Aspects of urbanism and political ideology in archaic Rome', in E. Robinson (ed.), *Papers on Italian Urbanism in the 1st Millennium BC* (Portsmouth, RI, 2014), 15–28

Cifani, G., 'L'economia di Roma nella prima età repubblicana (V–IV secolo a. C.): Alcune osservazioni', in M. Aberson, M. C. Biella, M. Di Fazio, P. Sánchez and M. Wullschleger (eds), *L'Italia centrale e la creazione di una koiné culturale? I percorsi della 'romanizzazione'. E pluribus unum? L'italie, de la diversité préromaine à l'unité Augustéenne,* vol. II (Bern, 2016), 151–81

Claridge, A., *Rome*, 2nd edn (Oxford, 2010)

Coarelli, F., *Il foro romano,* vol. 1: *Periodo arcaico* (Rome, 1986)

Coarelli, F., *Rome and Environs: An Archaeological Guide* (Berkeley, CA, and London, 2007)

Colantoni, E., 'Straw to stone, huts to houses: transitions in building practices and society in protohistoric Latium', in M. Thomas and G. Meyers, *Monumentality in Etruscan and Early Roman Architecture: Ideology and Innovation* (Austin TX, 2012), 21–40

Colonna, G., 'Nome gentilizio e società', *Studi Etruschi* 45 (1977), 175–92

Cornell, T. J., 'Aeneas and the twins: the development of the Roman foundation legend', *Proceedings of the Cambridge Philological Society*, 21 (1975), 1–32

Cornell, T. J., 'Etruscan historiography', *Annali della Scuola Normale Superiore di Pisa*, 6.2 (1976), 411–39

Cornell, T. J., 'The value of the literary tradition concerning archaic Rome', in K. Raaflaub (ed.), *Social Struggles in Archaic Rome* (Berkeley, CA, 1986), 52–76

Cornell, T. J., 'Rome and Latium', in *Cambridge Ancient History*, vol. 7.2 (Cambridge, 1989), 309–50

Cornell, T. J., *The Beginnings of Rome: Italy and Rome from the Bronze Age to the Punic Wars (c. 1000–264 BC)* (London, 1995)

Cornell, T. J., 'Ethnicity as a factor in early Roman history', in T. J. Cornell and K. Lomas (eds), *Gender and Ethnicity in Ancient Italy* (London, 1997), 9–12

Cornell, T. J. 'The city of Rome in the Middle Republic (c. 400–100)', in J. C. Coulston and H. Dodge (eds), *Ancient Rome: The Archaeology of the Eternal City* (Oxford, 2000), 42–60

Cornell, T. J. 'Coriolanus: myth, history and performance', in D. Braund and C. Gill (eds), *Myth, History and Culture in Republican Rome: Studies in Honour of T. P. Wiseman* (Exeter, 2003), 73–97

Cornell, T. J., 'Political conflict in archaic Rome and the republican historians', in G. Zecchini (ed.), *'Partiti' e fazioni nell'esperienza politica romana* (Milan, 2009), 3–10

Cornell, T. J. (ed.), *The Fragments of the Roman Historians* (Oxford, 2013)

Coulston, J. C., and Dodge, H. (eds), *Ancient Rome: The Archaeology of the Eternal City* (Oxford, 2000)

Crawford, M. H., *Roman Republican Coinage* (Cambridge, 1974)

Crawford, M. H., 'The early Roman economy, 753–280', *L'Italie préromaine et la Rome républicaine: mélanges offerts à Jacques Heurgon* (Paris, 1976), 197–207

Crawford, M. H., *Coinage and Money under the Roman Republic: Italy and the Mediterranean Economy* (London, 1985)

Crawford, M. H., *Roman Statutes*, 2 vols (London, 1996)

Crawford, M. H., *Imagines Italicae: A Corpus of Italic Inscriptions* (London, 2011)

Crawley Quinn, J., and Wilson, A., 'Capitolia', *Journal of Roman Studies* 103 (2013), 117–73

Cuozzo, M., 'Ancient Campania', in G. J. Bradley, E. Isayev and C. Riva (eds), *Ancient Italy: Regions without Boundaries* (Exeter, 2009), 224–67

D'Agostino, B., 'Military organisation and social structure in archaic Etruria', in O. Murray and S. Price (eds), *The Greek City: From Homer to Alexander* (Oxford, 1990), 59–82

David, J.-M., *The Roman Conquest of Italy* (Oxford, 1996)

Davies, J., *Rome's Religious History: Livy, Tacitus and Ammianus on Their Gods* (Cambridge, 2004)

De Franciscis, A., *Stato e società in Locri Epizefiri: l'archivio dell'Olympieion locrese* (Naples, 1972)

De Grummond, N., and Edlund-Berry, I. (eds), *The Archaeology of Sanctuaries and Ritual in Etruria* (Portsmouth, RI, 2011)

Dench, E., *From Barbarians to New Men: Greek, Roman, and Modern Perceptions of Peoples of the Central Apennines* (Oxford, 1995)

Dench, E., 'From sacred springs to the social war: myths of origins and questions of identity in the central Apennines', in T. J. Cornell and K. Lomas (eds), *Gender and Ethnicity in Ancient Italy* (London, 1997), 43–51

Dench, E., *Romulus' Asylum: Roman Identities from the Age of Alexander to the Age of Hadrian* (Oxford, 2005)

De Polignac, F., *Cults, Territory and the Origins of the Greek City-State* (Chicago, IL, and London, 1995)

Develin, R., 'The integration of plebeians into the political order after 366', in K. Raaflaub (ed.), *Social Struggles in Archaic Rome* (Berkeley, CA, 1986), 327–52.

Di Fazio, M., 'Callimachus and the Etruscans: human sacrifice between myth, history, and historiography', *Histos* 7 (2013), 48–69

Diffendale, D. P., Brocato, P., Terrenato, N., and Brock, A. L., 'Sant'Omobono: an interim *status quaestionis*', *Journal of Roman Archaeology* 29 (2016), 7–42

Di Maria, F. (ed.), *Ardea, la terra dei Rutuli, tra mito e archeologia: alle radici della romanità: nuovi dati dai recenti scavi archeologici* (Rome, 2007)

Di Siena, A., *Metaponto* (Taranto, 2001)

Donnellan, L., Nizzo V., and Burgers, G.-J. (eds), *Conceptualising early Colonisation* (Brussels, 2016)

Drews, R., 'The coming of the city to central Italy', *American Journal of Ancient History (AJAH)* 6 (1981), 133–65

Drews, R., 'Pontiffs, prodigies, and the disappearance of the *annales maximi*', *Classical Philology* 83 (1988), 289–99

Dunbabin, T., *The Western Greeks: The History of Sicily and South Italy from the Foundation of the Greek Colonies to 480 B.C.* (Oxford, 1984)

Eder, W., 'The political significance of the codification of law in archaic societies: an unconventional hypothesis', in K. Raaflaub (ed.), *Social Struggles in Archaic Rome* (Berkeley, 1986), 262–300

Edlund Berry, I., 'Early Rome and the making of "Roman" identity through architecture and town planning', in J. D. Evans (ed.), *A Companion to the Archaeology of the Roman Republic* (Malden, MA, 2013), 406–25

Erskine, A., *Roman Imperialism* (Edinburgh, 2010)

Fentress, E., and Bodel, J. P., *Cosa V: An Intermittent Town, Excavations 1991–1997* (Ann Arbor, MI, 2003)

Fentress, E., and Guidi, A., 'Myth, memory and archaeology as historical sources', *Antiquity* 73/280 (1999), 463–7

Flower, H. I., *Roman Republics* (Princeton, NJ, 2010)

Finley, M. I., 'The ancient city: from Fustel de Coulanges to Max Weber and beyond', *Comparative Studies in History and Society* 19 (1977), 305–27

Finley, M. I., *The Ancient Economy* (Berkeley, CA, and London, 1999)

Forsythe, G., *A Critical History of Early Rome: From Prehistory to the First Punic War* (Berkeley, CA, 2006)

Fox, M., *Roman Historical Myths: The Regal Period in Augustan Literature* (Oxford, 1996)

Frank, T., *An Economic Survey of Ancient Rome: Rome and Italy of the Republic*, vol. 1 (New York, 1933)

Franke, P., 'Pyrrhus', in *Cambridge Ancient History*, vol. 7.2 (Cambridge, 1989), 456–85

Fraschetti, A., *The Foundation of Rome* (Edinburgh, 2005)

Frayn, J., *Subsistence Farming in Roman Italy* (London, 1979)

Frederiksen, M., *Campania*, ed. N. Purcell (London, 1984)

Frier, B. W., *Libri annales pontificum maximorum: The Origins of the Annalistic Tradition* (Ann Arbor, MI, 1979)

Fronda, M. P., *Between Rome and Carthage: Southern Italy during the Second Punic War* (Cambridge, 2010).

Fulminante, F., *The Urbanisation of Rome and Latium Vetus: From the Bronze Age to the Archaic Era* (Cambridge, 2014)

Gabba, E., *Dionysius and the History of Archaic Rome* (Berkeley, CA, and Oxford, 1991)

Garnsey, P., *Famine and Food Supply in the Graeco-Roman World: Responses to Risk and Crisis* (Cambridge, 1988)

Garnsey, P., Hopkins, K., and Whittaker, C. R. (eds), *Trade in the Ancient Economy* (London, 1983)

Gierow, P., *The Iron Age Culture of Latium* (Rome, 1964–6)

Gill, D. W. G., 'Silver anchors and cargoes of oil: some observations on Phoenician trade in the western Mediterranean', *Papers of the British School at Rome* (*PBSR*) 56 (1988), 1–12

Ginge, B., *Excavations at Satricum (Borgo Le Ferriere) 1907–1910: Northwest Necropolis, Southwest Sanctuary and Acropolis* (Amsterdam, 1996)

Gjerstadt, E., *Early Rome*, 4 vols (Lund, 1953–7)

Gleba, M., *Textile Production in Pre-Roman Italy* (Oxford, 2008)

Glinister, F., 'Women and power in archaic Rome', in T. J. Cornell and K. Lomas (eds), *Gender and Ethnicity in Ancient Italy* (London, 1997), 115–27

Glinister, F., 'What is a sanctuary?' *Cahiers du Centre Gustave-Glotz* 8 (1997), 61–80

Gnade, M., and Rubini, M., *Satricum in the Post-Archaic Period: A Case Study of the Interpretation of Archaeological Remains as Indicators of Ethno-Cultural Identity* (Leuven, 2002)

Grandazzi, A., *The Foundation of Rome: Myth And History* (Ithaca, NY, and London, 1997)

Hanell, K., *Das altrömische eponyme Amt* (Lund, 1946)

Hansen, M. H. (ed.), *An Inventory of Archaic and Classical Poleis* (Oxford, 2004)

Harris, W. V., *Rome in Etruria and Umbria* (Oxford, 1971)

Harris, W. V., *War and Imperialism in Republican Rome, 327–70* (Oxford, 1979)

Häussler, R., 'At the margins of Italy: Celts and Ligurians in north-west Italy', in G. Bradley, E. Isayev and C. Riva (eds), *Ancient Italy: Regions without Boundaries* (Exeter, 2009), 45–78

Haverfield, F., *The Romanization of Roman Britain* (Oxford, 1923)

Haynes, S., *Etruscan Civilization: A Cultural History* (London, 2000)

Herring, E., 'Ethnicity and culture', in A. Erskine (ed.), *A Companion to Ancient History* (Chichester, 2009), 123–33

Herring, E., and Lomas, K., *The Emergence of State Identities in Italy in the First Millennium* (London, 2001)

Hodos, T., 'Intermarriage in the western Greek colonies', *Oxford Journal of Archaeology* 18 (1999), 61–78

Holloway, R. R., *The Archaeology of Early Rome and Latium* (London and New York, 1994)

Humm, M., *Appius Claudius Caecus: la république accomplie* (Rome, 2005)

Humm, M., 'Forma virtutei parisuma fuit: les valeurs helléniques de l'aristocratie romaine à l'époque médio-républicaine (IVe–IIIe siècles)', in H.-L. Fernoux and C. Stein (eds), *Aristocratie antique: modèles et exemplarité sociale* (Dijon, 2007), 101–26

Humm, M., 'Exhibition et "monumentalisation" du butin dans la Rome médio-républicaine', in M. Coudry and M. Humm (eds), *Praeda: butin de guerre et société dans la Rome républicaine* (Stuttgart, 2009), 117–52

Humm, M., 'Il comizio del foro e le istituzioni della repubblica romana', in E. Corti (ed.), *La città: com'era, com'é, e come la vorremmo* (Pavia, 2014), 69–83

Isayev, E., *Inside Ancient Lucania: Dialogues in History and Archaeology* (London, 2007)

Izzett, V., *The Archaeology of Etruscan Society* (Cambridge, 2007)

Jehne, M., 'Who attended Roman assemblies? Some remarks on political participation in the Roman Republic', in F. M. Simón, F. Pina Polo and J. Remesal Rodríguez (eds), *Repúblicas y ciudadanos: modelos de participación cívica en el mundo antiguo* (Barcelona, 2006), 221–34

Joncheray, C., 'Les plans des cités étrusques à la période classique de la réalité fantasmée aux nouveaux critères d'interprétation', in S. Guizani (ed.), *Urbanisme et architecture en Méditerranée antique et médiévale à travers les sources archéologiques et littéraires* (Tunis, 2013), 121–32

Jones, H. (ed.), *Samnium: Settlement and Cultural Change* (Providence, RI, 2004)

La Genière, J. de, 'The Iron Age in southern Italy', in D. Ridgway and F. R. Serra Ridgway (eds), *Italy before the Romans* (London, 1979), 59–94

La Grande Rome dei Tarquini (Rome, 1990)

La Rocca, E., 'Fabio o Fannio: l'affresco medio-repubblicano dell'Esquilino come riflesso dell'arte rappresentativa e come espressione di mobilità sociale', *Dialoghi d'Archeologia* 2 (1984), 31–53

Leighton, R., *Tarquinia: An Etruscan City* (London, 2004)

Lomas, K., *Rome and the Western Greeks: Conquest and Acculturation in Southern Italy, 350 BC–AD 200* (London, 1993)

Lomas, K., *Roman Italy, 338 BC–AD 200: A Sourcebook* (London, 1996)

Lomas, K., 'Ethnicity and statehood in northern Italy: the ancient Veneti', in G. Bradley, E. Isayev and C. Riva (eds), *Ancient Italy: Regions without Boundaries* (Exeter, 2007), *21–44*

Lomas, K., 'Italy beyond Rome', in A. Erskine (ed.), *A Companion to Ancient History* (Chichester, 2009), 248–59

Macmullen, R., *The Earliest Romans: A Character Sketch* (Ann Arbor, MI, 2011)

Malkin, I., *The Returns of Odysseus: Colonization and Ethnicity* (Berkeley, CA, 1998)

Mattingly, D. J., *Imperialism, Power and Identity: Experiencing the Roman Empire* (Princeton, NJ, 2011)

Mehl, A. (trans. H.-F. Mueller), *Roman Historiography* (Malden, MA, 2011)

Meyers, G., and Thomas, M. L., *Monumentality in Etruscan and Early Roman Architecture* (Austin, TX, 2012)

Miles, G. B., *Livy: Reconstructing Early Rome* (Ithaca, NY, and London, 1995)

Mitchell, R. E., 'The definition of *patres* and *plebs*: an end to the struggle of the orders', in K. Raaflaub (ed.), *Social Struggles in Archaic Rome* (Berkeley, CA, 1986), 130–74

Momigliano, A., 'The rise of the plebs in the archaic age of Rome', in K. Raaflaub (ed.), *Social Struggles in Archaic Rome* (Berkeley, CA, 1986), 175–97

Morel, J.-P., 'Études de céramique campanienne, I: l'atelier des petites estampilles', *MEFRA* 81 (1969), 59–117

Murray, C., 'Constructions of authority through ritual: considering transformations of ritual space as reflecting society in Iron Age Etruria', in D. Haggis and N. Terrenato (eds), *State Formation in Italy and Greece: Questioning the Neoevolutionist Paradigm* (Oxford, 2011), 199–216

Northwood, S. J., 'Grain scarcity and pestilence in the early Roman republic: some significant patterns', *Bulletin of the Institute of Classical Studies* 49 (2006), 81–92

Oakley, S., 'The Roman conquest of Italy', in J. Rich and G. Shipley (eds), *War and Society in the Roman World* (London, 1993)

Oakley, S,. *The Hill-Forts of the Samnites* (London, 1995)

Oakley, S., *A Commentary on Livy, Books VI–X*, 4 vols (Oxford, 1997–2005)

Ogilvie, R. M., *A Commentary on Livy, Books 1–5* (Oxford, 1965)

Ogilvie, R. M., and Drummond, A., 'The sources for early Roman history', in *Cambridge Ancient History*, 2nd edn, vol. VII (Cambridge, 1988), 1–29

Osborne, R., 'Early Greek colonisation? The nature of Greek settlement in the west', in N. Fisher and H. Van Wees (eds), *Archaic Greece: New Approaches and New Evidence* (Cardiff, 1998), 251–69

Osborne, R., *Greece in the Making, 1200–479* (London, 1998)

Pacciarelli, M., *Dal villaggio alla città: la svolta protourbana del 1000 a.C. nell'Italia tirrenica* (Florence, 2000)

Pagliara, A., 'Gli "Aurunci" in Livio', *Oebalus* 1 (2006), 11–19

Pallottino, M., *A History of Earliest Italy* (London, 1991)

Palmer, R. E. A., 'The censors of 312 and the state religion', *Historia* 14 (1965), 293–324

Palmer, R. E. A., *The Archaic Community of the Romans* (Cambridge, 1970)

Patterson, H., et al., *Bridging the Tiber: Approaches to Regional Archaeology in the Middle Tiber Valley* (London and Rome, 2004)

Pébarthe, C., and Delrieux, F., 'La transaction du plomb de Pech-Maho', *Zeitschrift für Papyrologie und Epigraphik*, 126 (1999), 155–61

Pedley, J. G., *Paestum* (London, 1990)

Pelgrom, J., and Stek, T. (eds), *Roman Republican Colonization: New Perspectives from Archaeology and Ancient History* (Rome, 2014)

Perkins, P., and Attolini, I., 'An Etruscan farm at Podere Tartuchino', *Papers of the British School at Rome*, 60 (1992), 71–134

Pina Polo, F., *The Consul at Rome: The Civil Functions of the Consuls in the Roman Republic* (Cambridge, 2011)

Potter, T., *The Changing Landscape of South Etruria* (London, 1979)

Poucet, J., *Les origines de Rome: tradition et histoire* (Brussels, 1985)

Pugliese Carratelli, G. (ed.), *The Western Greeks* (London, 1996)

Purcell, N., 'Forum Romanum (the Republican period)', in M. Steinby (ed.), *Lexicon Topographicum Urbis Romae* II (Rome, 1995)

Quilici, L., and Quilici Gigli, S., *I Volsci: testimonianze e leggende* (Rome, 1997)

Raaflaub, K., *Social Struggles in Archaic Rome: New Perspectives on the Conflict of the Orders*, 2nd edn (Oxford, 2007)

Rallo, A. (ed.), *Le donne in Etruria* (Rome, 1989)

Rathje, A., 'Oriental imports in Etruria in the eighth and seventh centuries: their origins and implications', in D. Ridgway and F. R. Ridgway, *Italy before the Romans: Iron Age, Orientalizing, and Etruscan Periods* (Edinburgh, 1979), 145–83

Rawlings, L., 'Army and battle during the conquest of Italy (350–264)', in P. Erdkamp (ed.), *A Companion to the Roman Army* (Oxford, 2007), 45–62

Rich, J. W., 'Fear, greed and glory: the causes of Roman war-making in the middle Republic', in J. W. Rich and G. Shipley (eds), *War and Society in the Roman World* (London, 1993), 38–68

Rich, J. W., and Shipley, G. (eds), *War and Society in the Roman World* (London, 1993)

Rich, J. W., 'Warfare and the army in early Rome', in P. Erdkamp (ed.), *A Companion to the Roman Army* (Oxford, 2007), 7–23

Rich, J. W., '*Lex Licinia, Lex Sempronia*: B. G. Niebuhr and the limitation of landholding in the Roman Republic', in L. de Ligt and S. Northwood (eds), *People, Land and Politics: Demographic Developments and the Transformation of Roman Italy, 300 BC–AD 14* (Leiden, 2008), 519–72

Richard, J.-C. 'Patricians and plebeians: the origin of a social dichotomy', in K. Raaflaub (ed.), *Social Struggles in Archaic Rome* (Berkeley, 1986), 105–29

Richardson, J. H., 'Rome's treaties with Carthage: jigsaw or variant traditions?', in C. Deroux (ed.), *Studies in Latin Literature and Roman History* XIV (Brussels, 2008), 84–94

Richardson, J. H., 'App. Claudius Caecus and the corruption of Roman voting assemblies: A new interpretation of Livy 9.46.11', *Hermes* 139.4 (2011), 455–63

Richardson, J. H., *The Fabii and the Gauls: Studies in Historical Thought and Historiography in Republican Rome* (Stuttgart, 2012)

Richardson, J. H., and Santangelo, F. (eds), *The Roman Historical Tradition: Regal and Republican Rome* (Oxford, 2014)

Ridgway, D. W., 'Italy from the Bronze Age to the Iron Age', *Cambridge Ancient History*, vol. 4: *Persia, Greece and the Western Mediterranean, c. 525 to 479* (Cambridge, 1988), 623–33

Ridgway, D. W., *The First Western Greeks* (Cambridge, 1992)

Ridley, R. T., 'The historian's silences: what Livy did not know – or did not choose to tell', *Journal of Ancient History* 1 (2013), 27–52

Riva, C., *The Urbanization of Etruria* (Cambridge, 2010)

Roma medio-Repubblicana: aspetti culturali di Roma e del Lazio nei secoli IV e III a.C. (Rome, 1973)

Roselaar, S., *Public Land in the Roman Republic: A Social and Economic History of 'ager publicus' in Italy, 396–89 B.C.* (Oxford, 2010)

Roth, R., *Styling Romanisation: Pottery and Society in Central Italy* (Cambridge, 2007)

Rüpke, J., *The Roman Calendar from Numa to Constantine: Time, History, and the fasti* (Hoboken, NJ, 2011)

Rutter, N. K., *Campanian Coinages, 475–380* (Edinburgh, 1979)

Rutter, N. K., *Historia Nummorum: Italy* (London, 2001)

Salmon, E. T., *Samnium and the Samnites* (Cambridge, 1965)

Salmon, E. T., *Roman Colonisation under the Republic* (London, 1969)

Salmon, E. T., *The Making of Roman Italy* (London, 1982)

Salmon, E. T., 'The Iron Age: the peoples of Italy', *Cambridge Ancient History*, vol. 4: *Persia, Greece and the Western Mediterranean, c.525 to 479* (Cambridge, 1988), 676–719

Santangelo, S., 'Fetials and their *ius*', *Bulletin of the Institute of Classical Studies* 51 (2008), 63–93

Scheidel, W., 'Human mobility in Roman Italy, I: the free population', *Journal of Roman Studies* 94 (2004), 1–26

Scott, R. T., 'The contribution of archaeology to early Roman history', in K. Raaflaub (ed.), *Social Struggles in Archaic Rome*, 2nd edn (Oxford, 2005), 98–106

Seager, R., '"Populares" in Livy and the Livian Tradition', *Classical Quarterly* 27.2 (1977), 377–90

Sewell, J., *The Formation of Roman Urbanism, 338–200 B.C.: Between Contemporary Foreign Influence and Roman Tradition* (Portsmouth, RI, 2010)

Shepherd, G., 'Fibulae and females: intermarriage in the western Greek colonies', in G. Tsetskhladze (ed.), *Ancient Greeks: East and West* (Leiden, 1999), 267–300

Sherwin-White, A. N., *The Roman Citizenship*, 2nd edn (Oxford, 1973)

Small, A. (ed.), *An Iron Age and Roman Republican Settlement on Botromagno, Gravina di Puglia: Excavations of 1965–1974* (London, 1992)

Smith, C. J., *Early Rome and Latium* (Oxford, 1996)

Smith, C. J., 'Early and archaic Rome', in J. Coulston and H. Dodge (eds), *Ancient Rome: The Archaeology of the Eternal City* (Oxford, 2000), 16–41

Smith, C. J., 'The beginnings of urbanisation in Rome', in B. Cunliffe and R. Osborne (eds), *Mediterranean Urbanization, 800–600* (London, 2005), 91–112

Smith, C. J., *The Roman Clan: The 'gens' from Ancient Ideology to Modern Anthropology* (Cambridge, 2006)

Smith, C. J., 'The religion of archaic Rome', in J. Rüpke (ed.), *A Companion to Roman Religion* (Oxford, 2007), 31–42

Smith, C. J., 'Latium and the Latins', in G. J. Bradley, E. Isayev and C. Riva (eds), *Ancient Italy: Regions without Boundaries* (Exeter, 2009), 161–78

Smith, C. J., 'Thinking about kings', *Bulletin of the Institute of Classical Studies* 54.2 (2011), 21–42

Staveley, E. S., 'The political aims of Appius Claudius Caecus', *Historia* 8 (1959), 410–33

Staveley, E. S., 'Italy and Rome in the early third century', in *Cambridge Ancient History*, vol. 7.2 (Cambridge, 1989), 420–55

Steinby, M. (ed.), *Lexicon Topographicum Urbis Romae* (Rome, 1993–2000)

Steinby, M. (ed.), *Lacus Iuturnae* (Rome, 2012)

Stek, T. D., *Cult Places and Cultural Change in Republican Italy: A Contextual Approach to Religious Aspects of Rural Society after the Roman Conquest* (Amsterdam, 2009)

Stek, T. D., 'The importance of rural sanctuaries in structuring non-urban society in ancient Samnium: approaches from architecture and landscape', *Oxford Journal of Archaeology* 34.4 (2015), 397–40

Stevenson, T., 'Women and early Rome as exempla in Livy, *Ab Urbe Condita* book 1', *Classical World* 104.2 (2010), 175–89

Spivey, N., and Stoddart, S. *Etruscan Italy: An Archaeological History* (London, 1990)

Tagliamonte, G., *I sanniti: caudini, irpini, pentri, carricini, frentani* (Milan, 1996)

Termeer, M. K., 'Early colonies in Latium (ca 534–338 BC): a reconsideration of current images and the archaeological evidence', *BABESCH* 85 (2010), 43–58

Terrenato, N., 'The auditorium site in Rome and the origins of the villa', *Journal of Roman Archaeology,* 14 (2001), 5–32

Terrenato, N., 'Early Rome', in A. Barchiesi and W. Scheidel (eds), *The Oxford Handbook of Roman Studies* (Oxford, 2010), 507–18

Terrenato, N., 'The versatile clans: Archaic Rome and the nature of early city-states in central Italy', in N. Terranato and D. Haggis (eds), *State Formation in Italy and Greece: Questioning the Neoevolutionist Paradigm* (Oxford, 2011), 231–40

Thiermann, E., 'Die Nekropole Fornaci in Capua im 6. und 5. Jh. v. Chr. Neue Forschungen zu alten Grabungen', *Neue Forschungen zu den Etruskern,* BAR Int. Ser. (Oxford, 2010), 101–5

Toms, J., 'The relative chronology of the Villanovan cemetery of Quattro Fontanili at Veii', *AION (arch)* 7 (1986), 41–97

Torelli, M., *Elogia tarquiniensia* (Florence, 1975)

Torelli, M. (ed.), *The Etruscans* (London, 2000)

Tuck, A. J., 'The performance of death: monumentality, burial practice, and community identity in central Italy's urbanizing period', in M. Thomas and G. Meyers, *Monumentality in Etruscan and Early Roman Architecture: Ideology and Innovation* (Austin TX, 2012), 41–60

Tuck, A. J., 'Manufacturing at Poggio Civitate: elite consumption and social organization in the Etruscan seventh century', *Etruscan Studies* 17 (2014), 121–39

Tuck, A. J., Glennie, A., Kreindler, K., O'Donoghue, E. and Polisini, C. 'Excavations at Poggio Civitate and Vescovado di Murlo (Provincia di Siena)', *Etruscan Studies* 9.1 (2016), 87–148

Turfa, J. M. (ed.), *The Etruscan World* (London, 2013)

Walbank, F. W., Astin, A., Frederiksen, M. W., and Ogilvie, R. (eds), *The Cambridge Ancient History*, vol. 7.2: *The Rise of Rome to 220 B.C.* (Cambridge, 1989)

Wallace, R. W., 'Hellenization and Roman society in the late fourth century: a methodological critique', in W. Eder (ed.), *Staat und Staatlichkeit in der frühen römischen Republik* (Stuttgart, 1990), 278–92

Wallace-Hadrill, A., *Houses and Society in Pompeii and Herculaneum* (Princeton, NJ, 1994)

Wallace-Hadrill, A., 'Rethinking the Roman atrium house', in R. Laurence and A. Wallace-Hadrill (eds), *Domestic Space in the Roman World: Pompeii and Beyond* (Portsmouth RI, 1997), 219–40

Wallace-Hadrill, A., *Rome's Cultural Revolution* (Cambridge, 2009)

Walsh, P. G., *Livy: His Historical Aims and Methods* (Cambridge, 1961)

Ward, L. H., 'Roman population, territory, tribe, city, and army size from the Republic's founding to the Veientane war, 509–400', *American Journal of Philology* 111.1 (1990), 5–39

Ward-Perkins, J. B., 'Veii: the historical topography of the ancient city', *Papers of the British School at Rome* 29 (1961), 1–123

West, M. L., *Iambi et elegi Graeci* (Oxford, 1971)

Willemsen, S. L., 'A changing funerary ritual at Crustumerium (ca. 625 BC)', in A. J. Nijboer, S. Willemsen, P. A. J. Attema and J. Seubers (eds), *Research into pre-Roman Burial Grounds in Italy*, 35–50 (Leuven, 2013)

Williams, J. H. C., *Beyond the Rubicon: Romans and Gauls in Republican Italy* (Oxford, 2001)

Wilson, J. P., 'The nature of Greek overseas settlement in the archaic period: *emporion* or *apoikia*?', in L. Mitchell and P. Rhodes (eds), *The Development of the Polis in Archaic Greece* (London, 1997), 199–216

Wiseman, T. P., 'The she-wolf mirror: an interpretation', *PBSR* 61 (1993), 1–6

Wiseman, T. P., *Remus: A Roman Myth* (Cambridge, 1995)

Wiseman, T. P., 'Reading Carandini', *Journal of Roman Studies* 91 (2001), 182–93

Wiseman, T. P., *The Myths of Rome* (Exeter, 2004)

Wiseman, T. P., *Unwritten Rome* (Exeter, 2008)

Witcher, R. E., 'Globalisation and Roman imperialism: perspectives on identities in Roman Italy', in E. Herring and K. Lomas (eds), *The Emergence of State Identities in Italy in the First Millennium BC* (London, 2001), 213–25

Zanker, P., *The Power of Images in the Age of Augustus* (Ann Arbor, MI, 1988)

Zevi, F., 'Considerazioni sull'elogio di Scipione Barbato', *Studi Miscellanei* 15 (1970), 65–73

Ziolkowski, A., 'Les temples A et C du Largo Argentina: quelques considérations', *Mélanges de l'École française de Rome–Antiquité* 98 (1986), 623–41

Ziolkowski, A., 'Ritual cleaning-up of the city: from the Lupercalia to the Argei', *Ancient Society* 29 (1998–9), 191–218

Ziolkowski, A., *The Temples of Mid-Republican Rome and Their Historical and Topographical Context* (Rome, 1992)

INDEX

Massalia 117, 125, 169

Mastarna (*see also* Servius Tullius) 129, 130, 141

Mater Matuta, cult of 64–5, 141, 144, 147, 232–3, 237, 316, 350, 355

meddix, meddices 163, 167, 240

Mediterranean 3, 5, 11, 18–19, 23–6, 28, 30–31, 33, 46–8, 50, 55, 59, 63, 68, 71, 73, 78–80, 95, 102, 107, 111, 121, 123–4, 126, 138–40, 150, 159, 169, 191, 214, 256, 266, 271, 273, 279, 309, 322, 325, 327, 339, 345, 347, 354, 359

Medma 29, 30

Mefitis, cult of 65, 162

Menenius Agrippa 187

Messana 288, 327

Messapians (*see also* Iapygians) 109, 215, 272, 347, 356

Metapontum 29, 30, 32, 64, 78, 82, 100, 102, 115, 117, 155–6, 240–41, 243

Mezentius 47

migration 7, 24, 30–31, 33, 49, 80–81, 123, 125, 131, 141, 149, 160, 164–9, 255, 265, 268, 286

Milan 169

military pay (*stipendium*) 212, 303

military service 194, 212, 264–5, 274, 303

mineral resources 5, 11, 18–19, 24–5, 30, 33, 79, 125

Minturnae 254, 276, 277

Minucius (Lucius Minucius) 183

mirrors 46, 116, 241

Monte Bibele 168

Monte Pallano 162

Monte Sannace 240

Monte Vairano 162

Motya 24

Mount Soracte 65

Mucius Scaevola (Gaius Mucius Scaevola) 151, 336, 338

municipia 265

Murlo 60–63, 65, 68–9, 71–2, 86, 93, 147, 349

myths, mythology 19, 27, 36–7, 43–4, 46–7, 46–9, 50–51, 89, 200, 241, 319–20, 335, 341–5, 347

    Greek 308, 320

N

Naevius 47, 50, 343

Naples (Neapolis) 29, 156, 165–6, 248, 257, 300, 309–10, 320, 358

Navies 200, 209, 234, 246, 255–6, 258, 303–4, 327

Nemi 65, 121

Nepet (Nepi) 17, 33, 44, 211, 241, 269, 346

nexum (*see also* Debt-bondage)

nobility, Roman 68, 225–6, 228–9, 234, 291, 304–7, 318, 323, 325–6, 337

Nola 81, 158, 248, 356

Nora 25

North Africa 5, 24

Nuceria 81, 158

Numa Pompilius 83–5, 93, 351, 355

Numitor 45, 47

O

oaths 201, 249

Ogulnii (Gnaeus and Quintus Ogulnius) 46, 315

olives, cultivation of 25, 33, 78–9, 104, 115–16, 241

oracles 28, 32, 324, 319, 338

orientalising culture 54, 59–60, 67, 69, 72, 77–80, 85–7, 89, 95, 110–11, 113, 116, 138, 149, 159, 322, 350

Oscan language and culture 155, 158, 161–7, 240, 242, 248, 255, 257, 281–3, 311, 320, 342, 354, 356, 362

Osteria dell'Osa 10, 21–2, 39, 52, 75, 346

Ostia 85, 137, 314

Ovid 45, 65, 316, 342, 352, 359

P

Pacuvius Calavius 286

Paeligni 252

Paestum (*see also* Poseidonia) 66, 105, 165–6, 230, 243, 260, 277, 281, 284

palaces 61, 65, 68, 86, 146

Palatine hill 36–45, 52, 90–91, 93, 111, 143, 146–7, 230–31, 235–7, 315, 334–5, 348–9, 351

Pandosia 243